Post-Keynesian Economics

by Kenneth K. Kurihara

MONETARY THEORY AND PUBLIC POLICY

INTRODUCTION TO KEYNESIAN DYNAMICS

THE KEYNESIAN THEORY OF ECONOMIC
DEVELOPMENT

NATIONAL INCOME AND ECONOMIC GROWTH

Post-Keynesian Economics

EDITED BY

KENNETH K. KURIHARA
Rutgers University

LONDON
George Allen and Unwin Ltd
RUSKIN HOUSE · MUSEUM STREET

FIRST PUBLISHED IN GREAT BRITAIN 1955
SECOND IMPRESSION 1962

330.1
K96p
Cop. 4

PRINTED IN GREAT BRITAIN
BY PHOTOLITHO
BY UNWIN BROTHERS LIMITED
WOKING AND LONDON

TO THE MEMORY OF

John Maynard Keynes

*May this volume prove a worth-while contribution
to the tradition initiated by him*

PREFACE

THE PRESENT VOLUME represents the extension of Keynes' *General Theory* by a group of well-known economists. The essays in this volume are entirely new materials, each taking Keynes' work as a frame of reference for searching criticisms, further explorations, imaginative extrapolations, and novel insights, yet all trying to add something to a superstructure on the foundation of the *General Theory*. Here is to be found the unity and import of the volume as a whole, despite the diversity of the topics discussed and the variety of the styles pursued. So that a maximum of coherence might be achieved, the contributors were asked to focus their essays on specific but related aspects of Keynes. In addition, part of the whole effort has been to appraise economic ideas on their own merits, whether or not those ideas are associated with the name of Keynes.

By way of stating the purpose, scope, and significance of this book, the editor may be allowed to justify the present undertaking on several grounds. In the first place, Keynes, while providing indispensable tools of analysis (Keynes' savings and investment functions are to income analysis what Marshall's supply and demand curves are to price analysis), raised more questions than he answered. Few would gainsay that Keynes "opened up new vistas and new pathways to a whole generation of economists," but many would now consider his analysis less than adequate for meeting such special problems as cyclical forecasts and controls, persistent inflation, the maintenance of full-employment booms, secular growth, nonlinear structural relations, and macrofunctional distribution. These problems lie largely outside the scheme of the *General Theory* and call for fresh approaches, as will be shown by the contributions in this volume.

Moreover, an extension of Keynes' *General Theory* can now have perspective, for enough time has elapsed and enough has happened since to enable writers to see more clearly what is his "contribution to fundamental economic thought" and what are the "limitations of Keynesian economics." In the third place, now that Keynes' seminal ideas have been absorbed into the general tradition of our discipline, economics and economists might inadvertently slip once again into that "dogmatic slumber" which, according to Professor Pigou, Keynes had broken "resoundingly." It was therefore both gratifying and reassuring that Professor Austin Robinson, who was closer to Keynes than most in pupildom and friendship, wrote to the editor that "the extension of Keynes' work by the younger generation is what Keynes himself would have most liked to see." In the fourth place, a symposium like this one has the unique advantage of varied insights into "the common concerns of mankind" in the economic field. For scholars of various international backgrounds have been brought together here by "the common love of truth, bred of a scientific habit of mind" which Lord Keynes delightedly found to be "the closest of bonds between the representatives of divers nations."

Finally, the spirit of Keynes seems to be the right and fitting one for coping with those problems peculiar to mixed economies, in which private initiative and public policy supplement and reinforce each other. For to secure the full and productive utilization of resources, the steady growth of output, and the equitable distribution of income and wealth "whilst preserving efficiency and freedom" is the *raison d'être* and *esprit* of modern economic analysis, at least in democratic societies. It is hoped that this volume will serve as a useful book of reference for seminars, the profession, and statecraft.

It may be helpful to say a word about each essay so that the reader may have some idea of what to expect. The level of abstraction is on the whole very high, especially in the technical recesses of this collaboration, but the reader will find in it a fairly balanced combination of the "Cambridge oral tradition" and mathematical propensities. Professor Bowen and Dr. Meier discuss cycle theories and stabilization policies in the broader perspective of institutional realities and urge us to take institutional change, not as a given datum for purely endogenous analysis, but as an object for countercyclical policy. Their essay richly supplements the pure theories of the trade cycle discussed by Mr. Matthews and Professor Ichimura. Mr. Matthews lets us have a taste of the latest British thinking on the subject. He analyzes the crucial role of investment both as an increasing function of income and as a decreasing function of capital in the trade cycle, and stresses the need for more effective control of investment activity than at present. Mr. Matthews' essay throws much light on how to maintain full employment without "war orders." Professor Vickrey's essay deals with the stability conditions of monetary equilibrium with continuous full employment. He treats the role of expectations, liquidity-preference, and fiscal-monetary reforms in a suggestive manner and with mathematical rigor. His essay can be profitably read in conjunction with those of Professors Timlin, Patinkin, Dillard and Bronfenbrenner. Miss Timlin does for Canadian stabilization policy essentially what Professor Tarshis does for American national income analysis, as far as econometric orientation is concerned. Miss Timlin attempts to synthesize Keynesian and classical teachings on monetary stabilization, while Professor Tarshis offers the hypothesis that corporate saving plays a causally more significant role in income determination than is commonly supposed—both providing relevant empirical evidence.

Professor Bronfenbrenner's essay contains a broad interpretation of the implications of persistent inflation for the future of our economic society, though with the cautious reservation that the Keynes-Hansen "stagnation thesis" may come of age. Professor Tsuru's essay is a rare treat for Western economists, especially for those who are acquainted with the works of Mrs. Joan Robinson and Dr. Paul Sweezy. Professor Tsuru clarifies the hitherto obscure differences and similarities between Keynes and Marx—so colorfully discussed in J. Schumpeter's *Ten Great Economists: From Marx to Keynes*. Mr. Streeten provides penetrating insights into the relationship between Keynesian and classical contributions to fundamental thought, between Keynes' analysis and changing social milieu—with an Oxford accent. Mr. Streeten's essay will be found as refreshing as Professor Dillard's essay, both of which deal with the deeper and mellower aspects of Keynes. Professor Dillard points out the unfilled promises of Keynes' *General Theory* in the same searching way as Mrs. Robinson did those of his *Treatise on Money*—a stream of thought running from a theory of money as a "veil" to a theory of output as a whole. Professor Murad elaborates on Keynes' long, long-run suggestion that economic progress will depend more on "changes

in technique, taste, population and institutions" and less on the
classical virtue of saving to accumulate capital for the sake of
progress. He exempts underdeveloped economies from all this,
however.

Dr. Klein's econometric contribution clarifies the empirical
basis of Keynesian operationalism for control and prediction.
His analysis throws a good deal of light on dynamics versus statics,
the respective roles of a priori and empirical equations in macro-
analysis, the econometric possibility of bridging the gap between
theoretical economics and practical statistics, and the possible
integration of the Keynesian "building-block theory" and the
Walrasian "mutual-dependence theory." Dr. Klein's essay, together with those of Professors Modigliani, Patinkin, Vickrey,
and Ichimura, befits the Econometric Society, of which Keynes
was a memorable president. Professor Modigliani and Mr. Brumberg offer an econometric testing of the controversial Keynesian
consumption function hypothesis. They advance the challenging
hypotheses concerning the causal significance of assets, age, and
expectations for the dynamic behavior of the consumption function. Professor Ichimura's explorations bring up to date, in a
more generalized form, the nonlinear trade-cycle theories of
Kalecki, Harrod, Kaldor, Goodwin, and Hicks. Professor Ichimura's essay, together with Mr. Matthews', clarifies the nature
of the endogenous instability of modern industrial society—that is
not explained by Schumpeter's exogenous theory or by Keynes'
linear savings-investment theory. Professor Patinkin offers an
ingenious extension of Keynes' suggestion that the quantity
theory may be an operationally meaningful way to express
money-price relations in conditions of full employment. His stability discussion stands in interesting contrast with Professor
Vickrey's. My own essay takes up income distribution as an explicit variable in the consumption and investment functions from
a long-run standpoint, and also attempts to indicate the operational significance of the Keynesian macrofunctional theory of
distribution for progressive equilibrium.

Such is the nature of each essay in relation to the others, as
I see it. If I have misinterpreted any of these essays, I wish to
apologize but not without expressing my hope that the reader
will set me aright by checking them himself.

May I take this opportunity to say that the present volume
owes its fruition not only to the cooperative endeavors of the

participating authors but also to the good will of Dr. Thomas
Balogh, Professor Kenneth Galbraith, Dr. Everett E. Hagen,
Professor Seymour Harris, Mr. Roy Harrod, Professors Albert
G. Hart, Abba P. Lerner, James E. Meade, Lloyd Metzler, and
Broadus Mitchell, Dr. Jacob L. Mosak, Professors Ragnar Nurkse
and Austin Robinson, Mrs. Joan Robinson, Professor Paul A.
Samuelson, and Mr. Piero Sraffa.

KENNETH K. KURIHARA

NOTES ON THE AUTHORS

HOWARD R. BOWEN, Professor of Economics, Williams College. Director, study of graduate education in economics, American Economic Association. Economic consultant, National Council of Churches. Trustee, National Opinion Research Center. Member, American Economic Association, Royal Economic Society, Econometric Society, American Finance Association (president, 1950). Author of *Graduate Education in Economics* (American Economic Association), 1953; *Social Responsibilities of Businessmen*, Harpers, N.Y., 1953; *Toward Social Economy*, Rinehart, N.Y., 1948; *English Grants in Aid*, 1939; *Iowa Income*, 1934; and numerous monographs on monetary-fiscal subjects. Co-author of *Report on Japanese Taxation* (Shoup Mission), 1949. Published articles in *Quart. Jour. Eco., Amer. Eco. Rev., Jour. Finance, Jour. Business, Bull. Nat. Tax Assn.*

MARTIN BRONFENBRENNER, Associate Professor of Economics, University of Wisconsin. Member, American Economic Association, Econometric Society. Published contributions include: "The Consumption Function Controversy," *South. Eco. Jour.*, Jan. 1950; "Price Control under Imperfect Competition," *Amer. Eco. Rev.*, Mar. 1947; "Some Fundamentals in Liquidity Theory," *Quart. Jour. Eco.*, May 1945; "Production Functions: Cobb-Douglas, Interfirm, Intrafirm," *Econometrica*, Jan. 1944. Also articles in *Jour. Pol. Eco., Rev. Eco. Stat., Rev. Eco. Stud., Eco. Internaz., Nat. Tax Jour., Jour. Business.*

RICHARD BRUMBERG, Graduate Assistant in Economics, Johns Hopkins University. Member, American Economic Association. Published contributions include: "*Ceteris Paribus* for Supply Curves," *Eco. Jour.*, June 1953.

DUDLEY DILLARD, Professor and Chairman, Department of Economics, University of Maryland. Member, Board of Editors, *Journal of Economic History*. Member, American Economic Association. Author of *The Economics of John Maynard Keynes*, Prentice-Hall, N.Y., 1948 (Japanese, Spanish, Italian eds.). Published articles in *Amer. Eco. Rev., South. Eco. Jour., Jour. Eco. Hist., Jour. Land and Pub. Util. Eco.*

SHINICHI ICHIMURA, Assistant Professor of Economics, Wakayama University, Japan. Staff reviewer, *Mathematical Review*. Member, Econometric Society. Co-author of *National Income and Resources* (with N. Kamakura), Tokyo, 1951. Published articles include: "Dynamic Multiplier Analysis," *Keizai Ronso,* 1952; "A Critical Note on the Definition of Related Goods," *Rev. Eco. Stud.,* XIII(3), 1950-51. Other articles in *Econometrica, Jour. Eco. Theory* (Japan).

LAWRENCE R. KLEIN, Lecturer in Economics, and Consultant, Survey Research Center, University of Michigan. Consultant, Cowles Commission for Research in Economics, University of Chicago. Counselor and Fellow, Econometric Society. Author of *Econometrics,* Row, Peterson and Co., Evanston, Ill., 1953; *Economic Fluctuations in the United States,* John Wiley, N.Y., 1950; *The Keynesian Revolution,* Macmillan, N.Y., 1947 (British, Japanese eds.). Contributor to *Conference on Business Cycles,* Nat. Bur. Eco. Res., N.Y., 1951. Published articles in *Econometrica, Amer. Eco. Rev., Rev. Eco. Stud., Jour. Pol. Eco., Jour. Eco. and Soci.*

KENNETH K. KURIHARA, Assistant Professor of Economics, Rutgers University. Vice President, Metropolitan Economic Association. Member, American Economic Association, Royal Economic Society, Econometric Society. Author of *Monetary Theory and Public Policy,* Norton, N.Y., 1950 (Allen and Unwin, London, 1951); *Labor in the Philippine Economy,* Stanford Univ. Press, 1945. Published articles in *Amer. Eco. Rev., Jour. Pol. Eco., Rev. Eco. and Stat., Metroeconomica, Indian Eco. Jour., Social Research.*

R. C. O. MATTHEWS, Lecturer in Economics, Cambridge University. Fellow of St. John's College, Cambridge. Assistant Editor, *Economic Journal.* Member, Royal Economic Society. Author of *A Study in Trade-Cycle History: Economic Fluctuations in Great Britain 1833-1842,* Cambridge Univ. Press, 1954. Published articles in *Eco. Jour., Rev. Eco. Stud., Oxford Eco. Papers.*

FRANCO MODIGLIANI, Professor of Economics, Carnegie Institute of Technology. Consultant, Cowles Commission for Research in Economics, University of Chicago. Fellow, Econometric Society. Member, American Economic Association. Co-author of *National Incomes and International Trade* (with H. Neisser), Univ. of Illinois Press, 1953. Published contributions in *Studies in Income and Wealth,* Nat. Bur. Eco. Res., *Econometrica.*

GERALD M. MEIER, Instructor in Economics, Williams College. Rhodes Scholar, Oxford (1948-52). Member, American Economic Association. Published contributions include: "Note on the Theory of Comparative Costs and Long Period Developments," *Eco. Internaz.,*

Aug. 1952. Other articles in *Amer. Eco. Rev., Oxford Eco. Papers, Rev. Eco. Stud., Canad. Jour. Eco. Pol. Sci.*

ANATOL MURAD, Associate Professor of Economics, Rutgers University. Member, American Economic Association, Metropolitan Economic Association. Author of *Private Credit and Public Debt*, Public Affairs Press, 1954; *Economics*, Ames, Iowa, 1952; *The Paradox of a Metal Standard*, Washington, D.C., 1939. Co-author of *Economics: Experience and Analysis* (with B. Mitchell, *et al.*), William Sloane, N.Y., 1950. Contributor to *The Economics of Inflation* (by Willis and Chapman), 1935. Published articles in *Amer. Eco. Rev., South. Eco. Jour., Jour. Business, Southwest. Soc. Sci. Quart.*

DON PATINKIN, Associate Professor of Economics, Kaplan School of Economics and Social Science, Hebrew University, Jerusalem. Fellow, Econometric Society. Member, American Economic Association, Royal Economic Society. Published contributions include: "A Reconsideration of the General Equilibrium Theory of Money," *Rev. Eco. Stud.*, May 1951; "The Invalidity of Classical Monetary Theory," *Econometrica*, Apr. 1951; "Involuntary Unemployment and the Keynesian Supply Function," *Eco. Jour.*, Sept. 1949; "Price Flexibility and Full Employment," *Amer. Eco. Rev.*, Sept. 1948. Other articles also in *Economica, Metroeconomica, Quart. Jour. Eco., Jewish Soc. Stud.*

PAUL P. STREETEN, Lecturer in Economics, Oxford University. Fellow of Balliol College, Oxford. Member, Royal Economic Society. Translator and editor of *The Political Element in the Development of Economic Theory* (by G. Myrdal), Kegan Paul, 1953. Published articles in *Oxford Eco. Papers, Bull. Oxford Inst. Stat., Quart. Jour. Eco., Rev. Eco. Stud., Manchester School, Jahrbucher fur Nationalokomomie und Statistik.*

LORIE TARSHIS, Professor of Economics, Stanford University. Member, American Economic Association, Royal Economic Society. Author of *Elements of Economics*, Houghton Mifflin, Boston, 1947. Co-author of *Mobilizing Resources for War* (with T. Scitovsky and E. Shaw), McGraw-Hill, N.Y., 1951. Published articles in *Eco. Jour., Amer. Eco. Rev., Quart. Jour. Eco., Rev. Eco. Stud., Canad. Jour. Eco. Pol. Sci.*

MABEL F. TIMLIN, F.R.S.C., Professor of Economics, University of Saskatchewan. Member, Econometric Society, Canadian Political Science Association, American Economic Association, Royal Economic Society, Canadian Institute of International Affairs, Royal Society of Canada. Author of *Keynesian Economics*, University of Toronto Press, 1942 (also Japanese ed.). Published articles in *Amer. Eco. Rev., Canad. Jour. Eco. Pol. Sci.*

SHIGETO TSURU, Professor of Economics, and Director, Institute of Economic Research, Hitotsubashi University, Japan. Executive officer, Japan Science Council, Japanese Economic Association, International Association for Research in Income and Wealth. Member, Econometric Society, American Economic Association. Author of *National Income and Economic Reproduction,* Tokyo, 1951; *Postwar Inflation in Japan,* Tokyo, 1949; *A Travelog on American Economics,* Tokyo, 1948. Contributor to *The Theory of Capitalist Development* (by P. Sweezy), 1942. Published articles in *Rev. Eco. Stat., Econometrica, Rev. Sci. et Leg. Finan., Indian Eco. Rev., Annals Hitotsubashi Acad., Hitotsubashi Univ. Eco. Rev.*

WILLIAM S. VICKREY, Associate Professor of Economics, Columbia University. Member, American Economic Association, Royal Economic Society, Econometric Society, Metropolitan Economic Association, American Statistical Association, National Tax Association. Author of *Agenda for Progressive Taxation,* Ronald Press, N.Y., 1947; *The Revision of the Rapid Transit Fare Structure of the City of New York,* 1952. Co-author of *Report on Japanese Taxation* (Shoup Mission), 1949. Contributor to *Studies in Income and Wealth,* X (1947), and *Goals of Economic Life* (National Council of Churches), 1952. Published articles include "Limitations of Keynesian Economics," *Social Research,* XV (1948). Other articles in *Econometrica, Amer. Eco. Rev., Rev. Eco. and Stat., Jour. Pol. Eco., Jour. Amer. Stat. Assn., Proc. Nat. Tax Assn.*

CONTENTS

xvii

Part III. Aggregative Economics and Testing

PART ONE

MONETARY THEORY AND POLICY

CHAPTER ONE

The Theory of a Monetary Economy

Dudley Dillard

". . . money is the father of private property."—Max Weber, *General Economic History.*

MONEY is the central concept in the economics of John Maynard Keynes. Viewing his work as a whole, this proposition seems hardly debatable. With respect to his general theory of employment, it may be less obvious, although the title of his book, *The General Theory of Employment, Interest and Money,* is primafacie evidence that money, along with interest, is the key to his explanation of employment. The present essay examines the hypothesis that the properties of money constitute the ultimate theoretical basis in Keynes' analysis for the tendency of the economic system to reach equilibrium at less than full employment. This idea is discussed in terms of the origin, evolution, exposition, evaluation and possible further development of what Keynes calls The Theory of a Monetary Economy, or alternately, A Monetary Theory of Production. Although the modern theory of income and employment was stimulated mainly by Keynes, it has departed from his primary emphasis on money. Consequently the present essay has meaning in relation to a clear distinction between Keynes' own theory and what is often referred to as Keynesian economics, that is, the modern theory of income and employment which uses Keynes' tools, in refined form, but departs from his fundamental thought, as here interpreted.

Although this essay is mainly concerned with an interpretation of Keynes' fundamental thought, as distinguished from the apparatus in terms of which this thought is expressed, the fact that he was a person of exceptional ability and perspicacious insight suggests the fruitfulness of pursuing further the original direction of his thought. In the vast literature on Keynes almost no recognition has been given to his Theory of a Monetary Economy, and the concept has not been developed anywhere. Keynes' most important statement of the task to be performed by such a theory appears to be largely unknown to the contributors to Keynesian literature in English, perhaps because the essay in which this was elaborated appeared in a German volume in 1933.[1]

From a Monetary Theory of Prices to a Monetary Theory of Output

During the early part of his career Keynes was preoccupied with technical monetary theory and policy. His economic writings of the 1920's are concerned mainly with monetary standards, domestic price levels, and foreign exchange rates. His criticisms of the gold standard stemmed from a conviction that what was gained from stability of foreign exchange rates was more than outweighed by the instability of domestic price levels under such a system. He argues in the *Tract on Monetary Reform* for a managed currency and in the *Economic Consequences of Sterling Parity* he inveighs against a return to the gold standard at pre-war parity.

The *Treatise on Money* (1930) marks a turning point from the earlier monetary theory of prices to the later monetary theory of output. This transition is described by Keynes as follows: "When I began to write my *Treatise on Money* I was still moving along the traditional lines of regarding the influence of money as something so to speak separate from the general theory of supply and demand. When I finished it, I had made some progress towards pushing monetary theory back to becoming a theory of output as a whole." [2] The so-called fundamental equations belong to the earlier, or price level theory. These equations are alternative forms of expressing the traditional quantity equation for analyzing changes in price levels. However, the *Treatise* also analyzes fluctuations in output as responses to profit disequilibrium and in this respect it makes a substantial contribution to a monetary explanation of the trade cycle. Keynes describes the weakness of the *Treatise* as a failure "to deal thoroughly with the effects of *changes* in the level of output." [3]

[1] Keynes' essay appeared in *Der Stand und die nachste Zukunft der Konjuncturforschung, Festschrift fur Arthur Spiethoff* (Munich: Duncker & Humblot, 1933), pp. 123-25. The only direct reference to this article known to the present author is Wolfgang Stolper, "Monetary, Equilibrium, and Business-Cycle Theory," *The Review of Economic Statistics*, February, 1943, p. 88.
[2] *The General Theory of Employment, Interest and Money*, p. vi.
[3] *Ibid.*, p. vii.

While the *Treatise* remained closer to price theory than to output theory, the *General Theory of Employment* (1936) completes the transition from monetary price analysis to monetary income analysis. Technical monetary theory falls into the background and is replaced by a monetary theory of output as a whole. It is not quite accurate to say that the *General Theory* integrates monetary theory into general economic analysis; more appropriately general theory is integrated into monetary theory (of a broad type). Not only is the theory of prices in the *General Theory* incidental to the theory of employment, but it has an entirely new look. Prices are determined mainly by labor costs associated with an adumbrated labor theory of value (sometimes confused with sticky or inflexible wages). The level of prices and the physical volume of output determine the quantity of money needed for active circulation, and the rest of the money supply is held in idle balances, where it operates on the rate of interest, which in turn is an important determinant of the volume of investment and employment.

The Task of a Monetary Theory of Production

"Monetary economy," which always remained a sort of will-o'-the-wisp in Keynes' writings, becomes an explicit notion only after the onset of the Great Depression. As a member of the Macmillan Committee to investigate unemployment in Great Britain, Keynes was very critical of Professor Pigou, who appeared as a witness, for analyzing unemployment and related questions on a "real" level and only subsequently introducing minor modifications occasioned by shifting to a money level of analysis. The unreality of the "real" approach is the burden of Keynes' questions and exposition—for he could not resist expounding his own ideas even when interrogating witnesses.

In his essay on Malthus (1933), Keynes praises Malthus for analyzing problems in terms of "the monetary economy in which we happen to live," and criticizes Ricardo for using "the abstraction of a neutral money economy." [4] From his monetary level of analysis Malthus was able to work out an explanation of fluctuations in output in terms of a theory of effectual demand, which Keynes felt that Ricardo was never able to comprehend. However, Malthus was unable to carry his analysis far enough to

4 *Essays in Biography*, p. 138.

provide a satisfactory theory because "Malthus's great defect lay in his overlooking entirely the part played by the rate of interest." [5] Keynes' critique of Malthus may be summed up by saying that the strength of Malthus' position lay in projecting his analysis on a monetary level and his weakness lay in the lack of a theory of interest. This evaluation anticipates Keynes' own theory of employment in terms of money and interest.

Keynes' clearest statement of the Theory of a Monetary Economy is given in his essay in the *Festschrift* for Arthur Spiethoff, already referred to above. The *Festschrift*, which appeared in 1933 on the occasion of Spiethoff's sixtieth birthday, is devoted to discussions and explanations of crises and business fluctuations. Keynes opens his contribution by stating: "In my opinion the main reason why the Problem of Crises is unsolved, or at any rate why this theory is so unsatisfactory, is to be found in the lack of what might be termed a Monetary Theory of Production." He develops this theme in terms of a distinction between Monetary Economics and Real-Exchange Economics. A Monetary Economy is defined as one in which "Money plays a part of its own and affects motives and decisions and is, in short, one of the operative factors in the situation, so that the course of events cannot be predicted, either in the long period or in the short, without a knowledge of the behaviour of money between the first state and the last." Money has a role *sui generis* in a Monetary Economy; it is not neutral; it is not just a device for facilitating transactions in real things.

Real-Exchange Economics, which is similar to what Keynes later called "classical economics," assumes away the whole problem of booms and depressions. The assumptions of Real-Exchange Economics are "precisely the same as those which will insure that crises do not occur." In Real-Exchange Economics money is neutral in the sense that it does not affect the essential nature of transactions—it is not allowed to enter into and help to determine motives and decisions which influence the volume of output. Money is important only in the sense that it is more efficient than barter.

Two other points in the Spiethoff essay are of special interest in connection with the Theory of a Monetary Economy which Keynes subsequently developed in the *General Theory*. The first concerns the relation of money to interest and of interest to out-

[5] *Ibid.,* p. 147.

put. The link between money and output via the rate of interest is quite explicit in the 1933 article. The difference between Real-Exchange Economics and Monetary Economics is "most marked and perhaps most important when we come to the discussion of the rate of interest and to the relation between the volume of output and the amount of expenditure." No mention is made of the savings and investment nexus which has been featured in most interpretations of Keynes' general theory of employment. The second point concerns the relation of Monetary Economics to policy. Although a Monetary Theory of Production is essential for explaining booms and depressions, Keynes does not view the business cycle as a purely monetary phenomenon nor does he espouse a purely monetary remedy. Finally in concluding the essay he poses the task later performed in the *General Theory*: "Accordingly I believe that the next task is to work out in some detail a Monetary Theory of Production, to supplement the Real-Exchange Theories. . . . At any rate that is the task on which I am now occupying myself, in some confidence that I am not wasting my time."

In the three years between the Spiethoff essay and publication of the *General Theory*, Keynes made occasional published references to his work, but there is no other statement in which the plan of the work is so clearly sketched as in the *Festschrift* contribution. However, by way of indicating the lines along which his Monetary Theory of Production was crystallizing, mention should be made of the *New Republic* article in 1935 entitled "A Self-Adjusting Economic System?" in which Keynes states he has found the answer to the paradox of poverty in the midst of potential plenty. The real issue between Keynes and the orthodox theory is not so much whether unemployment or full employment actually exists at any time, but whether there are automatic processes which always *tend* toward full employment. In this 1935 article, as later, Keynes rests his case for the lack of automaticity in the economic system on the monetary nature of the rate of interest. The "fatal flaw," as he calls it, of the orthodox theory has been its failure to provide a realistic theory of interest. Keynes' earlier concern with money and his new preoccupation with output (or the lack of it) were to be brought together through a monetary theory of the rate of interest.

In the "Preface" of the *General Theory of Employment, Interest and Money* Keynes stresses expectations as the distinguish-

ing characteristic of a monetary economy: "A monetary economy
. . . is essentially one in which changing views about the future
are capable of influencing the quantity of employment and not
merely its direction." The analysis of present economic behavior
in terms of changing expectations about the future "depends on
the interaction of supply and demand, and is in this way linked
up with our fundamental theory of value," which is part of a
more general theory in which the classical analysis becomes a
special case.

The notion of bringing traditional economic analysis, with its
emphasis on value and distribution, into an integrated Monetary
Theory is the subject of the first section of chapter 21 on "The
Theory of Prices" in the *General Theory*. In order to prepare the
ground for this task Keynes abandons the usual division of economics into the theory of value and distribution, on the one hand,
and the theory of money, on the other, in favor of a dichotomy
between the theory of the single firm (or industry) and the theory
of output and exployment as a whole. Money is not a separate
branch of the subject matter of economics, but is an integral part
of any realistic analysis. The properties of money are not so important to the theory of the firm, "But as soon as we pass to the
problem of what determines output and employment as a whole,
we require the complete theory of a Monetary Economy." The
influence of money on current expectations concerning the uncertain future is again emphasized. Money is an operative force
influencing these decisions. Since "money in its significant attributes is, above all, a subtle device for linking the present to
the future; and we cannot even begin to discuss the effect of
changing expectations on current activities except in monetary
terms."

Further evidence of the stress on money in relation to expectations is found in Keynes' first published reply to reviewers
and critics of the *General Theory*. The article, entitled "The
General Theory of Employment," reiterates "the comparatively
simple fundamental ideas which underlie my theory. . . ." [6]
Although the term "Monetary Economy" does not appear in this
article, the role of money and interest in determining output is
featured, as against, for example, the savings and investment
apparatus. After a brief reply to some specific criticisms, Keynes
launches into a discussion of "the simple basic ideas," including

[6] *The Quarterly Journal of Economics*, February, 1937.

uncertainty, expectations, money, interest, alternative forms of holding wealth, and their effects on fluctuations in the accumulation of capital as the cause of fluctuations in output as a whole.

Money and Unemployment

Keynes' most direct statement attributing unemployment to money appears in the chapter of the *General Theory* entitled "The Essential Properties of Interest and Money," where he states: "Thus with other commodities left to themselves, 'natural forces,' *i.e.*, the ordinary forces of the market, would tend to bring their rate of interest down until the emergence of full employment. . . . Thus in the absence of money . . . the rates of interest would only reach equilibrium when there is full employment." (p. 235) This rather striking statement that unemployment could not persist in the absence of money can be evaluated only in relation to the whole system of thought of which it is a part. In the absence of space for such a comprehensive evaluation, a few observations may suffice to indicate the place of money in Keynes' Theory of a Monetary Economy. The schedule of liquidity-preference, which is, of course, the crucial concept by which money is introduced into the theory of output, occupies a unique position in his system. It reflects the pragmatic nature of Keynes' thinking more than do other concepts of the general theory. It falls into line with a pragmatic maxim which Keynes quotes in his essay on Frank Ramsey to the effect that ". . . the meaning of a sentence [concept] is to be defined by reference to the actions to which asserting it would lead. . . ." [7] Keynes' concept of liquidity-preference appears to have been derived from a practical judgment concerning what might be done about the plight of the economy during the Great Depression, and more particularly during the financial crisis of 1931. He theorized along lines that gave logical coherence to his views on policy. In order to arrive at a determinate solution of the unemployment equilibrium, he needed a concept which would explain why investment was checked before the rate of interest fell to zero,[8] so he invented and injected liquidity-preference into his system to supply the missing link. Concepts arrived at in this manner have a rough-

[7] *Essays in Biography*, pp. 299-300.
[8] In this connection see Keynes' statement in the essay on Malthus: "Twenty years ago I should have retorted to Malthus that the state of affairs he envisages could not occur unless the rate of interest had fallen to zero." *Essays in Biography*, p. 147.

and-ready hue; they lack the refinement of concepts derived by proceeding in step-by-step logic from first premises to final conclusions. However, they have the great advantage of being relevant to actual experience, from which they are in fact derived, and may prove enlightening or useful, especially if the inventor [9] is an individual of discerning practical insight. The schedule of liquidity-preference suggests at once the possibilities of monetary policy (on the downward sloping range of the curve) and its limitations (on the flat range of the curve as well as the instability of the entire schedule), which together provide a rationale for monetary policy and, beyond that, for deficit spending in depression. The *General Theory* is another essay in persuasion. Probably not much significance can be attached to attempts at direct empirical verification or refutation of liquidity-preference. It has meaning in relation to other concepts in the system and to the theory as a whole, which in turn has operational meaning in terms of policies that may prove wise or unwise depending upon the results obtained in actual experience. This interpretation of the genesis and significance of liquidity-preference is intended to carry with it the suggestion that "stickiness" of the rate of interest is part of the structural pattern of the economic system as Keynes envisaged it, and not an abnormality.

Keynes' theory of interest is a corollary of his theory of unneutral money. On one occasion in order to highlight the strategic role of money in the theory of output, Keynes altered the terminology used in the *General Theory* to refer to the rate of interest as the marginal efficiency of money. He held that the orthodox view regards "the marginal efficiency of money as wholly different in character from the marginal efficiency of other assets." [10] In the orthodox view, the marginal efficiency of other assets varies with their quantity, whereas the marginal efficiency of money is held not to, since changes in the volume of money are assumed

[9] The word "inventor," rather than "discoverer," is used advisedly to stress the nature of such concepts. They do not involve the discovery of new laws, principles, or phenomena previously unknown, but are new contrivances or inventions which previously did not exist either known or unknown. Liquidity-preference reveals no new truth. It is a device for focusing the analysis on relations between aspects of known experience. The relevant test of such concepts is one of usefulness, not of validity in the sense of correspondence to experience. Any test of validity must be in operational terms after the meaning has been established, presumably in relation to the whole system of which individual concepts are a part.

[10] "The Theory of the Rate of Interest," in *The Lessons of Monetary Experience, Essays in Honor of Irving Fisher*, A. D. Gayer, ed. (New York, 1937), p. 151.

to affect prices but not the rate of interest. The level of the marginal efficiency of other assets depends on the scale of investment, which is assumed in the orthodox theory to be at a level corresponding to full employment. Following the equilibrium requirement that the marginal efficiencies of all assets, including money, must be at the same level (due to the attempts of wealth-holders to equalize advantages from all forms of ownership), the rate of interest is assumed to adjust passively to the level of the marginal efficiencies of other assets. Money is neutral; it plays no part in determining the level of output and employment.

In Keynes' own analysis, in which the marginal efficiency of money (rate of interest) does vary with the quantity of money, the distinction between active balances (M_1) and inactive balances (M_2) is absolutely essential. He is willing to accept the orthodox presentation that the marginal efficiency of money does not vary with its quantity so far as active balances are concerned, which means he accepts the view that the demand for money for transactions depends primarily on the level of money income. If all balances were active, changes in the quantity of money might not influence the rate of interest (even though the rate of interest would have some influence on the size of balances). Even in the case of inactive balances, he concedes the possibility of this being true if expectations were "constant and definite." But in a monetary economy where expectations cannot in the nature of the case be constant and definite, Keynes insists that the marginal efficiency of money depends on the quantity of money in the same way that the marginal efficiencies of other assets depend on their quantities.

Money lulls the disquietude of wealth-holders confronted with uncertain expectations. Since money cannot be produced by private enterprise, its marginal efficiency is not free to fall, whereas in the case of other assets additional production brings down their marginal efficiencies. However, since the marginal efficiencies of all assets, including money, tend to equality, the failure of the marginal efficiency of money to fall tends to halt the production of other assets (investment). ". . . the marginal efficiency of other assets falls into line with the rate of interest." [11] This is almost the reverse of the orthodox position which, as previously noted, holds that the marginal efficiency of money adapts passively to the marginal efficiencies of other assets.

11 *Ibid.*, p. 147.

Money in its role as a store of wealth stands as a barrier to full production, that is, unemployment is caused by money. Under laissez-faire this is inevitable. Some relief may come from appropriate monetary policy, but even this suffers from important limitations.

Elasticity in the supply of output and in the size of inactive balances provides the basis of flexibility whereby the economic system adapts itself to shocks which orthodox theory assumed could and would be absorbed by flexibility of prices. Elasticities in the scale of output and in the desire for money balances permit a degree of price stability not otherwise possible. "If these elasticities are zero there is a necessity for the whole body of prices and wages to respond immediately to every change in the quantity of money." [12] This analysis reflects again the shift from the traditional monetary theory of prices to a monetary theory of output. The essential distinction between active and idle balances is a further development of the earlier dichotomy between industrial and financial circulation. The nub of the economic *problem* lies in the financial (speculative) sphere, where the stress on fluctuating expectations is the key to Keynes' Theory of a Monetary Economy. As explained in the Spiethoff essay, Real-Exchange Economics, involving the assumption of neutral money, is a very blunt weapon for dealing with crises and most other disturbing features of the world of actual experience.

Monetary and Nonmonetary Economies

Chapter 17 in the *General Theory* on "The Essential Properties of Interest and Money" contains Keynes' most sustained effort to detail the Theory of a Monetary Economy. Failure to appreciate the significance of this chapter appears to the present author as one of the ironies in the history of economic thought. Perhaps its neglect can be explained by the tendency of modern economists to concern themselves with the apparatus of thought rather than with fundamental ideas. Professor A. P. Lerner alone among the commentators has devoted a full-length article to Chapter 17, and even his effort, while not without interpretative significance, is directed mainly at clarification of exposition and terminology. [13]

[12] *Ibid.*, p. 152.
[13] A. P. Lerner, "The Essential Properties of Interest and Money," *The Quarterly Journal of Economics*, May 1952.

Chapter 17 opens with a discussion of own-rates of interest, the purpose of which is to (a) generalize the theory of interest from money to all assets, and (b) to show why the own-rate of interest on money is the significant one which "rules the roost," "sets the pace," "carries the sting." Professor Lerner distinguishes three different aspects of Keynes' discussion of own-rates: the own-rate from *lending* an asset, which he calls the own-rate of interest in a proper sense; the own-rate from *holding* or possessing an asset, which he calls the marginal efficiency of holding; and the own-rate from *creating* new assets, which he calls the marginal efficiency of investment, a term equivalent to Keynes' marginal efficiency of capital. In Professor Lerner's terminology the significant concept for chapter 17 is the marginal efficiency of holding an asset. This terminology is helpful in clarifying Keynes' discussion of the essential properties of money and interest.

The total return or benefit expected from lending, holding, or creating an asset is equal to the algebraic sum of its yield (q), minus its carrying cost (c), plus its liquidity-premium (l). Characteristically the yield of an instrumental capital asset exceeds its carrying cost, and the liquidity-premium is negligible. Stocks of finished goods usually involve a carrying cost in excess of the expected yield plus the liquidity-premium, although under some circumstances the liquidity-premium may become significant. Money is peculiar in having a liquidity-premium that exceeds its carrying cost, and its yield is nil. Thus the total return on an instrumental asset is approximately q; of stocks approximately $-c$; and of money l, assuming the carrying costs are negligible. Own-rates may be expressed in terms of the asset itself or in terms of any other asset taken as a standard. As a rule, own-rates are expressed in money, but they might be expressed in wheat or houses or some other asset. The choice of standard is not particularly important in principle. If some assets are expected to appreciate (depreciate) in relation to the standard, an appreciation (depreciation) factor reduces them to comparable terms. Thus under normal circumstances in which money is the standard, its own-rate in terms of itself will be l (assuming no carrying costs). If an instrumental asset is expected to appreciate in terms of money at the rate a_1, its own-rate expressed in terms of money will be $a_1 + q$, as compared with q if it were expressed in terms of itself. Similarly if a stock of goods is expected to appreciate in terms of money at the rate a_2, its own-rate in terms of money will be $a_2 - c$, as compared with $-c$ expressed in terms of itself. In equilibrium the own-rates of all assets will be equal when expressed in terms of the same standard. Moreover, in equilibrium the own-rate of interest, the marginal efficiency of holding, and the marginal efficiency of investing are all equal to each other.

The strategic asset in relation to the scale of investment and employment is the one with an own-rate of holding most reluctant to fall as measured by the algebraic sum of $q - c + l$. This will be, according to Keynes, the asset with a liquidity-premium most in excess of its carrying cost. Some asset will occupy this position, and very probably although not inevitably, it will be what is usually called "money"; but whether or not this asset is called "money," it will perform the asset function of money in capitalistic societies. Presumably in an economy in which cattle or tobacco, for example, functioned as the standard of value, the precious metals or other durable assets with low maintenance would occupy the asset or store-of-value function of money. If there were no asset with a liquidity-premium in excess of its carrying cost, the economy would be described as nonmonetary, since money in the relevant sense would not exist.

By virtue of its essential properties the marginal efficiency of holding money of the conventional type tends to decline more slowly than the marginal efficiency of holding any other asset. In addition to a high liquidity-premium and a low carrying cost, the important properties of conventional money are its negligible elasticities of production and substitution. For ordinary commodities and most instruments of production an increase in demand will temporarily increase the price and call forth an enlarged output to bring down the higher price. In the case of money, however, an increase in demand will increase the price (rate of interest) but cannot result in an increase in the quantity of money, because money is not produced like ordinary commodities. It cannot be produced by diverting labor and other resources to its production. Some factors, like land, have a negligible elasticity of production, but when their price rises other factors can be substituted for them. This, however, cannot be done with money, which has a negligible elasticity of substitution as well as a negligible elasticity of production. By its nature money cannot respond to the ordinary forces of the market in a "normal" fashion. Institutionally speaking, it differs from all other assets. The institutional peculiarities of money provide the ultimate basis for Keynes' explanation of unemployment.

Even though the quantity of money is not changed by the forces of the market, the quantity of liquidity is capable of being increased by forces that in some sense are automatic. An increase in the demand for money will tend to increase its value via a fall in prices. At a lower price level less money will be required for transactions and more money will be available for inactive balances. Also at lower prices, the ratio of money to other forms of wealth will be greater. Without denying that some reduction will take place in the rate of interest and that some increase will occur in the volume of effective demand via these sequences, Keynes gives several reasons for believing that the nature and magnitudes of the change are not such as to assure full employment. If a rise in the value of money sets up expectations of a further rise, the marginal efficiency of holding money will increase. Moreover, the tendency for money-wage rates to be sticky for reasons that are inherent in the nature of money as a standard of value, and not just because of "rigidities" in the narrower sense of the term, limits the fall in prices and therefore limits the amount of funds transferable from active to inactive balances. More important, however, are the properties of money associated with high liquidity and low carrying costs, especially after the rate of interest on money has fallen to its "institutional minimum" (Modigliani), perhaps at 2 per cent. At this point the liquidity-preference schedule becomes horizontal. The demand for money becomes perfectly elastic in the sense that it can be exchanged for other forms of wealth in indefinite quantities without causing the terms of trade to become less favorable to money. Money becomes "a bottomless sink for purchasing power." [14] The liquidity advantage of money is not offset by carrying costs which make the storage of most assets for extended periods prohibitively expensive. Beyond a modest limit, wealth cannot be stored in the form of stocks without suffering losses. Large values stored up in real wealth take the form of instrumental capital-assets. However, this latter alternative may be unattractive if the terms on which their future output can be converted into money are definitely expected to be unfavorable or if there is considerable uncertainty as to whether or not they will be favorable, which is to

[14] *General Theory*, p. 231.

B

say that investment will not occur if the marginal efficiency of holding and of investing in instrumental assets is low.

Given the special properties of money—including its high liquidity-premium, low carrying cost, and negligible elasticities of production and substitution—the ordinary forces of the market, which would be effective in pushing down the rates of return on other assets, cannot operate to lower the marginal efficiency of holding money to a level which assures full employment. Not only money but any asset with the characteristics of money can prevent the system from reaching equilibrium at full employment. This flaw in the market mechanism, which Keynes otherwise accepts as largely free of major faults, prevents the economic system from being self-adjusting along the lines suggested by orthodox theory. Unemployment results because the owners of wealth demand what cannot be produced (money), and do not demand what can be produced (other forms of wealth).

The asset or store-of-value function is by far the most important aspect of money in relation to Keynes' explanation of unemployment. However, the properties of money arising from its being the *standard* of value interact with its properties as a store of wealth to enhance the strategic importance of the marginal efficiency of holding money. The advantages of holding assets in the form in which future obligations will fall due contribute to the liquidity-premium of money because such payments, including wages and other contracts, are normally payable in the standard of value. If wheat rather than money were the standard in terms of which contracts and wages were payable, wheat would enjoy a liquidity-premium which it does not normally have. However, as already noted, if wheat were the standard of value, it would not have the same significance as conventional money in determining employment, because the carrying cost of wheat is relatively high. What matters is not the absolute level of liquidity but the algebraic sum of $l - c$. Furthermore, the elasticities of production and substitution for wheat would prevent it from playing the crucial role of conventional money if wheat were the standard of value.

The liquidity of money is enhanced by the expectation that wages will be relatively sticky in terms of money. This expectation is not an accidental condition caused by trade unions and the like, but follows from the other properties of money. Money enjoys liquidity partly because a low elasticity of production means the supply cannot be easily increased, and because money, due to its low carrying cost, can be absorbed in large quantities without loss. In other words, the stickiness of wages is "a corollary of the excess of liquidity-premium over carrying costs being greater for money than for any other asset." [15] With other commodities, or at least most other commodities, a greater than negligible elasticity of production gives rise to the possibility of a large increase in their quantity, and their greater than negligible carrying costs means that any surplus in current production cannot be absorbed into stocks except at a loss. Money loses its liquidity when its quantity is expected to increase sharply.[16] In drastic inflation this is what actually happens. What has been called "money" ceases to function as money because it loses its liquidity-premium. The liquidity-preference curve falls through the bottom of the graph. In a somewhat similar fashion, the low elasticity of substitution of other things for money means that no rapid increase in other things can have much effect on the value of money.

Keynes defines a nonmonetary economy as one in which there is no asset with a liquidity-premium in excess of its carrying cost. Although this condition is difficult, and probably impossible, to realize under private ownership of the means of production, the concept of a monetary economy may be clarified by reference to a hypothetical nonmonetary economy. Such a state of affairs may be imagined to exist as a result of a sufficiently high artificial carrying cost on money and all substitutes for money. Silvio Gesell's proposal for stamped-money and similar suggestions by others are designed to increase the carrying cost of money, although not necessarily to a point exceeding the liquidity-premium. No attempt is made to evaluate these plans for creating artificial carrying costs on money, but it should be observed that there exists, so far as the present author is aware, no satisfactory

[15] *General Theory*, p. 238. Stickiness of wages has an entirely different significance in Keynes' Monetary Economy than in Pigou's Real-Exchange Economy. An understanding of the Theory of a Monetary Economy might have spared the journals the plethora of polemics on the so-called Pigou effect. In eschewing policy considerations and by invoking the stationary state, Pigou moves on a level of analysis totally different from Keynes' Monetary Economy. Harrod contends that Pigou, despite conciliatory statements, never understood Keynes' general theory of employment. See Harrod's review of Pigou's *Keynes's General Theory* in *The American Economic Review*, September, 1951, pp. 665-71.
[16] *General Theory*, p. 241 n.

refutation of these proposals on their own ground. This does not mean that the ideas are sound, or even "on the right track," as Keynes said, but merely records a fact. Administrative difficulties which are inevitably associated with stamped-money plans may render them too impracticable to merit serious theoretical treatment, although impracticability does not appear to inhibit theoretical discussions by economists. Possibly the utopian plans for monetary reform have not been satisfactorily refuted because of the underdeveloped status of monetary theory in relation to output and employment. Keynes' theory of own-rates of interest, which is intended to show that all assets contain qualities of moneyness, is a step in the right direction. Unfortunately it does not carry through far enough to refute the utopian schemes on theoretical grounds, and in fact is carried just far enough to suggest that the plans might be workable.

The general objective of plans calling for artificial carrying costs on money is to make money more like other assets, to take away its preferred position in the hierarchy of wealth. The question remains whether, even if such proposals were capable of realizing their objective, they would be desirable. Professor Simmons has contended "the gap between money and other things should be made as wide as possible." [17] To make other things more like money or money more like other things would, he argues, destroy the basis for successful monetary management. Keynes' position appears ambiguous. On the one hand, his explanation of unemployment in terms of the reluctance of the marginal efficiency of holding money to fall because of the excess of its liquidity-premium over its carrying cost led him to see logical merit in remedies involving the creation of artificial carrying costs.[18] On the other hand, he attributes stickiness of wages to the essential properties of money and sees in the stickiness of wages the basis for stability of prices, which is an important condition of general economic stability.

While Keynes avoids most of the pitfalls of utopian monetary reformers like Robert Owen, John Gray, John Francis Bray, Proudhon, and Silvio Gesell, his thought has much in common with theirs. All reject Say's law of markets because of its neutral money implications; all view interest as a monetary phenome-

---

[17] Edward C. Simmons, "The Relative Liquidity of Money and Other Things," *Readings in Monetary Theory* (Philadelphia, 1951), p. 33.
[18] See *General Theory*, pp. 234, 353-58.

THEORY OF A MONETARY ECONOMY 19

non; all are vigorously opposed to the gold standard; all are anti-*rentier* and pro-entrepreneur; all adhere to or are sympathetic to the labor theory of value; and they distinguish the financial and industrial spheres of capitalism, blaming the former for unemployment and other economic ills, while finding no major fault with industrial circulation. The purpose of their monetary reforms was an economic environment in which supply would create its own demand. John Gray, for example, said that if his monetary proposal for social reform were adopted, "to sell for money would be as easy as it is to buy for money; . . . production would become the uniform and never-failing cause of demand."

Overall, Keynes appears to have believed it impossible to create a nonmonetary economy even though it might be desirable to do so. In discussing the complete theory of a Monetary Economy, he says: "We cannot get rid of money. . . . So long as there exists any durable asset, it is capable of possessing monetary attributes and, therefore, of giving rise to the characteristic problems of a monetary economy." [19] The conclusion that Keynes did did not believe it possible, even though desirable, to create a nonmonetary economy is subject to the obvious qualification that a complete socialist economy with no privately owned means of production would be "nonmonetary." Under these institutional arrangements the ownership of money would not be an alternative to ownership of means of production and therefore could not provide a basis for withholding the latter from use in production. Liquidity is important to individual property-owners but not to the community as a whole. If it is true that Keynes did not believe it possible to create a nonmonetary economy within the limits of private ownership, his theory of a monetary economy turns out to be a theory of a private property economy.

Evaluation of Keynes' Contribution to the Theory of a Monetary Economy

The thesis of the present essay may now be restated. Money is the central concept in Keynes' general theory of employment in the sense that it is the strategic factor which, in continuity with his earlier writings, is "institutionalized," which "makes the difference." Money is the "institution" upon which the entire

[19] *General Theory*, p. 294.

analysis focuses and around which everything else "falls into place." The theory is oriented toward showing how money can be managed or manipulated to compensate for disturbing forces in the economy, but in contradistinction to his earlier ideas, the institutionalizing of money in the theory of employment suggests the inevitability of unemployment in a Monetary Economy except by measures that extend beyond conventional forms of monetary policy. By a logical development of Keynes' thought, monetary theory and policy are merged with fiscal theory and policy and are carried beyond monetary-fiscal measures. Unemployment is shown to be endemic in a monetary economy. Money holds the key to explaining unemployment but not to its remedy. Flirtation with the stamped-money proposal illustrates the dilemma. Failure of monetary measures to correspond to the monetary explanation suggests either a deep-seated inconsistency or the need for monetary remedies in a more fundamental sense than the term usually signifies. The latter position is nearer to the theme of the present essay than the former, although elements of inconsistency are not altogether lacking in Keynes' thought.

The meaning of the proposition that money is the central concept may be illustrated by contrasting its role with that of the consumption function. The propensity to consume, which Keynes describes as a "fundamental psychological law," is related, if not to human nature as such, at least to "the more or less permanent social structure of the community." [20] As a "fairly stable function," the propensity to consume is an important taxonomic device, but it lacks the operational and causal significance of the factors which determine the pace of unstable investment. The consumption function is not manageable to the same degree and with the same appropriateness as the quantity of money, the rate of government loan expenditure, and the "socialization of investment."

Rejection of Say's law of markets follows from the repudiation of neutral money associated with Real-Exchange Economics. The notion that supply creates its own demand is a corollary of the broader conception of economic activity on the analogy of a barter economy. In a barter economy, or one which behaves as if it were a barter economy, production represents demand for

[20] *General Theory*, p. 110.

other goods, hoarding cannot occur in any manner which is significant for unemployment, and wages may be viewed as involving a barter of wage-goods for labor services. No fault need be found with this type of analysis other than its irrelevance to problems such as crises, business cycles, and unemployment. Being oriented to policy considerations, Keynes' system places a high premium on relevance to real problems. Keynes' achievement on the critical side was to show that economic theory which operates with the assumption of neutral money cannot be very useful in explaining crises and unemployment.

Keynes' rejection of Say's law, and therefore of neutral money, is closely linked with his criticism of the orthodox theory of the rate of interest, adjustments in which are supposed in the orthodox scheme to equilibrate savings to investment at full employment. Unneutral money is invoked to account for the failure of the rate of interest to be self-adjusting to a level corresponding to full employment. Keynes attempts to remedy this "fatal flaw" in orthodox economics with a monetary theory of interest.

By virtue of choosing formal apparatus similar to that of his orthodox predecessors, Keynes, like most pathbreaking economists, suffered from a self-imposed handicap in the expression of his new ideas. The orthodox model, with its stress on the rate of interest and with no emphasis on money, was not wholly appropriate for demonstrating Keynes' insight concerning the role of money in economic activity. In providing an alternative to the classical theory of interest, Keynes was led to devote more attention to interest than is justified by its importance in policy questions, the criteria which usually guided his selection and emphasis. More important, however, by making the influence of money on production operate primarily through the rate of interest, Keynes limited the role of money more narrowly than would appear to be called for in working out a Monetary Theory of Production. From his original and ambitious objective of formulating the Theory of a Monetary Economy, he shifted in the *General Theory* to filling in the gaps in the existing theory. He thereby simplified his task but limited his achievement. Consequently many of the most significant ideas are found outside the formal model. As Arthur Smithies has observed of the *General Theory*, "Its true greatness could never have been achieved had its author been fully dependent on the analytic tools he forged . . . . any attempt to formalize the *General Theory* inevitably does it less than justice." [21]

In looking outside the formal apparatus of Keynes' system to the ideas already discussed in connection with the essential properties of interest and money, it seems evident that the genuine significance of money is associated with its role as a special form of property and that the over-all meaning of the theory may be described as a critique of money in a private enterprise economy. To money as property is assigned the ultimate theoretical explanation of unemployment. Money offers an attractive alternative to the ownership of real instrumental assets. The marginal efficiency of holding money can rise without limit but it can never fall below a certain minimum, whereas the marginal efficiency of holding other assets cannot rise very high and can fall almost without limit, even to negative rates. The store-of-value function of money is, significantly, its asset function. The distinction between M_1 and M_2 has its meaning in this connection. Under characteristic conditions of unemployment and uncertainty, money operates at a deeper level of motivation in lulling the disquietude of wealth-holders confronted with innumerable imponderables. As a link between the present and the future, money influences the expectations of wealth-owners both with respect to the form in which they choose to hold their assets and also with respect to the form in which they expect increments in wealth to accrue. The holder of wealth desires a future command of general purchasing power which will enable him either to consume some (presently) unspecified item or to increase further his accumulations. Keynes' discussion of the fact that capital accumulation is, from the motivation point of view, basically money accumulation is relegated to a chapter entitled "Sundry Observations on the Nature of Capital," which falls outside the main model. Very little stress is placed on money as the objective to be desired from the *production* of real wealth as distinguished from money as an alternative form in which to *hold* wealth.

Despite the lack of a theory of capital as such, Keynes' familiar proposition that employment depends on investment leads to a general critique of the whole capitalist process. Contradictions and tensions associated with the accumulation of wealth come to the forefront of the analysis. Instability becomes normal

[21] *The New Economics*, Seymour E. Harris, ed. (New York, 1947), pp. 559, 563.

rather than abnormal. Abundance of capital may interfere with the abundance of output, that is, old wealth may be a barrier to the production of new wealth. Accumulation by individuals may contribute to the impoverishment of society if the prospective benefit from owning money is more attractive than the prospective reward from creating new assets. Each addition to the stock of real capital-assets tends to lower the rate of return and to enhance the preference for liquid rather than illiquid wealth. Poverty in the midst of potential plenty finds a ready explanation. Thrift may impede and profligacy may promote the progress of wealth. This follows from the theory of effective demand according to which investment is important because it is a means for disbursing income most of which will be spent for consumption. At modest and higher levels of employment, those receiving income from consumers' goods activity will not spend enough to buy back all they produce; the deficiency in their spending must be compensated for by spending for consumers' goods on the part of those whose incomes are derived from an activity other than producing consumers' goods. Activity which results in the purchase but not the production of consumers' goods must be considered as "investment" for the purposes of the income analysis based on the proposition that employment depends on investment. The contribution of new investment to greater future production forms no part of the model.

Only to a limited extent did Keynes achieve a Monetary Theory of Production, the goal set out in the 1933 Spiethoff essay. Only in the financial sphere is money unneutral. In the sphere of production, or to use a cognate term prominently featured in the *Treatise*, in the Industrial Circulation, money remains neutral in much the same sense that it is neutral in Real-Exchange Economics. As already noted, in the main model the impact on production is through the rate of interest, operating in the financial sphere, to investment and output in the industrial sphere. That changes in the rate of interest can cause major changes in investment and employment does not carry conviction. One may accept a purely monetary explanation of interest, as Professor Schumpeter, for example, does, and yet assign only minor importance to interest rate policy and major importance to money and credit. Keynes has been criticized with considerable justification for assuming an interest-elastic schedule of the marginal efficiency of capital. If the investment-demand sched-

ule is interest-inelastic not much can be expected in the way of
increases in investment and employment from purely monetary
policy, no matter to what extent changes in the quantity of
money may affect the rate of interest. However, Keynes vacil-
lated in the importance of control of interest rates. The tone of
the *General Theory* is to play down the importance of changes
in the rate of interest because of the overriding influence on investment of instability in the entire schedule of the marginal
efficiency of capital. With respect to the schedule of liquidity-
preference, Keynes was more concerned with its shape and with
movements along a given curve than with shifts in the entire
schedule.

Instability of the marginal efficiency of capital calculated on
the principles of private enterprise is the occasion for Keynes'
extending his policy recommendations beyond financiel (*i.e.*,
monetary-fiscal) measures to what he calls "socialization of investment." This concept is interesting in relation to the view
expressed in the Spiethoff essay that a Theory of Monetary Production does not mean that the remedies for crises can be purely
monetary. In the *General Theory,* in the concluding paragraph
of the chapter on "The State of Long-Term Expectation," after
a vivid portrayal of the erratic and precarious basis of private
expectations, Keynes says he expects to see "the State, which is
in a position to calculate the marginal efficiency of capital-goods
on long views and on the basis of the general social advantage,
taking an ever greater responsibility for directly organizing investment; . . ." The distinction between the erratic expectations of private enterprise and the more constant expectations of
social (state) enterprise reflects the identification of Monetary
Economics with private enterprise. Private producers engage in
Monetary Production ("making money"), whereas social enterprise is directed toward a different objective.

Keynes' "socialization of investment" appears to represent a
compromise between private and social control of the means of
production. He is explicit in rejecting social ownership but is
not convinced that private enterprise, even with the aid of monetary and fiscal controls, can provide a satisfactory degree of
stability and continuity in production. It should be recalled that
Keynes was writing during the Great Depression of the 1930's,
when secondary deflation had pushed the economies of the Western world into an almost inextricable stagnation and when the

prospect of war, with its exhilarative influence on economic activity, was not yet clearly foreseen. For the future the relevance of "socialization of investment" would appear to be in relation to a situation in which failure to recognize soon enough the onset of a severe deflationary emergency would permit secondary deflation to set in so severely that monetary and fiscal measures would prove unequal to the task of recovery. "Socialization of investment" might turn out to be a constructive new form of mixed enterprise or it might degenerate to a fascist type of reconciliation between capitalism and socialism. In any event, it suggests an element in Keynes' thinking that carries beyond the more conventional monetary-fiscal programs usually associated with his position on policy. "Socialization of investment" would remove the monetary objective of production as a barrier to investment and would leave only the allocation and management of new investment to private decision. Ability to sell for money at a profit would no longer be the basis, or at least not the sole basis, for increasing the total stock of capital-assets. This position leads to a new set of considerations which, if pushed too far, raise questions of self-consistency in Keynes' thought. His system is not well suited to extending unneutral money directly into Industrial Circulation. "Socialization of investment" contains more promise than fulfillment.

Keynes' attention to the financial sphere and his neglect of the industrial sphere is a striking illustration of how social perspective influences the direction and emphasis of economic analysis. He was a consistent critic of finance, speculation and *rentierism* and an equally consistent champion of industry, enterprise, and functional participants in economic activity. When economists strike out into virgin territory, their views on social policy and their ethical values provide significant clues to the path they are likely to pursue.

The extent to which Keynes succeeded in developing a Theory of Monetary Economy may be summarized by reference to the following propositions:

(1) In the classical theory, money is neutral in both the financial and industrial spheres.

(2) In Keynes' general theory of employment, money is neutral in the industrial sphere and unneutral in the financial sphere.

(3) In a complete Theory of Monetary Production money would be unneutral in both the industrial and financial spheres.

Possible Further Developments of Keynes' Theory of a Monetary Economy

Keynes never completed the transition from a monetary theory of prices to a monetary theory of output. The task of constructing a Monetary Theory of Production was larger than could have been foreseen in his 1933 Spiethoff essay. It could hardly have been achieved satisfactorily in a work of the brevity of the *General Theory*, the substance of which is given within less than 250 pages (chapters 3 through 18). Keynes was not the patient scholar to elaborate a complete system of thought. Although not a system-builder, his writings abound with insights latent with promise for further development.

A major weakness of the *General Theory* is the lack of a theory of capital. As already noted, the chapter on "Sundry Observations on the Nature of Capital" contains a few illuminating hints but remains what its title suggests, a succession of obiter dicta which are not incorporated into the main scheme of the analysis. Keynes' most systematic discussion of the theory of capital is contained in the *Treatise on Money*, especially in Book VI on "The Rate of Investment and Its Fluctuations," which contains successive chapters on fixed capital, working capital and liquid capital. Interestingly, Keynes apologizes for including a long discussion of capital theory in a treatise on money. He says, "These chapters are in the nature of a digression, which is doubtfully in place in a Treatise on Money. . . ." [22] He justifies their inclusion on grounds that fluctuations in the rate of investment have not been treated adequately elsewhere for his purpose, and in conformity with this purpose the theory of capital is subordinate to a monetary theory of price levels.

One of the most useful extensions of Keynes' work would be to rewrite the detailed discussion of capital in the *Treatise* in terms of the theory of output in the *General Theory*. The task of reorienting capital theory from a position subordinate to price level analysis to an integral part of output analysis seems eminently feasible because of the very considerable unity of thought in the *Treatise* and the *General Theory*. Both contain a ready-made emphasis on real investment and capital accumulation. The most essential element which it would be necessary to provide would be a full treatment of money as a form of capital and

[22] *Treatise on Money*, Volume II, p. 95.

its relation to fixed, working and liquid capital. This would broaden the significance of money in the determination of output beyond its rather inconsequential impact through the rate of interest. While this task cannot be attempted here, the following paragraphs sketch a few suggestions concerning the relation of real capital and money capital which might prove useful in such an undertaking and might shed light on the nature of crises and unemployment.

A likely starting point might be the suggestion made by Keynes in the Spiethoff essay to the effect that money be directly related to the motives and decisions which determine employment and production. These, of course, are the motives and decisions of entrepreneurs seeking to maximize their returns, or at least who are concerned with "making money." Orthodox theorists like Professor Pigou fell into a wholly unrealistic explanation of unemployment by stressing the motives and decisions of workers with respect to the utility of real wages and the disutility of work. Realistic adherence to the motivation of entrepreneurs would assist in avoiding the substitution of teleological values for the institutional arrangements in the labor market which determine employment. If the expectation of being able to convert real goods into money at a profit is the significant motivation of entrepreneurs in hiring labor, it is pure euphemism to say that consumption is the ultimate purpose of production. A Monetary Theory of Production would stress pecuniary motivation.

The theoretical and practical importance which Keynes attributes to the terms on which assets (debts) can be converted into cash could be extended from financial transactions to all transactions. In Keynes' *General Theory,* uncertainty as to the terms on which bonds and other forms of debt can be exchanged for cash in the future is used to explain the existence of a positive rate of interest on money. While the speculative motive for holding cash and other activities associated with the money market and stock exchange are important in any explanation of crises, they are in a sense surface phenomena which are less essential for a Monetary Theory of Production than money flows and commodity flows through the Industrial Circulation. Ability to convert goods into money tests the wisdom of entrepreneurial activity in terms of the significant motive to produce (profit). If goods cannot be converted into money on favorable terms, "speculation" in production has been unsuccessful. Common language of the market is that profit is realized when goods or securities are converted into cash on favorable terms. In brief, the final test of the decisions of those who decide to employ or not to employ laborers is the conversion of product into money. Keynes' marginal efficiency of capital, the concept designed to deal with the expectations of sale of product (conversion from goods to money), could be developed in depth to show the monetary nature of production. On several occasions his near identification of a Monetary Economy with one in which expectations of the future determine the present level of employment suggests he had something like this in mind.

In connection with the proposition that the individual producer who employs labor achieves his purpose (profit) when his output is sold for money on favorable terms, there is a clear contradiction between the meaning of money and goods in their respective roles as real and artificial wealth. "Real goods" appear to the individual producer as an artificial form of wealth until they are converted into money, which appears as real wealth to the individual producer. Values are realized for the individual firm only if and when the conversion of goods to money occurs. Since the time of Adam Smith, however, the traditional view of economists has been that goods are real wealth while money is a superficial embodiment of real wealth. Actually the reverse would appear to be the case under production on private account. To the individual firm, money is genuine wealth and real goods are an artificial and transitory embodiment of hoped-for values to be realized by their conversion into money. Mercantilistic theory is based on the realistic view that money is wealth (to the individual merchant). Classical economics exorcised this notion from political economy, and Keynes, despite his sympathetic interpretation of mercantilism, failed to reiterate or reintroduce this aspect of mercantilistic thought. Max Weber, with characteristic insight, described mercantilism as "carrying the point of view of capitalistic industry into politics." The unreal wealth (stocks of goods) of individual firms gains social recognition only when it is sold, that is, converted into the unreal wealth of society (money). Real social wealth (stocks of goods) will be produced by entrepreneurs only if there is the expectation of transforming them into unreal social wealth (money). In brief, what is "real" to society is "unreal" to the individual producer; and what is "unreal" to society is "real" to the individual producer.

The contradiction between individual and social forms of wealth is more obvious in crises than in prosperity. The desire to "liquidate" stocks reaches a state of panic. Inability to sell goods (convert them into money) sets up a chain reaction, punctures the credit cycle, and brings the economy tumbling down on the heads of businessmen, farmers, workers and the general public. If the transformation from goods to money cannot be made quickly before others convert their goods into money, all will be lost. Since liquidity is not possible for the community as a whole, all probably will be lost to the group acting as individuals to become liquid at the expense of each other. Stocks of goods may be stored for later sale only on a limited scale, because the carrying costs for most goods are so heavy as soon to eat away the (normal) value of the goods. Keynes says in the *Treatise*: ". . . our present economic arrangements make no normal provision for looking after surplus liquid capital . . . . our present economic system abhors a stock of liquid goods. . . . An important factor of instability is thus introduced into our economic life. . . . We have, therefore, an adequate theoretical explanation of the violence and rapidity of the slump once it has begun."[23]

In view of the foregoing, every business transaction involves an embryo crisis which is averted if "real" goods are converted into money. With embryo crises always existing everywhere among firms with highly sensitive and intimately interwoven credit relations, slight provocation may set off a cumulative wave of liquidation motivated by the desire to hold the socially recognized form of wealth, that is, money. The paradoxical position of money as the universally recognized form of private wealth which is not really wealth at all from the social point of view lies, in undeveloped form, at the heart of Keynes' Theory of a Monetary Economy.

If every business transaction on the selling side involves an embryo crisis, so every transaction on the purchase side involves an increased risk arising from the conversion of capital from its money form into its "real" form. A purchase means a shift from a form of value which is socially recognized to a form which is not socially recognized. A sale reduces and a purchase increases risk. As Proudhon said, when capital leaves its "constituted form" (money) to become "engaged" (goods form), it cannot be dis-

23 Volume II, pp. 145, 146, 147.

engaged without difficulty by virtue of the higher degree of exchangeability of money as compared with products.[24] If Keynes' theory were to be extended from the Financial Circulation to include also the Industrial Circulation, the analysis of the purchase of goods with money would be as important as the analysis of the sale of goods for money. Commodity flows and money flows are an underdeveloped area of economic theory. Professors Kuznets and Copeland have dealt with commodity flows and money flows, respectively, but their empirical work awaits systematic incorporation into a causal theory of business activity. Discussions of time lags and the process analysis are related, but these are not sufficiently "institutionalized" to make their maximum contribution to the theory of capital forms and flows within the Industrial and Financial Circulation.

Money is not just another form of wealth; it is the standard of wealth and the universal objective of business activity. In a money economy all goods must assume a money form, that is, must be transformed from goods into money. Otherwise they remain unsold and lose all meaning since specialized producers have only negligible use for the things they produce. The only alternative is to barter the goods, but goods are not as a rule bartered in a money economy. These simple facts have not been incorporated into economic theory, perhaps because they are too obvious for sophisticated analysis, but perhaps for other reasons connected with the general neglect of money in relation to the motives and decisions which determine the level of output and employment.

Keynes' career as an economist unfolds in terms of a progressively subtle insight into the nature of money as the key institution of modern capitalism. He was always concerned primarily with money, but the monetary theory of the *General Theory* is wholly different from the monetary theory of his first book on *Indian Currency and Finance*. In Keynes' early thought money had significance in relation to price levels, but in the mature years monetary theory became the theory of output and employment as a whole. What ultimately emerged may be characterized as a highly sophisticated and original critique of money as a form of private property. This is the context in which has been chosen the quotation from Max Weber at the beginning of this essay.

[24] P. J. Proudhon, *System of Economical Contradictions* (Boston, 1888), Vol. I, p. 291.

CHAPTER TWO

Some Neglected Implications of Secular Inflation

Martin Bronfenbrenner

Lenin is said to have declared that the best way to destroy the Capitalist system was to debauch the currency. Lenin was certainly right. There is no subtler, no surer means of overturning the existing basis of society than to debauch the currency. The process engages all the hidden forces of economic law on the side of destruction, and does it in a manner which not one man in a million is able to diagnose.—J. M. Keynes.

The present inequality of income is more favourable to the growth of capital, than a more even distribution would be, but less favourable to the growth of human efficiency. The danger of checking the growth of capital has for so long been trotted out as a bogy for social reformers that we are in danger of forgetting that it is a far easier and quicker business to remedy a shortage of capital than the physical and mental shortcomings of a population.—Josiah Wedgwood.

The Problem

SECULAR INFLATION is a condition in which the general trend of prices is intermittently upward, like a flight of stairs. To put it differently, there is a jack or ratchet under the price level, whose nature we shall discuss more fully later, which hinders prices from falling although permitting them to rise.

Under secular inflation, the annual rate of price increase is highly irregular. It may be 10 per cent in one year, 5 per cent in the next. There may be frequent breaks, in the form of periods of stability, or even occasional moderate declines such as occurred in the United States in 1949. These declines, however, do not cancel out the increases which preceded them, and are themselves cancelled out by the increases which follow them in the course of secular inflation.

Because of its irregularity, secular inflation cannot usually be discounted adequately in ordinary commercial contracts, although "escalator clauses" in building contracts and "cost-of-living" clauses in wage contracts are important exceptions to this generalization. If secular inflation were more regular, so that price level changes could be anticipated with a high degree of certainty, the survival of our monetary and credit system would be more questionable than it is. Conceive a situation, for example, in which a price increase of approximately 5 per cent within a year was expected with confidence by everyone on the basis of facts known at the beginning of the year. An immediate result would be a wave of anticipatory purchases, of speculative accumulations of inventory, and of inflationary collective bargains which might stop at the 5 per cent level, but might equally well take on an explosive character. Under such existing arrangements as elastic currency and monetizable national debt, there could also be anticipated a currency and credit expansion which would decrease further the likelihood of prices remaining within the 5 per cent target area. If not in the first year, then surely in the second or third, the rate of price increase would rise to 8 or 10 or 15 per cent, and so on, probably at accelerating rates, until the currency was debauched or the experiment abandoned. Some authorities, notably Professor Sumner H. Slichter of Harvard University, have hopes for a workable system of controls which would combine the productive impetus of (almost) guaranteed inflation and high employment with insurance against the inflation becoming explosive, but the weight of professional opinion, including this writer's, is inclined toward pessimism.[1]

Secular inflation, even at irregular and uncertain rates, causes certain classes of durable goods and equity securities to be demanded more avidly, and therefore priced more highly, than their current income or utility yields would justify. The goods in question are called "inflation hedges." Real estate and common stocks are the most common inflation hedges, but a wide variety of durable consumer goods can serve the same purpose when held in inventory. Jewelry, objects of art, and rare postage stamps are examples. Since the prices of inflation hedges may be expected to decline if general prices are stabilized, the holders of these goods have a vested interest in continued inflation, which is only occasionally recognized, let alone admitted publicly.

In somewhat more technical terms, secular inflation implies that the short-run (and sometimes fairly long-run) supply functions of a large and increasing proportion of goods and services

[1] Sumner H. Slichter, "How Bad is Inflation?" *Harper's Magazine*, 1218 (August, 1952).

become highly elastic and highly irreversible at going prices. These going prices themselves increase irregularly over time, as from P_1 to P_3 in Figure 1, following increases in demand, *i.e.*, from D_1 to D_3 in the same figure. Decrease in demand, as from D_3 to D_1, results in underproduction (or underemployment) of AC at price P_3 rather than full production (or full employment) of B at price P_1. It is the combination of elasticity and irreversibility which produces the asymmetrical price movements we call "secular inflation."

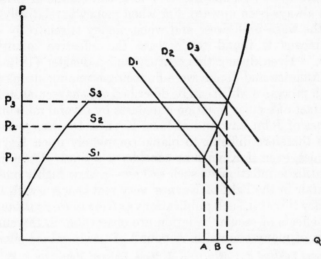

FIGURE 1

To sum up: under a regime of secular inflation, any war, calamity, or business boom causes a sharp rise in the general price level. Any recession or depression, however, results primarily in unemployment. Most costs and prices fall only moderately, if indeed they fall at all.

Historical Notes

In the sense discussed above, secular inflation has been the general rule throughout recorded financial history. The financial records of ancient Greece, Rome, and China abound with illustrations. Karl Marx could already write, in the 1850's: "The English pound sterling denotes less than one-third of its original weight; the pound Scot, before the Union, only 1-36; the French livre, 1-74; the Spanish Maravedi, less than 1-1000; the Portuguese

Rei, a still smaller fraction." [2] Periods of cyclical oscillation about a fairly constant long-term level have been few and far between. In Western Europe and North America, the period of long-term stability between the end of the Napoleonic Wars and the beginning of World War II, broken though it was by cyclical movements, was unusually long. This century and a quarter undoubtedly has warped the judgment of many present-day writers as to the nature of "normality" in financial history, although Keynes himself was among the minority with no illusions on this point. He wrote: "Thus the very long-run course of prices has almost always been upward. For when money is relatively abundant, the wage-unit rises; and when money is relatively scarce, some means is found to increase the effective quantity of money." [3] Even during this century and a quarter (1815-1940), Latin America and Japan were financing economic development through processes which can be described only as secular inflation.

The fact of secular inflation antedates by several millennia the doctrines of John Law and of Lord Keynes. Its resurgence after 1940 is therefore difficult to blame completely upon Keynesian economics, even if Keynes be considered a linear descendant of mercantilistic inflationists such as Law—a view highly one-sided and unfair in the light of Keynes' very real concern with the inflationary threat in such publications as *How to Pay for the War*. [4]

The effects of secular inflation are observable in the currency systems of many countries. A pound of newly-mined silver, for

[2] *Critique of Political Economy*, tr. N. I. Stone, Chicago, Kerr, 1918, p. 85.

[3] *The General Theory of Employment, Interest and Money*, p. 307.

[4] The fate of Hegel has overtaken Keynes increasingly since his death in 1946. His adherents have become increasingly divided, as far as policy considerations are concerned, between what are journalistically called the "Keynesian Right" and "Left" respectively. The terms "Keynesian" and "Keynesianism" have lost by the split much of whatever meaning they once possessed. Those who are associated with the Keynesian Right have taken policy positions on inflation control not greatly dissimilar from those of monetary theorists who have never seen the Keynesian light. They rely mainly on tight money, tax increases, and reduced public spending to curb inflation, look with equanimity at whatever unemployment may result from a "stabilization crisis," and distrust direct controls over individual prices. The Keynesian Left, however, is more sympathetic toward greater public control and will brook no significant cuts, however temporary, in the level of employment. Those associated with this latter group rely for the most part on such measures of direct control as price-fixing, allocation, rationing, and exchange control to suppress any inflationary pressure that may arise under full employment, and if the choice must be made they prefer inflation to underemployment. In the public and professional mind, the Keynesian Left has become identified with Keynesian orthodoxy. It would have been equally reasonable to identify the "Hegelian Left" (Marx) with Hegelian orthodoxy a hundred years earlier, in the 1840's.

example, is worth for currency purposes slightly more than $20 in the United States. A British pound sterling, once identical in value, is worth somewhat less than 15 per cent of that amount. A French franc, the linear descendant of Charlemagne's *livre* (pound) of silver of the early ninth century, has depreciated in 1,100 years to approximately one-fourth of an American cent. Small currencies have disappeared from circulation as prices have risen. The French centime, Greek lepton, Chinese cent, and Japanese rin are examples, while in the United States comedians express concern as to the survival value of the nickel and the penny.

Secular Inflation: Its Motivations

One cannot generalize with any confidence as to the motivations of secular inflation, for these have varied with place and time. Its appeal prior to the capitalistic era, however, may be safely ascribed to its efficacy as a substitute for taxation and for saving. This appeal survives today in many of the world's underdeveloped countries, who rely on "forced saving" for the internal financing of their ambitious projects. (At least the first two Soviet Five-Year Plans were cases very much in point.) In more advanced countries, the use of inflation as a substitute for taxation and saving has become limited largely to periods of war, or rearmament, and of reconstruction after warfare or major catastrophe.

Inflation is now perhaps more important, however, as a method of maintaining aggregate money demand and purchasing power, and forestalling any tendencies toward depression. In addition to increasing present income streams, inflation also increases purchasing power by reducing the rate of consumer saving and by encouraging the immediate investment of all sums saved. It chokes off, in other words, any tendency to hoard, and may operate in reverse to bring about dishoarding of sums set by in past periods.

Another social function of inflation, not stressed sufficiently in the recent literature, is as a method of mollifying class conflict in a capitalistic society. In its capacity as social mollifier or lubricant, inflation permits one pressure group, such as the trade union movement or the farm bloc, to increase its money income without decreasing the money income of anyone else, and therefore without arousing the volume and vehemence of opposition which might be expected. Strikes, for example, are short or non-existent when wage demands can be granted and then translated into price increases. Even if the bulk of the workers' or farmers' monetary gains are lost in these price increases, real gains remain in the lightened burden of their fixed money indebtedness and in the rising real value of whatever real estate or other inflation hedges they may own.[5]

Secular inflation has the net effect of permitting all "active" pressure groups to gain at the expense of the "dead hands" of the salariat, the *rentier,* and the pensioner. It offers to these active elements—farmers, workers, and industrialists alike—the same sort of incentive which compound interest offers to the passive saver and the passive *rentier.* It is then in a very real sense the social rebuttal to compound interest.

Secular Inflation or Secular Stagnation?

We look on secular inflation, not as strictly inevitable, but as likely to dominate economic life in capitalist countries for at least the next few years—say, through the decade 1950-1960. During war or rearmament or reconstruction emergencies, prices will rise. Between emergencies, the maintenance of full employment should bolster them against offsetting declines.

This forecast of secular *inflation* appears to conflict sharply with the forecasts of secular *stagnation* and the doctrine of "economic maturity" which gained wide currency in the decade following the publication of Keynes' *General Theory.* In my view, however, the conflict is more apparent than real.

As all economists are aware, the doctrine of secular stagnation envisages a steady drift toward depression and unemployment in peacetime, accompanied by some price deflation.[6] Three principal causes for this drift have been considered.

[5] Offsetting this real gain is an equally real loss in the value of whatever pension, insurance, interest, or other fixed money claims the workers or farmers may hold. These, however, are in many cases less in value than the inflation hedges, plus the fixed money debts. (Farmers, particularly, stand to gain on balance.) As for pensions, there is some justifiable confidence that money returns will be increased to some extent as prices rise. In other cases, there is simply forgetfulness, money illusion, or Böhm-Bawerkian "over-estimation of the future."

[6] In recent years, Professor Benjamin H. Higgins has become the leading expositor of this point of view. See his essays on "Concepts and Criteria of Secular Stagnation" in *Income, Employment and Public Policy: Essays in Honor of Alvin H. Hansen* (New York, 1948) and "The Theory of Increasing Under-Employment," *Economic Journal,* LX (June 1950).

(1) A long-term slackening in both the rate and eventually the amount of population growth. (Reliance upon this argument has lessened at least temporarily, due to the "baby boom" which followed World War II.)

(2) The passing of the frontier, or, more accurately, the closing of such existing frontier areas as Asiatic Russia and China to capitalistic development.

(3) Diminishing returns to investment, resulting from capital accumulation. (To this is sometimes added a pessimistic note that twentieth-century inventions require less heavy capital equipment by and large than their nineteenth-century ancestors. The writer doubts the accuracy of any generalization on this point.)

The stagnation thesis also assumes a thoroughgoing free enterprise economy, with the functions of government limited to those of, say, the United States in 1929, and carried on at approximately the 1929 scale. In particular, the thesis allows for no government guarantees of employment or output at any wage or price levels whatever.

Government, however, is at the very center of the argument for secular inflation. This argument assumes that, regardless of the hypothetical course of events in the hypothetical private economy, government will in fact act in such a way, albeit after a time lag, as to maintain aggregate money demand if it falls off, in the interests of maintaining a high level of employment. If prices rise, moreover, government is expected to act in such a way as to increase money demand and provide high employment at the higher price level. The monetary authority, in other words, is expected passively to "validate" pressure-group decisions making for higher price levels.

These two secular analyses apply essentially the same kind of macro-economic theory to two different institutional worlds. The world of secular stagnation is the world of sound finance and of the gold standard. It is not currently in existence. It passed into coma in 1933, when Roosevelt and Hitler came to power, and died completely on the several battlefronts of World War II. Its importance today may be largely "academic" in the derogatory sense antithetical to "realistic." The world of secular inflation, however, is the pressure economy of the present, including the political necessity of maintaining high employment at whatever cost.

Does the *de facto* guarantee of high employment arise from military urgency, or from political? The question is well worth asking; indeed, it is fundamental. If military urgency is responsible, partial reversion to the relative irresponsibility of the 'twenties is not only conceivable but highly probable when and if the armament boom declines. In which case, of course, the stagnation bogy may conceivably return to life. This writer, however, conceives the *de facto* high-employment guarantee as primarily political. No more can governments remain long in power in the United States, in the Commonwealth countries, or in Western Europe, if they rely primarily or exclusively on market mechanisms for high employment and high farm prices, or if they use their monetary authority deliberately to chastise inflationists with unemployment ("Don't let them take it away.") Full-employment practices, with their inflationary implications, are due less to the continuing atmosphere of "military Socialism" than to the fact that full employment has been tried and found good by those potent bodies, the farm and the labor votes. It seems reasonably safe to proceed on the assumption of secular inflation, not secular stagnation, as the dominant phenomenon which must be faced regardless of the state of the military arts or the definition of that elusive term "preparedness."

The Responsibility for Secular Inflation

There have been a number of attempts, both in America and elsewhere, to assess the responsibility for the inflationary trend which has set in since 1939 in the Western world, on the plausible supposition that, whatever may be the case for mild inflation, the existing inflation has passed the bounds of mildness and degenerated into a substantially unmixed evil.

It is a convenient escape for the economist, although not completely a realistic one, to ascribe the inflation completely to the military factors of war and rearmament. The inflationary movements of the war years and the period of restocking did not subside materially, as by this theory they should have done, during the two years of greatest relative peace immediately preceding the Korean War. The mild "recession" of 1949-50 was in no country equivalent to the drastic deflation of 1920-22. Indeed, prices had passed their trough and turned upward again in "wavelets" of inflation prior to the outbreak of hostilities in Korea.

Similarly, an eighteen-month lull in the Korean fighting, beginning in June of 1951, produced no substantial reversal of the inflationary trend of the previous year, although the pace of inflation was slowed considerably.

Above and beyond the factors of war and rearmament, economists are divided by what may well be a meaningless issue in accounting for secular inflation. The rival culprits, if we may call them such, are "pressure economics" and "Keynesian economics." To those who blame "pressure economics," the inflation could and should have been reduced sharply by a closer approximation to pure competition on the markets for goods and for labor. To those who blame "Keynesian economics," the inflation could and should have been reduced sharply by Governmental refusal to support effective demand and employment at inflated price levels, regardless of the degree of pressure-group organization.[7]

The case against "pressure economics" starts logically from the fact that consumers and fixed-income receivers are less completely and less firmly organized than the principal producer pressure groups of labor, industry, and agriculture. There are exceptions to this generalization; war veterans and old-age pensioners, for example, constitute formidable pressure groups, but they are as yet organized primarily like producer interests, bent on obtaining larger money returns for themselves rather than resisting the larger money returns demanded by others. Due to the weakness of consumer pressure groups, conflicts among labor, industry, and agriculture have come to be settled ordinarily by giving higher money incomes to all the combatants at the consumers' expense.

Of the producer pressure groups involved, the trade unions have been singled out for particular condemnation. This is to some degree natural, since their strength (in the United States) has grown more rapidly since 1939 than has the strength of organized industry or organized agriculture.

Economists of the anti-pressure-group persuasion stress the wage-price spiral rather than monetary expansion as their ex-

[7] For presentation of the "anti-pressure-group" position, see two studies by the present writer: "The Dilemma of Liberal Economics," *J.P.E.* LIV (August 1946); and "Post-war Political Economy: The President's Reports," *Ibid.,* LVI (October 1948). The "anti-Keynesian" position is expressed by Walter A. Morton, "Trade Unionism, Full Employment, and Inflation," *Am. Econ. Rev.* XL (March 1950); and "Keynesianism and Inflation," *J.P.E.,* LIX (June 1951).

planation of inflation. This is not to deny the proximate importance of changes in the money supply, for example, but rather to consider these changes as resultants of previous changes in wages and cost prices. The view of monetary changes as resultants is unrealistic for periods of actual warfare, such as 1939-45. It takes on more verisimilitude in connection with the events of 1946-50, when the expansion of commercial bank loans in the United States compensated for the reduction in the public debt. Even here, however, it may be objected that increased physical investment was more important than wage or other cost-price increases in swelling the demand for loan accommodation. Nevertheless, it is probably true that some finite fraction of the loan expansion represents adjustments to meet higher wages and other costs, which had been raised by organized pressure groups further and faster than they would have risen by the normal market forces of a purely competitive economy.

The anti-Keynesians, as has been said, blame the inflation, particularly its long-run character, upon the vogue of Keynesian economics, crudely and journalistically interpreted. More specifically, they interpret Keynesian economics as guaranteeing "full employment at whatever cost," to use Professor Viner's phrase.[8] In such a Keynesian regime, employment is effectually guaranteed, except for occasional brief lags and lapses, without reference to either the wage policies of unions or to the price policies of their employers.

According to this analysis, wage and price increases of even the strongest, most aggressive, and best-disciplined of the producer pressure groups were held in check, in the pre-Keynesian days, by limitations of demand. The supply of purchasing power was held in check by "sound finance" and the rules of the gold-standard "game," these restraints being in most cases more directly pertinent than those imposed by restrictive legislation typified by the Antitrust Acts. Under a Keynesian economy, however, any shortage of demand, almost regardless of cause, is expected to be remedied in fairly short order, usually by monetary expansion in the form of Federal deficit financing. Even when caused by price increases, demand failures are counteracted in this manner if a sufficiently large or strategic segment of the national economy is involved. Given this governmental psychology and the resulting expectations, it is only natural for inflation

[8] Jacob Viner, "Full Employment at Whatever Cost," *Q.J.E.*, LXIV (August 1950).

to accompany good times, for price and wage cuts to be resisted in depressions, and even for underemployment inflation to raise its head on occasion.

The elementary technical apparatus of Figure 1 can be used to illustrate the differences between these two positions. In Figure 2, we start from an increase in demand in a position of considerable unemployment, and in Figure 3, from a decrease in a demand after a temporary boom. In each case point A, at the intersection of D_1 and S_1, is the original position, point B is the higher-employment, lower-price solution, and point C the lower-employment, higher-price solution. To the anti-pressure-group economist, the likely consequences of either the situation of Figure 2 or that of Figure 3 can be tabulated:

Monetary-Fiscal Policy	Strength of Pressure-Groups	
	HIGH	LOW
Keynesian	C	B
Non-Keynesian	C	B

As seen by the anti-Keynesian economist, the table would appear as follows:

Monetary-Fiscal Policy	Strength of Pressure-Groups	
	HIGH	LOW
Keynesian	C	C
Non-Keynesian	B	B

To this writer, a distinction should be made between the case of increasing overall demand (Figure 2) and that of decreasing demand (Figure 3). In the first instance, underemployment inflation is relatively unlikely except in the presence of strong pressure groups in industry, labor, and agriculture. In the second instance, resistance to wage and price cuts can be expected, even on an individual basis in an atomistic economy, if there is confidence in early Government support. And whether we adopt an anti-pressure-group or anti-Keynesian ideology, it must be clear from Figure 2 in particular that a sufficient increase in money demand to D_3, such as occurred during World War II, must lead in any event to inflation, either open or suppressed by direct controls and rationing.

When we pass from formal economics to political economy, it becomes even less practicable to distinguish between pressure groups and Keynesian policy as scapegoats for secular inflation.

If essentially full-employment policies are in fact to become a permanent feature of our peacetime economy, as the prognosis of secular inflation implies, the political support for these policies will obviously come primarily from organized labor and agriculture, seconded by at least some sections of organized industry.[9]

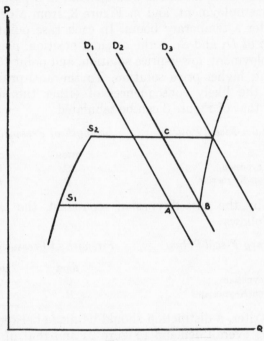

FIGURE 2

If economic pressure groups are responsible for maintenance of full-employment policies, any distinction between the pressure groups themselves and the policies they support seems more delicate than substantial.

Income Redistribution versus Secular Inflation

Among the motivations of secular inflation, we have mentioned (but too briefly) its appeal as a social lubricant, as a mollifier of

[9] In an atmosphere of competition between capitalist and Communist worlds, the loss of prestige involved in permitting unemployment to develop and endure may also operate to enforce full-employment policies in even the most atomistically competitive of capitalist economies.

conflict between economic classes regarding the distribution of the national income. This function appears to be underemphasized in modern monetary economics, with its tendency toward overaggregation. Carrying this thought a step further, may we not view secular inflation as the dominant manifestation or out-

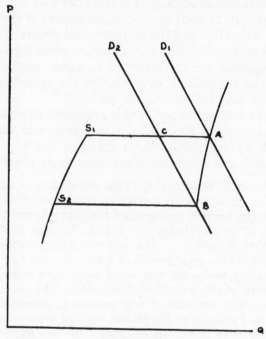

FIGURE 3

come, in the middle of the twentieth century, of the unsolved conflict or "contradiction" as to the distribution of income in capitalist society?

Wherein does this "contradiction" lie? The conventional Marxian formula of "socialized production" and "individual appropriation" has about it a certain aura of abstract, mechanical aridity, but it would be hasty to dismiss it as completely without significance. On the one hand, a highly unequal distribution appears to have been required, if it is not in fact still required, for the mechanical functioning of capitalism, for its functioning, that is to say, in the provision for economic progress. In the absence of a distribution so unequal, and so unrelated to present personal contribution as to be under constant attack on ethical grounds, the requisite supply of entrepreneurial and equity capital does not appear to be forthcoming. A more equal distribution of income may not produce so serious a diminution in the total volume of savings as has sometimes been supposed, at least in a prosperous country; the savings of the poor and the middle classes, however, are characteristically of the *rentier* and not the entrepreneurial variety. A shift in the major sources of savings from the wealthy individual and the undistributed profits of industrial corporations to middle-class individuals, savings banks, and insurance companies can be expected to lower materially their entrepreneurial component, even though the reduction in their total quantity may fall short of 10 per cent.[10]

Perhaps the best summary of this argument in standard economic literature is by Keynes—not the Keynes of the *General Theory* with its redistributionist rumblings, but Keynes in his thirties, writing the *Economic Consequences of the Peace*: [11]

It was precisely the *inequality* of the distribution of wealth which made possible those vast accumulations of fixed wealth and of capital improvements which distinguished that age [the century prior to 1914] from all others. Herein lay, in fact, the main justification of the Capitalist System. . . . The immense accumulations of fixed capital which, to the great benefit of mankind, were built up during the half century before the war, could never have come about in a Society where wealth was divided equitably. The railways of the world, which that age built as a monument to posterity, were, not less than the Pyramids of Egypt, the work of labor which was not free to consume in immediate enjoyment the full equivalent of its efforts.

Thus the return to pure "property" in the United States has amounted quite steadily, from the Civil War until World War I, to slightly less than 20 per cent of personal income. If thereto is added the property component of agricultural and other undifferentiated entrepreneurial income, the percentage may be approximately 25. The remaining 75 per cent we may call labor income, and the ratio between the two percentages, or 25/75,

10 This figure is but the vaguest guess. It is derived indirectly from the wartime Federal Reserve studies of personal consumption and saving, inflated by inclusion of some allowance for the corporate sector. See, *e.g.*, Harold Lubell's summary notes, "Effect of Income Redistribution on Consumer Expenditures," *Am. Econ. Rev.*, XXXVI (March and December 1946).

11 (New York, Harcourt, Brace, and Howe, 1920). Running quotation from p. 19.

may be looked upon as an estimate of the Marxian rate of surplus value. As an estimate, it is probably on the low side, since a certain portion of reported labor income in its higher brackets (salaries and bonuses) may represent property income in disguise. Let us accept a 35 or 40 per cent figure, then,[12] as representing the rate of surplus value in America, or the percentage by which, in the immediate run, labor income could be increased by appropriation of the property share.

Let us lay aside all doubts and fears as to the economic consequences of so high a property share, whatever the detailed figures may be. Let us ignore deliberately, in other words, any increased possibilities of economic instability, underconsumption, or stagnation engendered by so high a property share in the national income. (Professor Kurihara deals with certain of these very real problems in his contribution to this symposium.) Let us concentrate our attention rather upon the political or sociological fact, for we believe it to be a fact, that so high a property share is simply not acceptable to working people and their leaders, however it may be divided among the property-owners by income size classes.[13] It is all very well to demonstrate, with the aid of the marginal productivity theory and the Cobb-Douglas production function, that the productivity of "capital" in the abstract may justify, or at least correspond to, the returns actually achieved. The productivity of capital, however, is not the productivity of the capitalist. The institutions of private property and of inheritance come between. Few would claim that, in twentieth-century America, all or even most of the property share is genetically "functionless investment," completely divorced from the responsibilities of management or of that specifically entrepreneurial risk, investment without contractual return. But memories are short, and last year's active Schumpeterian entre-

---

[12] Estimates by avowed Marxists are usually substantially higher, possibly in part for propagandistic reasons. If only the labor income earned in *commodity production* (goods as distinguished from services) is taken as our denominator in the surplus value ratio, and all other income in society, including total income in services as well as property income in commodity production, is taken as the numerator, it is easy to compute rates in excess of 100 per cent. It is less easy to assign them any clear meaning after their computation.

[13] If this view is correct, the "economic revolution" involved in the falling share of the top 1 per cent and 5 per cent of American income receivers in total income and saving since 1929 is more or less irrelevant. But see Simon Kuznets, *Shares of Upper Groups in Income and Saving* (New York, 1950) and A. F. Burns' comments in "New Facts on Business Cycles," *30th Annual Report of the National Bureau of Economic Research* (New York, 1950).

preneurship is this year's Veblenian "absentee ownership" and next generation's "functionless investment."

The intensity of working-class resentment, and therefore of economic class antagonism or conflict, appears to be increasing for a number of reasons, of which three are perhaps particularly worthy of note. In the first place, the degree of mobility between the working class on the one hand and the propertied class on the other appears to be diminishing. Fewer workers see themselves, or see their children, as even small-scale capitalists in the future than saw themselves or their children in those positions one or two generations ago. Rising in the world has become gradually more a matter of rising with one's group or class, and less a matter of rising out of it. (Educational opportunity remains with us, indeed in increasing degree, but the economic advantage of the educated, or white-collar, way of life is falling correspondingly.) Secondly, the spread of organization to include labor in mass-production industries and a substantial percentage of the nation's farmers is reducing steadily the real gains obtainable, guild-fashion, by restrictionistic co-partnership between employer and employee at the expense of the unorganized public. Money gains can of course be made in the short run by craft-conscious or job-conscious subsections of the working class. Their requiting in higher prices has likewise become more rapid, more complete, and more inevitable, through the "wage-price-profit spiral" of secular inflation. The obtaining of real, as distinguished from money, gains is coming increasingly to transcend guildism and job-consciousness and to pass to class conflict on a broader scale. And thirdly, among the causes for intensification of class antagonism, we must list the proved viability of societies in which the propertied class is either dispensed with almost completely, as in the Soviet Union, or reduced to relative impotence as in Great Britain, Eastern Europe, and the mainland of China. The grievances of labor and agriculture under capitalism can no longer be shifted to Natural Law and Divine Providence, as they could when the alternatives were limited to primitive and feudal societies remote from the main centers of Western civilization.

This is not to imply that the representative American worker or farmer, or yet the American "labor intellectual," is inherently anticapitalist in his ideology. We have pictured him as demanding for his class a larger share in the product of industry; even this picture is somewhat too general and abstract for photo-

graphic realism. The A. F. of L. occasionally, the C. I. O. quite
regularly, speaks out for redistribution on ethical grounds, but
the individual worker, or union local, or even national union, has
no direct concern and at most but a propaganda interest in the
global labor share of the global national income. This must be
admitted, but at the same time the sum total of the demands of
individual workers and locals and national unions cumulates to
a demand for an increase in this share. A demand, moreover,
which seems to be increasing in intensity, to such an extent that,
if capitalism cannot operate without continuance of the existing
"unfair" system of distribution, so much the worse for capitalism
in the eyes of labor. And what has been said for labor applies in
only slightly less degree to agriculture as well.

In the days prior to the First World War, and even beyond to
the hungry 'thirties, this working-class resentment had not, for
the reasons suggested, developed in America, at least not to the
extent to which it has developed subsequently. Furthermore, it
was kept in check with relative ease by what can only be described as the religion of sound finance and the gold standard.
This religion involved the constant threat of mass unemployment
if wage demands became excessive, and periodic wage cuts in
depressed periods, when the "reserve army of the unemployed"
became a reality as well as a threat.

The religion of sound finance worked with reasonable effectiveness in restraining and modifying the immediate demands of the
labor movement. Even in the relatively few skilled trades, such
as railroading, construction, and printing, where a guild spirit
manifested itself in a highly restrictive unionism, the secular
gains in the economic position of the workers were achieved less
at the expense of their employers than of the consumers of their
products and the workers excluded from the craft unions. On
the other hand, each successive depression gave rise to stronger
long-run demands for the removal and replacement of the capitalistic system itself, so that the long-run effects of sound finance
were hardly as happy, from the capitalistic viewpoint, as were
the short-run ones.

In understandable worry about the consequences of labor organization, inflation, and the "Russian menace," Americans of
the 'fifties appear to have forgotten the 'thirties. In 1930-35, to
be precise, labor organization was weaker than we find it today.
The value of money was both higher and more stable. The ex-

ternal menace came from the extreme Right rather than the extreme Left. Yet so severe was the internal depression, and so profound the resentment against the system which had permitted it, that the internal position of American capitalism was not stronger but weaker than it is today.

Let us suppose, more generally, that the so-called "Austrian" remedy for industrial depressions is mechanically the quickest and easiest method of recovery. This remedy involves, as readers of Hayek's *Monetary Theory and the Trade Cycle* and *Prices and Production* will remember, temporary unemployment, wage cuts, tight money, liquidation, and what has been called "healthy bankruptcy" for the weaker segments of small business and of agriculture. The validity of this analysis has of course been subject to increasing question, particularly since the appearance of Keynes' *General Theory* in 1936, but let us suppose the "Austrians" to have won indisputably the theoretical battle in the pages of the learned journals. The fact still remains that the "Austrian" remedy will no longer be permitted to work for any length of time in a democratic society, despite such spectacular instances of success as the depression and recovery of 1920-22 in the United States. The consequences of attempting such a remedy, in an atmosphere of strong labor and agricultural organizations and resentment against the existing income distribution, can be predicted with high probability as either a Fascist or a Socialist revolution. A Fascist revolution will be required to put "Austrian" economics into effect; a Socialist revolution may be the answer of labor and agriculture to the attempt to do so.

The incompatibility of political democracy with the "Austrian" remedy for the business cycle is not limited to this single prescription of deflation and liquidation. It extends, we suggest, to the entire nineteenth-century mechanism of combating labor's demand for a higher share of the national income through the constant threat and occasional fact of mass unemployment. The "Austrian" cycle theory, however, is in a sense unique in its distastefulness because its combination of dearer money and cheaper labor proposes to bring about recovery through *increased* inequality of the income distribution.

Because of the anticapitalist resentment engendered by periodic unemployment, in the last quarter-century it has become increasingly passé as a check on the aspirations of labor and agriculture. And what has been its replacement? One thesis of this paper is precisely that inflation has replaced unemployment as the major instrument of "labor discipline."

The so-called "Keynesian revolution" may be looked upon as a landmark or milestone of this change. The Keynesian policy of full employment as applied both before and during the Second World War may with little exaggeration be credited with having saved capitalism in the 1930's. The astonishingly rapid and virtually complete eclipse of the previous orthodoxy of sound finance is evidence of its effectiveness; so is the mounting animus and resentment in the criticism of Keynes and all his works from the anticapitalist Left. At the same time, the inflationary consequences of this neo-Keynesian orthodoxy are beyond denial, particularly in a pressure-group economy. As pure economics the *General Theory* has little to say about underemployment inflation—although Keynes himself, fully aware of the secular rise in prices, never advocated for Great Britain the inflationary policies which would have been required to restore full employment to the deepest pockets of unemployment, the so-called "blighted areas," before 1939. And while we have argued that, in practice, the inflationary bias of the Keynesian faith might be materially less even at high employment under a regime of pure competition, this argument has little relevance to the questions of the day. For in their striving for higher wages, particularly with employment looked upon as guaranteed, and with trade union organization a necessary, publicly-encouraged offset to monopoly in labor markets, workers can hardly be restrained by the limitations of atomistic, pure, perfect or any other theoretical construct of economic competition.

A Venture at Forecasting

Social forecasting is a dangerous business, yet we may make bold to venture a gamble to the effect that, despite its impressive short-run record in the decade 1945-54, secular inflation will be no more effective in the long period as a social lubricant than was sound finance as a social bludgeon or battle-axe.

The short-term record of postwar inflation in the American economy during the years 1945-54 is doubtless far better in this connection than any but a small fraction of our economists would have dared to forecast in advance. Throughout this period, inflation has been effective in combining rising money wages, in particular, with a constant labor share in the national income. This share, while lower than during the suppressed inflation of the war itself and lower than the depressed years of 1932-33, has been higher than in previous periods of boom and has shown no tendency toward substantial decline as prosperity continued. There is reason in the Marxian reformulation which elevates the "fictitious values" of inflation to the position of principal weapon for extortion of surplus value, replacing the "reserve army of the unemployed," however uncanonical such reformulation may appear to the faithful.

But there are grounds for suggesting that the days of inflation's effectiveness are limited, and that when secular inflation ceases to be effective it will subside, be the economy formally regulated along Keynesian lines or not. These grounds lie primarily in increased familiarity with the workings of the inflationary spiral on the part of workers and farmers, which cannot but increase with each successive "round." This familiarity manifests itself in insistence, which to this possibly prejudiced ear appears already increasing in volume, for collective-bargaining or governmental administrative provisions assuring payment of money wage increases out of profits, or out of increased productivity, rather than out of consumer prices. The various "Nathan Reports" in the United States, prepared by the Robert R. Nathan Associates for the Congress of Industrial Organizations and individual member unions, are in the nature of straws in the wind, as are the "Mitbestimmungsrecht" movement in the labor movement of Western Germany and the concern of the British Trade Union with the price position of British export products. Consumer political pressure, meaning the threat to vote Conservative in protest against inflationary wage and price increases, is constantly being exerted in the same direction.

The Nathan Reports, which have become annual visitants to the American labor battlefront, call uniformly for wage increases and other benefits to be paid "out of profits" without price increases. That is to say, they call for direct redistribution within the productive process, and are concerned to show that the profits which would remain to the employers, after redistribution and after taxes, constitute a substantial and equitable amount. They are also of interest because of their stress on what capitalists *ought* to do, or should be *made* to do by their workers or the Government, rather than what they may be expected to do under the mechanical operation of the profit calculus. (Nowhere is absorption of wage increases suggested as the normal or expected outcome of pricing mechanics.)

Wage increases out of profits are submitted as means of restoring or, more frequently, retaining the level of high employment against a depression which lurks perennially around the same corner that concealed prosperity in 1930-32. This argument is supported by underconsumptionist arguments of the Hobsonian type, which appear to be exaggerated quantitatively in the light of the Federal Reserve findings referred to above (*vide supra,* n. 10). Despite this heavy intermingling of economic technicality, however, the fundamental argument appears to be ethical. (Professor F. H. Knight comments on the characteristic predilection of contemporary American thinking to clothe ethical arguments in economic terms, giving ethical appeals that "hardheaded," "realistic," "practical" disguise which seems prerequisite to their serious consideration.)

If I interpret Mr. Nathan and the C. I. O. correctly, they propose a fairly high ceiling on aggregate money profits, with redistribution achieved in increasing degree through the appropriation by labor and agriculture of substantially all future gains from technical improvements and other productivity factors.

The German "Mitbestimmungsrecht" (Co-Determination) movement carries forward more sharply and more openly the process of encroachment by organized labor upon traditional management prerogatives which many writers, perhaps most emphatically Professor Chamberlain of Yale,[14] have outlined in recent labor history in the United States and elsewhere. This movement seeks to achieve for organized labor an equal voice with management in setting output, setting product prices, and determining the volume of employment as well as in the determination of wages and other conditions of work.

Here again, more clearly than in the Nathan Reports, the purpose is to force the abandonment of profit-maximizing in employers' reactions to the wage gains of labor. The expected results are higher output and employment, and equally clearly lower prices, than achievable under the conventional model of the economic theorist. There is again to be redistribution in favor of labor. Wages are to be systematically higher than marginal

14 Neil W. Chamberlain, *The Union Challenge to Management Control* (New York, 1948).

products. Wages and employment are both to be increased steadily out of profits and with price increases held to a minimum.

Since labor, joined by at least a segment of the agricultural interest, has both ethical convictions which add to significant modifications in the traditional distributive system and also the normal voting strength necessary to back up these convictions, it is difficult to imagine any democratic system under which the relative share of labor will not begin to rise in the long run. The existing regime of inflationary shadowboxing, in particular, rests upon a partial "money illusion" on the part of labor—at least as regards the immediate effects of wages upon prices under the present economic arrangements. This illusion can hardly be expected to last for many wage-price rounds, let alone many generations, longer.

The next step, in such developed countries as the United States, appears to be either what Professor Slichter has christened "Laborism" [15] or some form of latter-day Fascism. Under Laborism, if I understand Professor Slichter's meaning, pressure politics and economics are dominated by the labor interest, usually but not necessarily operating through the forms of representative democracy. Under Fascism, the class aspirations of labor are effectively suppressed by some effective combination of nationalistic propaganda, force, and the threat of force. In countries with a recent history of foreign "exploitation," of course, the forces of Laborism and Fascism may unite in a joint venture of pillaging foreign capital under slogans combining class and patriotic ideas, producing such hybrid systems as prevail in Argentina, China, and Iran, and rendering inapplicable our tentative dichotomy between the Laboristic and the Fascistic solution.

Under "Laborism," to whatever extent the appearances and even the practices of private enterprise capitalism are maintained, mechanism can be anticipated which will increase the labor share of the national income. Even where the real income of the propertied classes is not cut severely, future increases due to innovations, technical progress, and economic development will be channelled almost exclusively to the laborer and small farmer, either by legislation or by state-supported collective bargains covering product prices, outputs, and employment as well as wages proper and working conditions in the narrow sense.

[15] S. H. Slichter, *The American Economy: Its Problems and Prospects* (New York, 1948), pp. 7-13.

Under Fascism, we may expect to see the share of at least the native property-holders maintained if not increased, and a mass base created among public employees both civilian and military, among pensioners and *rentiers,* and among other middle-class elements with interests in price stability.

In either case, secular inflation probably will grind gradually to a halt in developed countries, if indeed it does not cease abruptly. It will end at the expense of the property share if Laborism triumphs, and at the expense of labor's aspirations in Fascistic countries. (Our argument is purposely limited to developed countries. Elsewhere, inflation may well continue, under either Laborism or Fascism or any hybrid of the two, its additional historical role of accelerating the pace of economic development through forced saving and investment.)

The decline or demise of secular inflation may increase rather than decrease the importance of Keynesian economics in its original form in either a Laborist or a Fascist economy. By "its original form" we mean primarily a theory of employment and output at constant prices, as it was during the period prior to the Second World War. Its relevance, it is maintained, will be likely to increase if the price change factor can be left out of account.

Implications for Capitalism

The foregoing analysis has been influenced so greatly by, and leaned so heavily on, the sociology of Joseph Schumpeter and the economics of Karl Marx that the writer himself would be hard put to isolate important segments which might be considered at once significant and original. Yet, despite his indebtedness to Schumpeter and Marx, he does not see the development which has been outlined as leading with any certainty or inevitability to the termination of capitalism which Schumpeter has foretold with apprehension and Marx with jubilation.

Can capitalism first permit and then survive a major reduction in the property share in the income distribution? The problem of permission is one of politics and sociology rather than economics proper, and beyond our professional province here. It should be pointed out nevertheless that the fate envisaged for the capitalist class through income redistribution cannot by any means be equated to the expropriation and liquidation which,

Marx argues from history, no dominant social class has permitted peaceably to occur. Redistribution is far milder. The faster the rate of growth of the economy, the milder it can be made. Being milder, it has a greater chance for peaceful acceptance than would the drastic measures Marx presumably contemplated. The greater chance, however, remains far removed from certainty.

The more strictly economic problem can be rephrased. Will entrepreneurship and equity capital be forthcoming after redistribution in sufficient quantity to maintain an acceptable rate of progress in a capitalism of "low-profit" prosperity? Or if not, can satisfactory substitutes for entrepreneurship and equity capital be developed? Or the minimum acceptable rate of progress perhaps reduced? High authority can be appealed to on both sides of these propositions, and Keynesian authority into the bargain. In Professor Kurihara's essay on distribution in the present volume, Alvin Hansen's case for a high-wage, low-profit, full-employment, and largely capitalist economy as a target for the future is reviewed favorably. On the other side, David McCord Wright has become the principal academic spokesman denying the feasibility of income redistribution under capitalism [16]—a position shared not only by Chambers and Schools of Commerce throughout the land, but by Socialists as well.

The problem is of course largely a quantitative one. If only a small proportionate redistribution is required to appease the ethics of the farm and labor groups, the chances of Hansen and Kurihara being correct, Wright and Baran being mistaken, are fairly high. If appeasement and a slow growth rate require the share of labor to rise to substantially 100 per cent, the old Socialist "Right to the Full Produce of Labor," then Wright, Baran (and Marx) have the better of the argument. It would furnish an interesting exercise in survey research to ascertain as precisely as may be how high a proportionate share of capital would be tolerated as "equitable" by the majority of American or British workmen and their leaders. In the remainder of this essay, I am writing under the assumption that the shift required would be somewhat between 5 and 10 per cent of the national income, or

[16] Cf. D. M. Wright, "Income Redistribution Reconsidered," in *Income, Employment, and Public Policy, op. cit.;* also *Capitalism* (New York, 1951), pp. 107-29. A similar argument is spelled out, but from a Socialist viewpoint and with Socialist conclusions, by Paul Baran in his essay "National Economic Planning," in B. F. Haley, ed., *A Survey of Contemporary Economics,* vol. II (Homewood, Ill., 1952), pp. 374-77.

between 20 and 40 per cent of the present returns to property. Large enough, certainly, to be significant, but too small, certainly, to be called expropriation.

In considering these crucial questions, the supply of entrepreneurship and risk capital, we turn first to the classes now responsible for providing the bulk of these resources. These are the wealthy individuals and the managers of industrial corporations. And in considering the possible effects of redistribution, it would be well to distinguish between "sunshine countries" where expropriation or confiscation is not an imminent threat, and "thundercloud countries" where such risks should be taken into serious account by present or potential investors. As of the mid-twentieth century, the United States and Canada are examples of the first category of countries, while India and Indonesia may serve as examples of the second category.

Where the risk of confiscation can be neglected, the chances for continued entrepreneurial activity by these classes—wealthy individuals and industrial managers—appear fairly high in a capitalism of "low-profit" prosperity, quite as outlined by Hansen or Kurihara. If redistribution increases the quantitative importance of consumption, and particularly its more stable elements, relative to saving, investment, and luxurious (and therefore postponable) consumption, greater stability in the level of over-all income and employment can be expected with the confidence approaching certainty. In a more stable economy, the proportionate volume of equity and other investment dissipated periodically in depressions and stagnations would be reduced, and a reduction in the gross volume of investment counteracted. At the same time, entrepreneurial capital probably would be forthcoming at a lower real rate of return. The likelihood of this outcome is increased if the attractiveness of nonrisk investment is reduced at the same time by low interest rates and low rents. These latter reductions have been carried out to a considerable extent both in the United Kingdom and the United States without cutting off the supply of such relatively risk-free capital.

Underlying our analysis up to this point has been a theoretical model in which the division of upper-group income (including undistributed corporate profits) between consumption and investment appears practically independent of the complex of interest rates, but in which the further division of investment between equities and debts appears to depend on the relative rates

c*

of return anticipated in the two types of uses. When the pure or economic rate of interest approximated 5 or 6 per cent, a profit rate of 15 to 20 per cent may have been required to entice risk investment—with all the resulting inequality in the personal income distribution. But when the pure interest rate falls to 2 or 3 per cent under the influence of banking, monetary, and fiscal measures, it is possible for collective bargaining or direct controls to cut the gross profit rate to 5 or 10 per cent (with correspondingly greater equality of personal incomes) before the investing habits of the upper classes are changed materially.

Our model is characterized by both interest-inelasticity and profit-inelasticity in the aggregate consumption expenditures of capitalists generally. This seems realistic enough, for economies in which expropriation and confiscation need not be considered seriously by investors. It is not presented as realistic outside the "sunshine countries." Even with general prosperity and high employment, who will invest large sums for long periods at low profit or interest with confiscation in the offing? Reluctance to invest under these circumstances is not a matter of "monopoly," nor yet of "strike of capital," although elements of both monopoly and capital strike may be found in concrete cases. Reluctance results from a natural, or at least a rational, preference for immediate consumption, or for capital flight, under the circumstances we have mentioned.

Even in the "thundercloud countries," it would be a mistake to treat the risk of expropriation as given, not to be modified by concessions from the side of distribution. There may exist in any such country, regardless of its past history, some range of redistribution which will simultaneously satisfy the proletariat and peasantry while including adequate supplies of capital, both domestic and foreign, for venturesome investment. The existence of such an optimum has been neither proved nor disproved in any country of which this writer professes knowledge. If it does not exist, or cannot be identified in time, Marx and Schumpeter are probably right in their forecasts, and Hansen and Kurihara utopian in their pious hopes. Capitalism may well be doomed in any country once expropriation is weighed as a significant risk in framing investment plans, so that any reduction in the rate of return to the level corresponding to popular standards of equity would cut off the bulk of the private capital supply.

Now as to an aspect of the problem which is frequently overlooked. Continuance of equity investment by the wealthy, and by the re-investment of corporate surpluses, cannot in itself insure the continuance of this investment by society as a whole, if redistribution of the income reduces the relative share of the wealthy and of undistributed profits in the national product. This important point deserves more stress than it usually receives in discussions of the effects of redistribution, but here again, there are offsets to be considered. These offsets may bring within easily tolerable limits the reduction in the rate of progress under an equalitarian enterprise economy, even when they do not cancel the reduction entirely.

The first offset to be considered is increased labor productivity. The economic base for a longer effective working life for the laborer, for more health and strength and skill for his children, is ordinarily thought of as provided by economic progress—but in the short run, income redistribution may provide it as well. At the same time, whatever psychological brakes on productivity may be ascribed to resentment against the real or imagined injustices of the present distributive system will be removed.

Less certain, yet worthy of mention among grounds for hope, is the possibility that redistribution of income may result eventually not only in a greater volume of saving by workers and farmers but by a greater channelling of those savings into equity and entrepreneurial forms. This may come about directly, through more risk investment by low-income people themselves. It is more likely to come about indirectly, through such investments by savings banks, insurance companies, investment trusts, and other institutions in which the poor place their savings in the first instance. Here, of course, both psychological and legal changes are required before any important shift can be expected.

Entrepreneurship, entrepreneurial investment, risk investment, equity investment—we have used these terms, and others too, almost synonymously, doubtless more so than the facts warrant, and we have correlated them with unique closeness to invention, to innovation, and to economic progress. Such a correlation is in the Schumpeterian tradition, but it is far from perfect in the real world. For as we know, innovation can be financed by bonds or taxes, just as common stock investment may flow to extension or duplication or replacement of existing facilities. Furthermore, a modicum of growth and progress is obtainable in the private sector of an economy like the American even when the supply of entrepreneurship or innovation declines. A machine is productive even when it duplicates last year's model, and when it is purchased from debt instead of equity investment. Only in the stationary state of satiety and stagnation, with capital already accumulated to the point of zero productivity, does advance depend so exclusively upon the entrepreneur and the innovator as it does in the Schumpeterian System. Such a state, however close it may have appeared during the hungry 'thirties, has receded beyond the economic horizon of the 'fifties.

And finally, the desired rate of growth in real national income per capita over time is not a constant, but a variable. Part of the price paid, perhaps willingly, for a combination of the equalitarian distribution and economic stability of socialism with the individualistic liberties of capitalism may well be some reduction in the minimum acceptable rate of growth and change. Willingness to substitute equality and stability of the national income for size and rapidity of progress may be quite as "natural," and quite as "rational," as the opposite preferences generally assumed (as first approximations) by conventional welfare economics.[17] It may also be equally compatible with some form of capitalism. Surely no cosmic palmist has yet read in the indifference surface of the lines of the invisible hand a zero marginal rate of substitution between equality and progress.

[17] Professor Gottfried Haberler expressed quite well the assumptions of the conventional welfare economist when he wrote: "I think he relies, like most people, on over-all output and employment figures and concludes that everybody *could* be better off [*e.g.*, under freer trade]; if some people are actually worse off, well that is just too bad." "Welfare and Freer Trade—A Rejoinder," *Economic Journal* LXL (December 1951), p. 783. Compare also H. C. Simons, "Our primary problem is production. The common man or average family has a far greater stake in the size of our aggregate income than in any possible redistribution of income." *Economic Policy for a Free Society* (Chicago, 1948), p. 5f.

[CHAPTER THREE]

Monetary Stabilization Policies and Keynesian Theory

Mabel F. Timlin

So FAR AS it may be possible within this short space and from so near a view, it is the purpose of this paper to examine Canadian postwar stabilization policies and to relate these to theory and empirical evidence. In the pursuit of low interest rate policies through a series of years characterized by price inflation, what seems to have been overlooked in Canada and elsewhere have been the conditions set out in Section VI of Chapter 21 [1] of the *General Theory* and the nature of the confirmation of that position in the last published article of Lord Keynes. It is the essence of this position that while the "classical medicine" may not "work by itself" in the fashion expected by laissez-faire theorists, nevertheless it is the proper object of policy to attempt "to use what we have learnt from modern experience and modern analysis, not to defeat, but to implement the wisdom of Adam Smith." [2] If this view be accepted, policy makers must unite two quite different approaches to economic problems. For if the main problem of Keynesian economics has been the stabilization of output and employment at high levels, the main problem of neoclassical economics has been the proper allocation of resources. If we are to unite the two approaches, the reconciliation of these two ends, so far as they may be reconcilable, is the question set for economists and policy makers.

It would seem to be true that the *monetary* parallel to the classical and neoclassical problem of the allocation of resources is the problem of the structure of prices. But if this in turn be true, policy considerations no longer involve simple aggregates such as consumption, investment, saving, and "the" interest rate but rather rates of consumption of particular types of goods and services, investment in particular markets, and the *asset* struc-

---

[1] Macmillan & Co., Ltd., 1936, pp. 307-308.
[2] "The Balance of Payments of the United States," *Economic Journal*, June, 1946, p. 186.

ture as well as the *time* structure of market rates of interest.

Postwar policies require therefore to be examined from this point of view as well as with reference to the general underlying antagonism between aggregate investment and aggregate consumption which may assert itself once the economy has reached virtual full employment. If we reverse the order of Keynesian statements, while the "general price level depends partly on the rate of remuneration of the factors of production which enter into marginal cost and partly on the scale of output as a whole," the price level in a particular market will depend "partly on the rate of remuneration of the factors of production which enter into marginal cost, and partly on the scale of output." [3] Even if, in a period of full-cost pricing, the term "average cost" be substituted for "marginal cost" the principle is not different. But under conditions which approach full employment of the agents of production, the elasticity of supply in both Marshallian and Keynesian theory "depends on the elapse of time." [4] As a result any policy of the government or central bank which affects the rates of flow of available funds into these various markets will have a determining effect on both the structure of prices and on the general price level—as well as on the allocation of resources.

In the analysis of Canadian stabilization policies with respect to these effects, it will be the basic contention of this paper that the same principle of opportunity cost underlies the assets markets that is fundamental to substitution at the individual margin in both Marshallian and indifference curve theory. Under the conditions of 1936, the liquidity-preference demand for money constituted the neglected margin and the most important one for the conditions of the time. But under the conditions which followed World War II, other margins emerged as the ones upon which attention needed to be concentrated. Attempts to hold to policies of artificially low rates of yield on securities traded in by central banks could be expected to increase existing disequilibia in these markets. The writer has long been convinced of the *multiple* nature of these margins and of the necessity of paying attention to the full set if policy decisions are to be made upon rational bases.[5]

[3] *General Theory*, p. 294.
[4] *Ibid.*, p. 300.
[5] See M. F. Timlin, *Keynesian Economics* (University of Toronto Press, 1942), Chapter III and p. 184.

Application of the general principles set out above to Canadian policies will be undertaken in the five following sections of this paper. In the first section a general examination of Canadian policy is attempted. The second section examines certain changes in the relations between total means of payment and the Gross National Expenditure in current and constant dollars. The third section deals with the handling of the public debt with special reference to the connections between open-market operations and reactions in other debt and equity markets. The fourth section deals more generally with fiscal and other stabilization policies of the government. The fifth and last is devoted to certain general conclusions arising from the discussion.

Mr. A. F. W. Plumptre, writing in the *University of Toronto Quarterly* in October, 1951, expressed the opinion that in no other English-speaking capital in the world had Keynesian thinking had more effect on policy than in Ottawa.[6] This is not strange. Easy-money policies in Canada antedate the publication of the *General Theory* and may perhaps be officially dated from November, 1932, and the issue of thirty-five million dollars of Dominion notes under the Finance Act "through the compulsory discount by the banks of that amount of Dominion two-year treasury bills which they had been forced to buy from the government."[7] But even as lately as 1930-31 "sound" monetary policy had appeared to be the established view in Canada.[8] Nevertheless, following the Ottawa Conference of 1932 an easy-money philosophy established itself with enough celerity and firmness to enable the Governor of the Bank of Canada to state in the first *Annual Report* of the new central bank, issued under date of February 25, 1936, "A policy of cheap and abundant money is the orthodox contribution of a banking system towards recovering from a depression," and to hold further, "In Canada, the present high price of gilt edged bonds is an indication of the presence of money looking for employment."[9]

Thus the connection between bond yields and the "presence of money looking for employment" seems to have been realized at

[6] "A Prophet Not Without Honour," pp. 82-83.
[7] F. A. Knox, *Dominion Monetary Policy, 1929-1934*, Appendix to *Report of the Royal Commission on Dominion-Provincial Relations* (King's Printer, Ottawa, 1939), pp. 29ff.
[8] *Ibid.*, pp. 18ff.
[9] See p. 12 of *Annual Report*.

the Bank even prior to the publication of the *General Theory*. As the Bank was transformed, through the Amendments to the *Bank of Canada Act* in 1936 and 1938 [10] and then through the years of wartime co-operation into what the late Dr. W. C. Clark called "the channel through which the monetary policy of the government is put into effect," [11] the relationship of monetary policy to the underlying philosophy of the government became clearer. In the White Paper on *Employment and Income* presented to Parliament by the Minister of Reconstruction in April, 1945, the monetary aim of the government was set out as follows: "The Government desires and expects that low interest rates will continue after the war. It proposes to pursue a monetary policy which will encourage, through low interest rates, the investment of funds in productive capital contributing to employment." [12] It will be a contention of this essay that the postwar situation differed vitally from the prewar situation and that there was a theoretical flaw in this policy.

The policy was based upon the expectation, recognized in the White Paper and elsewhere, that "in the near future there is more danger of inflation than deflation, unless necessary price and supply controls remain effective until war-created shortages are overcome," *but* that "The backlog of demand will not be large in relation to productive capacity when industry has been fully reconverted and inventories built up to normal levels." [13] Concern was evidently felt respecting the effects not only of the levels of interest rates but also of their variability. Even earlier than in the 1945 *Annual Report* quoted above, in his *Annual Report* for 1943, the Governor of the Bank had made the following statement:

> Admittedly, the rate of interest is only one of many factors influencing Canada's economic position and it is probably not as important an instrument of control as was once supposed. It remains true, however, that the prospect of unstable interest rates could make it exceedingly difficult for business to formulate long-term plans. Moreover, high borrowing costs would hamper new investment in plant, equipment and housing, would restrict the expansion of em-

---

[10] Statutes of 1936, Chapter 32; Statutes of 1938, Chapter 42.
[11] Canada, House of Commons, 1944, *Proceedings of the Standing Committee on Banking and Commerce,* Vol. 1, p. 12.
[12] White Paper, p. 11.
[13] Bank of Canada, *Annual Report*, 1945, p. 10.

ployment and would seriously complicate the task of government financing. There can be little doubt that the easy-money policy which has been pursued since 1935 assisted in promoting recovery from the depression and facilitated the adjustments which have been required during the war period. Indication that the Bank intends to continue this easy money policy should be helpful in making plans for the future.[14]

What seems to have been overlooked in the implementation of this policy in the postwar period is that the success of the policy in prewar years had depended upon the presence of idle labour and equipment and on an easy expansibility of output and employment without great changes in costs and prices. In the war years, on the other hand, it had depended upon the strength of price and particularly of supply controls, and especially in the years 1943 and 1944, upon high levels of personal and business saving. The processes of decontrol were carried on with an admirable and orderly efficiency over the early postwar years, but controls were of course growing almost continuously less onerous over the period. The low interest rate policy was continued not only through the period of relaxation and final abolition of price and supply controls but beyond it.

Moreover the government was not content to leave interest rates at the coupon rates of the war issues. Thus in the series of yields published monthly by the Bank of Canada in its *Statistical Summaries,* the nine-year theoretical bond fell below the 3 per cent rate for the first time in January, 1943, and the fifteen-year theoretical fell below it in July, 1944. These yields reached their minimal levels of 2.21 per cent and 2.55 per cent in August and July of 1947, respectively, and the published series do not show them back again to the 3 per cent level until January, 1951, after the adoption of the floating-dollar policy. One hears occasionally in Ottawa the contention that because of public reaction to a fall of bond prices it would have been impossible for the government to have allowed interest rates to rise after the war. But the economist must wonder why it was necessary to let them go to premium levels and must suspect that the situation had some connection with the fact that low rates were a fiscal convenience and that higher ones "would seriously complicate the task of government financing."

[14] Bank of Canada, *Annual Report,* 1943, pp. 5-6.

Not until 1948, apparently, did Ottawa realize that inflation rather than deflation and employment would be the paramount problem for a long period. The question for the economist up to 1948 therefore concerns the rationality of a low interest rate policy seen against an expectation of a temporarily inflationary situation and of a deficiency of outlets for investment thereafter. The writer has come to hold that flexible rates of yield on bond prices are at least as important under such conditions as they are under conditions where expectations of resource development, expansion of population, rates of technological change and other long-term aspects provide more stability of inducements to invest.

This position implies that if there is under virtual full-employment conditions an even temporary overlap between the plans of investors and consumers under current prices and interest rates, Keynesian theory should make it the business of *monetary* policy to minimize the overlap. The ideal situation would appear to be one where a *sharp and sudden and once-for-all* rise in yields of securities entering into the portfolio of the central bank would hold the flow of funds into investment markets down to the level of current personal and business savings. A lagging and niggardly rise in rates, taking place by small degrees, might aggravate the problem not only because it would lead to increases in the quantity of currency and bank deposits, but also because it might create an expectation of rising rates and cause some disequilibrating transfers of investment planned for the future into the present.

Some adjustments of these aims might be necessary in a period like the postwar period in the face of wartime accumulations of currency and bank deposits, existing exchange rate commitments, and existing relationships between external and internal price levels. But the *minimum* sound objective in such a period would seem to be to prevent any extension of accumulations of currency and bank deposits; this would involve yields on securities entering into the portfolio of the central bank high enough to deter any flow of these securities toward the bank. Those who wished to liquidate their holdings would be compelled to offer them at prices that would be acceptable to other potential holders. The degree of inflation in various markets would be determined by the rates at which the existing quantities of currency and bank deposits entered these markets. But it should be the clear aim of both monetary and fiscal policy to hold such inflation to its practical minimum. It will be noticed later that high commercial bank reserve ratios may make some open market sales by the central bank a necessary part of this policy of control.

It is precisely because investment opportunities may be limited that this policy is urged as the rational policy from the economist's point of view. If existing investment opportunities are husbanded over a longer period of time, the chances for the occurrence of innovations or other autonomous supports to investment will be increased and in their absence opportunities for rational planning of public works will be augmented. Moreover, since elasticity of supply factors will be greater over a longer period, for a number of reasons the *magnitude* of investment, measured in constant dollars, may be greater under such a policy. Since marginal efficiency schedules of capital in particular investment markets will be reckoned on the *excesss of returns over costs of production,* the spinning out of existing investment opportunities may actually mean higher marginal efficiency schedules, taken on the average over a period of years. The point is that long-term planning of investment is not only a matter of the level and stability of interest rates to be paid on capital: the level and stability of costs of production and prices of output may be even more important. It is the connection *between* yields on portfolio securities of the central bank on the one hand and the quantity of currency and bank deposits, costs of production and prices of output in particular sectors of the national economy on the other that seems to have been overlooked in Canada, and elsewhere, in the period between the end of the war and Canada's return to a convertible dollar in December, 1951. Flexible rates of return on portfolio securities of the central bank may be the necessary price for even relative stability of costs and prices.

If therefore inflationary forces in the economy are expected to be short-lived, policy will need to be directed to the husbanding of existing inducements to invest. If they are on the contrary likely to be of a more permanent nature, the aim of policy must be the restriction of the rate of new investment to a level at once consistent with the propensity to consume and with a proper allocation of resources. Both general situations will be connected with the existing elasticities of supply in various markets and with the structure of both prices and interest rates.

It seems desirable in ending this section of the discussion to set out briefly the nature of the changes in the structure of Canadian prices as these show up in the *National Accounts*. Table I below, taken from Table 4 of the *National Accounts, 1926-1950,* and *Revised Preliminary,* 1951, shows the implicit price deflators relating current dollar values to constant dollar values for certain sectors of Canadian Gross National Expenditure for the years 1929, 1939, 1945, and 1951.

TABLE I. Implicit Price Deflators

1935-39 = 100	1929	1939	1945	1951
1. Personal Expenditure on Consumer Goods and Services	119.2	102.2	124.5	191.3
2. Government Expenditure on Goods and Services	108.4	99.1	131.6	189.4
Gross Domestic Investment				
3. New Residential Construction	115.4	102.8	154.1	268.9
4. New Nonresidential Construction	110.7	101.2	126.6	205.7
5. New Machinery and Equipment	103.8	102.8	123.5	198.4
10. Gross National Expenditure	115.3	100.0	127.0	193.3

The aspects of this table to be noted are the greater degree of distortion in the investment sectors in 1951 when that year is compared with 1929, and the reversal of relations between consumers' and investors' prices. No special case may be argued for the structure of prices in 1935-39, of course, and it is also true that the figures for the deflators may themselves reflect changes in weights over time, or even differences in methods of estimation between sectors in a field where statistical estimates are notoriously difficult to achieve with a very high degree of approximation. *But the nature of monetary and fiscal policies in the postwar period requires examination to see whether hypotheses may be arrived at respecting relationships between these and the differing degrees of inflation in various sectors of Gross National Expenditure when 1951 is compared with previous years.* Considerations of space will make it necessary in the main to restrict treatment to domestic policy. It is not overlooked that changes in international prices and in trade policies have undoubtedly limited freedom of action at the policy level in Canada. But it is possible to argue that the relations of various domestic policies among nations have been the chief determinants of the strength of the Canadian economy at the present time and that an earlier resort to some of the policies of 1952 might have been advisable. It is not necessarily wisdom which determines relative economic strength; it may be only the *comparative* degrees of indiscretion!

It is proposed below to inspect certain changes in the relations between total supplies of currency and bank deposits (active and inactive) and the current and constant dollar Gross National Expenditure in Canada, and to examine thereafter certain policy bases for these changes. Accordingly Table II below sets out the

TABLE II

MILLIONS OF DOLLARS Year	Gross National Expenditure Current Dollars	Constant Dollars	Currency & Active Bank Deposits (L_1)	Inactive Bank Deposits (L_2)	Total Means of Payment ($L_1 + L_2 = L$)
1938	$5,233	$5,246	$1,042	$1,352	$2,394
1939	5,707	5,664	1,211	1,435	2,646
1940	6,872	6,487	1,480	1,350	2,830
1941	8,517	7,481	1,825	1,345	3,170
1942	10,539	8,941	2,260	1,346	3,606
1943	11,183	9,374	2,627	1,542	4,169
1944	11,954	9,721	3,031	1,939	4,970
1945	11,850	9,315	3,365	2,255	5,620
1946	12,026	9,045	3,747	2,709	6,456
1947	13,768	9,165	3,723	3,002	6,725
1948	15,613	9,438	4,114	3,284	7,398
1949	16,462	9,722	4,167	3,628	7,795
1950	18,122	10,194	4,430	3,714	8,144
1951	21,241	10,731	4,608	3,753	8,361

basic data. Graph I which follows shows certain of these data on the basis of $1938 = 1.000$. Table III follows a cash balance approach and shows holdings of currency and bank deposits at the end of each year as percentages of the current and constant dollar GNE of the year just concluding. Graph II is based on this table. The figures for currency and bank deposits are taken from estimates of the Bank of Canada published in its *Statistical Summary* for September, 1952, pp. 145-46, and represent holdings of Canadian residents only, as at December 31 for the respective years. Figures for the GNE come from the *National Accounts*. The province of Newfoundland here and elsewhere is included only from 1949 onward.

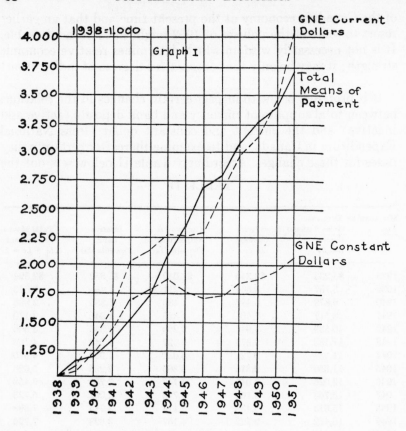

TABLE III. Cash Balance Relationships: Ratios of L_1, L_2 and L to Current Dollar GNE and of L ($= L_c$) to Constant Dollar GNE

Year	L_1	L_2	L	L_c
1938	.199	.258	.457	.456
1939	.212	.251	.463	.467
1940	.215	.196	.411	.436
1941	.214	.158	.372	.423
1942	.214	.128	.342	.403
1943	.235	.138	.373	.445
1944	.254	.162	.416	.511
1945	.284	.190	.474	.603
1946	.312	.225	.537	.714
1947	.270	.218	.488	.734
1948	.264	.210	.474	.783
1949	.253	.220	.473	.802
1950	.245	.205	.450	.799
1951	.217	.177	.394	.779

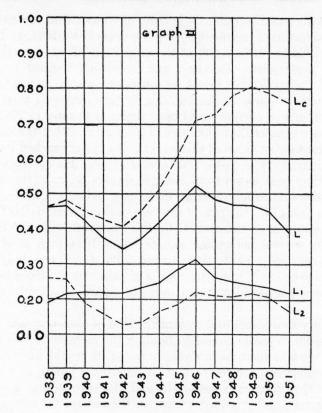

There are several conclusions to be drawn from the data above. In the first place it is to be noticed (see Graph I) that the first three years of the war, from the end of 1939 to the end of 1942, saw the highest rate of expansion in the constant dollar GNE. The data show also that this expansion was accompanied by a relatively modest expansion of total means of payments. Since easy-money policies antedated to a degree even the opening of the Bank of Canada in March, 1935, and since when the war began, the inactive balances actually exceeded in amount the holdings of currency and active bank deposits, it may be inferred that the discretion shown in the expansion of reserves by the central bank and of deposits by the chartered banks was to some extent owing to the generally liquid position with which the nation entered the war in September of 1939.

Policies in the years that followed seem to have been under-

taken with less discretion. It is true, of course, that increases in
the total means of payment during the years 1943, 1944, and 1945
may be held to be the result of the magnitude of war emergencies
during those years. Taxation and borrowing seemed to have
reached their effective limits as sources of war finance and the
consequent recourse to the banking system increased total resi-
dent holdings of currency and bank deposits at rates in 1943 and
1944 much greater than the rates of increase in either the current
or constant dollar GNE of these years. The latter reached its war-
period maximum in 1944, fell thereafter and did not return to
its wartime peak again until 1949, five years later. In the meantime, price and supply, foreign exchange, and export and import
controls held down the rate of increase in the current dollar GNE.
In the last year of the war, 1945, the constant dollar GNE had
fallen by several percentage points below 1944 to a level only
4.2 per cent over 1942; the current dollar GNE was only 12.4
per cent over 1942; but total means of payment at December 31,
1945, were nearly 56 per cent over the figure for December 31,
1942.

A policy as discreet and rational as that of the early war years
would seem to have counselled holding the increase to this level.
If this were to have been done, however, it would have meant
some pressure on the reserves of the chartered banks, in view of
the fact that reserve ratios at the end of 1945 stood at a liberal
11.5 per cent and provided a basis in themselves for substantial
further increases of bank deposits and currency in the hands of
the Canadian public. But the policy actually followed, through
a combination of reserve ratio adjustment and increases in reserves, induced by the end of 1951 an increase in total means of
payment over year-end figures for 1945 of nearly 49 per cent in
the face of an increase in the constant dollar GNE amounting
only to slightly over 15 per cent.

The situation seems to have come about through certain opinions held in the government respecting the "normal" relations
between Canadian and other price levels (particularly the American), through political and fiscal motives, and probably through
bad theory. With respect to the first, the advisers of the government (the ultimate determiner of monetary as well as fiscal
policy in Canada) seem to have held to the opinion that Canadian prices are so closely tied to external prices, especially
American prices, that they are to be expected "normally" to be

substantially the same when the exchange rate is taken into consideration. Yet the persisting differences which have held per capita money incomes in Canada lower than their American counterparts argue that the relation of domestic prices to the prices of internationally traded goods must be different in the two countries. Moreover, alterations in the trading positions and economic strength of nations which had formerly provided convertible currencies for the settlement of Canada's American deficit made changes in the total structure of world price levels appear a likely outcome of a return to stable trade and exchange-rate relationships. Thus it may be argued that substantial identity between Canadian and American price levels under conditions of a new world equilibrium could not be taken for granted. Since concentration in this paper is on Canadian domestic policies these possibilities cannot be further explored here. It is proposed rather in the third section to consider certain relationships between interest-rate policies, the handling of the public debt, and private investment in Canada.

In pursuing this aim, it is salutary to start with a comparison of gross domestic investment in the years 1929 and 1951. By Table 3 of the *National Accounts* (for references, see *supra*), in 1929 gross domestic investment, excluding inventory changes, formed 21.6 per cent of the current dollar GNE and 23 per cent of the constant dollar GNE. In terms of the prices of 1935-39, prices of investment goods in 1929 were lower than the prices of goods and services entering directly into consumption (see Table I above). But in 1951 the reverse was true. Moreover, in 1951, the same components of gross domestic investment formed only 17.9 per cent of the current dollar GNE and 16.7 per cent of the constant dollar GNE; yet in relation to the price structure of 1929 the implicit price deflators for gross domestic investment show themselves to be markedly higher. Conditions of space forbid detailed analysis of policy but questions arise as to the degree to which price increases and distortion of the price structure may be the result of policy decisions in the fields of monetary and fiscal policy and debt management. It is proposed below to examine briefly the effects of the low-interest-rate policy and certain aspects of the disposition of the budgetary surpluses in the postwar years. December, 1951, has been selected as the cutoff date for most aspects of this paper because it was in that month that the "floating" Canadian dollar was made fully convertible into other currencies at the market rate.

Table IV is set out below because it forms a handy scaffold for a brief account of the nature and effects of policy decisions. An attempt will be made in the discussion to show the probable directions of substitution at the margin in the assets market which may have been the consequences of these decisions. It is admitted with cheerfulness that the data upon which reasoning must be based are relatively crude from the statistician's point of view. It is the misfortune of the academic economist in Canada that his access to data is limited, just as it is on the other hand the misfortune of the government economist that any policy deductions he may draw from the data available cannot be set out in published work. On such subjects only Ministers may speak. And they usually regard the management of their own departments with optimism.

The changes in holdings of the public debt need to be seen not so much in terms of total changes over the period, but more analytically in terms of changes within the period. As has been pointed out in Section I of this paper, the period of lowest rates stretched through to early 1948. The period 1946-47 must in addition be viewed against certain events of 1946 and against the data already set out in Table II. The first of these events is the conclusion of the Savings Agreement with the chartered banks, announced by Mr. Ilsley, then Minister of Finance, on February 27, 1946.[15] The second is the revaluation of the Canadian dollar on July 6, 1946, to dollar for dollar parity with the American dollar.

The Savings Agreement contained two main provisions. Under one of these, the chartered banks consented to restrict their holdings of market issues of Government of Canada bonds to 90 per cent of their aggregate holdings of noncorporate notice deposits. Under the other, they agreed that their earnings from Government of Canada bond holdings should not exceed a moderate return over costs of operating their savings accounts. It is this latter part of the Agreement which was later described by Mr. D. C. Abbott as the "primary purpose" of the Agreement.[16] Its

[15] Department of Finance Press Release.
[16] Department of Finance Press Release. "Prices and Credit," an address to the Academy of Political Science, April 1, 1948.

intention was to keep the chartered banks from increasing the average maturity on such securities in their portfolios.

The significance of this latter provision needs to be seen in terms of the forces operating on the interest-rate structure after the war's close. At that time, it will be recalled that short-term rates on government securities were well below long-term rates. In the face of statements by the government and central bank respecting continuance of the low-interest-rate policy, ordinary operation of the principle of opportunity cost would imply that interest-sensitive holders would attempt to substitute issues carrying higher rates of return for those carrying lower rates, with consequent effects in straightening out the time structure of rates. The chartered banks in particular might be expected to take a large place in this process of substitution. Thus the Savings Agreement, though it may have been intended in part to turn the attention of the banks to the field of commercial credit, seems to have had as its "primary purpose" the support of the time structure of rates in existence at the end of the war. Since the market pressures were on the short- and medium-term rates and since the chief problems of redemption or refunding for some years would concern securities of short and medium durations, the motives would appear to have been fiscal.

In terms of this latter purpose, the results were disappointing. The banks allowed their security holdings to run off with redemptions in 1946, and in 1947 through sales in the market liquidated bond holdings to a considerable degree in excess of the redemptions of their holdings during that year. Pressure in the short- and medium-term government security market was offset to some degree by open-market operations of the Bank of Canada,[17] though these operations did not in 1947 completely offset the effects of redemptions upon its security account. In the longer-term markets support seems to have come from the government accounts, and in 1947 particularly from the Securities Investment Account. Of total purchases of bonds for all government accounts amounting to $497 million in that year, some $405 million were for this account. The principal evidence that government operations were chiefly in the longer-term market rests on the stability of bond yields for these maturities described below and on the fact that the budget speeches for the fiscal years 1948-49 and 1949-50 refer to *sales* from the Securities Investment Account as

[17] Bank of Canada, *Annual Report*, pp. 23-24.

TABLE IV. Changes in the Distribution of Government of Canada Direct and Guaranteed Funded Debt, December 31, 1945 to 1951 Inclusive

MILLIONS OF DOLLARS

A.	1945 (Total Amounts)	1946	1947	1948	1949	1950*	1951*	1951* (Total Amounts)	1945-51 (Total Changes)
	$	$	$	$	$	$	$	$	$
I. Bank of Canada	1842	+62	-23	+132	-4	-67	+249	2191	+349
II. Chartered Banks	3506	-189	-669	+311	+153	-33	-325	2754	-752
III. Government Accounts	821	+97	+497	-158	-461	+51	+162	1009	+188
IV. Nonresidents	1144	-53	-38	+105	+82	+126	-198	1168	+24
V. Resident Corporate (Private)									
1. Refundable Tax	184	+68	+6	-24	-64	-56	-90	24	-160
2. Life Insurance Companies	1659	+107	-12	-169	-171	-185	-149	1080	-579
3. Other Financial Corporations	573	+45	+23	-48	+30	+24	-8	639	+66
4. Nonfinancial Corporations	1195	-159	-309	-57	+45	+215	-10	920	-275
VI. Government Corporate									
1. Provincial	312	+4	+18	+29	+35	+29	-2	425	+113
2. Municipal	124	+5	-9	-18	-6	-15	-6	75	-49
VII. Resident Noncorporate									
1. Refundable Tax	260	+2	+22	-61	-223	....	....	....	-260
2. Other Nonmarket Issues	248	+475	+175	+55	+105	+46	+65	1169	+921
3. Market Issues	5611	-629	-288	-326	-180	-20	-280	3888	-1723
VIII. Total Debt Outstanding	17479	-165	-607	-229	-659	+115	-592	15342	-2137
IX.† Advances to (-) or funds returned by (+) Exchange		+25	+720	-520	-125	-515	-215		

MILLIONS OF DOLLARS

B.	1945 (Total Amounts)	1946	1947	1948	1949	1950*	1951*	1951* (Total Amounts)	1945-51 (Total Changes)
	$	$	$	$	$	$	$	$	$
I. Direct Funded Debt									
1. Special Banking Issues............	1796	−250	−346	+100	−100	+300	−100	1400	−396
2. Other Issues....................	15044	+179	−301	−295	−645	−178	−385	13419	−1625
3. Matured & Outstanding..........	15	+17	−10	+13	+18	−2	−30	21	+6
II. Guaranteed Unmatured.............	556	−39	+50	−47	+28	+29	−48	529	−27
III. Total Outstanding Excluding Exchange Rate Adjustment............	17411	−93	−607	−229	−699	+149	−563	15369	−2042
IV. Total Adjusted for Exchange Rate on Foreign Pay Securities...........	17479	−165	−607	−229	−659	+115	−592	15342	−2137

* Figures for 1950 and 1951 are preliminary and a number of those for 1951 are approximations. See Statistical Summary, Bank of Canada, September, 1952, pp. 145–46 for table from which the above calculations have been made.

† Data under IX of Part A were drawn from pages 5 and 8 respectively of the 1948 and 1950 Annual Reports of the Bank of Canada. Certain adjustments have been made in the figures for 1946 to 1948 inclusive to conform with the usages of the 1950 Report.

an important source of funds for redemption of other bonds.[18] It is possible that these operations were to some degree intended to relieve pressure on rates in the short-term and medium-term markets through the device of making rates on the longer-term securities less remunerative to other holders. But what happened was that the chartered banks turned not only to commercial credits but to corporation bonds, chiefly new issues, as alternative investments, again under the operation of the profit maximizing principle.

The revaluation of the Canadian dollar to dollar for dollar parity with the American dollar was undertaken as a cushion against the rapid rise in American prices which accompanied the collapse of price controls in the United States. But it was followed, it will be recalled, by a fall in Canada's reserves of gold and American dollars which culminated in the reimposition of exchange and certain import controls in November, 1947. This fall in reserves had the effect of bringing a flow of Canadian dollars to the Exchange Fund and resulted in a return of advances to the government amounting to $25 million in 1946 and $720 million in 1947. Taken in conjunction with the budgetary surplus of 1947, these funds enabled the government not only to make the purchases for the Security Investment Account referred to above but also to make a reduction of total debt outstanding amounting to $607 million in that year. Further effects on debt holdings need to be seen within the arena of these operations.

Since the government was in 1947 the only net large-scale purchaser of market issues, the problem is one of the effects of their purchases on bond yields and the consequences of these effects for other holders. Reference to series for the theoretical bonds in the *Statistical Summaries* of the Bank of Canada indicates that the downward movement in yields in the longer series, arrested in the spring of 1946, resumed its course and continued until July of 1947. From July through November, the yield for the fifteen-year theoretical stood consistently at 2.55 in the published series, rising slightly to 2.56 in December. The inference to be drawn from the fact that the only large operations in the market were for the Securities Investment Account must be that the government had through this account established a floor price on this maturity at this level and had taken corresponding action for other longer-term maturities.

[18] See *Budget Speeches*, March 22, 1949, p. 8; March 28, 1950, p. 7.

The question is whether these actions had consequences for other debt-holders. Inspection of Table IV will show that the Life Insurance companies which had been large-scale buyers in 1946 became small-scale sellers in 1947. More significantly, net disposal of these securities by nonfinancial corporations nearly doubled from $159 million in 1946 to $309 million in 1947. Since 1947 was the postwar year in which both current dollar and constant dollar investment was highest in the manufacturing industries,[19] three possible effects of government action in the bond market are the proper objects of scrutiny. First, did growing premiums on longer-term issues *accelerate* the disposition of these securities by nonfinancial corporations and the subsequent transfer of funds thus secured into private investment? Second, did low yields on Government bonds mean a readier market for the net new issue of $120.7 million of corporation bonds (as chartered bank purchases in the new issue market seem to indicate) and thus accelerate further the flow of funds into private investment? Third, did the redemption of some $301 million of market issues during the year mean a still further diversion of money in this direction?

Funds for redemptions came from the budgetary surplus, except in the years 1946 and 1947 when the return of advances by the Foreign Exchange Control Board provided funds for this and other purposes. The budgetary surplus came of course from the taxpayers, though that does not necessarily mean that payments were made from income, since funds to pay commodity taxes in particular may have come to some extent from the rapidly expanding commercial loans of the banking system or otherwise from an expansion of bank deposits. But even if this were not true, it is still a reasonable hypothesis that the national income was deflected toward private investment through both the low interest rate and the debt handling policies for which the government had final responsibility, and that one of the consequences of the deflection was a change in the relative prices of investment and consumer goods.

By early 1948, the generally inflationary trend was evident to the Government. As a consequence early in the year the Bank of Canada discontinued its practice of furnishing daily firm lists of the prices at which it was prepared to buy bonds and withdrew

[19] See *Private and Public Investment in Canada*, Department of Trade and Commerce, Ottawa, 1951, pp. 20-21.

sufficient support from the market to allow the published series for the fifteen-year, nine-year, and five-year theoreticals by March to show yields of 2.98, 2.81 and 2.26 respectively. Moreover, the Governor of the Bank intimated to the chartered banks his conviction that their purchases of corporation bonds were underwriting an undesirable rate of investment in fixed capital and "suggested" that they cease increasing their holdings of such securities. It is necessary to point out, however, that after March the Bank of Canada came back into the government security market presumably to limit somewhat the rise in yields and that by the end of December, 1948, its portfolio of government securities had increased by $132 millions over the previous year-end, the largest annual increase in the Bank's history except for 1951 and five of the six war years.

As a consequence of the easing of the reserve situation for the chartered banks and of the higher rates to be earned on government bonds, the banks paralleled an expansion of their Canadian deposits amounting to $626 millions over the year 1948 by an increase in their holdings of government bonds of $311 million. Demand for Canadian bonds by nonresidents also showed renewed strength.

An almost more important event in 1948 was the retreat of the Life Insurance companies from the government bond market, a consequence of their growing interest in the higher rates of return to be earned on urban mortgages. In 1947, rates of cost inflation in residential and nonresidential construction had been approximately the same. In 1948 the rise of costs in residential construction began to surpass the rate of rise in nonresidential construction. Table I will indicate the degrees of difference present in 1951. Moreover, operations of Central Mortgage and Housing Corporation under the National Housing Act of 1944 had increased demand for houses in terms of money in ways too complicated for analysis here. But the point again is that much of this increased demand was "spilled on the ground" through cost inflation. When in 1951 the Government withdrew its offer of second mortgages under Central Mortgage and Housing Corporation loans, and the Life Insurance companies began to restrict the aggregate funds going into urban mortgages, the artificial nature of the demand became evident. In that year, according to one estimate, only 6 per cent of new houses went to persons with incomes under $2700 a year and 63 per cent to persons with incomes of $3500 up.[20] Since Canadian incomes were considerably lower than American for the year in question, this would mean that new houses went preponderantly to higher-income groups.

It seems abundantly clear that changes in portfolio holdings of Canadian Life Insurance companies have been related to changes in the asset structure of interest rates over the postwar period, and therefore to government and central bank policies which have been connected with this rate structure. Thus the president of the Confederation Life Association of Canada reported in May, 1952, that in 1950 80 per cent of the increase in assets of Life Insurance companies went into new mortgages but that in 1951 this proportion fell to 65 per cent. One of the reasons given was that "in the past two years the interest rates on bonds have risen more than those on mortgages so that the latter are relatively less attractive than they were some time ago." [21] At present writing there is uncertainty respecting the volume of urban mortgage money which will be available from this source in 1953, an uncertainty founded in part on a disinclination of lending institutions to commit funds for mortgage lending too far ahead before they "see what other opportunities occur in the bond market and elsewhere," [22] and in part on the high proportion which urban mortgages now form of life insurance portfolios. At the end of 1939 first mortgages were less than 14 per cent of the portfolios of Canadian Life Insurance companies and at the end of 1952 they were over 30 per cent.

The question for the theorist is whether the artificially low rates on government bonds consequent upon operations for the government accounts in 1947 and the support brought to the government bond market by the Bank of Canada in 1948 may not have accelerated the flow of money into the housing market in a manner which not only contributed to the rate of rise in costs therein but also laid the basis for a later reaction. That is, might it not have been better to have transferred part of this flow of money into this market to some later period? The reaction which

[20] See the *Financial Post* for August 16, 1952, p. 16, "How the Mortgage Business Went in '51."

[21] T. K. Macdonald, "Life Insurance in the Economic Pattern of Canada," an address delivered at the Economic Conditions Conference, Toronto, May 25, 1952, and published in *Industrial Canada*, Vol. 53, July, 1952, pp. 98-100.

[22] *Financial Post*, March 14, 1953, pp. 1 and 3, "Who Will Put Up Money for Big Boom in Housing?" See also issue of April 4, pp. 19 and 28.

D

took place in 1951 was masked because of the increasing demands for men and materials from nonresidential construction and defense industries generally. But the *type* of reaction was one which in the past has only too often been connected with the turning point from boom to recession. There is a well-known proverb about "locking the door." Perhaps the logical time for the use of the interest rate as a regulator is *before* an inflationary rise in costs takes place. The threats to the housing program are real in 1953.

It is no part of the purposes of this paper to analyze the effects of the sterling exchange crisis of September, 1949, the devaluation of the Canadian dollar which accompanied it, the speculative inflow of capital from the United States which in the summer of 1950 forced the government, because of the exhaustion of its own cash resources, to turn first to the chartered banks for $200 million on the basis of Deposit Certificates, then to the Bank of Canada for Canadian dollars to finance the inflow, and finally on September 30, 1950, to the adoption of the floating dollar policy.

The only points to be made here refer to the security operations of the Bank of Canada. The first is that the large-scale open-market operations of the Bank of Canada, which between July 30 and October 18, 1950, caused the Bank to dispose of $337 million of securities as an offsetting operation to the acquisition of $393 million of net foreign exchange assets, were characteristically underdone. By coincidence, perhaps, the increase in the reserves of the chartered banks for the year was almost exactly equal to the difference between these two operations, namely $57 million! The second is that in 1951, although policy generally by that time was supposed to be "definitely restrictive," Table IV shows that the central bank that year acquired $249 million in government securities and that the government accounts also made large net purchases during the year. It is a matter to be observed that the increase of $82.2 million in chartered bank reserves that year is the second largest in the history of the Bank of Canada. Not until 1952, a year which generally comes outside analysis here because of the complications brought in by the return to convertibility, do we find a policy adopted under which the government bond market is allowed to take its own course.

The consequence to be expected theoretically from the combination of monetary, fiscal and debt handling policies outlined in this section would appear to be a deflection of the Gross National Expenditure toward the investment sectors. After the year 1947, the advance of funds to the Foreign Exchange Board by the government may have increased the deflection, since the increase in reserve holdings by the Board then so largely represented an inflow of capital funds into Canada. Table V set out below and drawn from the *National Accounts 1926-1950* and *Preliminary, 1952*, gives some indication of the magnitude of the deflection for the period.

TABLE V

MILLIONS OF DOLLARS

	I	II	III	Ratio of:	
			Gross Domestic	III	III
Year	Total	Consumer	Investment	to	to II
	Personal	Expendi-	Excluding	I	
	Incomes	tures	Inventory Changes		
1944	$9,002	$6,187	$859	.095	.139
1945	9,239	6,811	986	.107	.145
1946	9,761	7,977	1,398	.143	.175
1947	10,300	9,173	2,121	.206	.231
1948	11,943	10,112	2,685	.225	.266
1949	12,757	10,963	2,968	.233	.271
1950	13,483	11,994	3,216	.238	.268
1951	15,852	13,234	3,810	.240	.288
1952	17,146	14,290	4,138	.241	.290

Certainly with the decrease of government expenditures at the end of the war and with the relaxation of controls over materials and labor, a large-scale deflection was to be expected. But the data indicate that the deflection continued beyond that period and on into the period of increasing defense expenditures. Moreover, recourse to the table above will indicate that, except for the upward surge at the war's end when price controls were still in full operation, the rate of deflection was the greatest when prices were rising at the greatest rates. The ratios of Gross Domestic Investment to Consumer Expenditures shown in the table, with this exception, rise at the greatest rates in the years 1947, 1948, and 1951, precisely the years when the inflation of prices throughout the various sectors of the national income reached their highest rates of change. Lags between the receipt of funds and the execution of investment plans make it difficult to trace the relations between cause and effect. But 1947 and 1951

were also the only years during the period when the sum of security purchases by the central bank and government accounts
plus debt redemptions exceeded a billion dollars.

If the theorist, seeking to combine Keynesian and neoclassical
theory, looks at such a situation, he must see it from two standpoints: in the first place, he must look for the effects of policy
on the relation between plans for investment and plans for consumption. In the second place, in the face of such a deflection
he must look also for the effects of increased competition on prices
of factors specific to various investment goods industries. From
the first standpoint, under full-employment conditions the deflection will produce or increase an overlap of plans between investors and consumers if it is not fully covered by an equal and
opposite deflection toward saving. From the second standpoint,
the deflection may produce or increase distortion in the price
structure in accordance with existing short-period elasticities of
supply in the investment industries affected.

Moreover, neither examination can be made from the standpoint of static theory only. There will be dynamic aspects, even
aside from those connected with technological difficulties, which
may affect the short-period elasticity of supply of specific agents
of production. Changes in the timing of tax payments which have
resulted from World War II make it quite possible that the average dollar of government revenue may remain a shorter time in
the government's hand than was true formerly and even than it
otherwise would remain in the average taxpayer's hands. This can
be perhaps nowhere of greater importance than in Canada where
so large a fraction of budgetary revenues is derived from commodity taxation of the general sales type, payable at the manufacturer's level, typically "on sale or importation" under conditions
where a high rate of expansion of bank deposits has been supporting a high rate of increase in the current dollar GNE. If government policies are favoring a deflection toward investment in the
national economy, increasing government cash balances may be a
necessary element in the provision of the increasing magnitude
of saving necessary to match increasing investment and to the
stabilization of prices.

In its general program for stabilization, the reliance of the
Canadian government seems to have been based on the one hand

upon its budgetary surpluses [23] and on the other on "persuasion" of and "suggestions" to the chartered banks as substitutes for orthodox monetary operations of the central bank, with other special measures, such as consumer credit regulations and deferment of depreciation tax allowances, brought into use from time to time.

Data are extremely scarce respecting changes in cash balances of the government over the period under examination, but the data which are available indicate that by and large budgetary surpluses were *spent*. The budget speeches prior to March 22, 1948, lumped together the cash balances, Security Investment Account changes, and changes in advances to the Foreign Exchange Control Board under a single figure. But beginning with the 1948 budget speech, information respecting cash balances in the budget speeches gives the following data for March 31 of each fiscal year indicated:

March 31 of Year	Government Cash Balance
1947	$484.5 million
1948	35.9 "
1949	90.7 "
1950	67.0 "
1951	−25.4 "
1952	−66.0 "

There is no evidence here of any systematic build-up of cash balances to retard the counterflow of revenues back into the national income, as a counterbalancing measure to inflationary trends in the economy. On the contrary, the only year which does not show a fall in cash balances in relation to the preceding year is 1949, a year when inflationary forces seemed to be dying away.

The effectiveness of other methods of stabilization may be estimated to some degree with respect to the year 1951. In that year, in addition to certain changes in excise and sales taxation raising the prices of many "luxury" goods in relation to prices of "necessities," there were also in effect in comparison with the immediately preceding years higher personal income taxes, much

[23] The view that the budgetary surpluses which the Government has enjoyed since the end of the fiscal year 1945-46 are factors offsetting the powerful inflationary forces of the postwar period will be found consistently expressed throughout the series of budget speeches of these years and in public addresses of Ministers and Government officials up to and including the address which the late Dr. W. C. Clark had been scheduled to give to the American Economic Association on December 29, 1952. For the latter, see Department of Finance Press Release of the same date.

more stringent consumer credit regulations, the credit ceiling agreement with the chartered banks concluded in the early part of the year, and in addition a relatively high rate of consumer saving compared with 1950. The effects of this great arsenal of anti-inflation weapons may perhaps best be seen in terms of the magnitude of effects upon relative demands for consumers' Durables, as these are classified in Canada's National Accounts.[24]

TABLE VI

	MILLIONS OF DOLLARS					III	IV
	I		II			Ratio of	Ratio of
Year	Consumer Expenditures		Current Dollar Expenditures on			II (a)	II (a)
	Constant Dollars	Current Dollars	(a) Durables	(b) Nondurables	(c) Food & Shelter	to II (b)	to II (c)
1945	$5,471	$6,811	$338	$4,327	$2,713	.078	.125
1946	6,189	7,977	590	5,073	2,951	.116	.200
1947	6,478	9,173	852	5,776	3,361	.148	.253
1948	6,368	10,112	914	6,461	3,941	.141	.232
1949	6,612	10,963	1,084	6,799	4,072	.159	.266
1950	6,833	11,994	1,347	7,207	4,532	.187	.297
1951	6,828	13,234	1,399	7,904	4,983	.177	.281
1952*	†	14,290	1,567	8,397	†	.187	†

*—Preliminary.
†—Not available.

In an analysis of Table VI, attention must be called first to the comparative stability of consumer expenditures in constant dollars beginning with the year 1947. If high rates of population increase in Canada over the years 1947 through 1951 are taken into consideration in terms of *per capita* expenditures, the restrictions on real purchases become very obvious. Ordinary indifference curve analysis, taken in conjunction with these conditions and under the general assumption that the goods classed

24 This classification in Canada includes only jewellery, watches, clocks, silverware, home furnishings, furniture, household appliances, radios and automobiles. These goods, with small exceptions, were subject to the manufacturer's sales tax of 8 per cent up to April, 1951, and 10 per cent thereafter. Moreover, the special excise taxes of 10 per cent on a limited range of these goods were in September, 1950, extended to cover the whole range with very minor exceptions and the rate raised to 15 per cent. From April 10, 1951 through the early months of 1952, rates on many items were 25 per cent. On the other hand, commodity taxation on Nondurables affects only a portion of the category and in general has been falling in importance. Abolition of the general sales tax on most processed foods in early 1948, for example, left perhaps 95 per cent of food expenditures untaxed thereafter. The Food and Shelter components of the class of Nondurables have been set out separately, since this gives an aggregate which is virtually free of commodity taxation and which yet shows an almost identical pattern of change with the total class of Nondurables.

under Durables are "luxuries" and "elastic with income," would
hold that both income and substitution effects, operating in the
same direction, should have reduced expenditures on this class
of goods in 1951. These would be the effects to be expected both
from the higher prices on these goods resulting from higher sales
and excise tax rates and from the squeeze on money incomes resulting from increased income taxation, against *falling* real purchases on a per capita basis, when 1951 is compared with the year
1950. But what happened was that although the physical volume
of sales fell somewhat, expenditure actually increased by 3.8 per
cent and the ratio of expenditures to both Nondurables and to
Food and Shelter *remained the highest of the period up to this
time with the exception of 1950.*

The increase in expenditure may have been concentrated in
the first quarter of 1951, since the changes in taxation and credit
controls which took place in April of that year were fairly drastic.
Credit ceilings, consumer credit regulations, and the like may
serve only to cause substitution of demand over time and may
have disequilibrating effects in themselves upon the levels and
structures of costs and prices. Increased income taxation may fail
to have effect if it is not paralleled by an increase in the government's cash balances to the degree necessary to make the total
increase in saving equal the total increase in investment, public
and private. Excise taxation, unless carried to extremes, may be
offset in whole or part by the same underlying forces that cause
the real balances to fall. The community, turning away from
money as a store of value, may turn toward durable consumers'
goods as well as to investors' goods of various types. Moreover,
variable rates of excise taxation, in addition to bringing the ordinary disturbances to resource allocation that occur through
changes in relative prices, may bring special risks to the industries
subject to them and hence may further restrict their outputs,
raise prices, and affect unfavorably the allocation of resources in
the economy.

It is a long time since Wesley Clair Mitchell remarked that
every business cycle is unique. The unique characteristics of the
war and postwar period in Canada and other countries seem to
have been the extension of the practice of price administration
to the government bond markets and the adoption of other policies by central banks and governments designed to offset unde-

sired effects of the low-interest-rate policy. A scientifically sound appraisal of effects would require an extended comparison of current changes in economic magnitudes with those of previous periods having otherwise essentially similar characteristics. Yet in Canada at the present time this is impossible: the *National Accounts* go back only to 1926 and many of the statistical series published by the Bank of Canada only to 1938. Extension of these and other series backward toward the Confederation year of 1867 seems prerequisite to an extended study of Canadian cycles. Yet there is no indication at the present time that men and money will be available for such historical analyses. We are left for the present with the conclusions we may draw from the relations between theory and general empirical observations. The fit between theory and observation seems reasonably good. It supports the hypothesis that there is no real substitute for adequate control over the quantity of currency and bank deposits, exercised through flexibility of yields on the securities entering into the portfolios of central banks.

We may look at the situation briefly again in terms of a multiple set of margins. As the other margins of advantage in the assets market promise an increasing return over cost, causing a relative fall in the demand schedules for both bonds and money as stores of value, the attempt to hold to given rates of return in the government bond market can become successful only through the reduction of the volume of these bonds. This reduction must be of sufficient size to bring the market into short-period equilibrium again, since marginal holders must be those satisfied at the old rates. But if this reduction comes in whole or part through the central banking system a new element may enter which may lead to increasing disequilibrium. Additions to the amount of currency and bank deposits may result in inflation of prices and these may so shift expectations as to cause the demand for bonds and money to fall again. If this happens, the rate structure required to restore equilibrium in the government bond market may be higher than the structure which would have sufficed initially to preclude sales of securities to the central bank. The longer the policy of price administration continues in the bond markets, the greater the reductions that may be incurred in the demand schedules for bonds and money. The damages of the accompanying inflation may be far more important than those connected with the arbitrary redistribution of property and income. In the face of possible grave emergencies in a disturbed world, the narrowing of the bond market and distrust of the currency may carry a threat to national existence as a free society.

The process resembles a Wicksellian process, but the conditions required for equibrium are not so esoteric as an equality between the market and "natural" rates of interest! What is needed is only the recognition that while low rates of return on government bonds may lead to equilibrating movements in employment and output under conditions where there are ample supplies of unemployed agents of production, as the system approaches full employment, artificially low rates in the government bond market may set up conditions leading away from equilibrium. This is good Keynesian as well as good classical theory, for "if our central controls succeed in establishing an aggregate volume of output corresponding to full employment as nearly as is practicable, the classical theory comes into its own again from this point onwards." [25]

If Canadian policy has been the particular object of criticism in this paper, that does not mean that the practices outlined have not been nearly universal. Indeed the Canadian government began to turn away from administered prices for its bonds before either the American or the British government took the same step, and it may be just this priority in the return toward sanity which accounts in part for the current strength of the Canadian dollar in the world of today.

Debasement of the currency in the face of difficulties is a very old resort of princes. Modern methods through depreciation are more subtle, and modern treasuries, unlike medieval princes, need not choose between the costly recoinage of the whole money supply and the inconveniences involved in the simultaneous circulation of coins of the same names but of differing weights and fineness. For such reasons temptations to use these methods to meet contemporary fiscal or political problems may be relatively continuous. Governments may resort to them as drunkards may take to drink, little by little, under the plea of an imperative necessity. Yet if the position taken in this paper be a correct one, such policies are dangerous. It was back in the thirteenth century that Nicole Oresme, in the twenty-second chapter of his tract *On the First Invention of Money*, pointed out how infrequent deliberate alterations in the money of a community ought to be.

[25] *General Theory*, p. 378.

D*

Only "if the community has great need of a large sum of money for a war or for the ransom of its prince from captivity, or for some other emergency, then it might raise it by altering the money, and this would not be contrary to nature or usurious, since it would not be the act of the prince alone, but of the community to whom the money belongs. . . . And if the community should in any way make such an alteration, the money ought to be restored to its proper basis as soon as possible, and the making of gain in that way should cease." Perhaps there is not very much that is "new under the sun."

CHAPTER FOUR

Stability Through Inflation

William S. Vickrey

Price Trends and Equilibrium

IN most current macro-economic models, whether static or dynamic, equilibrium is explicitly or implicitly defined in terms of a stable price level. Even when the equilibrium is not a static one in the strict sense, in that it is thought of as occurring in a progressive economy in which the equilibrium is shifting more or less gradually through time as the exogenous parameters of the model change or as growth takes place within the model, some sort of a stable price level seems almost always to be taken for granted as part of the equilibrium picture.

To be sure, a "stable" price level may be defined in significantly different ways. Some, like Keynes, may prefer to consider, either as a datum or a desideratum, a stable level of wage rates (or perhaps of factor prices) as the norm, implied in the use of "wage-units" as a *numéraire* in which to express economic variables;[1] others may require a consumers' or cost-of-living price index to remain steady, and still others may fix on some index defined in terms of weights proportional to the volume of trading in various factors, intermediate and final commodities, and services. In a progressive economy, of course, with the purchasing power of labor presumably increasing, at least the wage-unit norm and the cost-of-living norm will mean substantially different things. Nevertheless in most economic discussion, equilibrium appears to imply the constancy of some significant price index, at least approximately.

Such concepts of equilibrium appear to be unnecessarily restrictive, both for the analysis of observed phenomena and for normative or prescriptive purposes. Particularly, as this paper will attempt to show, an economy in which prices are rising steadily may be more stable, in some significant respects, than

[1] J. M. Keynes, *The General Theory of Employment, Interest, and Money* (Harcourt Brace, 1936), chapter 4, esp. pp. 41-44.

comparable economies in which some kind of price index is kept approximately constant. If this be indeed the case, then it behooves us to broaden our horizons and admit a condition of specified, controlled, and generally anticipated inflation as a respectable and possibly even desirable condition, rather than to view inflation as being necessarily the result of fiscal immorality.

The key condition to the acceptance of this wider concept of stability is that the inflation be "generally anticipated." If we have a system whose stability depends on the steadily continuing inflation not being anticipated, there is on the one hand a considerable inequity involved as between debtors and creditors, and on the other, if the stability of the system is not upset for some other reason, it will be upset when individuals eventually learn, as in time they must, to expect the inflation. However, it is not at all difficult to construct models in which inflation is generally anticipated without this fact of itself producing any tendency to instability.

Consider, for example, an "economy of certainty" with a constant price level, in which all trading is planned and contracted for in advance along the lines of Hicks' "futures economy." [2] For such an economy in equilibrium, the real marginal productivity of capital will equal the money rate of interest. Consider on the other hand an economy in which the general price level rises at a rate of 10 per cent per year, in which all contracts are adjusted to make allowance for this price rise, and in which the money rate of interest is likewise adjusted, so that if, for example, in the constant price economy the rate was 5 per cent, the rate in the inflationary economy would be 15.5 per cent. The real aspects of the two economies would be precisely the same, aside from the effects of the higher rate of money interest on the velocity of circulation. For a monetary equilibrium to exist along with and compatible with this real equilibrium, it would be necessary only to have the real value of the amount of money in circulation somewhat smaller in the inflationary case than it would be with the stable price level, since the higher-money interest rate would in general induce a more rapid velocity of circulation.

If there is any difference in stability between these two economies, it must necessarily involve the monetary aspects of the model, since the real situation is almost exactly the same in both cases. The only necessary difference in the real situation is in the

[2] J. R. Hicks, *Value and Capital* (Oxford, 1939), pp. 136, 140.

amount of resources used up in the process of economizing the money supply and speeding up the velocity of circulation, which for most purposes is a negligible difference. Accordingly we will look to the monetary aspects of the situation for differences in stability. It may be noted at the outset that the monetary characteristics of an economy of steady anticipated inflation are rather closely comparable to those of an economy in which money is subjected to a tax or is otherwise devalued with the passage of time along lines suggested by Gesell, Dahlberg, and others.[3] In both cases the essential change is that the holding of cash balances is made more costly in real terms so that the velocity of circulation may be expected to increase.

An Equilibrium Model

The two types of economy may differ not only in their inherent stability but in their amenability to general controls through fiscal policy on the one hand and through monetary policy on the other. As this aspect of the question is somewhat easier to treat, and is itself involved in the question of stability, we will consider it first, using a simplified equilibrium model. The following model, while fairly simple and essentially static in nature, is yet broad enough to permit the illustration of a few elementary observations concerning the broad effects of monetary policy as contrasted with those of fiscal policy, according to both Keynesian assumptions and classical assumptions, with provision for comparison of inflationary and constant price-level economies.

For convenient reference, the symbols to be used in the various models in this paper are listed here; further explanation will be found in the context where necessary:

t time (in terms of a unit to be specified in alternative ways)

Y Y_t money income of individuals (for the period from t to $t + 1$)

P_t the general price level at time t, it being assumed that there is no significant divergence between different classes of prices

y y_t real income payments to individuals (for the period t to $t + 1$, the deflator being the geometric mean of the price levels at the beginning and end of the period)

[3] Arthur Dahlberg, *When Capital Goes on Strike* (Harpers, 1938); Silvio Gesell, *The Natural Economic Order* (tr. by Philip Pye from *Die Natuerliche Wirtschaftsordnung Durch Freiland und Freigeld*); see also Keynes, *op. cit.*, pp. 353-58.

i	i_t	the money rate of interest (for loans contracted at time t to be repaid at time $t + 1$)
k		the annual rate of inflation: $P_t = (1 + k)^t P_0$
r	r_t	the real marginal productivity of capital (from time t to time $t + 1$)
s		real savings
v		real private investment
M	M_t	the quantity of money in circulation (at time t)
m	m_t	the real value of the cash balances individuals want to hold (at time t)
F		fiscal deficits of public bodies on current account
X_t		outlays for consumption and investment for the period t to $t + 1$, planned at time t
h		the elasticity of price expectations
b		the elasticity of the demand for money
g		the volatility of outlays with respect to liquidity
j		the volatility of the credit supply
A		the (average) rate of growth or decline in individual entrepreneurial balances (without regard to sign)
q		the interval between financial transactions of individuals
C		the cost of a financial transaction
n		the elasticity of the cost of financial transactions with respect to the size of the transaction
T		the average size of financial transactions
K		the total cost of managing entrepreneurial balances
Q_t		the ratio of change in the money supply from time t to $t + 1$
Z		net national product at current prices
z		real net national product
P_{tu}		the expectation held at time u concerning the value which P is to have at time t, and similarly for other variables
w		the ratio of gross receipts to income payments
R_t		money gross receipts from time t to time $t + 1$

In the equilibrium model we will assume that the rate of inflation k is constant, and generally known and allowed for. Accordingly we can put $s = s(y,r)$; that is, the volume of real savings that individuals desire to make depends on their real income and on the real rate of interest, and is unaffected by changes in the money "veil." Similarly, private investment is also undertaken exclusively on the basis of real considerations. In this discussion the acceleration aspects of investment will be ignored, so that $v = v(y,r)$. Investment could, of course be written as a function of consumption expenditures rather than income, but since consumption is merely $y - s$ and s is in turn a function of y and r,

the relationship is capable of being reduced in any case to the form $v = v(y,r)$. It will further be assumed, for simplicity, that indirect taxes are kept at a level equal to government services to business (however defined), and that when the government deficit is equal to net government capital formation, so that $F = 0$, direct taxes can in effect be regarded as compulsory consumption outlays on government services to individuals. When this condition does not hold, y will more particularly be defined as the disposable income of individuals plus government services to individuals. This implies that a free government service has the same effect as the receipt of a comparable amount of income in determining savings of individuals; it will not matter if this assumption is unrealistic, since in any case it will be assumed that government outlays are kept constant. The net national product Z, to which the volume of employment is related, will then be $Z = Py - F = Y - F$, since the current account deficit F in effect represents that part of the savings of individuals that have no counterpart in real capital formation.

On the monetary side, the real value of the cash balances that individuals want to hold can be considered a function of the money rate of interest, since it is this rate that measures the sacrifice involved in holding money rather than interest-bearing securities. It is assumed here that money (including checking account balances) bears no interest. In general the demand for real cash balances will also be a function of real income, so that $m = m(y,i)$.

If now we regard the rate of inflation k as something exogenously fixed, as for example by the announcement and carrying out of an effective government policy to this effect, or if in particular we put $k = 0$, which is the case where a constant price level is presumed, then we have as two conditions for equilibrium (1) equality between the demand and supply of money, and (2) equality between savings and its offsets, as follows:

$$M = P \cdot m(y,i); \tag{1}$$
$$Ps = Pv + F. \tag{2}$$

If further we consider P as given (as will be the case if prices are not to deviate in the short run from the specified trend), we can consider the model consisting of the following seven relationships among the nine variables s, v, y, r, i, F, M, m, Z, with P and k being treated as parameters:

$$m = m(y,i) \tag{3}$$
$$(1 + i) = (1 + k)(1 + r) \tag{4}$$
$$Ps = Pv + F \tag{5}$$
$$s = s(y,r) \tag{6}$$
$$M = Pm(y,i) \tag{7}$$
$$Z = Py - F \tag{8}$$
$$v = v(y,r) \tag{9}$$

We can consider these six relationships as determining the six dependent variables s, v, y, r, i, m in terms of the two controllable independent variables F and M. Changing the variables F or M, corresponds, respectively, to pure monetary policy or pure fiscal policy. In pure monetary policy, government bonds are bought or sold on the market in exchange for cash, the cash being created or destroyed by the monetary authority while other operations of the Government are unaffected. It is assumed for the purposes of this analysis that some kind of 100 per cent reserve plan is in effect so that the creation or destruction of cash in this way is in the absolute control of a monetary authority and that banking operations cannot offset or magnify the operations of the Government. On the other hand, in pure fiscal policy taxes are increased or decreased and the sale of bonds is decreased or increased, in such a way that no money is created or destroyed, while government expenditures are maintained at the same level. An expenditure policy may also be postulated, consisting of expansion or contraction of government outlays accompanied by a corresponding increase or decrease in tax revenues, leaving the deficit and the money supply unchanged. In general any financial operation of the Government can be resolved into components each of which will be a pure "monetary," "fiscal" or "expenditure" policy; the present analysis is restricted to the monetary and fiscal components.

Equations (5) and (7) can now be differentiated partially with respect to F, considering M as a constant and all other variables to be functions of M and F; we thus get:

$$P(s_r - v_r) \frac{\partial r}{\partial F} + P(s_y - v_y) \frac{\partial y}{\partial F} = 1, \tag{10}$$

and

$$P\left[m_i(1 + k) \frac{\partial r}{\partial F} + (m_y) \frac{\partial y}{\partial F} \right] = 0, \tag{11}$$

where $s_r = \left[\dfrac{\partial s}{\partial r}\right]_y = \dfrac{\partial}{\partial r}[s(y,r)]$, and similarly for s_y, v_r, v_y, m_i, and m_y. These two linear equations in the unknown partial derivatives $\dfrac{\partial y}{\partial F}$ and $\dfrac{\partial r}{\partial F}$ can then be solved to give

$$\frac{\partial r}{\partial F} = \frac{m_y}{P[m_y(s_r - v_r) - m_i(1 + k)(s_y - v_y)]} \tag{12}$$

$$\frac{\partial y}{\partial F} = \frac{-m_i(1 + k)}{P[m_y(s_r - v_r) - m_i(1 + k)(s_y - v_y)]} \tag{13}$$

Similarly, differentiating (5) and (7) partially with respect to M, considering F constant and all other variables functions of M and F, and solving for $\dfrac{\partial r}{\partial M}$ and $\dfrac{\partial y}{\partial M}$, gives

$$\frac{\partial r}{\partial M} = \frac{-(s_y - v_y)}{P[m_y(s_r - v_r) - m_i(1 + k)(s_y - v_y)]} \tag{14}$$

$$\frac{\partial y}{\partial M} = \frac{s_r - v_r}{P[m_y(s_r - v_r) - m_i(1 + k)(s_y - v_y)]} \tag{15}$$

The right-hand side of each of these four equations involves only known parameters and the presumed known derivatives of the behavior functions $m(y,i)$, $s(y,r)$ and $v(y,r)$, so that from these expressions can be estimated the effectiveness of monetary policy and fiscal policy respectively on income and interest rates. For the more conventional analysis with the price level assumed constant, we can simplify these expressions somewhat by putting $P = 1$, $r = i$, and $k = 0$.

In any case, it is easy to see that if m_i becomes large (negatively, of course), or, in Keynesian terminology, if liquidity-preference "becomes absolute," then assuming that $v_y < s_y$, that is, that savings are more responsive to changes in income than is investment, then $\dfrac{\partial y}{\partial M}$ becomes small and accordingly monetary policy ceases to have much effect on income; indeed since $\dfrac{\partial r}{\partial M}$ is also small, monetary policy ceases to have much effect on interest rates either. Moreover from (8) we have $\dfrac{\partial Z}{\partial M} = P\dfrac{\partial y}{\partial M}$, so that mon-

etary policy has no greater effect on national product and employment than on income. On the other hand, under these circum-
stances (13) approaches $\dfrac{\partial y}{\partial F} = \dfrac{1}{P(s_y - v_y)}$ and hence

$$\frac{\partial Y}{\partial F} = P\frac{\partial y}{\partial F} = \frac{1}{s_y - v_y} = \frac{1}{1 - b - a} \tag{16}$$

where b is the marginal propensity to consume and a is the marginal propensity to invest; thus we obtain the familiar "Super-
multiplier." However, in this model this is an "income multiplier"
not an "employment multiplier," since from (8)

$$\frac{\partial Z}{\partial F} = P\frac{\partial y}{\partial F} - 1 = \frac{1}{s_y - v_y} - 1 = \frac{b + a}{1 - b - a} \tag{17}$$

and the employment multiplier is smaller by one than the income
multiplier. This is because so much of any increased income as is
represented by an increase in F consists of savings invested in government bonds that correspond to no net real capital formation.

The results in (12) to (15) also approach those of the simple
Keynesian analysis when $(s_r - v_r)$ becomes small, as is the case
when neither savings nor investment respond to changes in interest rates, or perhaps when a slight negative responsiveness of
investment is countered by a perversely negative responsiveness
of savings, with savings increasing with diminishing interest rates.
However, this result is not the one that is of interest here.

If we make the opposite assumption about liquidity-preference
and consider what happens when m_i is small, then we are back
to the classical case where the velocity of circulation is relatively
constant, or at least is not greatly affected by interest rates.
Equation (14) approaches $\dfrac{\partial y}{\partial M} = \dfrac{1}{P \cdot m_y}$ which can be interpreted
as the classical circuit velocity of money. Here income tends to
vary in proportion to the money supply. Further, at this end of
the spectrum $\dfrac{\partial y}{\partial F}$ becomes small, at least if m_i is small relative to
$(s_r - v_r)$, so that fiscal policy has little effect on real income.
Indeed, since $\dfrac{\partial Z}{\partial F} = P\dfrac{\partial y}{\partial F} - 1$, an increased deficit might have
so little effect on incomes that the net national product and with it
employment might actually decline if at the same time the money
supply were maintained strictly constant.

Fiscal Policy, Monetary Policy, and the Social Heritage

Now it is generally thought that at low rates of interest m_i is actually quite large and that therefore when the accumulation of capital has brought the marginal productivity of capital down to low levels, and with it, under constant price-level conditions, the money rate of interest, it becomes appropriate to abandon traditional monetary policy in favor of fiscal policy as a means of stabilizing the economy. What is perhaps not quite so often realized is that if conditions should occur where the productivity of capital is high, as it may be, for example, in underdeveloped countries, or as it may again become should we have a sudden spate of capital-requiring innovations, it would then be appropriate to return to a more complete reliance on monetary policies and expect less from the Keynesian fiscal policies.

If this were all, it would merely mean that we were equipped with two types of over-all control over the general pace of the economy which to a considerable extent complement each other in that the circumstances that impair the effectiveness of one method are generally favorable to the effectiveness of the other. The question would then merely be one of knowing which is the more effective to use at a particular moment or in a particular direction. And indeed, there would be no objection to combining both policies, as for example when taxes are reduced and the gap in revenue supplied by the creation of additional money.

But full employment (or the stabilization of some price trend) is not the only objective of fiscal and monetary policy. The way in which public expenditures are financed will also affect the rate of capital formation. If, for example, it is possible to maintain full employment and a constant price level either with a large deficit, low taxes, and high rates of interest, or with high taxes, no deficit or a surplus, and low rates of interest, the latter procedure will in general lead to a smaller consumption out of the full-employment net product, and to a larger rate of capital formation with possibly a more rapid rate of economic progress. To be sure, many other policies of government also affect the rate of capital formation and the social heritage passed on to future generations. The degree of progression of the tax system, for example, will affect individual savings and the amounts passed on in private estates to future generations. The degree to which the various governments engage in capital improvements and public works also

affects the way in which resources are apportioned between uses
that benefit present and those that benefit future generations. But
such policies are usually judged also by other criteria, and to
require that these policies be modified in order to achieve some
desired rate of capital accumulation will be *pro tanto* to interfere
with these other equally important goals. The decision as to
whether or not to undertake some construction project under
government auspices, or leave it to possible undertaking by
private enterprise, or perhaps to abandon the project entirely,
should be made preferably on the basis of the general desirability
of the project as compared with other uses of the required resources, or to the relative merits of private as compared with
public construction or operation; if possible, such decisions should
not be biased by the injection of considerations of desired aggregate capital formation if other independent means of adjusting
capital formation exist. If a desired level of aggregate capital
formation is secured through appropriate over-all monetary and
fiscal policies rather than through the warping of decisions on
other matters to this end, the social heritage probably can be
increased without impairing current standards of living. Similarly,
tax progression should be decided on the basis of prevailing concepts of social justice and incentive effects on productivity, rather
than in terms of effects on the social heritage, provided of course
that the provision of the desired social heritage can be taken care
of in other ways.

Accordingly, it is not a matter of indifference whether the over-
all stabilization of the economy is achieved through monetary or
through fiscal policy. If the economy is operated at a low-money
rate of interest, so that monetary policy is ineffective, fiscal policy
must be used to stabilize the economy while monetary policy lies
idle and useless; there is then nothing left in the field of over-all
controls that can be used to influence the rate of capital formation
within the framework of full employment. If the economy is operated at a high-money interest rate, however, where monetary
controls can be used to stabilize the economy, then fiscal policy
can be used, within limits, to influence the rate of capital formation. But if a level price trend is considered a *sine qua non*, a high-
money interest rate also implies a high real rate of interest which
in turn may discourage private investment and capital formation
to an undesirably large extent. With a level price trend there is a
certain minimum money rate of interest which must be main-

tained if monetary policy is to have room in which to operate in correcting downward tendencies in the economy. The desired level of capital formation may be much higher than could be secured within the limits imposed by requiring monetary policy to be kept effective in a level price trend economy.

Ease of Application of Monetary and Fiscal Policies

On a practical level, too, there are important differences in the ease with which monetary and fiscal policy may be applied. Monetary policy can be adjusted on extremely short notice, and moreover has a much more generalized impact on the economy than most forms of fiscal policy. Fiscal policy in the form of increased spending requires, if waste is to be avoided, that plans be made a considerable length of time in advance. Even under the best of circumstances, such stabilization spending cannot be turned on and off easily: congressional appropriations are required and personnel must be found, hired, and in some cases transported. Public works especially are slow to get started and sometimes even slower to get finished.

Increased attention therefore has recently been given to fiscal policy in the form of changes in taxes, and even to changes in "negative taxes" or subsidy and bonus payments of various kinds. But changes in excise tax rates, especially, involve either the use of floor stock taxes and rebates, or inequities and disturbances due to anticipatory or deferred buying. Changes in income tax rates require a certain minimum amount of time in order to allow for changes in withholding tax schedules and the like, although some announcement effect may be felt even before the changes in rates take place. Here too, however, arbitrary discrimination is likely to result between those earning incomes before and after the change in rates, and although this might in principle be remedied by some sort of averaging, the prospects for the adoption of the kind of averaging that would be appropriate for this purpose seem remote. Proposals for providing a series of alternative schedules legislated in advance so as to limit the delays due to legislative bickering over the distribution of the additional burdens or of tax relief are promising, but at best it seems probable that effective tax action will take a substantially longer time than would a corresponding change in monetary policy.

This is not to deny that there are also serious institutional difficulties in the way of carrying out changes in monetary policy, including the objections in financial circles to resulting fluctuations in security markets, changes induced in bank earnings, and possibly more immediate international repercussions. But these are in general obstacles to doing anything at all, rather than special difficulties in the way of prompt action, and if monetary policy can be carried through at all, it seems likely that it can be carried through with a promptness that is unobtainable with fiscal policy. On this basis it can be considered highly desirable to have available an effective monetary policy as a short term device to be backed up over longer periods by fiscal policy, even if only on grounds of administrative flexibility and promptness of response to indicated deviations of the economy from the predesignated path.

Monetary Instability

Still a third reason for wanting to operate a monetary economy with a high- rather than a low-money rate of interest is that there may be inherent in the low interest situation a source of instability that is absent or at least less intense in the high interest situation where the liquidity-preference curve is more nearly vertical instead of being nearly horizontal, *i.e.*, where the elasticity of the demand for money with respect to changes in money interest rates is smaller. While it may not be obvious a priori that the elasticity of the demand for money is smaller at higher interest rates, the probability that this is indeed so is greatly increased when it is discovered that the elasticity that appears to be relevant for the stability of the monetary system is not the simple elasticity relative to the interest rate itself, $-\dfrac{i}{m}\dfrac{dm}{di}$, but rather the elasticity referred to an origin taken at $m = 0$ and $1 + i = 0$, that is

$$- \frac{(1+i)}{m} \frac{dm}{d(1+i)} = - \frac{(1+i)}{m} \frac{dm}{di}. \qquad (18)$$

The general nature of this instability can be grasped by considering a classical economic market in which prices are completely flexible, and in which all resources are either fully employed or have a price of zero (or at most a price representing the marginal costs involved in providing for their use rather than their idleness). In such a market the quantities of goods offered for sale in a given income period are in the aggregate determined by the conditions of "full employment"; the prices they command in the aggregate will be determined by the total amount of money spent on them, which will in turn be the product of the quantity of money and a velocity of circulation determined by the money rate of interest. Money interest, in turn, will reflect the equilibrium rate of real interest that produces a balance between savings and investment, plus or minus an adjustment representing the anticipated rate of change in the price level. Expectations concerning the rate of change in the price level can be supposed to be the product of immediately preceding experience with the price level, and in general, for a sufficiently short time period, it can be assumed that the elasticity of price expectations will be positive: that is, if in the preceding time period prices prove to have risen by more than was previously expected, this will lead to an expectation that in the subsequent period the rate of price rise will be larger than was formerly expected.

Consider then an initial condition of equilibrium in which there is a given generally expected trend of the price level (which may be one of no change), accommodated by a money supply increasing at a rate just appropriate to the secular rise in real income compounded with this price trend, for the (steady) velocity of circulation determined by the equilibrium money rate of interest. If, then, through some chance variation, such as for example a bumper crop, the price level falls below the normal trend, a positive elasticity of expectations will lead to a further expectation of a lower than normal price rise in the subsequent period. If both savers and investors have the same anticipations regarding the price level, the equilibrium money rate of interest will fall, and with the fall in the rate of interest the willingness of individuals to hold cash rather than interest-bearing securities will increase, leading to a decrease in the circuit velocity of money and a decline in the rate at which purchasing power comes to the market, leading in turn to a further decline in prices. If this further decline in prices is large enough, a downward spiral may be set up that appears to have no inherent limit in the monetary structure. At some point in the process, money rates of interest will become so low, or even negative, that the investment market ceases to function, though even before this point is reached the repercussions of this monetary upheaval are likely to involve the underlying real structure of the economy, with possibilities for under-full employment.

A turning point may thus be reached through the repercussions in the real economy, but not before the monetary instability has produced real undesirable consequences.

There is considerably more likelihood that an upward spiral would become self-limiting, provided of course that fuel is not added to the fire by the expansion of the monetary supply at an abnormally high rate, either through the expansion of bank credit that might occur if a fixed rediscount rate is maintained, or through money creation impelled by fiscal emergencies. If the money supply is not thus expanded, money interest rates will eventually rise to a point where the demand for money is not very elastic and the velocity of circulation cannot readily be increased further, at which point the cycle probably will reverse itself. On the other hand, unless the equilibrium was established at a moderately high level of money interest, the cycle probably will overshoot on the downward side and possibly turn into a downward spiral with consequent unemployment. A limitation of this sort on the upward side seems likely if the official money continues to be used in trade. If, before the downturn comes, the rate of price inflation becomes so great that it becomes worth-while to use various money substitutes as a means of exchange, such as foreign currencies, commodities, interest-bearing notes, and the like, there may be no upper limit to the effective velocity of circulation and the inflation could conceivably continue through this "flight from the currency" until the abandonment of the original currency is virtually complete.

A Dynamic Monetary Model

To define the nature of this monetary instability more specifically, let us construct the following mathematical model:

Assume that all prices are perfectly flexible so that, whatever may happen to money incomes, real incomes stay at the full-employment level; that whatever expectations there may be regarding the future course of prices, these expectations are shared by both savers and investors so that the investment market is cleared at the same level of savings and investment as would be the case with a constant price level, the only difference being that the money rate of interest expected or contracted for is sufficiently higher to allow for the price increase that is expected by both parties to the contract. This price increase of course may or may not be realized in the event. The money rate of interest i_t refers to the rate of interest on loans for one "period" contracted at time t and payable at time $t + 1$. Similarly r_t stands for the equilibrium real rate of interest from t to $t + 1$, which, since we assume the real aspects of the economy to remain unaffected by monetary change, we will treat as an exogenous variable. If P_{teu} is the price which would obtain at time t if the expectations that are held at time u are realized, we can write the following relationship between money interest, real interest, and expected prices:

$$1 + i_t = (1 + r_t) \frac{P_{(1+t)et}}{P_t} \tag{19}$$

We will further assume that the "period" is sufficiently short so that there is no significant difference between the ratio of price increase expected to occur during the next period and that expected (at the same time) to occur during the second following period:

$$\frac{P_{(t+2)et}}{P_{(t+1)et}} = \frac{P_{(t+1)et}}{P_t} \tag{20}$$

Of course $P_{tet} = P_t$.

At time $t + 1$ prices are found to be P_{t+1} instead of the expected $P_{(t+1)et}$, and this experience will lead to a revision of expectations for the future. We can express this by

$$P_{(t+2)e(t+1)} = P_{(t+2)et} \left[\frac{P_{(t+1)}}{P_{(t+1)et}} \right]^h \tag{21}$$

where h can be called the elasticity of price expectations, measuring the strength of the influence of the surprise experienced at time $t + 1$ on the expectations for time $t + 2$. It will be assumed that h lies between 1 and 2; $h = 2$ would mean that people expect for the next period exactly the same rate of inflation as was experienced in the preceding one; $h = 1$ would mean that the rate of inflation expected for the next period is unaffected by what happened in the last, while $h = 0$ would mean that failure of expectations to be realized is considered entirely a temporary aberration from the expected trend and that the next period will see the lost ground made up with a return to the originally anticipated trend. This formulation of the formation of expectations seems completely inappropriate for values of h below 1, as this would imply that even if the price trend in fact was perfectly steady, any initial error made in forecasting the trend of prices would grow steadily worse as time goes on. Indeed such values produce a completely unstable model.

The course of the real elements in the economy being exogenously determined and known, we can put y_t for this known real income which is to be received during the period from t to $t + 1$. Expectations as to the price level coupled with this knowledge of real income imply expectations as to money income. Assume that income is valued at the geometric mean of the prices obtaining at the beginning and end of the income period; then the money income for the period t to $t + 1$ expected at time t will be

$$Y_{tet} = y_t[P_t P_{(t+1)et}]^{1/2} \tag{22}$$

The liquidity-preference function, representing the amount of real purchasing power individuals would like to have on hand at a given level of money income and money rate of interest, can be approximated over any small range of variation by a relation of the form

$$m_t = e^a y_t (1 + i_t)^{-b} = m(y,i) \tag{23}$$

Here e^a is a constant of proportionality, and b is the elasticity of the demand for money referred to in (18).

Further, suppose that at the beginning of each income period money outlays are planned according to the cash balances and the interest rate at time t, so as to exceed or fall short of expected receipts according to whether the money on hand at the beginning of the period, M_t represents a real purchasing power for the coming income period $M_t[P_t P_{(t+1)et}]^{-1/2}$ that exceeds or falls short of the purchasing power m_t appropriate to i_t and y_t. Expected receipts, in turn, will be assumed to be a constant multiple of expected income:

$$R_{tet} = wY_{tet}, \tag{24}$$

where w is a constant. The response of planned outlays to an excess or deficiency in liquidity may be considered to be approximately represented by:

$$X_{tet} = R_{tet}\left[\frac{M_t[P_t P_{(t+1)et}]^{-1/2}}{m_t}\right]^g \tag{25}$$

where g is a coefficient reflecting the elasticity of outlays with respect to liquidity.

These outlays are assumed to be actually made, their impact being absorbed by price adjustments; a fraction $1/w$ of these outlays is assumed to be made in the form of income payments, as would be required to satisfy the assumption that the real aspects of the economy are unaffected by monetary vagaries and are also fully anticipated. Accordingly we put

$$Y_t = \frac{X_{tet}}{w}. \tag{26}$$

And of course the analog of (22) for the actual money income is

$$Y_t = y_t[P_t P_{t+1}]^{1/2}. \tag{27}$$

Equations (19) through (27) then furnish 9 relationships between the 9 endogenous variables P_t, $P_{(t+1)et}$, $P_{(t+2)et}$, Y_t, Y_{tet}, X_{tet}, R_{tet}, m_t, and i_t. The remaining three variables that appear are exogenously determined: M_t by fiat of the monetary authority, r_t and y_t by the assumed determinate real equilibrium. $P_{(t+2)e(t+1)}$, and P_{t+1} do not count as additional variables, since they are merely $P_{(t+1)et}$ and P_t with the time variable shifted. To obtain a difference equation in a single variable P_t and its translations P_{t+1} and P_{t+2}, 8 of the variables are eliminated from these equations as follows. Put the value of Y_{tet} from (22) into (24), and the resulting value for R_{tet} into the right-hand side of (25), also substitute in (25) the value of m_t from (23); put the value of Y_t from (27) into (26), multiply the result by w and insert the resulting value for X_{tet} on the left of (25), then square both sides of (25) to eliminate the fractional exponents, getting:

$$w^2 y_t^2 P_t P_{t+1}$$
$$= w^2 y_t^2{}_t^2 P_t P_{(t+1)et} e^{-2ag} y_t^{-2g}(1 + i_t)^{2gb} M_t^{2g} P_t^{-g} P_{(t+1)et}^{-g} \tag{28}$$

Solving (19) for $P_{(t+1)et}$ and inserting the result in (28), shifting all terms to the right-hand side,

$$1 = P_{t+1}^{-1} P_t^{1-2g}(1 + i_t)^{1-g+2gb}(1 + r_t)^{g-1} e^{-2ag} y_t^{-2g} M_t^{2g} \tag{29}$$

To eliminate i_t from (29), first obtain from (19), (20) and (21) an expression involving only P_t and i_t and their translations. To do this solve (20) for $P_{(t+2)et}$ and insert the result in (21); solve (19) for $P_{(t+1)et}$ and obtain also an expression for $P_{(t+2)e(t+1)}$ by replacing t by $t + 1$, and insert these expressions in (21), getting

$$(1 + i_{t+1})(1 + r_{t+1})^{-1} P_{t+1}$$
$$= (1 + i_t)^{2-h}(1 + r_t)^{h-2} P_t^{1-h} P_{t+1}^h \tag{30}$$

We can now eliminate i between (29) and (30) by replacing t in (29) by $t + 1$, and also raising (29) to the $h - 2$ power (*i.e.*, multiplying all the exponents by $h - 2$); multiplying the two results together and multiplying by the $1 - g + 2gb$ power of (30). If we collect all the terms in P on the left, we have:

$$P_{t+2}P_{t+1}{}^{g-2+gh+2gb-2gbh}P_t{}^{1-3g+gh-2gb+2gbh}$$
$$= (1 + r_{t+1})^{2gb}(1 + r_t)^{2gbh-4gb}e^{2ag-2agh} \qquad (31)$$
$$y_{t+1}{}^{-2g}y_t{}^{4g-2gh}M_{t+1}{}^{2g}M_t{}^{2gh-4g}$$

The right-hand part of (31) is then entirely exogenous. If we take logarithms, (31) becomes a linear difference equation of the second order which can be written

$$[E^2 - (2 - g - gh - 2gb + 2gbh)E$$
$$+ (1 - 3g + gh - 2gb + 2gbh)] \log P_t = f(t) \qquad (32)$$

where E is the shifting operator having the effect of increasing the time argument by 1, and $f(t)$ is the exogenous driving function given by the right-hand side of (31).

Conditions for Monetary Stability

For the general linear difference equation of the second degree represented by $(E^2 - BE + C)\phi(t) = f(t)$, we have as conditions for the convergence of the transient part of the solution the following inequalities:

$$C \leqq 1; \quad -1 - C \leqq B \leqq 1 + C \qquad (33)$$

and if we substitute for B and C the respective coefficients appearing in (32), these conditions reduce to

$$0 \leqq 1 - g + gb(h - 1) \qquad (34a)$$
$$2bg(h - 1) \leqq 3 - h \qquad (34b)$$
$$0 \leqq 2g(h - 1) \qquad (34c)$$

It can be assumed that g is not negative, as this would imply a perverse response to excess liquidity. If g is zero, implying that individuals make no attempt to adjust their cash position, then the difference equation reduces to $(E - 1)^2\phi(t) = f(t)$, which gives $\phi = 0$ as the only solution of the reduced equation. If g is positive, then condition (34c) requires that h be greater than 1, as is to be expected since for h less than 1 the expectations are themselves unstable. With g and $h - 1$ both positive, solving (34b) for h gives

$$1 < h \leqq 1 + \frac{2}{2b + 1} \qquad (35)$$

Now h is a parameter reflecting fundamental psychological attitudes of the trading population, and while it is likely to be considerably affected by the measures taken for economic stabilization and by the confidence that individuals have in the effectiveness of these measures, and particularly on the promptness with which these measures will have their effect, on the whole there is relatively little that can be done to squeeze the value of h into the limits set by (35) for a given value of b. Indeed, for low rates of money interest the value of b may be fairly large, probably of the order of 10 or higher, so that h would be required to lie between 1.0 and 1.1 in order to satisfy the requirements for stability. Such a low elasticity of price expectations is by no means impossible, but such a range of values would seem to presuppose a continued sluggishness of response of economic units that would be a rather thin reed to rely upon for long.

On the other hand, if a rate of inflation is decided upon and maintained so that the normal money rate of interest in equilibrium would be 8 or 10 per cent or higher, even with a marginal productivity of capital down to as low as 2 per cent, it seems likely that the coefficient b would be small enough to allow a considerable range for h and still maintain stability. Indeed if b can be made as low as 1.0, then the range for h is widened to $1 < h < 1.67$, and continued stability seems much more probable.

Indeed, stability in this model is to a considerable extent autocatalytic, in the sense that if the system has the appearance of stability, creating confidence in the stability of the system in the minds of traders, then the elasticity of expectations will be reduced and the system made more stable.

A Liquidity-Preference Model

Some further light on the relation of the coefficient b to the level of money interest rates may be shed by considering the model suggested by William Baumol in which the theory of inventories is applied to cash balances.[4]

[4] William J. Baumol, "The Transactions Demand for Cash: An Inventory Theoretic Approach," 66 *Quarterly Journal of Economics*, 545 (November, 1952).

We may first suppose that the "entrepreneurial program" of an individual or firm calls for the making of certain outlays and the receipt of certain proceeds through time, and the net resultant of these entrepreneurial activities on his cash balance can be represented by an "entrepreneurial balance" which is a function of time. If this individual or firm makes no "financial transactions" outside of his entrepreneurial program, this entrepreneurial balance will be his cash balance at each point of time. If financial transactions were costless, while interest is paid on short-term loans, it would always be profitable to keep this entire entrepreneurial balance invested at all times, even though this in the limit would involve an exceedingly large number of financial transactions of small size.

If, on the other hand, financial transactions involve a cost, in general it will not pay to invest idle funds unless this investment can be held for some minimum period (though this period may vary depending on the directness of the access of the individual firm to the money market, and perhaps also on the size of the transaction involved). Moreover, if the cost of a financial transaction increases with the size of the transaction but less rapidly than in proportion to its size, then even if funds are to be invested for fairly long periods, it will not pay to make a large number of small transactions. Rather, transactions will be spaced at intervals, so as to take advantage of the lower unit cost of the larger scale transactions.

More specifically, let us assume that the real entrepreneurial balances of each individual are characterized by alternating periods of fairly steady growth and of fairly steady decline, each period being long enough to include several financial transactions. Assume further that the rate of growth or decline is fairly steady and can be represented by A. If the interval between financial transactions is q, and if the size of each transaction is such that the entrepreneurial balance just before or just after each transaction is zero, then the size of the transaction will be $T = Aq$, and the average (real) cash balance will be $m = Aq/2$. The total cost of managing the entrepreneurial balance can be considered the difference between the net proceeds from the investment of the balances and the theoretical proceeds if the balances could be kept fully invested without transaction expense. This cost will be the sum of the interest lost on the average cash balance, and the cost of the financial transactions. If the cost of the transactions is a function of their size, this relation may be approximated by a function of the form $C(T) = aT^n$ where n lies between 0, in which case the cost would be independent of the size of the transaction, to 1, where the cost would be proportional. In a unit interval of time there will be $1/q$ transactions, so that the total cost of managing entrepreneurial balances can be put at

$$K = im + \frac{C}{q} = \frac{iAq}{2} + \frac{a}{q}(Aq)^n = \frac{iAq}{2} + aA^n q^{n-1} \qquad (36)$$

If the total cost is to be a minimum, we must determine q so that

$$0 = \frac{dK}{dq} = \frac{iA}{2} + a(n-1)A^n q^{n-2} \qquad (37)$$

from which

$$i = 2a(1-n)A(Aq)^{n-2} = 2aA(1-n)(2m)^{n-2} \qquad (38)$$

If this relationship determines a liquidity-preference function, then for this function, considering m as a function of i,

$$\frac{dm}{di} = \frac{1}{\dfrac{di}{dm}} = \frac{1}{2aA(1-n)(n-2)(2m)^{n-3}(2)} = -\frac{m}{i(2-n)} \qquad (39)$$

On the other hand, from the liquidity-preference function assumed in the dynamic model, given in (23), we have

$$\frac{dm}{di} = -\frac{mb}{(1+i)} \qquad (40)$$

If then these two liquidity-preference functions are to approximate each other over a small range in the neighborhood of the point at which the economy is operating, they must have the same slope at this point, so that we must have

$$-\frac{mb}{1+i} = -\frac{m}{i(2-n)} \quad \text{or} \quad b = \frac{1+i}{i(2-n)} \qquad (41)$$

Obviously, on this basis the larger the rate of interest the smaller will be the coefficient b, and the larger will be the range of stability for h, the elasticity of price expectations, as given in (35).

It should be noted, however, that if the i occurring in (41) is to be consistent with the period used in (19), this i must be considered as representing the interest rate for a period of time corresponding to the planning period in terms of which the elasticity of price expectations is defined by (21) and during which the outlays are carried out as planned at the beginning of the period as assumed in (26). On the whole it seems unlikely that the period that would make the model most nearly realistic would be longer than one year, and accordingly the i of (41) is probably something smaller than the annual rate of interest. This in turn would seem to imply that even at best with a fairly high rate of interest of the order of 10 per cent per year or more and with the elasticity of the cost of transactions n close to zero, b would still be greater than 5 and the range of h for which the model is stable would still be uncomfortably narrow.

Monetary Instability in the Real World

Indeed, it would seem that the real world is in fact quite far from exhibiting the kind of instability predicted by this model. This model deliberately abstracts from all repercussions that take place through effects upon the real aspects of the economy as contrasted with the monetary aspects. This has been done, despite the drastic sacrifice of realism, in order to isolate the specifically monetary sources of instability. In the context of current economic conditions these monetary sources of instability may be insignificant or their effects may be completely masked by other effects. For example, a reduction in outlays may not in fact produce an immediate comparable reduction in prices, but rather prices may be somewhat sticky, giving rise to a reduction of real output and employment with a whole sequence of consequences quite outside the monetary sphere that will in turn react on the monetary equilibrium.

Nevertheless, it is felt that an analysis of this sort has a usefulness in pointing out factors that may be missed if attention is concentrated on the more immediately apparent instabilities. Indeed, if conditions are in fact such as would produce instability of the monetary system, either along the lines of the present model, or indeed of any other model in which monetary vagaries are prevented from affecting the real aspects of the economy, then in practice either the monetary divergence proceeds to a point where the model breaks down and real repercussions occur, or the monetary divergence is prevented by real repercussions outside the postulates of the model from the very start. In either event, disturbances arising in the monetary sector of the economy come to affect the real economy, presumably adversely, and the monetary system is then failing in its function of providing a mere medium of exchange or lubricant with the aid of which a stable pattern of "real" economic life is maintained. To have a minimum of disturbing effects on the real economy, it seems that the monetary system should be such as not to require real repercussions for the maintenance of its stability.

Actually a complete autonomous stability of the monetary system may not be required. Some degree of monetary control is likely to be needed in any case, even if this is nothing more than an agency charged with feeding an appropriate increment to the money supply into the economy, however rigidly this increment may be specified. If the endogenous elements in the monetary system do not themselves constitute too violently unstable a system, a proper adjustment of the monetary supply by the monetary authority may be able to maintain a reasonably steady price trend, even though the system if left to itself with an arbitrarily determined money supply would tend to go off to extremes. Moreover, it seems that the more nearly stable the endogenous system is, the easier would be the task of stabilization and the narrower the margin within which the prescribed price trend could be maintained. Even if stability is to a considerable extent dependent upon assistance from real repercussions, it appears likely that the more nearly stable the purely monetary model, the smaller would be the real deviations from optimum patterns. A system in which the norm is a steadily rising general price level and in which this trend is generally anticipated would, on the basis of the above discussion, appear to be more stable than a system in which it is attempted to keep the general price level unchanged.

Perhaps one consideration counter to the above conclusion should be noted, however. A level price trend is unique in a way that a specified upward price trend is not, and for this reason it may be easier to impress the public with the sacredness of the obligation upon the monetary authorities of maintaining this trend rather than allowing a rise or fall of, say, 2 per cent per year, than it would be to produce an equal firmness of conviction on the part of the public that an announced intention of maintaining a 10 per cent rate of inflation will actually be carried out and that equally strong steps will be taken to prevent the rate of inflation from falling to 8 per cent or rising to 12 per cent. Nevertheless confidence in the maintenance of a steady rate of inflation should be capable of being brought eventually to a comparable degree of firmness, particularly since this confidence would be based on greater underlying effective power in the hands of the authority entrusted with the responsibility.

Interest Bearing Forms of Money

While the above model indicates that as the price trend is made steeper the monetary stability of the system becomes greater, there are limits to this relationship. The model makes use of the money rate of interest as a measure of the cost of holding money, reflecting the usual tacit assumption that money will not earn interest. For currency this assumption seems tenable, even in the event of a fairly steep price trend. For demand deposits, however, this assumption can be made only with great caution. Banks have in the past paid explicit interest on demand deposits, and where such interest is paid the cost of holding such demand deposits would be merely the difference between the interest rate on term loans and that on demand deposits. Even at present, banks pay a form of interest in kind on demand deposits by allowing customers a measured amount of free service proportioned to the size of their deposits. In most cases the service allowed is measured by the minimum balance each month rather than by an average balance, but there is no inherent reason, aside from the possible expenses of computation, why this free service allowance should not be based on the average balance. If evaluated at the level of the service charge otherwise imposed for the same services, the interest in kind thus allowed on deposits may run up to 2 per cent per year. Many depositors, however, do not use the full amount of free service to which they are entitled, so that the size of their deposits cannot be considered to be influenced by the free service allowance, at least at the margin.

If money rates of interest were to rise substantially, competition among banks might well induce them to expand substantially the amount of free service they are prepared to render, even if they might still be prohibited by law from offering explicit interest in money. A possible means of offsetting this tendency would be to impose a tax on demand deposits, or perhaps to impose some kind of 100 per cent reserve requirement which would keep bank earnings to a level where only moderate amounts of free service could be offered.

In passing it may be noted that the essentially institutional nature of monetary theory, including much of the basic notions of the quantity theory and of the liquidity-preference theory, is brought out by considering how far either of these theories would be applicable to a situation in which all transactions are executed by check or some similar instrument, in which banks cover their operating expenses entirely from service charges and pay interest on average balances at rates reflecting the return on their investments, and in which overdrafts are honored fairly freely, possibly at graduated interest rates. It seems likely that for application to such circumstances the theories would have to be rather radically modified, if indeed they did not become entirely inapplicable.

Upper Limits to Money Interest Rates

While a moderate rate of inflation might be accommodated with minor adaptations in banking regulations and methods and in ways of handling transactions, too drastic an increase in the cost of holding money may lead to another kind of real repercussion and even to a more or less complete breakdown to the monetary system. As long as money takes the form of a mere paper fiat or credit balance, the cost to individuals of holding such balances in terms of the loss of interest represents no real social cost associated with the creation of such money, unlike the case where a commodity or representative money is in use and where the holding of a cash balance represents the holding out of use, directly or indirectly, of tangible productive capital resources. On the other hand, individuals incur costs, in keeping their cash balances down, that involve the use of real resources, as when making smaller but more frequent financial transactions, or adopting various devices to speed up the circulation of money, such as the use of telegraphic rather than mail transfers. This means that resources are used that might be diverted to more productive use if a larger volume of currency were supplied at negligible real cost in resources.

The net social loss arising from this diversion may be approximately represented by the area between the liquidity-preference curve, the money axis, and the two ordinates at the two alternative volumes of money. It may be that once the interest rate has been pushed to a point where the system is reasonably stable the liquidity-preference curve may be sufficiently inelastic so that changes in the rate of interest in this range would make relatively little difference in the social loss involved in the costly economizing of cash by individuals. At most, this loss is a relatively minor matter compared to the importance of preserving the stability of the economy as a whole.

A more important consideration tending to put an upper bound to the rates of inflation that will produce satisfactory results is the fact that there probably is a level of interest above which money tends to lose its acceptability as a medium of exchange. At very high interest rates, money would tend to be displaced, as a medium of exchange, by substitutes that are less costly in terms of loss of interest, such as foreign currencies not subject to the steady devaluation, securities, interest-bearing notes, or even commodities. The use of interest-bearing paper would be particularly likely for large transactions. The creation of money by commercial banks is after all nothing more than an exchange of promissory notes between depositor and banker, with the banker's undertaking to honor checks conveniently serving as money. It is conceivable that if the incentive were made strong enough by a sufficiently high interest rate, promissory notes of individuals and firms, securities, and even drafts on individuals might circulate as a medium of exchange for many purposes in spite of the credit risk and the inconvenience of computing the interest at each transfer. While the credit creation of commercial banks can be fairly readily controlled and regulated, the manifold varieties of "private coinage" that could arise under the incentive of a high rate of interest might be much more difficult to control. A general flight into such substitute currencies would of course mean that the problem of monetary stability would not be solved, but merely transposed to the new media, with the added difficulty that the volume of the new media would probably exhibit a pronounced perverse elasticity of supply.

As an offset, however, to the real net loss arising from these attempts to economize on the use of money, there is the net gain in resource allocation resulting from the reduction in taxes made possible by the absence of interest charges on that part of the national debt represented by the currency in circulation, plus whatever taxes are levied on demand deposits as a means of preventing banks from paying interest on them. If the marginal taxes that would be reduced on this account were completely neutral in their impact, then of course this offset would vanish, but since in practice all taxes have at the margin some unfavorable effects on resource allocation, this offset will exist. It is difficult to state a priori, however, whether this offset is likely to be large enough to cause any substantial modification of any conclusions regarding the most advantageous rate of inflation.

A Model with Exogenous Interest Rates

The above model is developed in terms of an exogenously determined money supply and with interest rates determined endogenously. In terms of actual institutions, this would imply something like a 100 per cent reserve banking system, the absence of any fixed rediscount rate or of any market peg on government bonds, and the use of open market operations as a control measure. It is possible to examine an alternative model in which the quantity of money is endogenously determined through the operations of banks in expanding credit, making use of rediscount facilities or selling or buying government bonds as their operations require, the rate of interest in this model being exogenously determined by the fixing of the rediscount rate and the pegging of government security prices. However, for such a model instability appears to occur for all reasonable values of the coefficients.

For such a model we may retain equation (21) defining the elasticity of expectations, but now instead of the interest rate being determined by this expected price change as in (19), price expectations together with the marginal productivity of capital in relation to the given rate of interest determine the rate at which the money supply expands. This can be represented by a new relation as follows:

$$M_t = \left[\frac{P_{(t+1)et}(1 + r_t)}{P_t(1 + i_t)} \right]^j M_{t-1} \tag{42}$$

This expresses the idea that the amount of credit demanded (and supplied) at time t will be greater or less than that for time $t - 1$ according as the expected increase in price from time t to time $t + 1$, compounded with the real productivity of capital, promises a money rate of profit on investment greater or less than the money rate of interest. The exponent j expresses the rapidity with which this expansion or contraction takes place, and can perhaps be called the volatility of the supply of credit. It should perhaps be noted that this volatility is by no means dependent upon there being borrowers ready to borrow directly from banks: banks can also expand their portfolio of private securities if expectations are such as to make this an attractive prospect. We can retain from the former model equations (20), (23), (24), (25), (26), and (27). If we put $Q_t = M_t/M_{t-1}$, these relationships yield the differential equation:

$$[E^2 - (2 - hg - g + 2jgh - 2jg)E \\ + (1 + gh - 3g)] \log Q_t = f(t) \quad (43)$$

where $f(t)$ is again a function of the exogenous variables. This equation is unstable for all values of h greater than 1, regardless of the values of the other variables provided only that g and j are both positive. In effect, any tendency of individuals to regard an unexpectedly large price rise as a sign of a steeper general trend of prices in the future is likely to produce instability.

Since a condition where h is greater than 1 seems more likely than not to be encountered, an attempt to exercise monetary control indirectly through the interest rate by means of the specification of market pegging levels and rediscount rates is likely to be somewhat more ticklish than the exercise of monetary control directly by policies aimed at a particular change in the volume of money. Even though the actual transactions in the two cases may be identical, the terms in which policy is couched may be a critical element. For example, it might be estimated that the sale in the open market of a given volume of bonds would raise the level of interest rates by a given amount. If the estimate is correct, then it may make little difference which way the policy is formulated. But if the estimate is in error, or if business fluctuations cause a deviation from the expected market conditions, so that the planned purchases would cause less than the desired increase in interest rates, then there is a great difference in the consequences of the two formulations of policy. With a quantity policy, purchases are stopped at the planned amount, regardless of what has happened to interest rates, at least until a revision of the policy is made; the economy may be relatively stable on the basis of such a datum. With a rate policy, such as the announcement of the maintenance of a fixed price on government bonds, purchases may be continued far beyond the volume originally contemplated, and in terms of the continuation of the specified policy the situation may well be quite unstable.

In effect, control through specifying the interest rate is somewhat like steering a car that is backing up. If the car is headed too far to the left, the front must be swung still further to the left in order to get the car headed back towards the center of the road. If it is desired to achieve a rising price trend and with it a high rate of interest, it will not do to raise the interest rate and expect the inflation to follow: on the contrary, it is necessary first to lower rates of interest so as to stimulate monetary expansion, and once expansion and inflation are under way the rates may be raised considerably above the original level without causing a contraction. On the other hand, any contraction that may have been initiated by raising interest rates will not be stopped merely by restoring the interest rates to the former level; indeed, once strong anticipations of a sharply downward price trend develop, there may be no monetary policy capable of reversing the trend.

Transition Problems

It is of course one thing to suggest that an economy in which an upward price trend has always existed and been anticipated will be more stable than one with a horizontal price trend, and another to propose that a transition be made from one to the other. The undesirable effects arising from the transition might well be such as to outweigh any possible ultimate benefits.

Ideally, perhaps, it should be possible to take the bull by the horns and make specific comprehensive legislative provision for the change in monetary policy, including a stipulation that all contracts calling for the payment of money that are outstanding on the effective date of the change shall be adjusted in specified ways to allow for the proposed change in the price trend. This might produce considerable confusion at the time of the change, but the confusion would be short-lived and equities would generally be preserved. There might be a constitutional conflict between the power to regulate the currency and prohibitions against the impairment of contracts; the gold clause precedent would seem to augur favorably. Another possibility would be to announce the change several years in advance; in this case the number of contracts that would not have been made with the benefit of advance notice of the change would be considerably reduced, although there might in some cases be inequities resulting from differences of opinion as to whether the announced change would actually come off.

A more likely development is that a transition might be made gradually over a period of years, so that in the main the injustices and dislocations caused would not be too severe, although individual cases of inequity might be substantial. Probably the dislocation and inequity could be kept to a level that would be fairly small compared to what has already occurred during wartime, particularly in countries less fortunate in this respect than the United States and Canada. Indeed, one may consider that some more or less unwitting progress in this direction has already taken place: while up to about 1935 or 1940 it was generally expected that the economic annals would continue, as in the past, to show periods of downward as well as upward price movements, it has become rather fashionable to talk about the general price level as being on a "ratchet" and that while it may rise rather substantially in some periods, it is not to be expected that there will be any further periods of substantial or protracted decline. The pressure for a full-employment policy, or for relief from high tax levels called for by expanded government services is expected to be such as to prevent the recurrence of a price decline such as that of the early 1930's, or even of the more moderate decline of the sort experienced in the later 1920's.

Of course, the nature of any transition will be strongly affected not only by the intended pattern of change, but by the confidence of the public in the firmness with which this intention is maintained and in the effectiveness of the measures available to carry it out. For a time, confidence in the carrying out of the proposed change may be self-justifying, as in the early days of the National Recovery Act. But such a psychological reinforcement is likely to be short-lived unless backed by adequate fiscal and monetary powers. On the other hand a general lack of confidence that the program will be carried through will make stronger measures necessary. In case such doubts are widespread, they may even threaten to cause such inequities and dislocations, if the program is carried through, as to make it necessary to abandon the program.

In any event, it is probable that the difficulties of carrying out such a deliberate change in the price trend are greater than those of maintaining a constant price level, though these difficulties would have the saving quality of being only temporary rather than permanent. In a period of serious depression, such as the early 1930's, the size of the fiscal operations that might have been needed to inaugurate such a policy might have been almost overwhelming as a result of the high liquidity-preferences. A price rise may take time to get under way, or may stall halfway up, particularly during a period when idle factors are being put to use; this would result in the disappointment of expectations based on the announced program. On the other hand, once the price rise is well under way and firmly established in general anticipations, the more rapid turnover of large cash accumulations as interest rates rise may require a careful but substantial contraction of the money supply lest the rate of inflation overshoot the mark. The remedy is one to be applied with great care!

Objections to High Interest Rates

At first sight it may seem that a policy that results in high money rates of interest would run counter to widely held objectives that are at present implemented at least in part by keeping interest rates low. Low interest rates are held to be needed (1) to keep down the interest charges on the national debt and thus avoid added tax burdens with their adverse effects on incentives and on the allocation of resources; (2) to keep the level of private interest charges and profits low, and so diminish the share of the national income going to property owners as against wage earners; and (3) to keep interest charges low so as to permit the financing of housing and other public works on a low-cost self-liquidating basis. Actually, however, it appears that all of these objectives could be better served in an economy with high interest rates and a corresponding inflationary trend, than in economies with level price trends.

First, it should be observed that as between an economy with a real marginal productivity of capital of 1 per cent, money interest at 10 per cent, and inflation at 9 per cent, and an economy with a level price trend and with marginal productivity of capital and money interest both at 1 per cent, the difference is purely nominal, assuming that the level price economy can be maintained stable. While in the inflationary economy investors will get a nominal return of 10 per cent on capital, this will be only a nominal return, and if they are to maintain their capital intact, they will

E*

have to reinvest 9 per cent, or have the real value of their capital impaired.

Public projects will have to pay a nominal 10 per cent on their borrowings, but of this 10 per cent, nine-tenths will in effect be amortization, and it would be generally proper to reduce any explicit amortization charge by this amount. Or, if 9 per cent exceeds the desired rate of amortization, it would even be quite proper under these new conditions, however unorthodox it might appear at present, to borrow further against the growing money value of the project to pay a part of the nominal interest. For example, of the 10 per cent nominal interest charge, 6 per cent could be reborrowed, and the remaining 4 per cent would represent 1 per cent interest plus 3 per cent amortization. Or bonds for such projects could call for relatively low coupons for the first few years with larger coupons in the later years to compensate: such coupons could be arranged to follow any real pattern of amortization desired.

Finally it should be noted that a nominal balancing of the budget in the inflationary economy would correspond in real terms to a very substantial surplus for a level price economy. Thus in the same way it would be perfectly appropriate, however odd it might appear, for a government to consider its real budget balanced even though it would have to borrow to pay nine-tenths of the nominal interest on the outstanding debt. If this were the attitude adopted, the higher nominal interest rate would have no untoward effect on tax revenue requirements, and moreover the additional loans would in fact be provided with a market by the need of investors to reinvest a large fraction of their interest payments if they should wish to maintain their real capital intact.

All of this is of course not to deny that the psychological impact of the upward price trend might be such as to cause substantial changes in the behavior of individuals, and if this is the case the real aspects of the economy would not in fact be reproduced exactly. In particular, the amount of what may be termed a "seigniorage gain" to the government, measured by the interest that does not have to be paid on the part of the public debt that is represented by money may be either higher or lower, reflecting a higher rate of interest applied to a smaller amount of money in circulation. But the rationales of the objections to high interest rates, while they may apply where a level price trend is assumed, do not carry over to the case where the increase in interest rates merely reflects the rate of inflation of the price trend.

Indeed, if the full possibilities of the two types of economy are examined, the shoe appears to be on the other foot. Actually it is unlikely that a level price economy can be maintained stable with an interest rate as low as 1 per cent. In practice, to maintain stability, or to restore full employment resulting from a downward divergence, it will be necessary to have deficit financing to absorb excess savings, and this is likely to have the effect of increasing the rate of interest to, say, 2 per cent, if indeed effective rates of interest ever got below 2 per cent. At this higher level of interest there would be less private capital formation, higher real profits, and higher interest costs to long-term public projects. Or another way of putting it would be to say that the liquidity-preference function may be such that no expansion in the money supply can lower the effective rate of interest much below, say, 2 per cent, and that the 1 per cent level is unattainable. It is then the inflationary economy that makes possible low real interest charges on the public debt, low-cost housing and the like, and a redistribution of income in favor of earned, as against property, incomes. Moreover, these effects are genuine and permanent, and do not in any way depend on the persistence of a "money illusion." Indeed, it is absolutely essential that the money illusion be eliminated if the inflationary economy is to operate in a rational and equitable manner.

Yet the inflationary economy does not require that real interest rates be low. It is perfectly possible, if desired, for the inflationary economy to retain a real interest rate of 2 per cent (or any other level) which would imply that with a 9 per cent rate of inflation the money rate of interest would be 11 per cent. The inflationary economy can establish any over-all real pattern that the level price economy can, and in addition has a further range of possibilities not attainable with a level price trend. At one extreme, either type of economy can operate with high real interest rates, a large government deficit (on a real basis) and consequent low level of private capital formation, with either consumption or public investment increased so as to create a full-employment situation. At the other extreme, an inflationary economy can operate with even a slightly negative real rate of interest. The real interest rate cannot be too negative, otherwise there would be an excessive amount of investment in the storage of nonperishable nonobsolescent commodities with low storage costs in relation to value (though even this might be economical under special conditions, as where scarcities are developing). With such a negative real rate of interest would go a relatively large government surplus and a large volume of private capital formation, financed in part by funds provided by the paying off of the government debt. In the long run this situation might even go so far as to involve the elimination of the interest-bearing government debt and the investment by the government of its surplus in the senior securities of private enterprise. Such a situation cannot be approached in a level price economy, for before this situation could be reached the monetary system would have been made unstable and the economy would have been broken down into either unemployment or unanticipated inflation.

An economy of steady, anticipated inflation is thus not only more stable, but can be made to develop in a much wider range of modes than can a level price economy. Nor is this range dependent upon freedom to choose among a number of different rates of inflation: this wider range of possible modes is obtained even if a particular rate of inflation is specified and is adhered to indefinitely, and as strictly as the effectiveness of the available controls permits.

It may be some time before any such controlled inflation is adopted in any country as a deliberate and explicit policy, as contrasted with inflationary policies adopted under duress and as a *pis aller*. This should not prevent our studying models of such economies as a means of getting a clearer insight into economic fundamentals and freeing ourselves from traditional shibboleths regarding the nature of economic stability. For the present, at least, it seems that wartime destruction and the demands of rearmament have pushed the productivity of capital up into the range where even with a level price trend an equilibrium money rate of interest is possible that gives some margin for the operation of monetary controls. But the long-term trend seems still to be one in which the accumulation of capital, combined with the shift towards capital-saving innovations, drives the real marginal productivity of capital down to a level where a reasonable degree of stability and the freedom to choose the form and amount of capital formation will be difficult to secure with a level price trend.

CHAPTER FIVE

Keynesian Economics and the Quantity Theory [1]

Don Patinkin

Introduction and Summary

KEYNESIAN ECONOMICS criticizes the quantity theory of money on two distinct grounds. First, it argues that the velocity of circulation is not a constant of economic behavior, and so questions the usefulness of the quantity theory as a device of applied economic analysis. Second, it insists that the theory is valid only under highly restrictive assumptions, and so questions even its theoretical usefulness.

In this paper we shall not, except indirectly, be concerned with the first of these criticisms. It should, however, be noted that implicit in this criticism is the assumption that the economic variables specified by the Keynesian analysis provide more dependable interrelationships than does the velocity of circulation. In other words, it is assumed that a breakdown of the flow of expenditure into the sum of consumption and investment is more useful an analytical device than its breakdown into the product of the stock of money and the velocity of circulation. This is clearly an issue that can be settled only by extensive empirical study.

This paper will deal only with the second of the criticisms listed above. We explicitly exclude from the discussion restrictions on the validity of the quantity theory which were fully recognized by the exponents of this theory themselves. Thus, for example, there is no need to discuss here the fact that under conditions of unemployment an increase in the amount of money need not bring about a proportionate increase in prices. [2] Instead it will be assumed throughout this paper that conditions of full employment always prevail. Our main task will be the examination of Keynes' criticism that even under this assumption the

---

[1] I am indebted to E. Fuerst, A. Gaaton, I. R. Kosloff, and N. Liviatan for their valuable criticisms of an earlier draft of this paper.
[2] Cf., e.g., Knut Wicksell, *Lectures on Political Economy: II: Money* (London, 1935), p. 195.

quantity theory is not valid unless other conditions also are met. Specifically, at one point Keynes attempts to prove that an additional necessary condition is that "the propensity to hoard [that part of the demand for money which depends on the rate of interest—M_2] will always be zero in equilibrium." [3] At yet another point he argues that an additional necessary condition is that effective demand increase in the same proportion as the quantity of money; and that the fulfillment of this condition, in turn, is dependent upon the forms of the liquidity-preference function, marginal efficiency of capital, and consumption function.[4]

The plan of this paper is as follows: In Part 2 a simplified model describing the functioning of the economy is set out. This model is essentially Keynesian in nature, in so far as its basic components are an aggregate demand function and a liquidity-preference function which depends upon the rate of interest. Nevertheless, it also has important non-Keynesian elements, which are duly noted. In Part 3 the effects of an increase in the amount of money in this model are examined. It is demonstrated that, regardless of the values of the marginal propensities to invest and consume, and regardless of the existence of a nonzero propensity to hoard, such an increase must ultimately bring about a proportionate increase in prices and leave the rate of interest unaffected.[5] Thus Keynes' arguments are seen to be incorrect.

The crucial assumptions from which these results follow are then examined in Part 4. It is seen that the basic assumption is that of absence of "money illusion." This concept is defined and discussed at length. It is also seen that absence of rigidities, as

[3] *General Theory*, pp. 208-209. Note the explicit statement on p. 209 that this assumption is necessary in addition to the assumption "that there is always full employment."

[4] *Ibid.*, pp. 292-306. Note in particular pp. 305-306, where Keynes explicitly states that even in the case of full employment ($e_o = 0$, in his notation), prices will not rise proportionately unless effective demand increases in the same proportion as the amount of money ($e_d = 1$, in his notation).

Item (c) on p. 298 is "the investment multiplier." Since, however, this is dependent upon the marginal propensity to consume, it has been replaced by "consumption function" in the text here.

[5] This was demonstrated previously for a general equilibrium model of n-2 goods, bonds, and money. The present paper gives the proof diagrammatically for a much simpler model, which is a special case of the general model already considered. See my "Indeterminacy of Absolute Prices in Classical Economic Theory," *Econometrica*, Vol. 17 (1949), Section 14; "Reconsideration of the General Equilibrium Theory of Money," *Review of Economic Studies*, Vol. 18 (1950-51), Sections 5-8; "Further Considerations of the General Equilibrium Theory of Money," *ibid.*, Vol. 19 (1952-53), pp. 186-95.

such, is not a necessary condition for the validity of the quantity theory. Furthermore, the quantity theory is seen to hold even in the extreme Keynesian case where the initial increase in the amount of money directly affects only the demand for bonds. Finally, an explanation is given of the fact that a change in the amount of money does not ultimately affect the rate of interest, even though a change in the rate of interest does affect the amount of money demanded.

The Model

Let us assume that the economy consists only of four markets: those for finished goods, labor services, bonds, and money,[6] respectively. In each of these markets we have a demand function, a supply function, and a statement of the equilibrium condition: namely, a statement that prices, wages, and the interest rate are such that the amount demanded in the market equals the amount supplied. By virtue of what has come to be called Walras' Law, we know that if equilibrium exists in any three of these markets, then it must also exist in the fourth. Hence, in examining the equilibrium of the system as a whole, it suffices to concentrate on the markets for finished goods, labor services, and money, respectively, and to exclude from our explicit consideration the market for bonds.[7]

Consider now the market for finished goods. For our present purposes it is not necessary to discuss separately the consumption, investment, and government demand components of this market. It is only the sum of these components—Keynes' aggregate demand function—which interests us. Following Keynes, assume that the real amount demanded of finished goods (E) varies directly with the level of real national income (Y), and inversely with the rate of interest (r).[8] Assume further that E

[6] For simplicity, assume that there are no banks, and that the only money in circulation is legal tender issued by the government.

[7] For a particularly lucid explanation of Walras' Law see J. R. Hicks, *Value and Capital* (Oxford, 1939), pp. 155–57. Actually, it would seem more natural to conduct the analysis in terms of the markets for finished goods, labor, and bonds, and to consider that for money as the residual one. This is, indeed, the procedure followed in a larger work on which I am now engaged. But since this approach deviates from the traditional one, and hence requires a more extended presentation than can be permitted here, it has not been considered advisable to follow it explicitly in the present article.

[8] Even if the amount demanded for consumption should decrease with a fall in the rate of interest (cf. *General Theory*, pp. 93–94), the amount demanded for investment is assumed to increase sufficiently to offset this.

also depends directly on the real value of cash balances held by the community ($\frac{M_0}{p}$, where M_0 is the amount of money in circulation, assumed constant, and p is an index of finished-goods prices). That is, a decrease in the price level, which increases these real cash balances, is assumed to cause an increase in the aggregate amount demanded, and conversely.[9] Thus we can represent the real aggregate demand function for finished goods by

$$(1) \qquad E = f\left(Y, r, \frac{M_0}{p}\right).$$

It should be emphasized that this formulation hides many simplifying assumptions. First of all, it presumes that only the total of real income or real balances matters, and not the respective distribution among the members of the economy. This is equivalent to the assumption that the marginal propensity to spend out of real income—or out of real balances—is constant and the same for every member of the community. Secondly, it assumes that debtors are discouraged by their indebtedness to exactly the same extent as creditors are encouraged by the amounts due them; otherwise the distribution of bonds in the economy would also have to appear in the expenditure function. These are all complicating factors which will be ignored here. It should, however, be noted that account can be taken of these factors without affecting our basic conclusions.[10]

By assumption, there exists a state of full employment, and this is presumed to remain unchanged during the discussion. Hence the supply function of finished goods can be written quite simply as

$$(2) \qquad Y = Y_0,$$

[9] Actually, the expenditure function is also assumed to depend on the real value of physical assets held by the community; but since this is assumed to remain constant throughout the discussion, it has not been explicitly introduced into the following function. For the rationale of the assumption in the text see A. C. Pigou, "The Classical Stationary State," *Economic Journal*, vol. 53 (1943), pp. 343-51.

This assumption is not made by Keynes. For him a change in the amount of money affects aggregate demand only through its effect on the interest rate via the liquidity-preference function (*General Theory*, p. 298). As will be shown in Part 4 below, the dropping of this assumption does not affect the basic properties of our model.

[10] See the second reference cited in note 5 above.

where Y_0 is the level of real national product (equal, by definition, to the level of real national income) corresponding to full employment. The statement of equilibrium in this market is, then, that the amount demanded equals the amount supplied; that is,

(3) $E = Y.$

Graphically, we obtain the following familiar representation of these conditions:

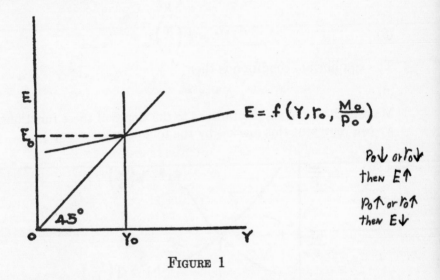

FIGURE 1

The aggregate demand—or expenditure—function in this diagram is drawn for a given price level, p_0, and a given rate of interest, r_0. For other levels of these two variables, the expenditure function shifts either upwards or downwards. For example, if the price level were lower than p_0 (thus increasing the real value of cash balances), or the rate of interest lower than r_0, then, by our previous assumptions, the expenditure function would lie above the one depicted in Figure 1; and conversely, if the price level or rate of interest were higher. In the diagram it is assumed that for the price level p_0 and the rate of interest r_0, aggregate demand is such as to generate an equilibrium position at full employment; that is, at $p = p_0$ and $r = r_0$, the aggregate demand function intersects the 45° line through the origin [representing equation (3)] at a level of real national income corresponding to full employment—the economy is willing to purchase the entire output corresponding to full employment.

Let us now consider the market for labor services. Assume that both the amount demanded (N^d) and the amount supplied [11] (N^s) of labor depend on the real wage rate, $\frac{w}{p}$ (where w is an index of money wages). That is,

$$(4) \qquad N^d = g\left(\frac{w}{p}\right) \qquad \text{and}$$

$$(5) \qquad N^s = h\left(\frac{w}{p}\right).$$

The equilibrium condition is then

$$(6) \qquad N^d = N^s.$$

Making the usual assumptions as to the slopes of these functions, we can represent this market by the following diagram:

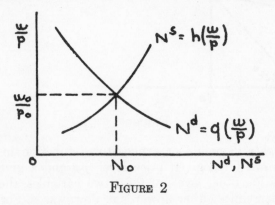

FIGURE 2

From the diagram we see that the market is in equilibrium when the real wage rate $\frac{w_0}{p_0}$ prevails. To this equilibrium real wage rate corresponds the equilibrium level of employment, N_0. By definition, this is the full-employment level, since anyone who wishes to work at the prevailing real wage is employed. The full-employment level of real national income, Y_0, which appears in the market for finished goods, clearly is directly related to the full-

[11] This assumption is not made by Keynes, who assumes that "labour stipulates (within limits) for a money-wage rather than a real wage" (*General Theory*, p. 9).

employment level of employment, N_0. Specifically, given the latter, the former is uniquely determined by the production function, which tells us the national output that will be forthcoming when full employment prevails. For simplicity, this production function has not been explicitly introduced into the preceding analysis.

Finally let us consider the market for money. Assume that the individual is concerned solely with the real value of the cash balances he holds. Denote this demand for real balances by $\dfrac{M^d}{p}$, and assume, with Keynes,[12] that this is divided into a transactions and precautionary demand, varying directly with the level of national income Y; and a speculative demand, varying inversely with the rate of interest. Thus

$$(7) \qquad \frac{M^d}{p} = L_1(Y) + L_2(r).$$

For our purposes, it will not usually be necessary to distinguish between these two components, so we can write, more generally,

$$(7a) \qquad \frac{M^d}{p} = L(Y,r).$$

Alternatively, we can describe the demand for nominal cash balances by writing

$$(7b) \qquad M^d = pL_1(Y) + pL_2(r) = pL(Y,r),$$

and this is the form [13] we will find most useful for our purposes.[14]

[12] On the following see the *General Theory*, chap. 15.

[13] This probably differs from the demand function Keynes gives on p. 199 of the *General Theory*. In terms of our notation here this formula is

$$M^d = L_1(pY) + L_2(r).$$

In contrast with equation (7b) of the text, the preceding equation is not free of "money illusion". The meaning and significance of this fact are discussed below.

This interpretation of Keynes' formula is based on the assumption that his M represents nominal balances and his Y, money income. This is consistent with his use of these symbols later on p. 209. However, it is not consistent with Keynes' earlier statement in Chapter 6 that he will express all magnitudes in wage units. This whole question requires further study.

[14] The preceding exposition has been oversimplified to the point of inaccuracy. From equation (7b) it would appear that the demand for money in a system free of "money illusion" is proportionate to the price level. But this clearly cannot be

By assumption, the nominal amount of money in circulation is fixed at the constant level M_0. Hence the supply function is simply

$$(8) \qquad\qquad M^s = M_0,$$

and the equilibrium condition is

$$(9) \qquad\qquad M^d = M^s.$$

The situation in this market is represented diagrammatically in Figure 3.

This diagram incorporates Keynes' assumption that the amount

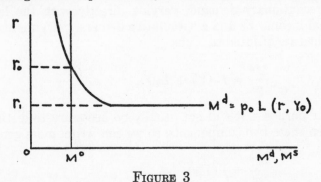

FIGURE 3

true. For from equation (1) we see that a change in the price level affects the demand for goods, hence Y, and hence the demand for money as well.

Actually, the demand for money, like the demand for goods, also depends on the real value of the initial assets held by the economy (see note 9 above), and on the real value of cash balances in particular. The same holds true for the labor market functions. Thus in its correct form equation (7b) should read

$$M^d = pL_1\left(Y, \frac{M_0}{p}\right) + pL_2\left(r, \frac{M_0}{p}\right) \equiv pL\left(Y, r, \frac{M_0}{p}\right).$$

This form makes it clear that the demand for money is *not* of uniform unitary elasticity.

For the limited purposes of the present article this complication can be ignored. It is, however, discussed in section 4 of the last reference listed in note 5 above, and in my "Dichotomies of the Pricing Process in Economic Theory", *Economica*, vol. 21, 1954. It will also be explained fully in the work referred to in note 7 above.

The second inaccuracy occurs in the graphical description of the demand function for money. It can be shown that this curve does not have the property usually ascribed to it of becoming horizontal at a minimum rate of interest. But since this requires a lengthy explanation, and since the resulting modification does not affect any of the basic conclusions of Keynesian monetary theory, a full discussion of the matter has also been deferred to the larger work already referred to. Hence the demand curve for money in Figure 3 has been drawn in the usual—though incorrect—manner.

demanded of money increases as the rate of interest falls, and that at a certain minimum rate the demand becomes infinitely elastic. In the particular case presented in the diagram the equilibrium rate of interest is r_0.

The demand curve in Figure 3 is drawn for given levels of real national income and prices. Were the level of income below Y_0, the transactions demand at every rate of interest would be less, and the whole curve would shift to the left. Since we are assuming that the economy always remains at the full-employment level Y_0, this type of shift does not interest us. Of much greater importance, for our purposes, is the effect of a change in the price level. Specifically, we see from equation (7b) that if the price level increases, the whole demand curve in Figure 3 shifts over to the right; conversely for a price decline.

So far we have considered each market separately. To complete this stage of the analysis we must now examine the model from the viewpoint of general equilibrium analysis. The preceding discussion has described the hypothetical economy by a system of nine equations in nine variables $(E, Y, p, N^d, N^s, w, M^d, M^s, r)$. By substituting (1) and (2) into (3); (4) and (5) into (6); and (7a) and (8) into (9) these can be readily reduced to the following system of three equations in the three variables p, w, and r:

$$(10) \qquad f\left(Y_0, r, \frac{M_0}{p}\right) = Y_0,$$

$$(11) \qquad g\left(\frac{w}{p}\right) = h\left(\frac{w}{p}\right),$$

$$(12) \qquad pL(Y_0, r) = M_0.$$

These are the conditions for equilibrium in the markets for finished goods, labor services, and money, respectively.

Assume that there exist a certain price level, wage rate, and interest rate at which this system is in a position of static equilibrium. That is, assume that there exist a price level, p_0, a wage rate, w_0, and an interest rate, r_0, whose joint existence simultaneously satisfies the equilibrium conditions for all three markets. In other words, the same set of values—p_0, w_0, and r_0—simultaneously (a) causes the aggregate demand function in Figure 1 to intersect the 45° line at the full-employment level, Y_0—indicating that aggregate amount demanded is equal to the full-employment output; (b) equilibrates the amounts demanded and supplied of labor, in Figure 2; and (c) equilibrates the amounts demanded and supplied of money, in Figure 3.

Under certain, simple dynamic assumptions, the equilibrium position just described must be a stable one. Specifically, assume that an excess demand for finished goods drives up the absolute price level; that an excess demand for money drives up the rate of interest (*i.e.*, individuals increase their sales of bonds in order to satisfy their needs for cash); and that the labor market is always in equilibrium (*i.e.*, there is very little lag between money wages and prices). Assume also that there are no destabilizing expectations. Then the assumptions previously made as to the slopes of the various demand and supply functions insure the stability of the system. This is proved below in the mathematical appendix.[15] Some further discussion of the dynamic process involved is provided in the next part of this paper.

The Effects of an Increase in the Quantity of Money

Assume that the equilibrium position just described prevails during a certain initial time period. Let this position now be disturbed by the injection of an additional quantity of money into circulation. Let us now investigate the effects of this disturbance.

The following discussion is divided into two parts: comparative statics and dynamics. First, the existence of a new equilibrium position is established, and its properties are examined. Second, use is made of the discussion at the end of the preceding section to state that the system is stable and does indeed converge to this new equilibrium position. (This clearly requires the additional assumption that the system has only one solution.) A description of some simple cases is then provided in order to illustrate the nature of the dynamic forces at work.[16]

[15] The nonmathematical reader can establish this convergence for himself by adapting to the present analysis the neat diagrammatic device presented by Lloyd A. Metzler in his "Wealth, Saving, and the Rate of Interest," *Journal of Political Economy,* vol. 59 (1951), p. 104, Figure 3.

[16] Neither the comparative statics nor the dynamic analysis to be presented depends upon the demand for money having the form specified by equation (7b) above. In particular, the reader can readily establish for himself that the comparative statics argument holds just as well for the form specified in note 14 above. The dynamic argument also holds, provided that an increase in the price level increases the amount of money demanded. See also the mathematical appendix.

Thus the reader should keep in mind, while reading this part of the paper, that though the argument is, for simplicity's sake, presented in terms of equation (7b) above, it is actually independent of it.

Assume, in particular, that the amount of money in circulation increases from M_0 to $(1 + t)M_0$, where t is a positive constant. It can easily be shown that a new equilibrium position exists in which prices and wages have risen in the same proportion as the amount of money, and the rate of interest has remained unchanged. For consider equations (10)-(12) above, and assume that when the amount of money in circulation is M_0, these equations are satisfied by the price level, p_0, wage rate, w_0, and rate of interest, r_0. By inspection it is then readily seen that where the amount of money is $(1 + t)M_0$, these equations are satisfied at the price level, $(1 + t)p_0$, wage rate, $(1 + t)w_0$, and interest rate, r_0.[17]

Graphically, the argument can be presented in the following simple way. If prices rise in the same proportion as the amount of money, then the real value of cash balances is exactly the same as it was in the initial period. At the same time the rate of interest has remained unchanged. Hence, the new aggregate demand curve must be identical with the one which existed in the initial period; it must coincide with the one represented in Figure 1. Hence, since the market for finished goods was initially in equilibrium, it must also be in equilibrium now.

The argument for the labor market is similar. If wages and prices rise in the same proportion, then the real wage rate remains the same as it was initially. From Figure 2 we see that at this initial real wage the labor market was in equilibrium. Hence it must also be in equilibrium now.

The situation in the money market is only slightly more complicated. True, the amount of money supplied has increased from M_0 to $(1 + t)M_0$; and *if* the demand schedule for money remains in its original position, equilibrium cannot be achieved at the initial rate of interest, r_0 (see Figure 4). But, by our previous assumptions, the demand schedule for money cannot have remained in its original position. For the nominal amount of money demanded depends upon the price level; and if this increases, so must the demand for money. Specifically, if when the price level was p_0 and the rate of interest r_0, people wished to hold M_0 dollars; then, at the same rate of interest, but at the price level $(1 + t)p_0$, people must wish to hold the larger amount

[17] Note that it is necessary only to assume that the system has a solution for $M = M_0$. This suffices to establish the existence of a solution for $M = (1 + t)M_0$. No additional assumption on this score is required.

of money, $(1 + t)M_0$. That is, by our previous assumptions, the demand curve for money corresponding to the price level $(1 + t)p_0$, must have shifted over to the right in such wise as to intersect the new supply curve—$M^s = (1 + t)M_0$—at precisely the same rate of interest as before (see Figure 4). Hence, when the amount of money in circulation is $(1 + t)M_0$, the money market, too, is in equilibrium at the price level $(1 + t)p_0$ and the rate of interest r_0.[18]

So much for comparative statics. Let us now examine the dynamic process by which the new equilibrium position is reached.

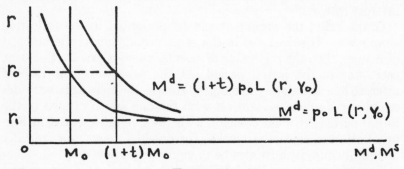

FIGURE 4

The following discussion does not attempt to prove this convergence rigorously; for such a demonstration the reader is referred to the mathematical appendix.[19] Instead, as was indicated above, the main purpose of what follows is to describe some simple cases in order to illustrate the way in which the dynamic forces work themselves out.

For convenience, call the initial period of equilibrium (during which the amount of money M_0 is in circulation) Period I. Assume that in Period II the government suddenly increases its expenditure on public works, and finances this increase by printing and paying out tM_0 new dollars—where t is a positive constant. In Period III, and in subsequent time periods, the govern-

<hr />

[18] The ease with which these conclusions are obtained makes it unnecessary to adopt the more traditional—and more complicated—technic of differentiation. However, by differentiating system (10)-(12) with respect to M, the interested reader can readily see that $\frac{dp}{dM}\frac{M}{p} = 1$, $\frac{dw}{dM}\frac{M}{w} = 1$, and $\frac{dr}{dM} = 0$—which agrees, as it must, with the analysis of the text.

[19] See also note 15, above.

ment reverts to its previous level of expenditures and no further net injections of money into the economic system take place. In this way the amount of money in circulation increases from M_0 to $(1 + t)M_0$.

Concentrate first on the market for finished goods. The curve $E(I)$ in Figure 5 represents the aggregate demand curve during Period I, and is identical with the corresponding curve which appears in Figure 1 above. Assume that in Period II there has not yet been time for prices, wages, or interest to change; nor has there been time for the increased value of cash holdings in

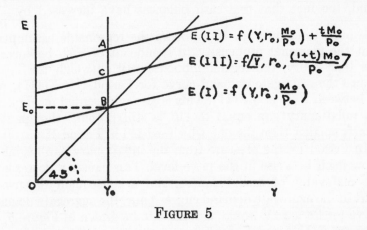

FIGURE 5

the hands of the public to exert its influence on the demand for finished goods. The aggregate demand function during this period thus lies above $E(I)$ by the amount of additional government purchases measured in real terms; *i.e.*, by $\dfrac{tM_0}{p_0}$. This is represented by the curve $E(II)$ in Figure 5. Despite the increase in aggregate demand, the level of real income cannot, by definition, increase above the full-employment level Y_0. Thus the economy in Period II will continue to produce the output Y_0; but, in distinction to period I, the aggregate amount demanded is now greater than Y_0. That is, an inflationary gap has been created: at the prevailing price level and interest rate, there will not be a sufficiently large output to enable all buyers to effect their planned purchases. This inflationary gap is represented in Figure 5 by the distance AB. By assumption, the upward pressure of this inflationary gap on the price level does not become effective during Period II itself.

This last assumption is maintained also for Period III; but we now drop the assumption that the increased holdings of real balances do not affect the amount demanded. As a result, there are, then, two forces operating on the aggregate demand curve of this period, relative to that of the preceding one. On the one hand, government expenditures have returned to their level of Period I; and this causes the curve to drop by $\dfrac{tM_0}{p_0}$. On the other hand, the fact that real cash balances have increased by $\dfrac{tM_0}{p_0}$ will push the curve up. If we make the reasonable assumption that the marginal propensity to spend out of cash balances is less than unity, the former influence will outweigh the latter. Hence the aggregate demand curve for Period III, $E(\text{III})$, will lie between $E(\text{I})$ and $E(\text{II})$. This is also represented in Figure 5. An inflationary gap equal to CB is still present, though it is clearly smaller than the one which existed in Period II.

In Period IV the pressure from the inflationary gap begins to show itself in a rise in the price level. This causes a decrease in the real value of cash balances, and a consequent downward shift in the aggregate demand curve. Thus, the aggregate demand curve for Period IV would, if it were to be drawn in Figure 5, lie between $E(\text{III})$ and $E(\text{I})$.

The essential point to be noted now is that—on the assumption that the rate of interest remains at r_0—an inflationary gap must persist until the price level has risen to the level $(1 + t)p_0$. For until this level is reached, the real value of cash balances is higher than it was in Period I, and hence the corresponding aggregate demand curve must lie above $E(\text{I})$. Thus, as long as the price level does not rise in the same proportion as the amount of money, there will exist forces constantly pushing it upwards. At the same time, the rise in the price level itself is the primary means by which the inflationary pressures themselves are eliminated. For when the price level has risen to $(1 + t)p_0$, the real value of cash balances will be exactly the same as in the initial period, so that the aggregate demand function will coincide with that of the initial period, and the inflationary gap will disappear. Thus, on the assumptions that no destabilizing expectations are created, and that no further net injection of money into the system takes place, the inflation itself sets into operation equilibrating forces which tend to bring it to an end.

Let us now drop the assumption that the rate of interest remains constant at r_0, and consider what is likely to be happening meantime in the market for money. During Periods II and III, when the price level is still assumed to be at its original level, the demand curve is in the same position it was in Period I. Thus the curves for $M^d(\text{I})$, $M^d(\text{II})$, and $M^d(\text{III})$ in Figure 6 coincide, and this is the same curve depicted in Figure 3 above.

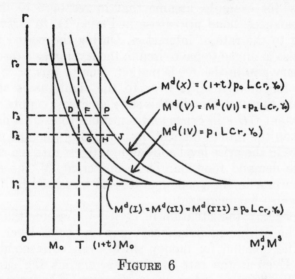

FIGURE 6

At the same time, the supply curve for money has shifted over to the right and is now represented by the vertical line at $(1 + t)M_0$. At the original rate of interest, r_0, and price level, p_0, individuals are now holding more money than they desire to in the light of their transactions and speculative needs. Consequently they use these excess money balances to increase both their demand for finished goods and their demand for bonds. This causes a corresponding increase in the general price level and in the price of bonds. The former effect has already been taken into account in our examination of the market for finished goods. The latter effect is, of course, identical with a fall in the interest rate.

The effect of this decrease in the rate of interest is to push the aggregate demand function upward. It may well be that in the early stages of the dynamic process this upward movement will more than offset the downward one generated by the rising price level, and thus increase the inflationary gap in the goods market. The essential point to note here, however, is that even in this case the price level effect must ultimately dominate. For as long as an inflationary gap exists, the price level must be rising; as the price level rises, the demand curve for money shifts to the right; and this must ultimately eliminate the excess supply of money and restore the rate of interest to its original level.

Let us, for example, assume that in response to the excess money balances, bond prices rise in Period IV to a level corresponding to the rate of interest r_2. During the period the price level is also assumed to have risen to the level p_1 as a result of the inflationary gap in the goods market. Due to this price rise, the demand for money shifts over to the right, as is shown by $M^d(IV)$ in Figure 6. Despite this shift, an excess supply of money to the extent GH still exists and continues to exert a downward pressure on the rate of interest. Assume, also, that the net result of the rise in the price level and fall in interest rate is a rise in the aggregate demand function. Thus, in Period IV, the extent of disequilibrium in the goods market—as measured by the inflationary gap—has increased.

Consider now the situation in Period V. Assume that as a result of the continued inflationary gap the price level increases to p_2. The demand for money shifts over, correspondingly, to $M^d(V)$. Even if the rate of interest remains the same as in Period IV, there is now an *excess demand* (HJ) for money balances; this is a fortiori so if the rate of interest has decreased below r_2. In order to bring their cash balances back to the desired level, individuals begin to sell bonds, and this reverses the downward trend in the interest rate. Thus ultimately the movement in the interest rate must reinforce the downward pressure on the aggregate demand function exerted by the rising price level.

As an extreme case let us assume that in Period VI the rate of interest rises to r_3, while the price level remains at p_2. The demand curve for money in Period VI, $M^d(VI)$, is thus identical with $M^d(V)$. From Figure 6 it would appear that the money market is now in equilibrium. However, it can easily be shown that such an equilibrium can be only a temporary one. The essential point is that p_2 must necessarily be less than $(1+t)p_0$. For from our previous discussion of comparative statics we know that at the rate of interest r_0 and the price level $(1 + t)p_0$ the amount of money demanded is $(1 + t)M_0$, in accordance with the schedule $M^d(X)$. From Figure 6 we see that at the rate of interest r_0 the amount demanded at the price level p_2 is OT, less than $(1 + t)M_0$. Hence p_2 must be less than $(1 + t)p_0$.

Since p_2 is less than $(1 + t)p_0$, it follows that the real value of cash balances held by the public— $\dfrac{(1 + t)M_0}{p_2}$ —is greater than in Period I. Similarly, by assumption, the interest rate is less than in Period I. Hence the aggregate demand curve for Period VI must be above $E(I)$; that is, an inflationary gap still exists in the goods market. Hence the price level will rise above p_2, thus shifting the money demand curve to the right of $M^d(VI)$. This will cause the rate of interest to rise once more. Clearly this process will continue as long as the rate of interest remains below r_0, and the price level below $(1 + t)p_0$.

Thus, under the stated assumptions, the typical time paths of the variables are as follows: the price level rises continuously toward its new equilibrium level, and the same is true for the wage rate. The interest rate first declines, and then rises once again to its original value. It is possible that the system may "overcompensate," and that the price level and interest rate may at some stage rise above their equilibrium values. But this will then generate equilibrating forces which will lower them once again.

Thus we see that an increase in the quantity of money causes a proportionate increase in the price level and in money wages, but leaves the rate of interest unaffected. The analytical framework is that of the modern income-expenditure approach; but the voice that emerges is that of the traditional quantity theory.[20]

[20] The preceding analysis agrees with the traditional quantity theory not only in its description of the new equilibrium position, but also in its derivation of the time-paths followed by the variables. In particular, quantity theorists emphasized that in the initial stages after an increase in the amount of money the rate of interest would decline; but that, when prices began to rise, the rate, too, would rise again to its original level. Cf., *e.g.;* D. Ricardo, *The High Price of Bullion,* as reprinted in *The Works and Correspondence of David Ricardo* (ed. Sraffa, Cambridge, 1951), vol. 3, p. 91; J. S. Mill, *Principles of Political Economy* (ed. Ashley), pp. 646-47; A. Marshall, *Money Credit and Commerce* (London, 1923), p. 257; Wicksell, *op. cit.,* pp. 197-98.

The Assumptions

Let us now examine the nature of the assumptions on which the preceding analysis is based. Before doing so in detail, we should note that there is nothing fundamentally surprising about the conclusions of this analysis. The relationship which the traditional theory found between the quantity of money and the level of prices was not based on any mystic quality attributed to money. Instead it was based on the concrete assumption that the individual's spending behavior is affected by the amount of money he holds. Hence there is no logical reason why a model which is based on a Keynesian "income and expenditure" approach should necessarily yield results differing from those of one based on a traditional "quantity of money" approach.[21]

Many assumptions are required for the validity of the argument in Parts 2 and 3 above. Thus we must assume that an initial equilibrium point exists; that the system is stable, and that, in particular, destabilizing expectations do not prevail; and, finally, that no other factors, except those which are specifically assumed to do so, change during the course of the discussion. All these assumptions are of a general nature and must be made for almost every type of economic analysis. What is of greater importance to us here are those other assumptions which are specific to the problem at hand. These will now be listed and discussed:

(a) A state of full employment continuously exists. The validity of the quantity theory is being discussed only under conditions of full employment. It must be recalled (see Part 1, above) that Keynes explicitly questioned its validity even under these conditions.

(b) The expenditure function remains stable. This assumption is really subsumed under the last of the general assumptions listed above. However, since it deserves some separate discussion, it has been listed again here.

Clearly, there is no empirical basis for believing this stability to hold for the investment component of this function; and in recent years doubt has even been cast as to its validity for the

[21] Cf., e.g., Knut Wicksell, *Interest and Prices* (tr. R. F. Kahn, London, 1936), pp. 39-41; Irving Fisher, *The Purchasing Power of Money* (New York, 1911), pp. 152-54.

For the definitive treatment of this point, see the comprehensive examination of the literature in A. W. Marget, *Theory of Prices*, vol. 1 (New York, 1938), chaps. 12-13, *et passim*.

consumption component. In the more traditional terminology of the quantity theory, this assumption implies that the income velocity of money is constant, for the expenditure function shows the rate at which a given *stock* of money—other factors constant —generates a corresponding *flow* of expenditure on finished goods. If the expenditure function is stable, the ratio of this flow to the stock of money—*i.e.*, the income velocity—must also be stable.

It should be emphasized that if the stability of the aggregate demand function is necessary for the validity of the quantity theory, it is even more necessary for the Keynesian one. Furthermore, as was pointed out in Part 1 above, it is on the alleged stability of this relationship that Keynesian economics must base its claim of superiority over the quantity theory.

(*c*) There are no "distribution effects." This assumption has already been referred to—though not in these terms—in Part 2 above. It is a very wide-reaching one; hence, a full discussion of its implications cannot be undertaken here. In brief, it consists of the following two propositions: (1) The level and composition of aggregate expenditures are not affected by the way in which the newly injected money is distributed among initial recipients. (2) The reactions of creditors and debtors to a changing price level offset each other.[22]

There can be no doubt that this assumption is unrealistic. On the other hand, there can be even less doubt that classical advocates of the quantity theory fully recognized this fact, and, indeed, showed how the simple quantity theory results would not obtain in the absence of this assumption. Thus, for example, the whole classical doctrine of "forced savings" was directed toward showing that, in the absence of the second proposition just listed, an increase in the amount of money was not neutral; that in certain circumstances it could increase the amount of real capital in the economy; and that in this way the rate of interest could also be permanently affected.[23]

[22] For further discussion see the second reference cited in note 5 above.

[23] For examples of classical and neoclassical economists who explicitly recognized the effect of "forced savings" on the interest rate, see J. S. Mill, *Essays on Some Unsettled Questions of Political Economy* (reprinted, London, 1948), p. 118; Wicksell, *op. cit.*, pp. 198-99; A. C. Pigou, *Industrial Fluctuation* (London, 1927), p. 253.

On the classical lineage of the doctrine of "forced savings," see F. A. Hayek, *Prices and Production* (London, 1931), pp. 8-11; "A Note on the Development of the Doctrine of 'Forced Savings,'" *Quarterly Journal of Economics*, Vol. 47 (1932-33), pp. 123-33; Jacob Viner, *Studies in the Theory of International Trade* (New

(d) There is no "money illusion." It must be emphasized that this term is not being used in its traditional sense. In this sense a "money illusion" exists if the quantities of goods which an individual demands are affected by any change in circumstances which does not affect relative prices, the rate of interest, and real income. It is, however, readily apparent that, in this sense, there cannot be a money economy without a "money illusion"! For consider a proportionate change in money prices and income. Clearly, this leaves relative prices and real incomes constant. Nevertheless, such a change affects the real values of cash balances held by the individual; hence it is completely rational for him to react by changing his purchases of goods and services.[24]

Instead we make use of the following definition: A "money illusion" is said to exist if a change which affects neither relative prices, the rate of interest, real income, nor the real value of assets, nevertheless causes a change in some real (as distinct from monetary) aspect of an individual's economic behavior. Inspection of the system used in the preceding analysis shows that it is free of money illusion in this sense. It also shows that if money illusion were present, then the results obtained above could no longer hold.

York, 1937), pp. 187-97. Clearly, any classical economist who held the doctrine of "forced savings" also held—by implication—that changes in the amount of money could affect the rate of interest. However, only few of them were explicit on this point.

Metzler (op. cit., p. 95, note 7) considers the above-cited passage from Pigou to be a "nonclassical reservation" which stands in contrast with Pigou's "usual" classical position. The present discussion shows that no such contrast exists, and that Pigou's analysis in this passage is entirely in the classical tradition. The present discussion also shows that there is no basis for Metzler's unqualified assertion that the distinguishing characteristic of classical monetary theory is the proposition that the "interest rate cannot [permanently] be influenced by changes in the amount of money" (ibid., p. 94). Correspondingly, there is no basis for Metzler's insistence that a model in which real balance appears in the expenditure function must be termed "nonclassical" just because such a model implies that open-market operations can permanently affect the rate of interest (ibid.).

On classical recognition of the first proposition listed in the preceding paragraph of the text, see the references cited in Marget, op. cit., pp. 307, 501-506.

[24] For examples of explicit and implicit uses of the traditional definition of "money illusion," cf. W. Leontief, "The Fundamental Assumption of Mr. Keynes' Monetary Theory of Unemployment," Quarterly Journal of Economics, vol. 51 (1936-37), pp. 192-97; J. Marschak, "Money Illusion and Demand Analysis," Review of Economic Statistics, vol. 25 (1943), pp. 40-41; P. A. Samuelson, Economics: An Introductory Analysis (Second Ed., New York, 1951), p. 346.

For further discussion of this question, see the references cited in note 5 above.

Assume, for example, that the expenditure function is influenced by the nominal, and not real, money holdings of the community, and that all other functions are the same as above. Then it is clear that when the amount of money in circulation increases, a new equilibrium position cannot be reached at the same rate of interest and a proportionately higher level of prices. For in the latter situation the expenditure function would still be above its original position; this is, of course, the indication that money illusion is present. Thus an inflationary gap would still exist, so that prices must continue to rise. As prices rise, the demand for money shifts to the right and the rate of interest rises too. In this case the whole brunt of eliminating the inflationary gap is on the interest rate; and this must rise above its former value to the extent necessary to bring the expenditure function down to its original level. Thus the increase in the amount of money causes a proportionately greater increase in prices and wages, and an *increase* in the rate of interest! [25]

Or assume that money illusion exists in the market for money itself.[26] Specifically, assume that the demand for money has the form Keynes himself attributes to it, so that the equilibrium condition in this market is

$$(13) \qquad L_1(pY_0) + L_2(r) = M_0,$$

where $M_1 = L_1(pY_0)$ is the transactions and precautionary demand for money, and $M_2 = L_2(r)$ is the speculative demand.[27] In real terms this equilibrium condition can be written as

$$(14) \qquad \frac{L_1(pY_0)}{p} + \frac{L_2(r)}{p} = \frac{M_0}{p},$$

where the first term on the left-hand side is the demand for real transaction balances, and the second term, the demand for real speculative balances.

[25] Note that the argument of footnote 17 above no longer holds, so that there is no certainty that a new equilibrium position even exists. This same observation holds true for the next case discussed in the text.

[26] An economically meaningful discussion of money illusion in the supply function of labor cannot be given within the framework of the preceding analysis. For a result of money illusion in this market is that the real wage rate in the new equilibrium position is less than in the old one. Hence the level of employment must be higher. This contradicts the simplifying assumption of the preceding model that the level of output is fixed at Y_0.

[27] Cf. above, note 13.

F

Assume that the amount of money and the price level increase in the same proportion. From (14) we see that the real value of cash balances that people desire to hold for the transactions motive may or may not change. If $L_1(pY_0)$ is of the form $pL_1(Y_0)$, then it does not. That is, if the transactions demand increases in the same proportion as the quantity of money and the price level, then it is free of money illusion. Be that as it may, it is clear from (14) that the real amount of money people desire to hold for speculative purposes must change. Thus the basic assumption of (14) is that there exists money illusion in the speculative demand for money. If we accept the Keynesian position that there is an obverse relationship between this demand and that for bonds, we can just as well say that the basic assumption of (14) is that there exists money illusion in the demand for bonds.[28]

Before examining the implications of this assumption it might be useful to clarify somewhat further the meaning of money illusion in the speculative demand for money. As has been pointed out above, such a money illusion does not exist if the demand for money is represented by equation (7). By comparing this equation with (14) we see that the fundamental difference is that in the former the demand for *real* speculative balances is independent of the price level, whereas in the latter it varies inversely with this level.

To bring out the significance of this distinction, assume that in a certain economy the old currency is abolished and replaced by a new one. For example, assume that all dollars are suddenly recalled, and replaced by pesos, at the rate of two pesos for every dollar turned in. Correspondingly, whatever previously cost one dollar, now costs two pesos, and every contractual obligation in dollars is replaced by a corresponding one in twice as many pesos. Only the rate of interest is permitted to remain unchanged. Clearly, in such a case there would be no reason for the real quantities of goods demanded and supplied to change. Neither would there be any reason for anyone to change his mind about the net amount of real indebtedness which he considers desirable. It is also clear that the real amount of money demanded for transactions purposes would not change; hence, it is equally clear that the real amount demanded for speculative purposes will not change. That is, the nominal amount demanded will increase in

[28] In connection with this and the following paragraphs it is advisable to refer again to note 14 above.

the same proportion as the quantity of money and the price level. This is the situation described by equation (7). On the other hand, equation (14) states that the *real* balances which individuals desire to hold for speculative purposes are smaller when the unit of currency is called the peso than when it is called the dollar. This is the essence of being involved in a money illusion.

Alternatively, we can look at the matter in this way: whatever reasons an individual has for holding bonds, they must be connected with the real purchasing power of either the interest receivable on them or the proceeds obtainable by selling them. Correspondingly, the margin on which the individual compares the relative advantages of holding bonds and holding cash must be a margin concerned with real quantities. Just as for the transactions motive he considers the advantages of holding "command over a fixed amount of real goods" in the form of cash, so for the speculative motive he considers the advantages of holding "command over a fixed amount of 'real' bonds." Hence, if the amount of money and the price level of goods increase, while the price of bonds remains unchanged, the real amounts of cash he wishes to hold for the transactions and speculative motives, respectively, must remain unchanged. Correspondingly, the real value of bonds he desires to hold must also remain unchanged. In such a case the individual is free of money illusion both in the demand for money and in the demand for bonds.

Consider now the effects of an increase in the amount of money. This creates an inflationary gap in the market for finished goods, driving up prices there. Assume prices to rise in the same proportion as the amount of money. From (13) we see that the amount of money demanded for transactions purposes increases. If there is no money illusion connected with this demand, it will increase in the same proportion as the supply of money. Even on this assumption, the *total* demand for money does not increase in the same proportion; for the speculative demand has not changed at all. Part of the resulting excess supply of money will be diverted to the bond market, driving down the rate of interest there until the increased speculative demand for money resulting from the lower rate of interest, and the increased transactions demand resulting from the higher price level suffice to absorb all of the increased supply of money. In this way a new equilibrium position is reached with prices having increased more than in proportion to the increase in the amount of money, and the interest rate having fallen below its initial position.[29]

The essential point to be noted in the preceding argument is its complete dependence on the crucial assumption of money illusion. If the speculative demand were free of this illusion— *i.e.*, if the amount of money demanded for speculative purposes were proportionate to the amount of money and the price level— then it would no longer be true that the only way this demand could absorb part of the increase in the amount of money would be through a fall in the rate of interest. For, even at the same rate of interest, the rise in prices and amount of money would cause the amount of speculative demand to increase. Hence the rate of interest need not change.

This completes our description of the four specific assumptions which must be made in order to insure the validity of the quantity theory. It is equally instructive to discuss some assumptions which need *not* be made for this purpose:

(*1*) Aside from the absence of money illusion, there is no need to place any further restriction on the form of the aggregate demand function, or any other function.

Our main interest at this point is in the aggregate demand function. In the preceding analysis this has been assumed to have a rather general form. In particular, there was no need to assume that an increase in the amount of money causes a proportionate increase in the aggregate amount demanded.

At the same time it should be noted that aggregate monetary expenditures in the new equilibrium period (what Keynes called "the effective demand" [30]) have increased over those of the initial period in the same proportion as has the amount of money. For by denoting the real aggregate expenditure in the initial equilibrium position by E_0 (see Figure 1 above), aggregate money expenditures in this period can be represented by $p_0 E_0$. Now assume that the amount of money in circulation increases from M_0 to $(1 + t)M_0$. The preceding analysis has shown that aggregate money expenditures in the new equilibrium position increase proportionately to $(1 + t)p_0 E_0$.

Superficially, there seems to be a paradox here. But the follow-

[29] The analysis just presented is adapted from *General Theory*, p. 200. It must, however, be emphasized that Keynes' discussion on this page is based on assumptions which are completely different from those posited here. In particular, Keynes is considering a situation of unemployment and, possibly, price rigidity.

[30] *General Theory*, p. 25.

ing simple explanation immediately resolves it. In brief, the two preceding statements actually correspond to two completely different conceptual experiments. In the first we take a given group of consumers with given real incomes and nominal money balances, and confront them with a given rate of interest and price level. For this given situation we ask them how much (in real terms) they would like to buy. We then increase the nominal amount of their money balances, *holding all other variables constant*, and ask them again the same question. In general, we should expect them to answer that they would like to increase their real purchases. If it should turn out that they increase their desired real purchases in the same proportion in which their nominal balances have grown, then we say that, at the point in question, the aggregate demand function has unitary elasticity with respect to nominal money balances.

Consider now the second experiment. Here we are concerned not with a group of consumers, but with the economy as a whole. Into an economy at equilibrium we introduce a disturbance in the form of a once-and-for-all increase in the quantity of money. We let this disturbance work itself out in all its various ramifications, and then examine the economy in its new equilibrium position. The analysis of Part 3 above has shown that in this new equilibrium position consumers are faced with prices that have risen in the same proportion as the amount of money in their possession, while the rate of interest has remained unchanged. Under these circumstances, if they are free of money illusion, consumers continue to buy the same quantities which they originally bought. But the prices they pay are higher. Hence, their money expenditures are proportionately higher than those of the first period.

In other words, the consumers in these two experiments are not confronted with the same changes. The variables held constant in the first case are not held constant in the second. Hence the results of the first experiment imply nothing about the possible results of the second; and conversely.

Thus, in a certain sense, Keynes was right in insisting that the validity of the quantity theory was connected with the condition that effective demand increase in the same proportion as the amount of money.[31] But what he failed to realize is that this is not an additional *assumption*, but a necessary *consequence* of

[31] Cf. the references in Part 1 above.

the three rather general assumptions listed above. In other words, this condition is not at all unlikely, and is in no way dependent upon the values of the elasticities yielded by the first type of experiment just described.[32]

(2) It is not necessary to assume that the aggregate demand function depends on the real value of money balances.

The reader can readily establish for himself that the preceding results follow even in the case where the aggregate demand function depends only on the level of real income and the rate of interest. The fundamental point is that even in this case there is no money illusion. Hence all of our preceding analysis is valid.

In particular, consider system (10)-(12) above, modified so that the argument $\frac{M_0}{p}$ does not appear in the left-hand side of equation (10). Assume that when $M = M_0$, this modified system is in equilibrium at $p = p_0$, $w = w_0$, and $r = r_0$. Then it is readily seen that when $M = (1 + t)M_0$, the system must be in equilibrium at $p = (1 + t)p_0$, $w = (1 + t)w_0$, and $r = r_0$.

Nor does this modification affect the stability of the system. This is shown in the mathematical appendix. Clearly, however, the dynamic forces at work differ from those described above. In particular, the effect of an increase in the amount of money does not act directly through aggregate demand, but indirectly, through the liquidity-preference function. The increased holdings of money increase the demand for bonds, and thus cause the rate of interest temporarily to decline. This shifts the expenditure function upward, creating an inflationary gap, and a consequent rise in the price level. As a result of the increased price level, the demand for money shifts to the right. This eventually puts an end to the decline in the interest rate, which now begins to rise. Clearly this process must continue until the rate of interest rises once again to its original level. For at any lower rate an inflationary gap will still exist, causing prices to rise more, and the demand for money to shift over still further to the right.

[32] The absence of money illusion can also be described in terms of elasticities: namely, an elasticity of zero of a real quantity demanded with respect to a proportionate change in the amount of money and prices, the rate of interest held constant.

Note that the absence of money illusion from the aggregate demand function alone is not sufficient to provide the results described in the second conceptual experiment above (namely, a proportionate increase in effective demand). As our preceding discussion has shown, these results will not follow unless *all* markets are free of money illusion.

Thus the validity of the quantity theory holds even in the extreme Keynesian case in which an increase in money balances is directed—in the first instance—only toward the market for bonds. All that is necessary is that this market be free of money illusion. In such a case borrowers and lenders will both increase their offers in the same proportion as the increase in the amount of money and the price level, so that the rate of interest is not ultimately affected.

(*3*) It is not necessary to assume the absence of rigidities *as such.*

The italicized phrase is here essential. Consider, for example, the labor market, and assume that there are rigidities on the supply side. There are two possibilities: The rigidity may be one of the real wage rate, or it may be one of the money wage rate. In the first case unions are assumed to follow the policy of tying their money wage demands directly to the price level. In this case the supply function becomes

$$(15) \qquad \frac{w}{p} = \text{constant.}$$

If, however, unions insist on a definite and rigid money wage regardless of the price level, then the supply function becomes

$$(16) \qquad w = \text{constant.}$$

Clearly, in the first case, none of the conclusions in the preceding analysis will change; for equation (15) is free of money illusion. It is equally clear that in the event equation (16) holds, money illusion is introduced into the system, and the conclusions must change accordingly. The important fact, however, is that the failure of the quantity theory to hold in this case is due to the presence of money illusion, and not to rigidities as such.

(*4*) It is not necessary to assume that the demand for money is independent of the rate of interest.

(*5*) It is not necessary to assume that "the propensity to hoard will always be zero in equilibrium." [33]

The dispensability of both of these assumptions follows from the same fact: the preceding analysis is based on a perfectly general liquidity-preference function. It is a function that has a speculative component (propensity to hoard) dependent on the

---

[33] *General Theory*, pp. 208-209. Cf. above, Part 1.

rate of interest—$L_2(r)$. At no point in the argument was it necessary to assume that this component is zero in equilibrium.

Here, too, there superficially appears to be a paradox. For even though the amount of money demanded is dependent on the rate of interest, the analysis shows that the rate of interest is not dependent on the amount of money. Once again, this paradox is easily resolved by a realization that these two statements correspond to two different conceptual experiments in which different variables are held in *ceteris paribus*.

Consider again a given group of individuals with given real incomes and nominal money balances, and faced with a given interest rate and price level. Assume that these nominal money balances are increased, while real incomes and the price level are kept constant. We now ask these individuals: what change, if any, is required to take place in the rate of interest in order to make you willing to hold on to this increased amount of money? In general, we expect to receive the answer that only at a lower rate of interest will there be a readiness to hold on to these increased balances. This is what is meant by the statement that the demand for money is dependent upon the rate of interest.

Let us now conduct a second experiment. Just as with the second experiment described under heading (*1*) above, this one is made on the economy as a whole. It consists of introducing a disturbance in the form of a change in the amount of money, and comparing the rate of interest on which people will insist in order to hold on to the existing quantity of money in the new equilibrium position, as compared with the initial one. By the analysis of Part 3 above we know that individuals in the new equilibrium position are confronted with prices that have risen in the same percentage as the quantity of money. Hence, if they are free of money illusion, they will be willing to hold on to the increased quantity of money at the same rate which originally prevailed. Thus an increase in the amount of money does not affect the equilibrium rate of interest. Furthermore, this result obtains no matter what the results which emerge from the first type of experiment.

Appendix

The dynamic system of the text is represented by the following system of differential equations:

(a)
$$\frac{dr}{dt} = K_1\left[L(r,Y_0) - \frac{M_0}{p}\right]$$

(b)
$$\frac{dp}{dt} = K_2\left[f\left(Y_0,r,\frac{M_0}{p}\right) - Y_0\right]$$

(c)
$$0 = g\left(\frac{w}{p}\right) - h\left(\frac{w}{p}\right)$$

A linear approximation to this system—in the neighborhood of the equilibrium point r_0, p_0, w_0—is given by the following:

(d)
$$\frac{dr}{dt} = K_1L_1(r - r_0) + \frac{K_1M_0}{p^2}(p - p_0)$$

(e)
$$\frac{dp}{dt} = K_2f_2(r - r_0) - \frac{K_2M_0}{p^2}f_3(p - p_0)$$

(f)
$$0 = -\frac{(g' - h')w}{p^2}(p - p_0) + \frac{(g' - h')}{p}(w - w_0)$$

where L_1 represents the partial derivative of $L(\ )$ with respect to its first argument, etc. By assumption, $L_1 < 0, f_2 < 0, f_3 > 0, g' < 0$, and $h' > 0$. The condition that this system be stable is that the real parts of the roots of the following determinantal

(g)
$$-\begin{vmatrix} K_1L_1 - \lambda & \dfrac{K_1M_0}{p^2} & 0 \\[2mm] K_2f_2 & -\dfrac{K_2M_0f_3}{p^2} - \lambda & 0 \\[2mm] 0 & -\dfrac{(g' - h')w}{p^2} & \dfrac{(g' - h')}{p} \end{vmatrix} = 0$$

equation in λ be negative (for convenience this has been multiplied through by -1).[34] Upon expansion, this yields

(h)
$$a\lambda^2 + b\lambda + c = 0$$

where

(i)
$$a = -\frac{(g' - h')}{p}$$

[34] Cf. P. A. Samuelson, *Foundations of Economic Analysis* (Harvard, 1947), pp. 269-71.

F*

(j)
$$b = \frac{g' - h'}{p}\left(K_1 L_1 - K_2 \frac{M_0 f_3}{p^2}\right)$$

(k)
$$c = \frac{K_1 K_2 (g' - h') M_0}{p^3}(L_1 f_3 + f_2)$$

By assumption as to the sign of the partial derivatives, a, b, and c are all positive. Hence the real part of the two roots of equation (h) must be negative, so that the system is stable.

If, in accordance with Part 4, heading (2) above, the aggregate demand function is assumed to be independent of the money holdings of individuals, then $f_3 = 0$. By inspection of (i), (j), and (k), we see that none of the signs is affected by this change. Hence the system is stable under this assumption too.

If we take account of the point discussed in note 14 above, then the form of the liquidity-preference function becomes $L\left(r, Y, \dfrac{M_0}{p}\right)$. The only change this requires in the preceding determinant is that the element in the first row, second column, now becomes $\dfrac{K_1 M_0 (1 - L_3)}{p^2}$. The sign of this element clearly depends on the value of L_3. If $L_3 < 1$, then the element is positive; the signs of a, b, and c, above, are also positive; and the system converges as before.

This clearly must be the case; for part of any increase in real balances will be spent on commodities and bonds.

Needless to say, we have abstracted through this appendix from the possible influence of destabilizing expectations. More generally, the stability of the system has been established only under some very simple dynamic hypotheses. This in no way assures its stability under more complicated, and, presumably, more realistic, hypotheses.

PART TWO

ECONOMIC FLUCTUATIONS AND GROWTH

[CHAPTER SIX]

Institutional Aspects of Economic Fluctuations

Howard R. Bowen and Gerald M. Meier

THE SUSCEPTIBILITY of a modern economy to fluctuations in income and employment—and the character of these fluctuations —is due in large part to the underlying institutional structure. For this reason fruitful efforts toward economic stabilization usually will involve significant (and perhaps painful) institutional changes. In the following pages, we shall consider the role of *institutions* as a condition or determinant of economic fluctuations—and as a factor in stabilization policy. In so doing, we shall refer especially to the theories of Wesley C. Mitchell, Lord Keynes, J. R. Hicks, and J. A. Schumpeter.

In this context, an institution is defined as a stable pattern of behavior that is widely prevalent and socially approved. It is a practice that is customary and sanctioned by well-defined and persistent social attitudes.

The Possibility of Economic Fluctuations

A preliminary but important part of cycle theory is to explain why economic fluctuations are possible, or conversely, under what conditions they would be absent. It is probable that fluctuations would occur in any economy in which there is *change,* regardless of the character of its institutions. Such fluctuations would result from time-space frictions, *i.e.,* from imperfect foresight, impediments to the mobility of resources, or time lags between recognition of need for adjustment and resultant action. Fluctuations would be absent only in a stationary (or possibly uniformly progressive) economy in which adjustment would be unnecessary, or in an economy free of all space-time frictions. Neither of these is a realistic possibility—especially in a society practicing detailed specialization and employing advanced technology.

But the ability of an economy to adjust to change, *i.e.,* the degree of friction in its operation, may be strongly influenced by its institutional structure. The institutional servo-mechanism may not be able smoothly and promptly to correct divergences between actual and ideal conditions, because of "gaps in communication" or "clumsiness of effectors."[1] While time-space frictions are partly the result of inherent physical and psychological conditions that are independent of institutions, they are also partly the result of the underlying institutional structure. In this sense, the effects of a given disturbance will depend upon the responses of existent institutions. And the institutions may be such that, from the viewpoint of prompt and adequate adjustment, the responses are either inconsistent, perverse, ineffectual, or delayed.

The theories of Wesley Mitchell and of J. M. Keynes were designed primarily to explain the relations between the institutions of modern capitalist society and susceptibility to economic fluctuations. Mitchell expressed this idea when he said:

> Business cycles do not become a prominent feature of economic experience in any community until a large proportion of its members have begun to live by making and spending money incomes. On the other hand, such cycles seem to appear in all countries when economic activity becomes organized predominantly in this fashion. These observations suggest that there is an organic connection between the elaborate form of economic organization which we may call "business economy," and recurrent cycles of prosperity and depression.[2]

Mitchell regarded cyclical movements in economic activity as due primarily to lags in institutional responses. Specifically, he regarded as most significant the lag of consumption expenditures behind income receipts, the lag of investment expenditures behind investment decisions, fabrication or production lags, differential movements of component parts of the price-cost structure, and differential responses in the monetary sphere. These lags were believed to be sufficiently pervasive, persistent, and interrelated to allow self-generating and self-perpetuating fluctuations.[3]

[1] For discussions of the economic system viewed as a servo-system, see R. M. Goodwin, "Econometrics in Business Cycle Analysis," in A. H. Hansen, *Business Cycles and National Income* (New York, 1951), pp. 436-42; and K. E. Boulding, *The Organizational Revolution* (New York, 1953), Chapter V.

[2] *Business Cycles, the Problem and its Setting* (New York, 1927), p. 182. For Mitchell's other writing on this subject, see also: *Business Cycles* (Berkeley, 1913); *Business Cycles and their Causes* (Berkeley, 1941); *What Happens During Business Cycles* (New York, 1951).

[3] In appraising Mitchell's contribution, Professor Milton Friedman has said: "Mitchell's 1913 volume contains practically every element that is significant in the

The principal contribution of Keynes' *General Theory* also was to demonstrate the relation between institutions and susceptibility to fluctuations. From his early work on *Indian Currency and Finance* onwards, Keynes revealed "an outstanding gift for penetrating the secrets of how institutions actually work." [4] Though he adhered to traditional theory, "he clearly thought that its proponents took too facile a view about how long-run beneficent forces operate through particular institutions." [5] His interest in institutions, his skill in analyzing their effects, and his keen sensitivity to trends in institutional evolution are abundantly clear in his *Essays in Persuasion*.[6] As he observed in the essay "Am I a Liberal?" "We have changed, by insensible degrees, our philosophy of economic life, our notions of what is reasonable and tolerable; and we have done this without changing our technique or our copybook maxims. Hence our tears and troubles." [7]

The *General Theory* was, of course, Keynes' culminant attempt to change our technique and copybook maxims. Here he emphasized the main characteristics of a modern business economy that subject it to instability, showed how stringent the conditions must be if the economy is to avoid instability, and how unlikely it is that these conditions will be fulfilled without the adoption of contracyclical policies.

Significantly, the major characteristics of the economy upon which Keynes concentrated are all institutional in form. Foremost was his observation that the act of saving is largely unrelated to the act of investment, being carried on by different persons with different motives. In so far as the classicists had assumed that "an act of individual saving inevitably leads to a parallel act of investment," Keynes was correcting a misconception regarding the effective consistency of a set of institutions.

---

business cycle theories that are currently prominent. Here are the multiplier process, the acceleration principle, the Pigouvian cycles of optimism and pessimism, the Marshallian and Hawtreyan drain of cash from the banking system and the resultant tightening of the money market, a decline in the expected yield from new investment at the peak that is the counterpart of the Keynesian 'collapse of the marginal efficiency of capital' except that it is a continuous decline rather than a discontinuous 'collapse,' the Keynesian changes in liquidity-preference." "The Economic Theorist," in A. F. Burns (ed.), *Wesley Clair Mitchell, The Economic Scientist* (New York: 1952), p. 271.

[4] R. F. Harrod, *The Life of John Maynard Keynes* (New York, 1951), p. 163.
[5] *Ibid.*, p. 164.
[6] New York, 1932.
[7] *Ibid.*, pp. 337-38.

The monetary system allows the link between saving and investment to be cut, not only by permitting investment without saving and saving without investment (as many monetary theorists had noted), but also by enabling savers to hold idle funds at no cost except risk of bank failure. This means that when the marginal efficiency of capital drops to a point where expected returns no longer exceed the necessary risk premium, investment is less attractive than liquidity. Thus, an increase in the propensity to save will not necessarily lead to a balancing increase in the propensity to invest. On the contrary, the decrease in the propensity to consume may reduce the prospective net yield of physical assets and thereby reduce the propensity to invest. Thus, the institutions underlying saving and investment help to explain the possibility of economic fluctuations.

Further, in emphasizing the role of investment as a main determinant of the level of income and employment, Keynes revealed additional institutional obstacles to the achievement of full employment. On the one hand, the rate of interest is a highly conventional phenomenon. He said, "the most stable, and the least easily shifted, element in our contemporary economy has been hitherto, and may prove to be in future, the minimum rate of interest acceptable to the generality of wealth-owners," [8] and "institutional and psychological factors are present which set a limit much above zero to the practicable decline in the rate of interest." [9] On the other hand, the marginal efficiency of capital is highly unstable. "The association of a conventional and fairly stable long-term rate of interest with a fickle and highly unstable marginal efficiency of capital" may, therefore, place difficulties in the way of maintaining effective demand at a level high enough to provide full employment in the short period; it is also possible that the rate of interest "may fluctuate for decades about a level which is chronically too high for full employment." [10]

Not only is investment an extremely volatile variable, but it is also limited in amount, in so far as in a business economy only those investments are considered feasible which are self-liquidating during the relatively short planning horizons of businessmen.[11] Such conventional behavior will exclude two important

[8] *General Theory,* p. 309.
[9] *Ibid.,* p. 218.
[10] *Ibid.,* p. 204.
[11] *Ibid.,* pp. 157-58.

classes of investments: those which are self-liquidating only over periods extending beyond the range of ordinary business planning and those investments which though socially valuable are nevertheless nonself-liquidating.

In contrast to the variability of the propensity to invest, "the propensity to consume is a fairly stable function." [12] This is because the subjective factors on which the propensity to consume depends "include those psychological characteristics of human nature and those social practices and institutions which, though not unalterable, are unlikely to undergo a material change over a short period of time except in abnormal or revolutionary circumstances." [13]

Finally, by considering institutional factors in the labor market, Keynes reached his conclusions regarding the effect of the wage bargain on real wages.[14]

The foregoing reveals Keynes' basic concern with the *possibility* of fluctuations due to internal inconsistencies in a set of institutions. This in itself did not, however, provide an "explanation" of the disturbances underlying economic fluctuations. It showed only the *possibility*, and the likelihood, of such variations in national income.

Disturbances

A complete theory of economic fluctuations must consider the cycle as part of the underlying processes of growth and institutional change in which it is embedded. Many disturbances which cycle analysts for convenience consider "exogenous" are actually changes in the structure of demand, changes in factor supply, and technological innovations. And these are closely related to institutional changes: sometimes they are causes of changes in institutions, and sometimes effects. If, by assuming technical and institutional conditions as given, such disturbances are relegated to the realm of the "exogenous," the analysis will then abstract from those very aspects which are of major importance in the explanation of cyclical phenomena.

Much of recent cycle theory has attempted to build a theory of fluctuations upon the foundation laid by Keynes. Perhaps the leading example is Professor Hicks' recent theory of the trade

---

[12] *Ibid.*, p. 96.
[13] *Ibid.*, p. 91.
[14] *Ibid.*, pp. 11-15.

cycle.[15] With its explicitly dynamic analysis of the connection between the magnitude of behavior coefficients and the amplitude and turning points of the cycle, Hicks' model does much to clarify the cyclical process. But it still suffers from deficiencies common to most macrodynamic models—inadequate attention to exogenous variables, simplified institutional postulates, and abstraction from changes in the institutional environment. It is unquestionably useful and necessary, methodologically, to base analysis on simplified postulates. Yet, when variables relating to growth and institutional change are assumed out of cycle theory, resulting generalizations are bound to be tenuous and artificial. As Professor Haberler remarked in his survey of various cycle theories:

> Even those writers whose theory centers round one single factor which they make responsible for the business cycle—*e.g.*, crop variations, or inventions, or the acceleration of derived demand, or changes in demand, or waves of optimism and pessimism—are forced to admit that what they call *the* cause of the business cycle can produce its effect only in a certain economic institutional environment. They assume, explicitly or implicitly, a certain structure of the exchange economy, a certain rigidity of wages and contracts, a certain behavior of investors, the presence or absence of a certain amount of knowledge and foresight amongst entrepreneurs, a certain monetary organization, etc. The business cycle might well not appear (a) if those "active" forces (crop changes, inventions, changes in demand, etc.) were absent, or (b) if one or several of the significant features in the economic institutional framework were changed. . . . It might therefore just as well be maintained that the rigidity of our economic system, or its financial or monetary organization, or particular features of the latter, are the causes of the cycle as that inventions or crop changes or changes in demand are responsible.[16]

It is true that Hicks' model considers the vital question of fluctuation about a rising trend, and demonstrates the restrictiveness of the conditions under which an economy may be "regularly progressive." Yet the treatment of the trend in the form of autonomous investment remains arbitrary. In attempting to give precision to the cyclical process, the formal and simplified character of the model necessarily abstracts from many of the variables associated with growth and institutional change. The funda-

15 J. R. Hicks, *A Contribution to the Theory of the Trade Cycle* (Oxford, 1950).
16 Gottfried Haberler, *Prosperity and Depression*, 3rd ed. (Geneva, 1941), p. 6.

mental issue is the relative importance of these variables as compared with the multiplier-accelerator mechanism.[17]

To Schumpeter, a multiplier-accelerator model was unconvincing alongside the more basic forces of technological innovation, institutional evolution, entrepreneurial activity, and the credit system.[18] As he pointed out, analysis of these more basic forces requires attention to social relationships and to the institutional framework. Thus, the analysis of business fluctuations merges into economic history. Only by so broadening and deepening the analysis of cyclical phenomena may the underlying causes of fluctuations be adequately explained for purposes of prediction and effective policy decisions.

There is still need, therefore, to combine the theories of Keynes and of Schumpeter. The short-period analysis of the former is inadequate to solve the long-period problems of the latter, and both points of view are required for an adequate cycle theory. Austin Robinson, in a recent review dealing with the relationships between the theories of Keynes and Schumpeter, questioned the feasibility of integrating these two theoretical systems when he made the astonishing statement: "There will always be the little men to make synthetic intellectual mixtures out of the immiscible ingredients that the great men have given us." [19] In our judgment, the ingredients are far from immiscible; indeed, the next steps forward in cycle theory will be precisely the mixing of these ingredients. As Schumpeter suggested, a full-blown theory of economic fluctuations will require nothing less than a theoretical, historical, and statistical analysis of the capitalist process. In such an analysis, the ideas of both Keynes and Schumpeter can serve as mutually supporting foundations. Each particular episode in the course of business fluctuations is likely to be the result of a unique set of underlying "causes." Each occurs at a particular stage in economic development and under a particular institutional structure; and each is generated by a particular combination of more or less adventitious forces. Among these may be

[17] *Ibid.*, p. 64.
[18] Cf., D. H. Robertson, "The Trade Cycle—an Academic View," *Lloyd's Bank Review*, September, 1937, p. 506. As Robertson said, "the phenomena of boom and slump are . . . a matter . . . of the inevitable discontinuity which attends the efforts of man to achieve material progress." Keynes in an early essay also referred to the cycle as reflecting "the growing pains of overrapid changes." (*Essays in Persuasion*, p. 358.) See also, Knut Wicksell, *Lectures on Political Economy*, edited by Lionel Robbins (London, 1935), vol. 2, p. 211.
[19] *Economic Journal*, March 1953, p. 129.

technological innovations, changes in governmental policies, war or rumors of war, wage policy of labor unions or price policy of business, speculative frenzies, climatic variations, etc. Because of the nature and variability of these forces, a single general theory of the causes of business fluctuations appears to be as infeasible as a general theory of historic causation. Indeed, economic fluctuations may perhaps be regarded most usefully as part of the process of general historic change.

An important factor determining the degree of economic stability is the sensitivity of the social servo-mechanisms which partly determines how deep and prolonged a depression may be before recovery sets in and how high and prolonged a boom may be before decline sets in. Some of the factors bringing about turning points are imbedded deeply in the basic physical characteristics of the economy. But some are related to the psychological attitudes of its people, the extant social institutions, and the political system. For example, one of the factors determining the course of business fluctuations is the extent to which upward or downward movements will be allowed to proceed before conscious action is taken to end them. This will be determined primarily by the attitudes of people toward fluctuations. If they regard them as "acts of God" about which nothing can or should be done, or if they are imbued with a laissez-faire philosophy, the course of economic fluctuations may be quite different from what it may be if they believe that something can be done about them. There will be differences, also, among different peoples, and at different times, in the amount of depression or inflation which will be tolerated before action is demanded. As Professor Swan has suggested, "Is it not time . . . to forget the glittering prize of achieving *the* theory of the trade cycle, and concentrate upon the systematic and pedestrian attempt to discover how the economy works and grows in its parts and as a whole?" [20]

Institutions and Economic Stabilization

Fortunately, a general theory of the causation of economic fluctuations is by no means a necessary prerequisite to stabilization policy. Even though we are unable to understand—much less

[20] Trevor Swan, "Progress Report on the Trade Cycle," *Economic Record*, Dec. 1950, p. 200. Cf. W. W. Rostow, "Notes on Mr. Hicks and History," *American Economic Review*, June 1951, pp. 316-24; W. C. Mitchell, *Business Cycles, the Problem and Its Setting, op. cit.*, pp. 55-57.

control—the basic causes, there may be useful things we can do toward ameliorating economic fluctuations. It may be possible to contrive compensatory schemes to offset or counteract the forces giving rise to economic fluctuations; and it may be possible to identify the institutions which permit or accentuate economic instability, and to design appropriate changes in these institutions. The theories and recommendations of Keynes were precisely of this character. His proposals regarding compensatory fiscal policy were designed to offset, rather than remove, the forces underlying business fluctuations. His analysis of savings and investment was essentially an effort to identify those institutional factors which permit or accentuate economic instability, and the recommendations flowing from his analysis—recommendations designed to achieve closer correlation between planned saving and planned investment—were proposals designed to overcome the destabilizing effect of these institutional factors.

The aspect of Keynes' thought that excited the greatest interest was the implication that stable prosperity might be approached largely through compensatory fiscal and monetary policy. During the 1930's his emphasis was upon public spending as a means of combatting depression.[21] This idea stirred the imagination of economists and others because it seemed a method of ridding capitalism of its greatest weakness, namely unemployment, without requiring significant institutional changes. It was, in other words, a promising answer to the socialist critics who argued that unemployment is inherent in capitalism and can never be overcome without a major institutional overhauling.

The experience of the 1930's and 1940's was a convincing demonstration that Keynes was technically correct. It showed that public spending on a sufficient scale can raise output and income from depression to full employment. And there are few economists today who would deny that a large deficit produced by reducing taxes while holding expenditures constant would accomplish a similar result. But from this one cannot conclude that compensatory fiscal policy is a way to economic stability

[21] There is no doubt that Keynes placed great store in fiscal policy as a means of combatting depression, and that much of his influence was used to encourage compensatory fiscal policy. Yet it is significant that his *General Theory* scarcely mentions fiscal policy as a remedy, but rather suggests more basic institutional changes such as redistribution of income and other devices to discourage saving or hoarding, public control of investment, and low interest rates.

involving no significant institutional reform. The history of the last twenty years also teaches us that painful changes in deeply-rooted institutions are involved in any effort to achieve stability via fiscal policy. The history of this period demonstrates the tenacious persistence of such institutions and the difficulties in changing them, and it suggests that only in a grave social crisis can these institutional obstacles be overcome even temporarily. Even the deep depression of the 1930's, devastating as it was, was not in itself a sufficient crisis to override these institutional resistances. Only the supreme crisis of war was able to break down inhibitions and to permit spending of sufficient magnitude to restore full employment.

What are the institutions to which fiscal policy runs contrary? First, it is contrary to the institution of *budget-balancing*. This is a well-established and strongly sanctioned behavior pattern which imposes the following three budgetary rules: (1) that a government, like a household, should spend no more than its current income except in time of war; (2) that a government should not tax in excess of current expenditures except to retire debt; and (3) that debt should be avoided, but if there is debt it should be retired as rapidly as possible. The institution of budget-balancing places grave obstacles in the way of compensatory fiscal policies such as deficit spending, tax reduction in the face of declining revenues, and creation of surpluses. Despite all the persuasion of economists and the experience of recent decades, the public and their representatives cling to a belief in the soundness of budget-balancing and in the evil of debt. The arguments "that we owe it to ourselves" or "that for every liability there is a corresponding asset" have fallen on skeptical and unwilling ears.

Second, fiscal policy runs squarely into ponderous legislative procedure and prerogatives which virtually preclude long-term planning of public works, flexibility in the rate of public spending, or prompt adjustment of tax rates.

Third, fiscal policy is hampered by the nature of our established institutions for the finance of local government and our strong attachment to local autonomy. Local government appears destined, for many years to come, to manage its financial affairs in ways that accentuate rather than counteract economic fluctuations.

Fourth, fiscal policy on the expenditure side is hampered by the institutional pattern which prevents government from assuming functions that have traditionally been carried on by private enterprise. The dichotomy between state and private industry is scarcely less sharp than the separation between church and state. Every encroachment upon the traditional domain of private enterprise produces the strongest resistance. This resistance appears even in minor cases such as prison industries and housing activities of universities, and in intensified form in connection with public ownership of power facilities, public housing, public health services, etc. Government spending thus tends to be restricted to those relatively limited projects which are traditionally governmental or which are not likely to be commercially profitable. With the re-entry of private enterprise into the provision of highways, it is even possible that public spending in this field will sometimes be resisted. As a result, expenditure for defense remains about the only large item of outlay which can be substantially increased without taint of infringement on private enterprise. The attitude is also prevalent that the production of nonmarketable goods or the provision of facilities that are not self-liquidating are inherently wasteful as compared with the production of goods that are marketable at a price to cover cost. This tends to create a bias against the kinds of goods which the government is able to provide without infringing upon private enterprise. Moreover, there is a strong and inherent suspicion of "big government," and therefore resistance to increases in public activities which are likely to extend the scope of government even when they do not invade the private domain.

Fifth, and finally, fiscal policy may be frustrated, as full employment is approached or attained, by the effort of vigorous trade unions to raise money wages.

In listing some of the institutional factors which tend to prevent effective fiscal policy in peacetime, we do not condemn these institutions. Some of them are, in our judgment, eminently sound even though they get in the way of fiscal policy. Their effect on economic stabilization via fiscal policy is not the only criterion by which they should be judged. Our only purpose in listing them is to show that there are important obstacles to successful fiscal policy, and that these obstacles are in the form of well-established and persistent institutional patterns. It was a delusion to have supposed that fiscal policy does not require major institutional changes. Fiscal policy of a magnitude necessary to overcome deep depression in peacetime would even today be confronted with strong institutional resistances not unlike those faced in the 1930's.

Paradoxically, experience has taught us that fiscal policy is a technically feasible method of achieving economic stability, but at the same time that it requires institutional changes that we are not altogether prepared to make in peacetime. Keynes himself was well aware of this problem. He wrote in 1940, "It appears to be politically impossible for a capitalistic democracy to organize expenditure on a scale necessary to make the grand experiment which would prove my case except in war conditions." [22]

A means of economic stabilization that is alternative or supplementary to compensatory fiscal policy is to modify those basic institutions which permit or accentuate economic fluctuations. Foremost among these, as Keynes pointed out, is the drastic separation between the economically related functions of saving and investment. These two functions, which must be closely coordinated if stability is to be achieved, are drastically separated in our institutional structure. One way toward economic stabilization, then, is to modify the institutions relating to saving and investment so that these two functions can be more closely coordinated, so that saving cannot be attempted unless there are planned investments to absorb them or so that investment plans cannot be made unless there are savings to be absorbed, or so that any socially desirable discrepancy between planned savings and investment can be arranged.

The coordination of savings and investment would require control over saving so that its amount might be adjusted to planned investment, or control over investment so that its amount might be adjusted to planned saving, or both. Keynes made various suggestions toward control of both savings and investment, but he did not develop them into a coherent plan. Moreover, he conceived the basic and continuing social problem to be underemployment. Hence his proposals were designed mainly to curtail saving and to encourage investment. Since he believed that the community's stock of capital ought to be increased fairly rapidly, he concluded that primary emphasis ought to be given to adjusting the rate of investment to the rate of saving rather than vice versa. Accordingly, he offered public control of investment

[22] *New Republic,* July 29, 1940, p. 158.

(presumably including direct investment by government) as his major recommendation. He said,

> In conditions of *laissez faire* the avoidance of wide fluctuations in employment may, therefore, prove impossible without a far-reaching change in the psychology of investment markets such as there is no reason to expect. I conclude that the duty of ordering the current volume of investment cannot be safely left in private hands.[23]

And in another passage:

> Furthermore, it seems unlikely that the influence of banking policy on the rate of interest will be sufficient by itself to determine an optimum rate of investment. I conceive, therefore, that a somewhat comprehensive socialization of investment will prove the only means of securing an approximation to full employment; though this need not exclude all manner of compromises and of devices by which public authority will cooperate with private initiative.[24]

Keynes also toyed with the idea of controlling or influencing saving, though he did not specifically endorse the proposals offered by others, *e.g.*, the stamped-money plan, taxes or subsidies on unspent receipts, or direct control of saving. He also often referred to greater equality in the distribution of income.

As Keynes well realized, to achieve coordination between saving and investment would require institutional changes of the first order. It seems obvious that the American people are not prepared to relinquish the freedom of saving and investment which these changes would inevitably involve. Even the relatively innocuous provisions of the Employment Act of 1946 have not been accepted wholeheartedly. Hence, the radical separation and independence of the functions of saving and investment, which is characteristic of the American economy, are likely to persist and to permit wide fluctuations in economic activity.

The Strategy of Stabilization Policy

We have chosen to discuss economic fluctuations and the problem of economic stabilization in an institutional context to emphasize that fluctuations occur or are possible because of the character of the existing institutional framework, and that stabilization necessarily involves change in firmly established insti-

[23] *General Theory*, p. 320.
[24] *Ibid.*, p. 378.

tutions and is therefore likely to be difficult of attainment. We do
not mean to imply, however, that institutions are all equally
resistant to change. In fact they differ from one another in this
respect, and the pliability of any one institution varies from one
time to another. This suggests that the strategy of stabilization
policy is to select those proposals which are likely to encounter
the least institutional inertia. No doubt those who have advocated fiscal policy have been right in their assumption that this
method would encounter less formidable institutions than any
alternative.

Since institutions are more likely to give way in time of social
crisis than at any other, one test of the strength of an institution
is the degree of crisis required to change it. Total war, the supreme social crisis, is clearly capable of producing at least temporary change in most of the institutions relevant to economic
stabilization. Up to now, however, wars have been regarded as
exceptional and temporary emergencies—as occasions when accustomed modes of behavior may be suspended but not ended—
and normalcy is expected to return after the cease-fire. The other
great social crises are deep depression or hyper-inflation. Both of
these are also likely to be considered temporary emergencies,
and to call forth a suspension rather than a termination of accustomed modes of behavior. However, deep depressions occur with
sufficient frequency—once or twice in a normal life span—that
they may come to be regarded as recurring phenomena and continuing problems. For example, the depression of the 1930's did
leave a substantial residue of institutional change bearing upon
stabilization. Among these changes were: social security, social
welfare legislation, financial reform, and revision of the tax structure.

Because the memory of the 1930's is still vivid in the minds
of many older adults, it is probable that if a deep depression
were to begin in the near future, institutional changes would be
feasible which were not possible in the 1930's. In this sense, resistance to institutional change relating to stabilization is doubtless less potent than it was prior to 1929. Perhaps also the
resistances have been softened up a little by the arguments of
economists. In this connnection, the famous words of Keynes in
the closing paragraphs of the *General Theory* are pertinent:
". . . the ideas of economists and political philosophers, both
when they are right and when they are wrong, are more powerful

than is commonly understood. Indeed the world is ruled by little else. Practical men, who believe themselves to be quite exempt from any intellectual influences, are usually the slaves of some defunct economist." [25]

But if depression is staved off for many more years, the recollection of the 1930's and the memory of the economic Cassandras who gave warnings and proposed remedies will be forgotten, and institutional resistances will be back at par. By that time Keynes himself may be one of the "defunct economists."

One of the characteristics of the development of business cycle theory has been the tendency for theories emerging at a given time to be descriptions of the most recently observed cycle. Thus, cycle theory from 1913 to 1929 was strongly colored by events in 1907 and 1921, and cycle theory since 1929 has been dominated by events in the '30's. Just as generals are said to prepare for the last war, economists tend to prepare for the last depression.

[25] *General Theory*, p. 383.

CHAPTER SEVEN

Capital Stock Adjustment Theories of the Trade Cycle and the Problem of Policy [1]

R. C. O. Matthews

THE HISTORY of economic thought furnishes us with plentiful evidence that when economists agree it by no means follows that their conclusions will be vindicated by the test of experience. Agreed conclusions have not infrequently proved an obstacle to the advancement of knowledge by creating prematurely the impression that an issue is closed and discouraging further research upon it. In surveying the present state of trade cycle theory, this is a point which it is well to bear in mind; for there is an increasing measure of agreement among theorists on the essentials of the problem. What we propose to do in the present paper is to take as our starting point the basic idea which underlies most modern theoretical writing on the trade cycle, and see what are the conclusions for policy that appear to follow from models of the cycle built upon it as a foundation. The policies suggested will be no better than the models from which they are derived, and if these models do not present a fair approximation to "what happens during business cycles," the policies derived from them will likewise fail to provide a proper starting point for the practical policy maker. The many issues of policy on which the models give no guidance serve to remind us of the many respects in which they are incomplete as explanations of the facts of business cycles. But since the models are seriously advanced as explanations of reality, albeit simplified and schematic explanations, it is legitimate to use them in seeking a guide to policy, so long as we recognize that their empirical basis is as yet extremely unsure and that at best they can do no more than provide an outline of the solution required. Thus we shall not in this essay be treating such problems as wage-induced inflation or complications arising out of international trade, nor shall we discuss the issue

[1] I am indebted to Dr. R. M. Goodwin and to the editor for valuable suggestions and criticisms.

between the different fiscal and monetary means by which a given policy may be implemented. We shall assume that the objective of policy is the maintenance of full employment, without discussing, save incidentally, the problems raised by the definition of the word "full."

The simplest form of the acceleration principle, that investment is a function of the rate of growth of output, has come in for a good deal of criticism, mostly deserved. But there is wide acceptance of its underlying postulate, that there is a certain level of capital capacity which is "appropriate" to a given volume of output, and that the trade cycle occurs from the interaction between efforts to achieve this appropriate level of capacity on the one hand and the working of the multiplier on the other. The special assumption of the acceleration principle—or rather its chief special assumption—is that on day $n - 1$ capacity was appropriate to the then prevailing level of output, so that the investment required by day n is merely that called for by any increase in output that may have occurred between the two days. A more general formulation allows for the possibility that capacity on day $n - 1$ was already excessive or deficient in relation to current output, as well as for the possibility of lagged reactions and other complications. An example of such a more general formulation is the statement that investment decisions are a diminishing function of the size of the stock of capital in existence and an increasing function of the national income. This is the formulation of Kalecki, adopted with modifications in the models¡ also of Kaldor and Goodwin.[2] The element in these models which gives rise to cyclical movements is essentially the same as the acceleration principle, whether as used in its pure form, for example in the Hansen-Samuelson model,[3] or in models like that of Hicks [4] in which it is qualified in a number of respects. The feature common to the five models mentioned and others similar to them will be conveniently indicated if we refer to them collectively as capital stock adjustment models.

It should be observed that the two principal assumptions of

[2] M. Kalecki, *Essays in the Theory of Economic Fluctuations* (1939), pp. 116-49; N. Kaldor, "A Model of the Trade Cycle," *Economic Journal*, 1940, pp. 78-92; R. M. Goodwin, "Econometrics in Business-Cycle Analysis," in A. H. Hansen, *Business Cycles and National Income* (1951), pp. 417-68.
[3] P. A. Samuelson, "Interaction between the Multiplier Analysis and the Principle of Acceleration," *Review of Economic Statistics*, 1939, pp. 75-78.
[4] J. R. Hicks, *A Contribution to the Theory of the Trade Cycle* (1950).

capital stock adjustment theories of the cycle, namely that investment decisions are a function of the relation between the amount of capacity in existence and the level of output or income, and that investment generates income through the multiplier, are not in themselves sufficient to lead to cyclical fluctuations; [5] some further conditions are required, and in most models these are supplied by the assumption either of a lag somewhere in the process (*e.g.*, between investment decisions and investment, as in Kalecki's model, or between the receipt of income and its expenditure, as in the Hansen-Samuelson model) [6] or else of a nonlinear investment function (as in the models of Kaldor and Goodwin), or finally of both (as in Hicks's model). Disagreements as to which of these conditions should be given chief prominence are largely responsible for the differences between the various capital stock adjustment models that have been propounded.

Not all models of the trade cycle, of course, belong to the capital stock adjustment class. The character of the innovatory investment which Schumpeter casts as the leading actor in the cycle is such that its profitability is not determined, except to a subsidiary extent, by the current level of income and output, and Schumpeter's model of the cycle therefore differs in essentials from the capital stock adjustment theory. But for better or for worse, it is capital stock adjustment theories that predominate in current thinking, and it is with them that we shall be concerned in the following pages. The common practice amongst present day writers on business cycle theory is to devote a few respectful sentences to Schumpeter, without endeavoring to relate or compare his views with those of others, and then pass on and forget all about him. This practice we shall on the present occasion regretfully follow.

The problem to which the Keynesian theory of the 1930's—what may be called proto-Keynesian theory—was chiefly addressed was how to rescue an economy which had got into a grave depression. In the light of *The General Theory* this problem seemed in principle tolerably easy to solve, and the various

[5] In terms of difference equations, the two principal assumptions stated lead by themselves only to a first-order linear difference equation, whereas a second-order equation is required to yield the sought-for results.
[6] To be strictly accurate, the working of the Hansen-Samuelson model is conditional not only on the lag mentioned but also on investment being a function of the rate of change of consumption, rather than a function of the rate of change of income.

fiscal and monetary measures suggested are now universally familiar. Preoccupation with the problem of the slump and the excess capacity associated with it caused less attention to be paid to the more difficult problem of how to keep the economy in a boom situation once that had been attained. To approach this problem, we need a more explicit treatment of the factors affecting the marginal efficiency of capital than is provided in *The General Theory*—a need which the acceleration principle and related formulations purport to fill. In order that full employment should be maintained, it is necessary not merely that *ex ante* investment should be equal to *ex ante* savings at a high enough level, but also that the current level of investment should not be such as to cause the stock of capital to increase so rapidly that a decline in its marginal efficiency occurs.

Apart from times of war and its aftermath and of preparations for war, full employment in the past normally has been attained only at the peak of business cycle booms, if then. Therefore, it appears that if investment is below its boom-time level, the level of national income generated will not be high enough to give full employment. But the boom level of investment is not maintainable, for reasons which the capital stock adjustment theory makes plain. It is found that the carrying out of investment at that rate causes the growth of capacity to outstrip requirements, despite the high level of income which it creates, and profit rates therefore fall. Hence follows a fall in investment which initiates the contraction phase of the cycle. If the boom rate of investment were to continue permanently, the amount of capital capacity in existence would soon become overpowering, even in relation to the requirements of a full-employment level of incomes and output. The profit rate remains relatively stable over the long period only because the high investment of the boom alternates with low investment or even negative net investment in the slump.[7] The dilemma is, then, that a rate of investment high enough to give full employment leads to excessive capital accumulation and is not maintainable; whereas if investment were kept steady at a level intermediate between boom and slump, there would not be full employment, although there

[7] Perhaps the first explicit statement of this point and its consequences is to be found in the article "Full Employment by Stimulating Private Investment?" by M. Kalecki, *Oxford Economic Papers*, 1945, pp. 83-92. See also *idem*, "A Note on Long-run Unemployment," *Review of Economic Studies*, 1949-50, pp. 62-64.

might be a fair chance that this moderate pace of investment would preserve the marginal efficiency of capital roughly constant and so not be inconsistent with stability.

To state the problem in this way, as we must do if we accept the essentials of the capital stock adjustment theory of the cycle, is already to suggest the broad lines of the solution. We wish investment to be stable; on.the other hand we wish income to be at a higher level than history would lead us to expect to be created by a maintainable level of investment. If the ratio of capital to output is taken to be fixed within limits at any one time by technical factors—though the ratio need not be changeless through time—it follows that to seek to keep private investment permanently at its high boom-time proportion to income is unpromising, and the endeavor must be instead to render a lower level of private investment consistent with full-employment income. The consumption function must be raised, or else government spending must fill the gap between the income level normally attained somewhere midway between boom and slump and the level of income set as the objective.[8] The consumption function is thus seen to be no less relevant to trade cycle policy than it is to longer period problems.

The purpose of the present paper is to consider more closely some of the theoretical implications of the policy just sketched in outline. The essence of this policy is that that part of investment which is subject to the capital stock adjustment principle should run at a rate which is sufficient but not more than sufficient to provide for depreciation and for the needs of secular growth, while the consumption function and/or the level of government expenditure are adjusted in such a way as to render this rate of investment consistent with the desired level of employment.[9] If the policy is to be carried out in its simplest form, it

[8] The government spending may take the form of investment, so long as it is not of a type to compete with private investment, since it is recognized by all exponents of the acceleration principle that there are certain types of investment which are not subject to the principle and which will therefore not lead to burdensome accumulation of capital.

[9] It will be perceived that the policy under discussion has much in common with the old-fashioned prescription of stopping slumps by stopping booms. There are, however, certain differences. Older writers often were more concerned with the unsound quality of the investment carried out at the peak of the boom than with its excessive quantity; and furthermore their policy appeared to condemn the economy to a permanent state of semislump, which under the present scheme is avoided by engineering a permanent rise in the consumption function or by having a permanently high level of government spending.

is important also to ensure that when it is first put into execution, the capital capacity available is of an amount more or less appropriate to the current level of income and output; if it is not, there will be arrears or surpluses to be worked off before investment can settle down to its proposed normal level.

The first and principal question to which we shall address ourselves is whether the policy position (as we shall describe the position attained as the result of the execution of the policy in question) would be stable in the sense that any chance departure from it would set up forces causing the economy to return to it rather than to deviate from it by increasing amounts.

The concept of stability in trade cycle theory is closely connected with the problem of damping, the Achilles heel of early capital stock adjustment models. As is well known, the simplest type of difference equation model based on the acceleration principle and the multiplier, if it gives rise to cyclical fluctuations at all, may yield either cycles of diminishing amplitude (damped cycles) or cycles of increasing amplitude (antidamped cycles), according to the values of the parameters, with cycles of constant amplitude a unique and not especially likely intermediate case. In either instance there will be a certain notional equilibrium level of investment and income about which the system fluctuates, this position being that represented in a trendless economy by zero net investment, or otherwise by a level of net investment just sufficient to provide for the needs of secular growth. The same tendency to damped or antidamped fluctuations about a notional equilibrium is manifested also in capital stock adjustment models such as Kalecki's where the acceleration principle is not explicitly used. Now since historically cycles have not shown any clear tendency either to diminish or to increase in amplitude, and since it is unreasonable to suppose that the parameters of the system have for some 150 years been by chance at or near the unique level which would yield cycles of constant amplitude, the question of damping has created something of a problem for all mathematically explicit cycle theories. Two attempts have been made to meet it. The first hypothesis, due to Wicksell and Frisch,[10] is to suppose that the cycle is inherently damped, but that it is prevented from reaching or remaining at its notional

[10] R. Frisch, "Propagation Problems and Impulse Problems in Dynamic Economics," in *Economic Essays in Honour of Gustav Cassel* (1933), pp. 171-205.

G

equilibrium by the constant recurrence of arbitrary "shocks," due to wars, innovations, etc., these shocks sustaining the cyclical tendency when it might otherwise disappear. The second hypothesis, found in the models of Kaldor, Goodwin, and Hicks, is that the inherent tendency of the system is to produce anti-damped cycles or even explosive expansion or contraction, but that the amplitude of the cycle is subject to certain constraints, imposed, for example, by the approach to full employment in the boom, and by the difficulty of reducing net investment in fixed capital very much below zero in the slump.

The stability or instability of the notional equilibrium position about which the system fluctuates depends on which of these two alternative hypotheses is accepted; and the stability of the policy position largely, though not entirely, depends on the stability of the notional equilibrium position.

Consider first the Frisch hypothesis of a damped cycle sustained by erratic shocks. In order for the equilibrium position to be attained, it is necessary that investment decisions should be at a level corresponding to zero net investment (abstracting from the consequences of secular growth) and also that the current level of income should be such as to create planned savings of the same amount. The latter condition will not be satisfied if current investment differs significantly from current investment decisions, or if, as a result of lags in the circular flow of incomes, the income level is determined by the level of investment at an earlier date, when it was running significantly higher or lower than it is at the time in question. (It is for this reason that equilibrium is not attained at the points during the representative trendless cycle when net investment passes through the zero level.) But supposing the equilibrium position to be once fairly and truly reached, it would be stable in the sense that any deviation from it would set up forces causing the system to tend to return to it, not indeed smoothly, but by a path of cycles of diminishing amplitude, so long as no further shocks supervened; and moreover a substantial cyclical movement would be brought about only by a substantial shock (or by a number of shocks whose aggregate effect was substantial).

What is the relation between the equilibrium position just discussed and the policy position? In both there is zero net investment (abstracting from secular growth), but in the policy position consumption and aggregate national income are higher than in the equilibrium position by an extent sufficient to ensure full employment. Consequently the required capital capacity is also greater, and zero net investment will therefore represent a somewhat higher level of gross investment. This, however, is an unimportant difference. As far as stability is concerned, the two positions may at the present level of abstraction be considered fundamentally similar.

If, therefore, the damped cycles plus erratic shocks hypothesis is a correct approximation to reality, the principal problems facing the authorities would be how initially to arrive at the policy position without setting up maladjustments on the way, and how to provide means of insulating the economy against major erratic shocks and the cyclical movements which the latter might set up if not prevented or offset.

However, there is some doubt whether the erratic shocks hypothesis as an explanation of reality is tenable. Hicks, in particular, has advanced some cogent objections to it, into which we need not here enter.[11] Largely as a result of Hicks's book, opinion has now swung somewhat in favor of the alternative hypothesis, which postulates the existence of antidamped cycles or explosive tendencies prevented by various constraints from proceeding beyond a certain point. We must therefore pass now to consider what is implied by this hypothesis with respect to the stability or otherwise of the policy position.

The answer is much less clear than it is in the case of the erratic shocks hypothesis just considered. It is obvious enough that on the assumptions in question the equilibrium about which the system fluctuates is an unstable one, and that if it were by chance attained even a small disturbance would be sufficient to start the cycle off anew with an amplitude that would soon or immediately reach its former dimensions. But it is not so clear whether the same is true of the policy position. The reason for this is that whereas the constraints which prevent the cycle from growing in amplitude beyond a certain range are *ex hypothesi* not in operation at the intermediate point in the cycle represented by the equilibrium position, it *is* possible that they will operate in the policy position. It depends on what exactly the constraints are supposed to be.

The problem can perhaps be most conveniently approached by the use of a diagram similar to that employed in the Kaldor

11 Hicks, *op. cit.*, pp. 89-91.

model. Some differences between the assumptions underlying it and those underlying other analogous models will be touched on later. For simplicity, we abstract from secular growth.

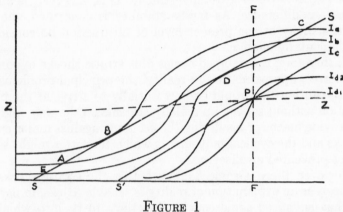

FIGURE 1

Income in money terms is measured along the horizontal axis, savings and gross investment in money terms along the vertical axis. The line *SS* represents the amount saved at any level of income, the function being assumed for convenience to be linear. It is postulated that investment is a positive function of the level of income and a negative function of the quantity of capital in existence. Each of the curves I_a, I_b . . ., of which there are in principle an infinite number, indicates how much investment will be undertaken at different income levels supposing that the quantity of capital is fixed at a given amount. If the quantity of capital is relatively low, the functional dependence of investment on income will be shown by a curve relatively high up on the diagram, such as I_a. If the quantity of capital is rather higher, investment will be *ceteris paribus* rather less profitable, and the amount undertaken will be at the point on the curve I_b corresponding to whatever is the level of income; and so on. The flattening out of the *I* curves at their lower and upper extremities, which is crucial to the argument, is attributed on the one hand to the difficulty of bringing about any further reduction in gross investment, when net investment has already fallen to zero in some or all sectors of the economy, and the consequent slackening in the rate of decline of investment which occurs at the bottom of the contraction phase of the cycle; and on the other hand to the various obstacles to the further expansion of investment that are likely to arise at the top of the boom, in particular the approach to general or partial full employment of labor and other resources. The dotted line ZZ shows the level of zero net investment, which will be rising slightly as income rises. At such a point as A the situation will be stable in that the SS curve is steeper than the I curve; the marginal propensity to save exceeds the marginal propensity to invest, and the multiplier is finite. However, at A, net investment is negative and the quantity of capital tending to fall. The I curve is therefore tending to shift upwards, and presently the point B will be reached. Here there is instability upwards, and the economy will rapidly proceed to C. At C the rise in income and investment will be arrested and temporary stability attained. But with net investment now positive, the I curve will tend to sink till it reaches the level I_c and the economy arrives at the point D, where there is downwards instability. E will mark the trough of the cycle, whence the system will proceed again to A and B and the cycle will recommence with the same amplitude as before.

The level of investment which will maintain the stock of capital constant and so keep the system on a single unaltering I curve is that marked by ZZ. The objective of policy is to make this level of investment consistent with full employment. The vertical dotted line FF is taken to mark the full-employment level of income. In order to reach the policy position, the authorities will seek to effect a shift in the savings function to such a position as $S'S'$, so that it passes through the point P where FF and ZZ intersect.

P, then, represents the policy position, and the question is whether it is stable. According to the principles of the Kaldor model, there is stability at a point on the savings function if the I curve on which it lies slopes less steeply at the point in question than the savings function. Thus, at P, if the relevant curve were I_{d1} there would be stability, whereas if it were I_{d2}, there would be instability.[12]

Which of the two possible positions of the I curve at P, I_{d1} and I_{d2}, is the more plausible, is not immediately apparent from

[12] It is evident from this that the stability of the policy position depends partly on the exact nature of the shift effected by policy in the savings function, a point not treated in the text. If the reduction in the average propensity to save, which is the objective of policy, carries with it also a reduction in the marginal propensity to save, the chances of the policy position being stable are *pro tanto* reduced.

the diagram. The question turns on whether the factors responsible for the flattening out of the curves in their upper reaches are brought into operation primarily by a high level of income or by a high level of investment. In the former case the points at which the curves severally begin to flatten out will stand in an approximately vertical line; the I curve passing through P in Figure 1 will then most nearly resemble I_{d1}, and there will be stability. If, on the other hand, it is a high level of investment which makes the I curves flatten out, the points of inflection will stand roughly horizontal to one another; the I curve at P will then approximate to curve I_{d2}, which yields instability.

It is therefore necessary to look rather more closely into the factors supposed to be responsible for the flattening out of the investment schedule at the top of the boom—in Hicks's terminology, the factors responsible for the existence of the "ceiling." If the principal stress is laid on the appearance of bottlenecks resulting from the approach to full employment, it is perhaps at first sight most natural to think of the ceiling as being imposed by a general shortage of factors of production, and hence as being a function of the over-all level of income rather than of the level of investment. This view is one for which quite a good case can be made. It is, however, subject to the objection that, according to Keynesian theory, general full employment of factors of production is likely to transform the boom into a cumulative inflation of wages and prices rather than to check or reverse its progress. There are a number of possible replies to this objection. Hicks mentions the significance of wage lags: [13] a stabilizing influence may be exerted by the shift to profit which accompanies inflation, since this may, by lowering the marginal propensity to consume, assist in providing the stabilizing increase in savings in real terms, which, once full employment has been reached, can no longer be relied upon to result from increase in the over-all national income.[14] It is likewise quite possible that the approach to full employment will cause costs to be raised and discourage investment, especially if the elasticity of expectations is low, without going to the stage that would threaten out-and-out inflation. These and similar arguments suggest that the possibility

[13] *Op. cit.*, pp. 126-27.
[14] The stabilizing effect of the shift to profits will, however, be subject to qualification insofar as it stimulates extra investment by raising expectations or by providing corporations with additional finance.

of a ceiling created by the approach to general full employment is not to be ruled out. If it corresponds to the facts, the prospects for the policy position being stable are favorable. However the objection mentioned above does have a certain amount of weight, and in that respect the alternative hypothesis that would make the ceiling a function of bottlenecks in the investment industries alone has more to recommend it.

This is, in fact, the view favored by Hicks.[15] He argues that on account of the well-known greater cyclical variability of investment relatively to consumption, the "investment ceiling," imposed by the full employment of factors attached to the investment industries, is likely to be reached before the "consumption ceiling," so that the cost of investment goods relatively to consumption goods will rise in the late stages of the boom, and investment will be discouraged. Now this view avoids the objection mentioned in the last paragraph; but it is subject to certain objections of its own. In the first place, the hypothesis appears to rest on the assumption that the elasticity of demand for investment goods with respect to changes in the ratio of their prices to the prices of consumption goods exceeds unity, which, to say the least, remains to be proved. In the second place, although, as Hicks remarks, a priori reasoning would lead one to expect the prices of investment goods to fluctuate more than the prices of consumption goods, and hence to rise relatively to them in the boom, the empirical evidence can scarcely be said to give this a great deal of support. Mills gives 39 as the measure of the amplitude of reference-cycle fluctuations in the prices of capital equipment in the United States, as compared with a reference-cycle amplitude of 40 in commodity prices generally.[16] The difference between the two is thus negligible, and, such as it is, is in the opposite direction from that suggested by theoretical reasoning. Capital equipment is admittedly not quite the same as "investment goods," but it is sufficiently close for some doubt to be cast by these figures on Hicks's hypothesis.

Let us, however, ignore these objections, and accept for the sake of argument the contention that the investment ceiling constitutes the upper boundary of the cycle. If we simply follow Figure 1 it appears that the policy position will then be unstable, since investment will not be high enough for the investment

15 *Ibid.*, pp. 127-32.
16 F. C. Mills, *Price-Quantity Interactions in Business Cycles* (1946), p. 76.

ceiling to be reached. However, this way of arguing is rather artificial. What we are interested in is not the situation which occurs in actual cycles under *laissez-faire*, but what is likely to occur as a result of a full-employment policy. Now full employment must surely mean a situation in which there is not more than a small amount of slack in either investment or consumption goods industries. Under *laissez-faire*, investment output may still be readily expansible when it is at the moderate level which we are taking as our policy objective; but this is because the investment goods industries and the labor force attached to them are geared to the very high rate of output which they are accustomed to attain at the peak of the boom. Abstracting from transitional difficulties, this would not be the case in the proposed policy position. Therefore if the ceiling is supposed to be created and stability assured by the relative absence of slack in the investment goods industries, the prospects for stability appear not too unpromising. However, if we take seriously the argument that general full employment creates a tendency to cumulative price inflation—this being the main argument in favor of emphasizing the investment ceiling rather than the general ceiling as the upper buffer of historical cycles—we are liable to run into that sort of inflationary instability, applicable only to upwards movements away from the policy position, which is distinct from the cyclical instability we have been mainly concerned with, and which we may call in contrast Wicksellian instability. The danger of instability of this sort would, indeed, on such assumptions be an objection to any full-employment policy.

To summarize the consequences for our present purposes of assigning to ceilings a strategic place in the explanation of the cycle: whether the ceiling is a function of general full employment or of full employment in the investment industries alone, the prospects of avoiding cyclical instability at the policy position are quite good. But if the approach to full employment is really so important in the mechanism of the cycle as the ceiling hypothesis implies, Wicksellian instability in an upwards direction, while admittedly not inevitable,[17] must be a serious threat to any full-employment position. The supposition that it is the sectional investment ceiling, rather than the general ceiling, which is the upper buffer of historical cycles does not help the policy position to avoid Wicksellian instability, unless the full-

[17] See above, pp. 180-81.

employment objective is compromised to an extent sufficient to allow the requisite slack in the consumer goods industries.

However, it cannot be taken as by any means certain that the assumption of a full-employment ceiling as an upper buffer of the cycle corresponds to reality. In addition to the objections already advanced against each of the two particular forms of the hypothesis, there is a more general objection. If the approach to full employment has the significance assigned to it, we should expect to find the rise in prices accelerating to a marked degree in the last stages of the upswing. Now the amount of evidence we have about price movements is more ample than on almost any other aspect of cyclical behavior; and it quite decidedly does not support this contention. Instead we most commonly find that the most rapid rise in prices comes at the beginning of the expansion stage of the cycle; there is then a certain slackening, followed by a more or less steady rise till the peak.[18] It is possible that means can be found to reconcile this result with the ceiling hypothesis; but the observed behavior of prices constitutes a prima-facie objection to the doctrine that it is the encounter with more steeply sloping supply curves which checks and finally reverses the upswing of activity. It remains to be disproved that, even when the economy is running at or near what is thought to be a full-employment level, it still for various reasons retains sufficient slack to avoid both an encounter with a restraining ceiling and the danger of Wicksellian instability, at least as far as temporary increases in effective demand are concerned.

Duesenberry has shown that the rejection of the ceiling hypothesis does not necessarily oblige us to revert to the erratic shocks theory, since the presence of a lower constraint or floor will, despite the absence of a ceiling, be sufficient to prevent the amplitude of the cycle expanding beyond a certain point, even if it is inherently antidamped.[19] It should be pointed out that this possibility is not directly applicable to Figure 1, which is based on the Kaldor model, since in the latter, if there is no ceiling, there will be nothing to stop the boom from expanding ad infinitum. The reason for this is that lags do not enter the model, and therefore, unless the investment function is nonlinear in its upper reaches, there can be no upper turning point. (See p. 172

---

[18] Cf. Wesley C. Mitchell, *What Happens during Business Cycles* (1951), p. 37.
[19] J. S. Duesenberry, "Hicks on the Trade Cycle," *Quarterly Journal of Economics*, 1950, pp. 467-68.

G*

above.) The model can, however, readily be amended in such a way as to admit the possibility of lags and hence of an upper turning point without a ceiling. The upper turning point of historical cycles is then explained simply as in the Kalecki or Hansen-Samuelson models.[20] What does this imply with regard to the stability or otherwise of the policy position? It means that at the policy position there is liable to be instability, not indeed in the most extreme sense that the economy is subject to explosive expansions or contractions, for that would be inconsistent with the proposed explanation of the upper turning point, but in the sense that the economy is prone to antidamped cycles. A small disturbance would not in that case immediately send the system into a fully fledged trade cycle, but it would set in train cyclical fluctuations which would grow in amplitude. Since the policy position, which is the starting point of the system, is assumed to be at or near full employment, there is also obviously the danger of Wicksellian instability if equilibrium is departed from by too great an extent in the upwards direction.

Even the consolation that the system is at least not subject to explosive contractions or expansions (apart from explosions of the Wicksellian type) cannot be entirely relied on. It is possible that historically there has been a tendency not merely to antidamped cycles but to explosions, these being restrained by an upper buffer which is a function of the level of investment in a way quite independent of the investment ceiling and having nothing to do with bottlenecks or full employment. In the absence of a ceiling (*i.e.*, an investment function that flattens out at the top) the upper turning point can be explained only by the assumption of lags in the system, as was noted above. In discussions of this sort where some temporal content is always present and explicit, the concept of lags is essentially a relative one, referring to the speed of one type of adjustment as compared with another. When it is asserted, for example, that the Kaldor model abstracts from lags, what is meant is that it is assumed in that model that such intervals as that between investment decisions and investment, and that between the occurrence of an increase in investment and the rise in incomes to an extent

[20] This view of reality is, of course, not without other difficulties: for example, it provides no answer to one important question which the ceiling hypothesis can explain, at least in principle; namely, why it scarcely ever happens that an ordinary commercial boom reaches the stage of inflation or hyper-inflation. See Hicks, *op. cit.*, pp. 134-35.

sufficient to create *ex ante* savings of the same amount, are short relatively to the time required for changes in the stock of capital to bring about a significant shift in the investment function: relatively, that is to say, to the time required for the *I* curve in Figure 1 to shift significantly. When net investment is very high and the rate of change in the stock of capital correspondingly rapid, the time required for the *I* curve to shift to any given extent is shorter than when net investment is lower. Lags in adjustment which were unimportant when the *I* curve was shifting more slowly now take on a new significance. It is possible that only when net investment is very high—appreciably higher than is planned for the policy position—do adjustment lags assume sufficient importance to bring the cumulative upward movement to a turning point.[21] In that case a small disturbance from the policy position would immediately send the system into a full-scale cycle, and cyclical instability would be complete. This is irrespective of the amount of unemployment of frictional or similar character budgeted for in the policy position.

From the preceding review, it is clear that cyclical instability of varying degrees at the policy position is not at all unlikely, though it is also not inevitable. This is in addition to the Wick-

[21] This may be expressed diagrammatically in terms of the Kaldor model.

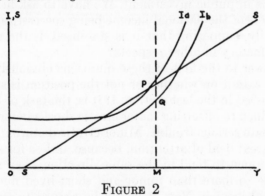

FIGURE 2

In Figure 2 the *I* curves and the *SS* curve bear the same general significance as in Figure 1. The upward instability at *P* is due to the assumption that the increase in incomes caused by the tendency for investment to exceed savings proceeds much more rapidly than any fall there may be in the *I* curve as a result of the high level of net investment. It is assumed, for example, that, by the time income has risen to *OM*, the *I* curve has shifted little if at all downwards from I_a. If instead, when income reached *OM*, the *I* curve had shifted down to I_b, investment would be at the point indicated by *Q* and the cumulative process would be arrested and reversed.

sellian instability which is always a danger to any full-employment position as such. The implications of this will be further
pursued in the next section.

If the authorities are content to sit back and do nothing once
they have brought the policy position into being, there is evidently every likelihood of the cycle recommencing, perhaps not
immediately with full force, but with the danger that full-sized
cycles will develop after no great interval. This, indeed, is much
as one would expect from more elementary considerations. In
place of doing nothing, there are broadly two types of policy
that the authorities may adopt. The first and more radical is for
them to make it their main endeavor to prevent private investment from departing from the desired level in either an upwards
or a downwards direction. Alternatively, they may, while seeking
to reduce the amplitude of fluctuations in private investment as
far as possible, place their principal reliance on compensatory
spending policies designed to stabilize aggregate national income
in default of stabilizing private investment. Let us consider this
latter alternative first.

Suppose that the government sets out to compensate for any
fluctuations that may occur in private investment by contrary
fluctuations in public investment. We have to ask first, what are
the prospects of the national income being successfully stabilized,
and secondly, supposing that it is stabilized, is the result likely
to be satisfactory in other respects?

The answer to the first of these questions obviously turns to a
very large extent on whether or not the position is stable in the
sense discussed in the last section. If it is, the task of the authorities is confined to offsetting major erratic shocks before they have
time to create serious trouble. Minor erratic disturbances will not
require a great deal of attention, because, unless for some reason
they all happen to tend in the same direction, they are unlikely
to give rise to more than minor and short-lived fluctuations in
the national income. Now it would be absurd to suppose that,
even in such relatively favorable circumstances as this, the execution of the policy would not in practice be attended with many
difficulties. But the difficulties would be very much greater if the
system were of a character to produce antidamped cycles, or,
a fortiori, constrained explosions. In that case even the smallest
shock would be capable of leading to large fluctuations, and

would call for immediate remedial action. And if the authorities' compensatory measures were either lagged or too violent, their intervention might well aggravate rather than mitigate the instability of the system.[22]

Supposing that, despite the formidable difficulty of their task, the authorities contrived to react to erratic disturbances with sufficient promptitude and accuracy to prevent major fluctuations in the national income, would all cyclical elements in the system be overcome? If there remained substantial fluctuations in private investment, which required to be offset by contrary fluctuations in government expenditure, there might be stability in the aggregate national income and a high level of employment; but if this high employment were achieved only at the cost of large and continuous structural shifts between the public and the private sectors of the economy, it is debatable whether the result could really be said to constitute full employment as commonly understood, for the elimination of avoidable instability within individual industries is an integral part of a full-employment policy. Moreover, enforced discontinuity in the investment program of the public sector could scarcely fail to react adversely on its social utility.

In all the capital stock adjustment models of the cycle quoted so far in this paper, the elimination of fluctuations in the aggregate national income would prevent fluctuations in private investment; and it might therefore be inferred that the danger mentioned is not a real one so long as the national income is successfully stabilized. But, although this is not what is normally assumed in capital stock adjustment models, it is perfectly possible for lags in the adjustment process to create cyclical fluctuations in an industry independently of fluctuations in the general level of incomes. The ordinary cobweb cycle is the best known case; but probably more important is the modified form of the cobweb cycle that is applicable to the production of durable goods. A model of this sort has sometimes been used to explain the seeming partial independence of fluctuations in the building

---

[22] For a good discussion of this latter point, cf. Goodwin, *loc. cit.*, pp. 465-67. It may be pointed out that Hawtrey's theory of the trade cycle, insofar as it is dependent on lags in the reactions of the monetary authorities to international bullion movements and lags between the taking of decisions by the monetary authorities and the consequent changes in traders' inventory investment, may be regarded as an example of a model in which the intervention of the authorities is in part responsible for the cyclical tendencies of the system.

industry from the general pattern of the business cycle.[23] Departing further from the capital stock adjustment concept, it is clear that innovations are liable to cause substantial fluctuations in investment, even if we do not go the whole way with Schumpeter in assigning to them causal primacy in the business cycles as a whole.

It cannot be considered, therefore, that the policy of offsetting variations in private investment with contrary variations in public spending is altogether satisfactory. Such a policy would no doubt be capable of preventing really catastrophic slumps; but the attainment by these means of stability in the national income might well be extremely difficult, and even if stability in the national income were attained, there might remain fluctuations in private investment necessitating substantial and disturbing structural shifts between the public sector and the private sector.

A case can therefore be made in favor of the alternative and more radical policy of preventing rather than offsetting fluctuations in private investment. This policy does not, of course, necessarily imply the elimination of all variations in private investment. A new invention or the occurrence of an urgent new need might well justify the authorities in sanctioning an increase in investment which would be understood from the first to be of a temporary character,[24] and the appropriate steps would then be required to reduce to the minimum the structural disturbances involved. The amount of flexibility to be allowed on this account would evidently raise some difficult problems for the authorities, who would have to try to steer a middle course between stifling promising innovations by an excessively rigid policy and leaving the door open for the return of unnecessarily disruptive fluctuations by erring in the opposite direction.

It must be recognized that for a policy of this sort to be effective, fairly close control over private investment probably would be required. Interest rate manipulation and similar liberal expedients undoubtedly would not be without effect on the course of private investment, and could with advantage be made use of; but taken by themselves they are subject to some of the same disadvantages as the policy of contracyclical government spend-

[23] Cf. J. Tinbergen and J. J. Polak, *Dynamics of Business Cycles* (1950), pp. 241-45.
[24] Cf. G. Haberler, "Cycles in a Planned Economy," in *Conference on Business Cycles,* Universities-National Bureau Committee for Economic Research (1951), p. 400.

ing already discussed. Their *modus operandi* is essentially to direct private investment *back* to the desired level when it has already shown tendencies to diverge from it; and for this reason both the timing of the measures to be adopted and the magnitude of the stimulus or check to be applied would present great difficulties. A policy of direct control of investment, designed to prevent private investment from diverging from the desired level in the first place, would be free from at least some of these difficulties, whatever its other drawbacks. Such a policy would be easier to execute in face of a threatened increase of private investment above the desired level than it would be as the means of preventing undesirable reductions in private investment, since it is easier to stop entrepreneurs from doing investment they consider profitable than it is to induce them to do investment which they expect to be unprofitable.

This last point raises further issues of some importance. Neither of the two types of policy described (stabilization of aggregate national income and stabilization of private investment) as such imposes on the authorities a persistently inflationary or deflationary role, apart from the initial need to raise the consumption function and/or the normal level of government spending so as to arrive at the policy position. The government's role is simply to offset or prevent departures from the norm in whichever direction they may tend to occur. But if we relax a little the strict assumptions of capital stock adjustment theory, this conclusion is liable to be somewhat altered.

In the first place, the danger of Wicksellian instability is applicable only to disturbances in an upwards direction, since unemployment will serve to prevent this type of instability from developing in a downwards direction. Therefore, particularly if the situation corresponds to that postulated in models where *cyclical* instability does not present a problem, it may be more important, *ceteris paribus,* for the authorities to restrain upwards movements than to restrain downwards movements, since the latter are likely in such a case to be self-righting, whereas the former may not.

In the second place, we may accept the central doctrine of capital stock adjustment theory, that the chief determinant of investment decisions is the relation between the level of income and the quantity of capital equipment in existence, without necessarily maintaining that this is the complete and sole reason why investment is high in the boom and low in the slump. Older writers on the trade cycle were wont to recite a variety of reasons why high investment should tend to be associated with general prosperity and low investment with general depression, and some of these reasons have a certain relevance in the present context. In times of prosperity profits are high and firms can more readily set aside funds with which to finance investment, whether that investment is principally intended to cope with an expansion in demand or to provide the means with which to obtain for the firm an increased share of a constant market. Moreover a generally high level of incomes is likely to cause entrepreneurial expectations to err in the direction of excessive optimism rather than the reverse. For these and similar reasons, it seems plausible to suggest that in the policy position, with income high and the capital stock at an appropriately high level also, private investment might, if left to itself, tend normally to exceed the level required to make good depreciation and to provide for such long-run factors as technical progress and population growth. If so, it again follows that the task of the government would more often be to restrain than to stimulate; private investment would often have to be run on the brake.

This may be an unwelcome conclusion inasmuch as it implies that, for reasons quite unconnected with the wage spiral, the price of full employment may be a permanent danger of inflation. But on the other hand a bias in this direction is not entirely a disadvantage; in one important respect it is likely to make a full-employment policy easier to execute. As has already been pointed out, a policy of direct control would probably be more effective in restraining than in stimulating private investment. Moreover, if the economy is *normally* being run on the brake, the authorities will be in a better position to counter a downward tendency if one should appear. This applies even if direct controls are not the chief means used for the control of private investment; for example, if interest rates paid by borrowers are usually pretty high, it will be easier to check a chance fall in investment by interest rate manipulation than it would be if the usual rate of interest were 2 or 3 per cent.

It is time now for an observation that has probably already occurred to the reader. The results of carrying out the type of policy, which, we have suggested, follows logically from the capital stock adjustment theory of the trade cycle, appear likely to bear a good deal of resemblance to what has actually happened in a good many countries since the end of the late war. Arrears of investment accumulated during the war, high consumption levels due to greater equality of incomes and other causes, and above all military expenditures, have together caused full employment to be maintained in many western countries without private investment proceeding so fast as to threaten general exhaustion of investment opportunities. There can be little doubt that the high levels of government expenditure, and in some cases of consumption, have restrained the expansion of private investment, and so have postponed the prospect of a serious recession. The means by which the expansion of private investment has been restrained have involved various degrees of governmental control and intervention in different countries; but in none has the role of the government been unimportant.

When attention is given to the determinants of the marginal efficiency of capital, as analyzed in the capital stock adjustment theory, the maintenance of a high and steady level of employment is seen to be a much more difficult task than was at one time supposed, and the concept of "a nice balance of over-all supply and demand" becomes an extremely elusive one. According to the argument presented in this paper, the most promising line of approach may require the government to exercise a fairly close control over the volume of private investment, a control which we suggested would most often take the form of restraint, but might also sometimes operate in the opposite direction. If close governmental control over private investment is socially or politically unacceptable, severe slumps can still doubtless be avoided, but continuous full employment may be unattainable. In addition to exercising control over private investment, the government will also, if our analysis is correct, either be obliged itself to be responsible for a large and continuous flow of expenditure, or else will have to bring about a substantial shift in the consumption function. It may be that in the immediate future the problem of rendering a moderate level of private investment consistent with full employment will be more than looked after by rearmament expenditure. But we must not shirk contemplation of the time when this will not be so; otherwise we shall be giving substance to the charge that full employment under capitalism can be assured only by war or preparation for war.

[CHAPTER EIGHT]

Toward a General Nonlinear Macrodynamic Theory of Economic Fluctuations [1]

Shinichi Ichimura

Introduction

IN NO THEORETICAL ANALYSIS of the economic phenomenon called industrial fluctuation, the trade cycle, business cycles, or economic fluctuations, can considerable idealization be avoided. For the process of economic fluctuations involves so many complexities and interdependencies of economic society that it is impossible to understand, much less control, that process without properly abstracting from realities. As J. A. Schumpeter said, "analyzing business cycles means neither more nor less than analyzing the economic process of the capitalistic era." The formidable dimension of this task almost by necessity requires macroscopic theories—an extremely high degree of idealization. The kind of idealizations to be selected and the elements to be omitted or underscored depend on the questions at issue. This dependence of idealization on the relevant questions may not even be unique. There may be and usually are some idealizations or different degrees of idealization even on the same questions to be answered. No theory, therefore, could claim to be *the* theory of economic fluctuations.

Theories of economic fluctuations are what Max Weber called the *idealtypische entwicklungskonstruktion* of the process of economic fluctuations. They could claim the highest value as heuristic measures and serve as means for describing or investigating history. In other words, the historical facts could be examined in the light of the hypothetically adequate causation of theory but

[1] This study was undertaken during the writer's tenure of the Industrial Relations Fellowship at the Massachusetts Institute of Technology. He had the benefit of having the original manuscript read by Professor P. A. Samuelson, and of receiving many helpful criticisms from Professor K. K. Kurihara while completing a final draft. Had it not been for Professor Samuelson's stimulating guidance and Professor Kurihara's patient encouragement, this paper would never have seen the light. Needless to say, any errors or opacity remaining is solely the responsibility of the writer.

could not be explained as the manifestation of the laws enunciated by theory. In this sense, as Professor J. R. Hicks observed, "the place of economic theory is to be the servant of applied economics." What theorists can do is then to consolidate a system of theories and clarify the hypotheses and the causation in each theory.

Theories of economic fluctuations are usually classified as over-investment, underconsumption, monetary, and psychological theories. They point to seemingly different phenomena in the course of economic fluctuations, but actual economic fluctuations probably contain all the phenomena discussed by those theories. In fact, any theory falling within the above categories presents the skeleton and then qualifies it by adding the elements of the other theories. The problems in most controversies are concerned with matters of degree or emphasis, for every theory contains a few grains of truth. What really matters is to make clear the basic differences in hypotheses and causation of each type of theory.

A coherent theory of economic fluctuations must be *determinate* in the sense that it has to involve the same number of equations as the unknowns in the system characterizing an economic model. As Professor R. Frisch pointed out, older theories are not very clear in this respect. And yet most literary theories could often be formulated in terms of some different systems of equations. Thus there is a definite advantage in presenting a cycle theory in terms of a determinate system of equations. It would be unnecessary to argue that such a system must be *dynamic*, because the inter-temporal relationships of the variables involved must come into the analysis in an essential way.[2] Keynes' concern with the trade cycle is clear in his *Treatise* and *General Theory*. The *Treatise* was, as Mr. Harrod suggested, primarily a diagnosis of the trade cycle for the purpose of stabilizing the price level. Though Keynes' direct contribution to trade cycle theories should by no means be minimized, his greatest achievement lies in his analysis of the determination of the level rather than fluctuation of economic activity. Dynamization of Keynesian economics has therefore been one of the major subjects of recent economic discussion, but most of the attempts have been either its literary elaboration or linear dynamic theories.

[2] Cf. R. Frisch, "On the Notion of Equilibrium and Disequilibrium," *Review of Economic Studies*, 1935-36, pp. 100-106; also P. A. Samuelson, *Foundations of Economic Analysis*, 1947, pp. 313-17.

Mathematically, dynamic theories can be formulated in terms of linear functional equations or nonlinear functional equations. They can be purely endogenous or exogenous, or mixed endogenous-exogenous. Pure exogenous theories such as the sunspot theory are of minor importance. Endogenous linear theories are not very satisfactory, for such theories cannot give rise to maintained oscillations with finite nonzero amplitudes—unless the coefficients and the structural relations of the system are just such as to lead to zero dampening between stability and instability, which is infinitely improbable.[3]

There is, however, another more fundamental difficulty in accepting endogenous linear theories. In practice, any mathematical description of structural relations is merely an approximation. The standard procedure of economic theory is to consider an economic system as isolated from other factors of a noneconomic nature and ignore the secondary effects of those factors on the economic system. Hence, whatever is significant in the economic system must remain unchanged when the functional shapes of the equations in the system are slightly changed. Moreover, any variable in the system should not go to infinity, as time passes by. Endogenous linear theories do not satisfy these two a priori restrictions. For a slight change of structural relations will make the system with zero dampening explosive. In general, the economic systems satisfying these two conditions are said to have *structural stability*. It may be said specifically that the economic systems to be analyzed by economic dynamics are the systems with structural stability.[4]

There are only two ways of escape from this difficulty of purely endogenous linear systems. One is to expose the stable linear system to external shocks which may or may not be cyclical in character. This makes the system a mixed endogenous-exogenous one. Whether the system is combined with quasi-oscillatory impulses or with erratic shocks, there will be a great deal to be said for such systems. But we are not concerned with such linear systems here.[5] This paper tries to investigate the matter in an-

[3] Cf. P. A. Samuelson, *op. cit.*, pp. 335-40.
[4] See H. F. DeBaggis, "Dynamical Systems with Stable Structures," in *Contributions to the Theory of Non-Linear Oscillations* (S. Lefschetz, ed.), Vol. II, Princeton Univ. Press, 1952, pp. 37-59. Also see A. Andronow and S. Chaikin, in *Theory of Oscillations*, Moscow, 1937 (English translation, 1949), pp. 183, 337-40.
[5] Cf. R. Goodwin, "Innovations and the Irregularity of Economic Cycles," *Review of Economics and Statistics*, May 1946.

other way; that is, by dropping the assumption of linearity. Any structural relations in economic dynamics can hardly be linear, as a matter of fact. It is only for simplification that linear functions are assumed. It would be enough to recall, for example, the irreversibility of the accelerator in the downswing. As Professor Samuelson has observed, a careful examination of various literary theories would show that they are essentially nonlinear theories.[6] What he called "billiard table theories" offers a class of nonlinear theories.

As early as 1933, a French physicist by the name of LeCorbeiller suggested the possibility of analyzing business cycles by applying the theory of oscillations in nonlinear mechanics which was still in its cradle. Probably owing to the formal difficulties involved in the mathematical solution of nonlinear functional equations, very little had been done before 1950, when a few economists began seriously pondering over this possibility. Their contemplations bore fruit in the subsequent writings of Professors N. Georgescu-Roegen, R. Goodwin, and J. R. Hicks.[7] Even prior to these mathematical arguments, however, Dr. N. Kaldor had presented a neat nonlinear theory of the trade cycle.[8] The present paper is intended as an attempt to explore further the possibility of post-Keynesian nonlinear theories of economic fluctuations, and also to re-examine the well-known classical theories of trade cycles in the light of recent theoretical developments along the lines of nonlinear macrodynamics. As will be shown, most classical theories can be formulated in terms of nonlinear differential equations, and the essential features of those theories can clearly be demonstrated. Finally it will be shown that there is a possibility that the economic system in which most of the elements of various theories coexist may still possess a unique limit cycle.

[6] P. A. Samuelson, *op. cit.*, p. 340.

[7] N. Georgescu-Roegen, "Relaxation Phenomena in Linear Dynamic Models," *Activity Analysis* (T. Koopmans, ed.), 1951; R. Goodwin, "The Non-Linear Accelerator and the Persistence of Business Cycles," *Econometrica*, January 1951; J. R. Hicks, *A Contribution to The Theory of The Trade Cycle*, 1950.

[8] N. Kaldor, "A Model of the Trade Cycle," *Economic Journal*, March 1940. A mathematical formulation of the Kaldor theory was given by Professor T. Yasui, to which contribution the discussion of the present paper owes not the least: T. Yasui, "Self-Excited Oscillations and Business Cycles," *Riron Keizai Gaku*, November 1952 (translated and reprinted in Cowles Commission Discussion Paper, No. 2065).

Nonlinear Accelerator and Relaxation Oscillations

Let us begin by analyzing a simple economic system in which the investment function is nonlinear but in which the saving function is linear:

$$(1.1) \qquad \mu\dot{Y} = I - S$$

$$(1.2) \qquad I = F(\dot{Y}) + \beta$$

$$(1.3) \qquad S = sY - \alpha$$

Here Y stands for national output or real income; I, investment; and S, savings. In (1.1) it is assumed that the rate of change in real income ($\dot{Y} = dY/dt$) is proportional to the difference between investment and savings *ex ante*. $1/\mu$ means, therefore, the speed of adjustment of output per unit of excess Effective Demand. In the investment function (1.2), $F(\dot{Y})$ is the induced investment, and β is the autonomous part of investment which is assumed to be constant. The functional form of $F(\dot{Y})$ is shown in Figure 1. It implies that $F(\dot{Y}) = 0$ for $\dot{Y} = 0$; $F(\dot{Y}) = b\dot{Y}$ for $-\dot{Y}_1 < \dot{Y} < \dot{Y}_2$; $F(\dot{Y}) = b_1 < 0$ for $\dot{Y} < \dot{Y}_1$; and $F(\dot{Y}) = b_2$ for $\dot{Y} > \dot{Y}_2$. The second condition is the normal accelerator, that is, $\dot{Y}$ times the coefficient measuring the optimal relation between the change in capital stock and the change in output. The third condition is due to the fact that output, and hence investment, cannot increase beyond a certain level, which fact deters the uncompleted part of investment. The fourth restriction shows that disinvestment cannot be carried out below depreciation that is assumed to be constant. (1.3) is the linear saving function in which s: the marginal propensity to save, is constant, and α: the autonomous part, is constant and positive.

Induced Investment

The equilibrium level of Y is given by $Y(t) = Y^0$ which makes $\dot{Y} = 0$:

$$(2.1) \qquad Y^0 = \alpha + \beta/s.$$

Accordingly the equilibrium investment and savings are:

$$(2.2) \qquad I^0 = \beta; \qquad S^0 = sY^0 - \alpha.$$

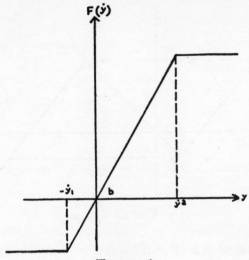

FIGURE 1

Taking the deviations of Y, I, and S from Y^0, I^0, and S^0 respectively, and denoting

(3.1) $$y(t) = Y(t) - Y^0,$$

we have from (1.1,2,3):

(3.2) $$\mu\dot{y} = F(\dot{y}) - sy, \text{ or}$$

(3.3) $$y = \{F(\dot{y}) - \mu\dot{y}\}/s.$$

Since (3.3) involves y and $\dot{y}$ only, it can easily be solved on the phase plane, as shown in Figures 2 and 3. Clearly the origin in

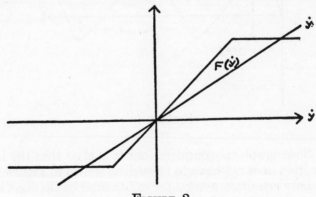

FIGURE 2

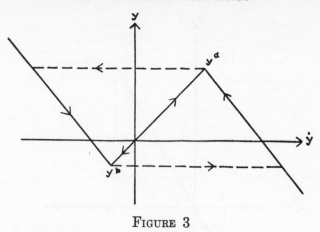

FIGURE 3

Figure 3 corresponds to $Y = Y^0$ and $\dot{Y} = 0$. As the arrows in the diagrams indicate, y must be increasing when $\dot{y} > 0$ and decreasing when $\dot{y} < 0$. When y reaches y^a, it suddenly turns down and starts declining. But when it comes down to y^b, it abruptly goes up again. Thus the cycle repeats itself once it is displaced from the equilibrium point. This is a typical relaxation or self-excited oscillation. (See Figure 4.)

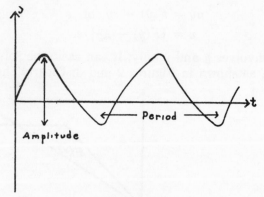

FIGURE 4

From these graphical considerations it is clear that the investment function does not have to be such as shown in Figure 1, and that the only condition needed for self-excited oscillations is that which makes the slope of the investment function steeper around the equilibrium point but less steep around the points far from the origin. It is also obvious that the linear saving function is not necessary, and that the dependence 'of $\dot{Y}$ on $I - S$ may not be proportional, if $\dot{Y}(I - S) > 0$ for $I \neq S$. It is to be noticed that given any initial value of y, the movement of y will sooner or later come back to a unique limit cycle, and that any special explanation of the turning points is unnecessary. The elements to explain . the turning points are built in, as it were. Thus, this cycle has a definite amplitude and a fixed period independent of initial conditions, in short, the *regularity*. Parenthetically, irregularities of cycles may be considered due to external erratic shocks, as illustrated in Figure 5. For erratic shocks may be regarded as shifting the origin of the phase plane.

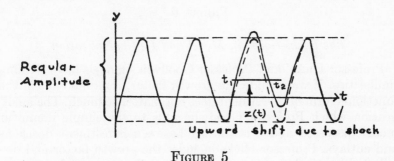

FIGURE 5

The nonlinear accelerator, however, does not necessarily lead to a unique limit cycle. Take, for example, an investment function like that in Figure 6. Here the induced investment becomes less proportional to $\dot{y}$ as soon as $\dot{y}$ becomes negative. Then the solution of the system on the phase plane would be the one given in Figure 6. The equilibrium point (the origin) is stable *in the large*, although in the small it is unstable for the upward displacement and stable for the downward displacement. For when y is displaced upward it goes around a cycle and comes back to stay at the origin. In order to keep cycles alive in this case, constant displacement upward is needed. If there were no growth of effective demand, then the low level of economic activity would, in this case, become chronic. It may be noted here that Professor Goodwin's investment function is of the type indicated in Figure 1, whereas Professor Hicks' seems to have the investment function similar to that in Figure 6.

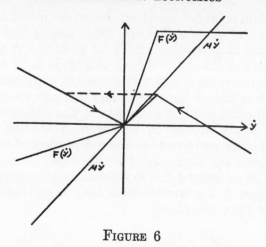

FIGURE 6

The Hicks-Goodwin Model and Its Generalization

Professor Hicks' and Professor Goodwin's models have striking similarities. If we include the growth factor, the difference in the functional form of investment does not matter so much. The modification which Professor Goodwin adds to the simple nonlinear model discussed above is the lag between investment decisions and outlays. Professor Hicks includes the growth factor and distributed lags in his model, and discusses the trade cycle in terms of nonlinear difference equations. Here we shall try to reformulate the Hicks-Goodwin theory in terms of nonlinear differential equations, and then offer a more general theory of the nonlinear accelerator-multiplier. In the light of this generalized model, we shall show that some classical trade cycle theories fall under the category of this nonlinear macrodynamic theory.

Let Y, C, I, and A stand for output (real income), consumption, induced investment, and autonomous effective demand. Then we can write the Hicks-Goodwin model as

$$(4.1) \qquad Y_t = C_t + I_t + A_t$$

$$(4.2) \qquad C_t = (1 - s)Y_{t-h}$$

$$(4.3) \qquad I_t = \varphi(\dot{Y}_{t-\theta})$$

$$(4.4) \qquad A_t = Ae^{g(t-\theta)}$$

where A is a constant, h is the income-expenditure lag, and θ is the lag between investment decisions and outlays and may be assumed to be greater than h. Let us assume that the induced investment function has the following properties:

$$(4.3)' \quad \varphi(\dot{Y}_{t-\theta}) = \begin{cases} b_1 \dot{Y}_{t-\theta} & (b_1: \text{small}) & \text{for } \dot{Y}_{t-\theta} \leqq 0 \\ b_2 \dot{Y}_{t-\theta} & (b_2: \text{large}) & \text{for } 0 < \dot{Y}_{t-\theta} \leqq \dot{Y}_{t-\theta}^m \\ b_3 e^{gt} & (b_3: \text{constant}) & \text{for } \dot{Y}_{t-\theta} > \dot{Y}_{t-\theta}^m, \end{cases}$$

where $\dot{Y}_{t-\theta}^m$ and other constants will be further specified later.

From $(4.1,2,3,4)$ we have:

$$(5.1) \qquad Y_{t+\theta} = (1 - s)Y_{t+\theta-h} - \varphi(\dot{Y}) - Ae^{gt}.$$

Taking the first *two* terms of the Taylor expansion of leading terms, we have

$$(5.2) \qquad \mu\dot{Y} - \varphi(\dot{Y}) - sY = Ae^{gt}, \text{ where}$$
$$\mu = \{s(\theta - h) - h\}.$$

Taking the first *three* terms, we have

$$(5.3) \qquad \nu\ddot{Y} - \mu\dot{Y} - \varphi(\dot{Y}) - sY = Ae^{gt}, \text{ where}$$
$$\nu = \{\theta^2 - (\theta - h)^2(1 - s)\}/2.$$

Needless to say, (5.3) gives a better approximation to the original nonlinear difference-differential equation (5.1).[9]

If it is assumed that [10]

$$(6.1) \qquad b > \mu; \ (\mu - b)g + s > 0, \text{ or}$$
$$(6.2) \qquad b > \mu; \ \nu g^2 + (\mu - b)g + s > 0,$$

then (5.2) and (5.3) will have their respective particular solutions such that they give the moving equilibrium path of $Y(t)$:

$$(7.1) \qquad Y_t^m = Ee^{gt} \qquad [E = A/(\mu - b)g + s] \text{ and}$$
$$(7.2) \qquad Y_t^m = E'e^{gt} \qquad [E' = A/\nu g^2 + (\mu - b)g + s].$$

---

[9] If the time lag, θ, is not short, the solution of (5.1) will not safely be approximated by (5.3). Mr. F. E. Bothwell attempted the approximation of Professor Goodwin's model by means of the equivalent linearization technique and derived very useful and interesting results. (See F. E. Bothwell, "The Method of Equivalent Linearization," *Econometrica*, April 1952, pp. 269-84.) If, however, we could use an electronic analogue computer or differential analyzer, we could directly solve (5.1) after eliminating Ae^{gt} as we shall do. For the discussion of more general nonlinear difference-differential equations, see F. H. Brownwell, "Non-Linear Difference-Differential Equations," in *Contributions to the Theory of Non-Linear Oscillations*, Vol. I, 1950.

[10] The first condition of (6.1) or (6.2) implies the assumptions of Professors Hicks and Goodwin. Professor Goodwin's assumption: $b > s\theta + \epsilon$ is implied if ϵ is understood as $(1 - s)h$. Professor Hicks' difference equation in the elementary case implies $\theta = h = 1$ so that $b > s(\theta - h) + h > 1$.

This gives the value of Y_t^m in (4.3)'.

Define the new variable y_t such that

(8) $$y_t = Y_t - Y_t^m,$$

then (5.2) and (5.3) become respectively

(9.1) $$\mu\dot{y} - F(\dot{y}) + sy = 0$$

(9.2) $$\nu\ddot{y} + \{\mu\dot{y} - F(\dot{y})\} + s\dot{y} = 0$$

Here, if $b_3 > sE$ or SE', $F(\dot{y})$ will have the shape such as given in Figure 7. Since (9.1) is of the same type as (3.2), we can solve

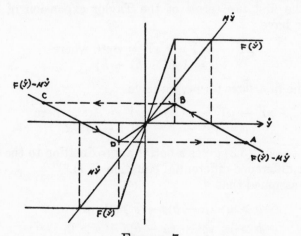

FIGURE 7

it on the phase plane. (See Figure 7.) Thus, it has a unique limit cycle. Output repeats a self-generating cycle $ABCD$.

As for the equation (9.2), the function

(10) $$f(\dot{y}) = \mu\dot{y} - F(\dot{y})$$

is called the *characteristic* of (9.2). If the characteristic is of the form indicated in Figure 7, it is clear that a self-sustained oscillation will occur.[11] This can easily be seen by transforming the

[11] $$\frac{dE}{dt} \equiv \frac{d}{dt}\left\{\frac{1}{2}\dot{y}^2 + \int_0^y \frac{s}{\nu}x\,dx\right\} + \left\{\ddot{y} + \frac{s}{\nu}y\right\}\dot{y} = -\frac{1}{\nu}f(\dot{y})\dot{y},$$

and (the rate of change of the energy in the system) > 0 for $|\dot{y}|$ small enough, $\dot{E} < 0$ for $|\dot{y}|$ large enough. Hence, one should expect the amplitude of y to increase when $\dot{y}$ is small and to decrease when $\dot{y}$ is large. Under this circumstance, a steady vibration of a certain amplitude would occur after some transients die out.

Rayleigh type of equation (9.2) into a *Van der Pol* type of equation. By differentiating (9.2) with respect to t and substituting x for $\dot{y}$, we have

(11) $$\nu\ddot{x} + f'(x)\dot{x} + sx = 0.$$

If $f(x)$ is of the type indicated in Figure 8.1, $f'(x)$ will appear as in Figure 8.2.

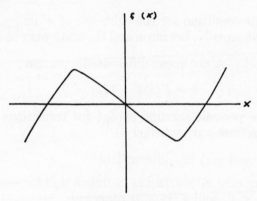

FIGURE 8.1

From the solution of a linear differential equation of the second order with constant coefficients, it is easy to see, by analogy, that the amplitude of x increases or decreases according as $|x|$ is small or large. The interplay of these two counteracting effects might be expected to result in a steady oscillation of a certain amplitude.

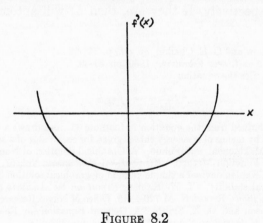

FIGURE 8.2

But the uniqueness of such periodic solutions is not obvious. Nor is the rigorous proof of existence of a limit cycle and its uniqueness very easy. Nevertheless there are a few methods of graphical solution of (9.2) or (11); hence it is not too difficult to decide practically whether a closed solution curve exists or not. The graphical methods known thus far are those of isoclines,[12] the Lienard method,[13] the E-function method,[14] and the Kaplan method.[15]

A sufficient condition for the existence of a unique limit cycle given by Professors N. Levinson and O. Smith may be stated here.

THEOREM I. A nonlinear differential equation:

$$\ddot{x} + f'(x)\dot{x} + g(x) = 0$$

has a unique periodic solution except for transitions in t, if the following conditions are satisfied:

1) $f'(x)$ and $g(x)$ are differentiable.

2) There exist $x_1 > 0$ and $x_2 > 0$ such that for $-x_1 < x < x_2$, $f'(x) < 0$, and $f'(x) \geqq 0$ otherwise.

3) $xg(x) > 0$ for $|x| > 0$.

4) $\lim_{x \to \infty} f(x) = \lim_{x \to \pm \infty} G(x) = \infty$, where $G(x) = \int_0^x g(x)dx$.

5) $G(-x_1) = G(x_2)$.

It may be noted that $f'(x)$ and $g(x)$ are not required to be even and odd respectively. If they are, then 5) will automatically be satisfied.[16]

---

[12] A. A. Andronow and C. E. Chaikin, *op. cit.*, p. 248-52.

[13] J. J. Stoker, *Non-Linear Vibrations*, 1950, pp. 31-36.

[14] This method uses the equation

$$\frac{dE}{dx} = -\frac{1}{\nu} f'(x)\dot{x}$$

which can be derived from the equation in footnote 11, and draws a limit cycle on the (E,x) plane by means of isoenergy curves given for each value of x as a parameter. Cf. Tsumura, Makinouchi, and Fukuo, "A Graphical Solution of Non-Linear Oscillations—the E Function Method," *Kikaigak-kai Ronbunshu*, Vol. 57, No. 17.

[15] Professor W. Kaplan devised a simple method of graphical solution by making full use of structural stability. Cf. W. Kaplan, *Report on the Analysis of Non-Linear Differential Equations*, Report N. M 720-1 R5, Office of Naval Research, April 1947.

[16] Cf. N. Levinson and O. K. Smith, "A General Equation for Relaxation Oscillations," *Duke Mathematical Journal*, Vol. 9, 1942, pp. 382-403.

In (9.2) we may slightly change the corners of the characteristic without loss of substance so as to retain the differentiability of $f'(x)$. Then the first four conditions will be satisfied, but the fifth condition may not be satisfied. This seems to leave a possibility that there may exist two or more stable limit cycles. The graphical solution of our specific equation (9.2) seems to confirm the conjecture that there still exists a unique limit cycle.[17]

The above completes our reformulation of the Hicks-Goodwin theory. Thus, output Y fluctuates around the moving equilibrium path. Some reflection may be made here upon the mechanism of this theory which causes the trade cycle. The *recovery* takes place due to growth, and the *breakdown* occurs because investment

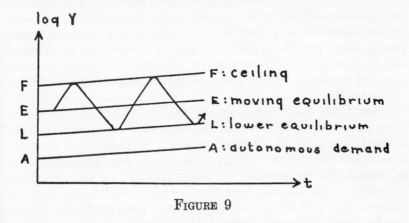

FIGURE 9

cannot exceed a certain level determined by the ceiling of output. The regularity of the trade cycle is maintained because of the fact that the ceiling of output changes parallel with the moving equilibrium path. (See Figure 9.) If the growth of autonomous demand is mainly due to the growth of population, and the ceiling

[17] On the assumption that the minimum point of the damping coefficient is on the positive side of y but otherwise the damping coefficient is of the general form as indicated in Figure 8.2, a spiral starting from a point in the neighborhood of the origin in the phase plane approaches one stable limit cycle. And a spiral from a point far from the origin approaches another stable limit cycle which is outside the first cycle. If nonsymmetricity regarding $f'(x)$ and $g(x)$ is not very great, these two cycles come very close. For practical purposes, therefore, it would be good enough to regard the area encircled by two stable limit cycles as a stable limit cycle zone. The writer did not work on the graphical solution of many cases with different characteristics; it is quite possible to obtain a unique limit cycle even though condition 5) is not satisfied, as was the case with Professor Goodwin's graphical solution.

is primarily determined by the full employment of labor, then there is very little doubt that the various growth rates (AA, LL, EE, and FF in Figure 9) can be approximately the same. But, as Professor Hicks observed, "in cases of constant (or declining) population the possibility of such parallelism is not at all clear."[18] In fact the parallelism will not be maintained unless technological progress or "innovations" is introduced as being in harmony with population growth and capital accumulation, because a large productive factor, land—in the sense of classical economists—is limited. As K. Wicksell indicated,[19] there must be a certain lack of such harmony. This "difference between technical progress and human wants causes a jerk" in the economic system. Owing to the inherent structure of the economic system, such irregular impulses are transformed into quasi-regular cycles. Irregularities of trade cycles, therefore, may best be understood as due to the irregular shocks which produce jerks in the growth of autonomous demand and in the ceiling. It is intuitively obvious, however, that even then the nonlinear system discussed above generates more or less regular cycles.[20]

Apart from the external shocks due to innovations, there are some other factors which restrict the growth of output. As Professor Hicks is aware, the ceiling is not necessarily an absolute upper limit but rather "a fairly wide zone in which the expansion of output will be impeded by real scarcities" or/and monetary constraints. The scarcity of productive factors will begin affecting the economic activity of one industry and then gradually spreading to other industries through the changes of relative prices. Moreover, the monetary factor will also become operative as the level of output rises and the supply of money becomes less elastic.[21] This further inspection immediately suggests a generalization of the Hicks-Goodwin model.

[18] J. R. Hicks, op. cit., p. 96n.

[19] K. Wicksell's lecture before the Norwegian Statsokonomiska Forening, published in Statsokonomiska Tidskrift, 1907, and Ekonomiska Tidskrift, 1924 (quoted by R. Frisch in H. W. Spiegel's The Development of Economic Thought, John Wiley, 1952).

[20] This requires the mathematical analysis of nonlinear stochastic models which is too difficult to be attempted in the present stage of knowledge. See, however, P. A. Samuelson, op. cit., pp. 344-49. For discussions of less difficult linear stochastic models, see R. Frisch, "Propagation Problems and Impulse Problems in Dynamic Economics," Economic Essays in Honor of Gustave Cassel, London, 1933; P. A. Samuelson, ibid., pp. 342-44; R. Goodwin, "Innovations and the Irregularity of Economic Cycles," op. cit.; G. H. Fisher, "Some Comments on Stochastic Macro-Economic Models," American Economic Review, September 1952.

[21] Cf. J. R. Hicks, op. cit., Chap. X.

Considering the gradual shrinkage of the accelerator after a certain level of output, we may write our new induced investment function as

(12) $$I = \varphi(Y_{t-\theta}, \dot{Y}_{t-\theta})\dot{Y}_{t-\theta}, \text{ where}$$

$$\partial I/\partial \dot{Y}_{t-\theta} \begin{cases} b_1\text{: small, for } \dot{Y}_{t-\theta} < 0 \\ b_2\text{: large, for } \dot{Y}_{t-\theta} \geqq 0 \end{cases}$$

$$\partial \varphi/\partial Y_{t-\theta} \leqq 0.$$

Substituting (12) instead of (4.3) into (4), and following the same procedure as we did before, we have

(13.1) $$\{\mu - \psi(y,\dot{y})\}\dot{y} + sy = 0$$

(13.2) $$\nu\ddot{y} + \{\mu - \psi(y,\dot{y})\}\dot{y} + sy = 0,$$

where it is assumed that the moving equilibrium path falls within the zone in which $\partial \varphi/\partial \dot{Y}_{t-\theta} = 0$; y and $\psi(y,\dot{y})$ are the deviations of Y and $\varphi(Y,\dot{Y})$ from the moving equilibrium path.

The equation (13.1) can be solved on the phase plane. Assume, for instance, $\psi(y,\dot{y})$ to be such as shown in Figure 10.1. Then the

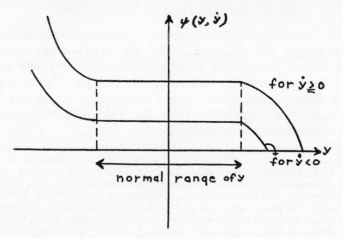

FIGURE 10.1

solution will be given as in Figure 10.2. It should be noticed that the conditions (see equation (12)) constraining $\partial I/\partial \dot{y}_{t-\theta}$ are not at all necessary; the only necessary condition is $\psi(y,\dot{y}) > \mu$ for the normal range of y. The discussion of the equation (13.2) will

H

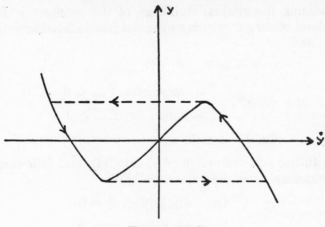

FIGURE 10.2

not be attempted until we reach the final section of this paper, for such a discussion is more fruitful after the subsequent analysis and interpretation of the Kaldor model and other nonlinear models.

The Kaldor Model and its Reformulation

In Dr. Kaldor's theory, the gross investment depends on the *level*[22] of output (Y) and capital stock (K). For a given quantity of real capital, investment depends on the level of profit which in turn depends on the level of activity. But Dr. Kaldor argues that on closer examination neither investment nor saving is a linear function of output (Y). Thus, Dr. Kaldor's investment and saving functions may be written as

[22] Dr. Kaldor rejects the general validity of the "acceleration principle" presumably on grounds similar to those of Professor J. Tinbergen ("Critical Remarks on Some Business-Cycle Theories," *Econometrica*, April 1942), and instead he makes use of a "simpler assumption—*i.e.*, that an increase in the current level of profits [as represented by the level of real income] increases investment demand." (See N. Kaldor, "The Model of the Trade Cycle," *op. cit.*) Professor Hicks in his footnotal reference to Dr. Kaldor's assumption observes that after all, in the Kaldor theory, "a certain amount of what is really 'acceleration' is allowed to go on, as it were, behind the scenes." (See J. R. Hicks, *Trade Cycle*, p. 9n.)

The real difference between these two theorists lies in the fact that Dr. Kaldor, following Dr. M. Kalecki ("A Macrodynamic Theory of Business Cycles," *Econometrica*, III, 1935), takes into account the effect of capital accumulation on investment, whereas Professor Hicks does not, at least explicitly.

Furthermore, in the actual world, investment is more likely to be induced both by the level of output and by the rate of output change. This synthetic view will be elaborated in the last section of this paper.

(14.1) $I = I(Y,K)$

(14.2) $S = S(Y,K)$, where it is assumed

(14.3) $\dfrac{\partial I}{\partial Y} > 0,\ \dfrac{\partial I}{\partial K} < 0,\ \dfrac{\partial S}{\partial Y} > 0,\ \dfrac{\partial S}{\partial K} > 0,$ and $\dfrac{\partial I}{\partial Y} > \dfrac{\partial S}{\partial Y}$

for the normal range of Y.

It seems useful to indicate below Dr. Kaldor's specific reasons for assuming the above functional forms:

(1) Given the amount of real capital, "low levels of activity can be carried out by existing capital so that they will not induce net investment. At the same time, gross investment will not be zero, for there is always some investment undertaken for long-run development purposes which is independent of current activity."

(2) Gross investment is small for unusually high levels of activity, owing to the increasing costs of borrowing and construction, and also to increasing difficulty in both.

(3) "The accumulation of capital, by restricting investment opportunities, will tend to make it [investment] fall." [23] In familiar Keynesian terminology this means that the marginal efficiency of capital tends to decline with the rapid growth of real capital, as it demonstrably does in highly industrial economies.

(4) There is a "customary standard of living" based on the normal level of income, corresponding to which there is the normal rate of saving. Below that level of income, saving will be cut down drastically, and above that level it will be increased considerably. Moreover, during high activity real income is redistributed in favor of profits, thus tending to increase the aggregate propensity to save, while during low activity "an increasing proportion of workers' earnings are paid out of capital funds," thus tending to decrease the aggregate propensity to save. As for the effect of capital on saving, there is, by hypothesis, a positive correlation between saving and capital. But Dr. Kaldor does not give us any convincing explanation of why saving and capital should move in the same direction. [24]

[23] This assumption is, in the history of economic thought, of course associated with the names of Ricardo, Marx, Mill (J. S.), and more recently Keynes, Robertson, and Kalecki.

[24] This assumption of Dr. Kaldor's is at variance with the usual assumption associated with Professor A. C. Pigou $(\partial S/\partial K \leqq 0)$. But we shall later have a chance to use Dr. Kaldor's assumption under a different interpretation. Even though we change to the Pigouvian assumption, it would not make a crucial difference to the Kaldor theory so long as $\partial I/\partial K < \partial S/\partial K$. As a matter of fact Dr. Kaldor alludes to this possibility.

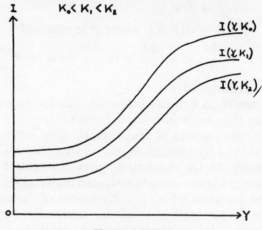

FIGURE 11.1

On these assumptions, investment and saving in (14.1) and (14.2) appear as in Figure 11.1 and Figure 11.2.

Assuming that the rate of change in output is proportional to the difference between investment and saving *ex ante*, we have

$$(15) \qquad \mu\dot{Y} = I(Y,K) - S(Y,K).$$

Whether K is increasing or decreasing depends on the current gross investment *ex post* being below or above the replacement

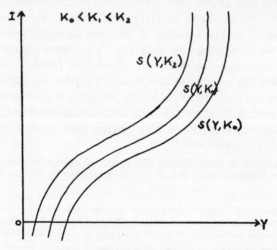

FIGURE 11.2

investment. Suppose that the replacement investment (R) depends on the existing capital stock and the level of economic activity. We then have

(16) $$R = R(Y,K).$$

The long-run equilibrium will be determined by

(17) $$R(Y,K) = I(Y,K) = S(Y,K).$$

The roots of (17) in Y and K: Y^0 and K^0, yield the long-run values of Y and K. From Figure 12 it is clear that this long-run equilibrium is unstable since a slight upward or downward displacement of Y would cause $I > S$ or $I < S$, with the result that Y runs away from the equilibrium point (Y^0,K^0). In Figure 12, there seem to be two other equilibrium points: Y^1 and Y^2, but output cannot stay there, since the increasing or decreasing capital stock due to net investment or net disinvestment shifts the investment and saving functions. So long, however, as the I-curve cuts the S-curve from the left, Y will slowly rise from Y_1 or fall from Y_2; hence one may roughly say that the changes are merely quantitative. But when K crosses certain critical values called "branch points" (or *bifurcations* in Poincaré's terminology), the behavior of Y changes radically; hence the very

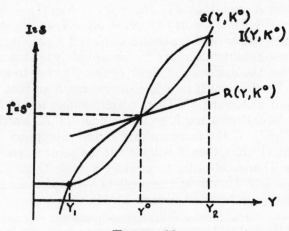

FIGURE 12

qualitative nature of the system changes. All this can be further clarified in terms of the following diagrams.

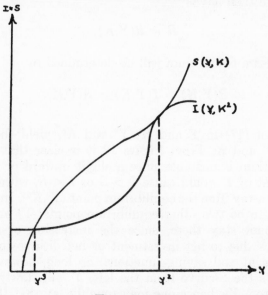

FIGURE 13.1

Considering K as a parameter in $I(Y,K) = S(Y,K)$, we can get the equilibrium values of Y ($\overline{Y}$ in Figure 13.3) corresponding to each value of K. And the branch points of K will be given by the values of K such that $\partial \overline{Y}/\partial K = (I_k - S_k)/(I_y - S_y) = \infty$, where $S_y = \partial S/\partial Y$, $I_y = \partial I/\partial Y$, $S_k = \partial S/\partial K$, and $I_k = \partial I/\partial K$. These branch points of K are shown as K_1 and K_2 in Figure 13.3.[25]

From these considerations we can immediately tell the necessary condition for the existence of limit cycles. That is to say, when Y reaches Y^2, there must be a force increasing K so that Y^2 drops rapidly from Y^2 toward Y^3. Then, corresponding to (Y^3,K^2) there must be a force decreasing K so that a point (Y,K) slowly moves toward (Y^1,K^1). If the force making K fall disappears before or at the point (Y^1,K^1), then Y will stay at the point where the force disappears. Hence, in order to produce a cycle there must be a force to decrease K even at the point (Y^1,K^1). If there is, Y will abruptly jump up from Y^1 toward Y^4.

[25] The discussion of what happens at the multiple points of $I = S$ may be carried quite far, but this need not be done here since such cases do not seem likely to occur in practice.

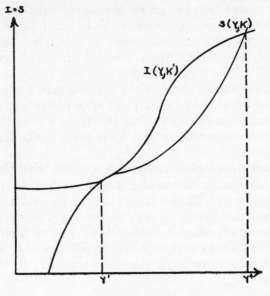

FIGURE 13.2

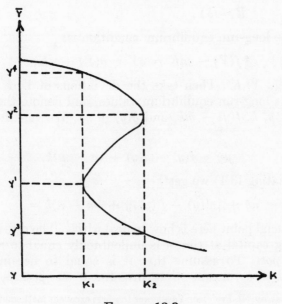

FIGURE 13.3

All this means that the gross investment equal to replacement or depreciation must lie between (Y^2, K^2) and (Y^1, K^1). In other words, the replacement investment at any point between these two should be smaller than $I = I(Y^2, K^2)$ and greater than $I = I(Y^1, K^1)$. The former condition is very likely to be satisfied but the latter may not hold. Then the economic system will settle down at the lower equilibrium point with possibly chronic under-employment. If we assume with Dr. Kaldor that this does not happen, then the existence of a limit cycle in the Kaldor model is guaranteed.

The above topological analysis has to do with the necessary conditions for the existence of a *unique* limit cycle. It is not yet certain whether the Kaldor theory has or has not a unique limit cycle. To see this clearly, it may be necessary to reformulate the Kaldor theory on simpler assumptions. Let us therefore try to formalize Dr. Kaldor's theory analytically so as to simplify the forms of functions to some degree. Assume I, S, and R to be of the forms:

(14.4) $I = \varphi(Y) - mK$ $(m > 0)$

(14.5) $S = \psi(Y) + nK$ $(m > n \geqq 0)$

(16.1) $R = \delta Y.$

Hence the long-run equilibrium condition is:

(17.1) $f(Y) - mK = \delta Y = g(Y) + nK,$

which yield Y^0, K^0. Then take the deviations of Y, K, I, and S from their long-run equilibrium values, and denote them respectively by y, k, $f(y) - mk$, and $g(y) + nk$. We can then rewrite (15) as

(15.1) $\mu\dot{y} = f(y) - g(y) + (n - m)k.$

Differentiating (3.1) we get[26]

(15.2) $\mu\ddot{y} + \{g'(y) - f'(y)\}\dot{y} + (m - n)\dot{k} = 0$

The crucial point here is how to deal with $\dot{k}$. The rate of increase of existing capital at time t is undoubtedly equal to net investment *ex post*. To assume that it is equal to net investment: $f(y) - mk - \delta y$ means that investment *ex post* is equal to

[26] Cf. T. Yasui, *op. cit.* Professor Yasui gave the first excellent mathematical formulation of the Kaldor theory on the assumption that $S = sY$, $R = \delta K$.

investment *ex ante*, whereas $k = g(y) + ny - \delta y$ implies that saving *ex post* is equal to saving *ex ante*. The first hypothesis will make the movement of y along the investment curve, whereas the second will make it along the saving curve. For simplicity we shall adopt the second hypothesis and assume that the capital accumulation over a cycle is zero: $\int k\,dt = 0$.[27]

Then we have

(15.3) $$\ddot{y} + F'(y)\dot{y} + G'(y) = 0, \text{ where}$$

$$F'(y) \equiv \frac{1}{\mu} \{g'(y) - f'(y) - \mu n\}$$

$$G'(y) \equiv \frac{1}{\mu} \{n[f(y) - \delta y] + m[g(y) - \delta y]\}$$

Notice that equation (15.3) is the *Van der Pol* type of nonlinear differential equation which we discussed in the third section of this paper. Now the question is whether or not it has a unique periodic solution. Following the argument in that section, we know that if $g'(y) > \mu n$ and $f(y)$ is of the type indicated in Figure 12, then the characteristic $F'(y)$ is of the form given in Figure 8.2. By graphical solution we could obtain limit cycles. As we discussed before, there may or may not be a unique limit cycle.

The period of the cycle can be calculated by

(18) $$T = \int dt = \int dy/v, \text{ where } v = \dot{y},$$

and the integral is taken along the closed integral curve in the direction of increasing t. By observing (15.1) and (18) it is clear that the larger the value of μ is, the longer will be the period of the cycle. Thus we may assert that the slower the adjustment of output is, the longer will be the period of the cycle. The amplitude will also be decreased, for larger μ makes y smaller for any time; the time lag has damping effect. It can be seen, too, that the greater the value of m, the smaller will be the amplitude.

---

[27] In the first case, the gap must be filled with the decumulated or accumulated stocks. There is no reason to believe that the decumulation during the upswing will be cancelled out exactly by the accumulation in the downswing of a cycle. In the second case, existing stocks will be unchanged. A third alternative would be to assume that k is equal to some value between planned investment and intended saving: $k = \sigma\{f(y) - mk\} + (1 - \sigma)\{g(y) + nk\}$, where σ is determined so as to make the sum of k over a cycle equal to zero: $\int k\,dt = 0$. This is the most proper assumption to make.

H*

The effects of the changes in the forms of I and S curves can be observed from Figure 13. Similar remarks could be made *mutatis mutandis* for the Hicks-Goodwin theory.

Now the nature of the Kaldor theory is very clear. Its essence lies in the facts that I is nonlinear and that K has counteracting effects on I. If it were not for those latter effects, the system would stay at one of the stable equilibrium points. Compared with the Hicksian theory, it is purely an endogenous model and does not depend on the growth factor at all. But earlier we showed that the system may not come out of the lower equilibrium level, if the depreciation is exceeded by gross investment in the neighborhood of the lower branch point. This possibility is very great in an economy where constant autonomous investment is large. Then a question may be posed: What happens if the growth factor is imposed on the Kaldor model? This can be analyzed in the same way as we did in connection with the Hicksian theory, provided that the ceiling or the level of activity where the tapering-off of investment occurs shifts upward consistently with autonomous investment. In such a growing Kaldor system, the difficulty with the Kaldor theory mentioned above would disappear. The cycle could then be seen as repeating itself around the moving equilibrium path in such a system.

A General Nonlinear Macrodynamic Theory of Economic Fluctuations

From the above discussion of the Kaldor theory and the Hicks-Goodwin theory, a mechanism which produces a limit cycle can be seen emerging in the form of a combination of a nonlinear investment function and investment-depressing factors. In the Hicks-Goodwin theory, the accelerator is combined with the depressing effect of real scarcity at high levels of output, whereas in the Kaldor theory a nonlinear investment function is conflated with the counteracting influence of capital accumulation. The former has very much to do with familiar "overinvestment" theories. Apart from their unfortunate reliance upon Say's Law, Tugan-Baranowsky, Spiethoff, Wicksell, and Professor Hayek seem to agree that as output advances to a very high level, the shortage of productive factors including skilled labor is bound to prevail and spreads itself through the changes in relative prices due to disproportionate productive activities in various industries. What Aftalion calls the *théorie de l'épargne*, or otherwise known as "undersaving" theories, emphasizes that the exhaustion of past savings during the boom raises the rate of interest to entail deficient investment, while the accumulated savings during the downswing lower the rate of interest to stimulate excessive investment. By contrast, the overinvestment theories of the Spiethoff variety are more inclined to stress the difficulty due to *real* factors as primarily responsible for the downturn and to regard the shortage of money capital as aggravating that "real" difficulty. As a matter of fact this appears to be the position taken not only by Spiethoff and Wicksell but, more recently, by Professors Harberler and Hicks, Mr. Harrod,[28] Mrs. J. Robinson, and many others. Thus it is clear that the Hicks-Goodwin theory covers much of the territory familiar to the student of traditional overinvestment-undersaving theories.

It may be of some interest to note that the Kaldor theory is flavored with the color of underconsumption theories, for in that theory the oversaving of the past which made capital accumulation possible is what causes the breakdown of an uncontrolled boom. Somewhat akin to underconsumption theories is another group of economists who explain the breakdown on a different basis. Aftalion, Schumpeter, Foster and Catchings, Professors D. H. Robertson and A. C. Pigou thus emphasize the fact that the upper turning point occurs when the roundabout process of production started during the upswing is completed and when the resulting output begins to pour out into unsuspecting markets. If excess supplies occur with respect to consumption goods, then the deficiency of consumption demand characterizes the early phase of the downswing. If, on the other hand, capital goods pour out of new production processes, then overinvestment relative to the current demand for capital goods is characteristic of the upper turning point. In what follows immediately we shall endeavor to formulate these types of theories in more rigorous terms.

The formulation of this theory, however, involves two con-

---

[28] Cf. R. F. Harrod, *The Trade Cycle*, Oxford, 1936. Mr. Harrod's cycle theory is really a forerunner of the Hicks-Goodwin type of nonlinear macrodynamics, though he presented it verbally. Mr. Harrod combines the multiplier and the accelerator, which latter is made nonlinear by reason of the following effects of the changes in the level of output on the acceleration coefficient: (1) the influence of the rising rate of interest in the upswing and that of the falling rate in the downswing; (2) the changes in the relative prices of capital goods; and (3) the variations in profitability due to the law of diminishing returns and the elasticity of demand.

ceptual problems to be noticed at the outset. The first of these is whether the Kalecki-Kaldor type of investment function or the investment function based on the acceleration principle should be assumed. The second is the treatment of the time lag; that is, the gestation period. Aftalion tends to discuss investment demand in terms of the acceleration principle, whereas Professor Robertson seems to think that such a relation may be very loose. For the moment, let us assume an investment function of the Kaldor type. Although the full treatment of the gestation period cannot be attempted here, we may, as a first approximation, assume that the investment made at time $t - \theta$ (θ: the gestation period) increases *capital equipment available for production* at time t, and that not only the increase of existing capital, as in the Kaldor theory, but also that of *capital available for production* exercises an investment-depressing effect. On this supposition, we may write our new investment function as:

$$(19) \qquad I = f(Y) - mK - p(K - \theta \dot{K}),$$

where $(K - \theta \dot{K})$ is an approximation to $K_{t-\theta}$ and p is a positive constant. It should be noticed that the above hypothesis involves two unsatisfactory aspects of the treatment of the gestation period. In the first place, it does not consider the gestation period as a period in which some investment plan is made at the beginning of the period and in which the investment so planned is carried out subsequently and completed all at once at the end of the period. In the second place, the application of the same formula to the downswing implies that disinvestment at time t decreases the quantity of capital available for production at time $t - \theta$. This is apparently inadequate because there should not be any time lag in this case. Despite all these defects, we may still claim that the hypothesis does take into account the effect of the gestation period better than any other models so far presented. As for S, K, $\dot{K}$, $\dot{Y}$, and replacement investment, we assume the same conditions as we did before in connection with the Kaldor model. Denoting the deviations of Y, I, S, K, and replacement from their long-run equilibrium values by the same symbols as in the Kaldor model, we have

$$(20) \qquad \mu \ddot{y} + F'(y)\dot{y} + G'(y) = 0, \text{ where}$$
$$F'(y) \equiv \{p\theta[g'(y) - \delta] + g'(y) - n\mu - f'(y)\}$$
$$G'(y) \equiv (m + p)\{g(y) - \delta y\} + n\{f(y) - (1 - \theta p)\delta y\}$$

The formal similarity of this nonlinear equation to the equation in the Kaldor model is very clear. We need, however, the larger slope of the investment function in the neighborhood of the long-run equilibrium; that is, $F'(y) < 0$. If this holds, our generalized Kaldor model can have a limit cycle. The Kaldor model so generalized covers many grounds of overinvestment theories in which the investment function is based on the profit principle rather than the acceleration principle (*e.g.*, in the models of Professor Tinbergen and Dr. Kalecki and in some models of Dr. L. R. Klein), but there exists the gestation period, regardless of whether capital accumulation has a depressing effect on investment or not.

At this juncture a question arises whether or not it is possible to formulate such a general theory as would include both types of nonlinear theories (based on the acceleration principle *and* the profit principle). The answer is that in some limiting cases the synthesis can be done within the mathematical knowledge of the present paper, as will be demonstrated subsequently.

Suppose an economic system in which there are two groups of industries, one of which is of the Kaldor type based on the profit principle and the other of the Hicks-Goodwin type based on the acceleration principle. Suppose, further, that investment in both of these industries is measured in *net* terms but includes the intra-transactions of capital goods within each group of these industries. (See Figure 14.)

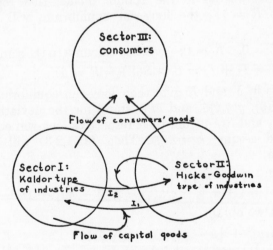

FIGURE 14

We now assume that the first of these two groups of industries, that is, of the Kaldor type, makes up a part of total investment (I_1), and the second, that is, of the Hicks-Goodwin type, therefore, the rest (I_2). This division of total investment may vary as the level of output changes. In addition to the same hypotheses as we made in our generalizations of the Hicks-Goodwin and Kaldor models, we assume that the speed of output adjustment in Sector I is the same as that in Sector II. For simplicity, moreover, we shall assume that there is no effect of capital accumulation on saving. But we consider three time lags: the investment planning period, the income-expenditure lag, and the gestation period. The first one refers to the time lag between the decision-making of investment and the actual order of the investment demand; this time lag is assumed to be equal to the income-expenditure lag (ϵ) but shorter than the gestation period. Lastly we neglect the growth factor to simplify the argument. Then such an economic system will be characterized by the following system of equations:

(21.1) $\mu \dot{Y}_{t+\epsilon} = I_1 + I_2 + S$

(21.2) $I_1 = \varphi(Y) - mK - p[K - (\theta - \epsilon)\dot{K}]$

(21.3) $I_2 = \psi(Y, \dot{Y})\dot{Y},$

where p, θ, m, μ, K, and S are used in the same senses as before. Assuming, as we did in the Kaldor model, that replacement investment $R = \delta Y$, the long-run equilibrium will be determined by

(22.1) $\dot{Y} = 0, \quad \dot{K} = 0,$ or what amounts to the same,

(22.2) $I \equiv I_1 + I_2 = S \equiv S(Y) = R \equiv \delta Y,$

whose roots in Y and K give their long-run equilibrium values. Let y, k, $f(y)$, $g(y, \dot{y})\dot{y}$, and $h(y)$ stand for the deviations of Y, K, $\varphi(Y)$, I_2 and $S(Y)$ from their respective long-run equilibrium values, and assume $\dot{k} = h(y)$. Then (21.1,2,3) will be transformed into:

(23.1) $\mu\epsilon\ddot{y} + \{\mu - g(y, \dot{y})\}\dot{y}$
$\qquad\qquad + \{(1 + \theta - \epsilon)h(y) - f(y) - \delta y\} + (m - p)k = 0,$

from which we obtain

(23.2) $\begin{cases} \mu\epsilon y^{(3)} + \{\mu - g(y, \dot{y}) - g_v(y, \dot{y})\}\ddot{y} \\ + \{(1 + \theta - \epsilon)h'(y) - f'(y) - g_v(y_1, \dot{y}) - \delta\}\dot{y} \\ + (m + p)\{h(y) - \delta y\} = 0, \end{cases}$

where $g_\nu = \dfrac{\partial g}{\partial y}$, and $g_y = \dfrac{\partial g}{\partial y}$.

It is apparent that this equation (23.2) contains most trade cycle theories as special cases. Then the question arises as to whether such a general theory produces a limit cycle. For the establishment of this general theory, it is most important to analyze the solution of (23.2) in rigorous mathematical terms and to envisage the behavior of the economic system represented by the equation. Let us begin with the analysis of a simple case. Suppose that the Hicks-Goodwin type of industries is predominant in the system, and that the impact of the gestation period is negligible. Then we may safely assume $0 = m = p = f(y)$. Hence, we have from (23.1):

$$(23.3) \qquad \mu\epsilon\ddot{y} + \{\mu - g(y,\dot{y})\}\dot{y} + h(y) = 0.$$

It should be remembered that formally this is also the equation (13.2) given for generalized Hicks-Goodwin theory. From the qualifications to the above general theory it is easy to see what is left out in the Hicks-Goodwin theory. We now attempt the mathematical analysis of this equation (23.2). For such a general equation of relaxation oscillations, Professors Levinson and Smith gave the following system:[29]

THEOREM II. Equation:

$$\ddot{x} + \phi(x,\dot{x})\dot{x} + G'(x) = 0,$$

has a limit cycle if the first group of conditions is satisfied, and has a unique limit cycle if the second group of conditions is satisfied.

Conditions for existence:

1) $xG'(x) > 0$ for $|x| > 0$.

2) $G(\pm\infty) = \infty$.

3) $\phi(0,0) < 0$.

4) There exist some $x_0 > 0$ such that $\phi(x,\dot{x}) \geqq 0$ for $|x| \geqq x_0$.

---

[29] Levinson-Smith, *op. cit.* Their Theorems I and III are combined into Theorem II here.

5) There exist an M such that for $|x| \leqq x_0$, $\phi(x,\dot{x}) \geqq -M$.

6) There exist some $x_1 > x_0$ such that

$$\int_{x_0}^{x} \phi(x,\dot{x})dx \geqq 10Mx_0,$$

where $\dot{x} > 0$ is an arbitrary decreasing positive function x in the integration.

Conditions for uniqueness:

7) There exist an $x_1 > 0$ and an $x_0 > 0$ such that $\phi(x,\dot{x}) < 0$ for $-x_1 < x < x_0$ and $\phi(x,\dot{x}) \geqq 0$ otherwise.

8) $\dot{x} \dfrac{\partial \phi}{\partial \dot{x}} = 0.$

9) $G(-x_1) = G(x_0).$

If the investment function $g(y,\dot{y})\dot{y}$ is of the general character which we discussed at the end of the third section, then the first eight conditions in Theorem II are likely to be satisfied so that the system (23.3) will have at least one limit cycle. Since, however, the last condition may not hold, the existence of one unique limit cycle is not certain. There remains a possibility of multiple limit cycles. It would be unnecessary to argue again about the case in which the Kaldor type of industries is more predominant. As we discussed before, such a system has a limit cycle which may or may not be unique.

As for the general equation (23.2), there does not seem to be any established theorem, that is, to the writer's knowledge. Nevertheless the above analysis of two special cases seems to allow a conjecture that such a general system has also at least one limit cycle. We can merely offer a mathematical conjecture and an economic argument which suggest a possible existence of a stable limit cycle. Mathematically, it can easily be seen that the amplitude of y cannot become infinite. This is so because for the large values of $|y|$, it may be assumed $g = g_v = g_y = f' = 0$ so that all the coefficients of $\dddot{y}$, $\ddot{y}$, $\dot{y}$ may be regarded as positive constants. Moreover, $h(y)$ for large values of $|y|$ may safely be approximated by $sy - \alpha$ (s and α: positive constants), and most likely $(1 + \theta - \epsilon)(s - \delta)\mu - \mu(m + p)(s - \delta)$; namely, $1 + \theta + \epsilon p > \epsilon(m + 1)$. If these conditions hold, then the Routh-Hurwitz theorem tells us that the system is asymptotically stable. Thus the amplitude of y is finite. On the other hand, for the small values of $|y|$, the coefficients of $\ddot{y}$ and $\dot{y}$ are negative so that the system is asymptotically unstable in the neighborhood of singular points. By our hypothesis that there exists the long-run equilibrium of Y and K, $(\ddot{y} = 0,\ \dot{y} = 0,\ y = 0)$ is a unique singular point for the equation (23.2). Thus, an ordinary point in the three-dimensional phase space, if located in the neighborhood of the origin, must run away therefrom but stay within the finite value of y. Since, moreover, we may assume the structural stability of the system, the ordinary point will have at least one stable cycle in its infinite future. We cannot say any more than a conjecture. But the two counteracting tendencies mentioned above may be expected to result in a steady motion to which an ordinary point in the neighborhood asymptotically approaches. Needless to say, there may be, and most likely will be, multiple limit cycles.[30]

Economically, the existence of a limit cycle may be seen in the following way. (See Figure 15.) Suppose that the economic system is slightly displaced upward from the long-run equilibrium point. Then the upward movement of y will be much more rapid than the simple Kaldor model because the accelerator intensifies the effect of I_2. But sooner or later the high level of economic activity will lower the accelerator coefficient so that y will come to the upper equilibrium point; for example, to A' in Figure 15. The depressing effect of capital accumulation will, however, cause the breakdown. In the downswing the system behaves as the Kaldor model does, for the accelerator is very small. The movement of y in Figure 15 will be roughly from A' to A and then to B (the upper branch point). If there is net investment at B, then y will rapidly shift to C' in Figure 15, owing to the downward shift of the I-curve caused by the depressing effect of capital accumulation and the small accelerator at work. If there is net disinvestment at C', then the Kaldor type of investment function will turn up

[30] The interested reader may try to analyze a nonlinear equation of the third order:
$$y^{(3)} + f(y,\dot{y})\ddot{y} + g(y,\dot{y})\dot{y} + h(y) = 0,$$
on which at least the following conditions may be imposed:

1) $f,\ g,\ h$ are all differentiable;
2) $h(y)y > 0$ for $|y| > 0$;
3) at least one of $f(0,0)$ and $g(0,0)$ is negative and finite;
4) $\dfrac{\partial f}{\partial v} \cdot v \geqq 0,\ \dfrac{\partial g}{\partial v} v \geqq 0$, where $v = \dot{y}$.

Such a mathematical analysis will be most welcome.

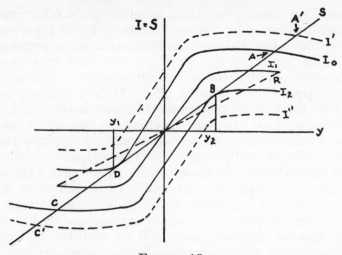

FIGURE 15

the movement of y. Here the strong accelerator becomes operative. The upswing of y carries it away to A' in Figure 15. Thus there will result a self-generating cycle. Though the lower branch point D in Figure 15 does not appear to play its role as it did in the Kaldor model, such actually is not the case. For if there is no net disinvestment at D, and given the initial condition such that $\dot{y} < 0$ and y is slightly above y_1 in Figure 15, then the system may settle down at a lower level of output.

Now the condition necessary for the existence of a limit cycle is clear; that is, replacement investment between two branch points is less than the corresponding values of I_2. But the existence of a unique limit cycle is by no means certain. If there are some stable limit cycles, that implies something interesting about the behavior of the economic system. For an external impulse will shift the cyclical movement of output to another stable cycle. In such a system, output fluctuations will be more irregular than in a system with a unique limit cycle. (See Figure 16.1 and Figure 16.2.) This completes a tentative analysis of our general nonlinear macrodynamic model of economic fluctuations.

We have certainly come a long way toward establishing a general theory in the course of exploring the possibility of constructing nonlinear macrodynamic theories. So long, moreover, as we remain in the domain of macrodynamic trade cycle theories in which we deal with total investment, savings, and output, this seems to be almost as far as we can go. Though the introduction of distributed lags will further complicate the model and will thereby make it more realistic, it would not alter the essence of our main argument. The only possibility to be exploerd further in

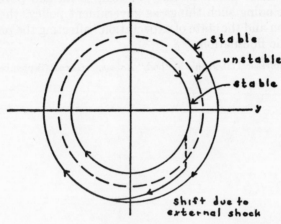

FIGURE 16.1

nonlinear macrodynamics would be that of exposing this general theory to random shocks. Even apart from such a theoretical possibility, the analysis of a general model attempted in the present paper is undoubtedly far from complete. All the same it poses a problem whose more rigorous solution must continue to occupy

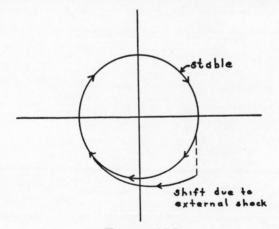

FIGURE 16.2

the minds of all those seriously concerned with the phenomenon of economic fluctuations and with their stabilization.

We may conclude this highly formal discussion by reminding ourselves of Keynes' allusion to the possible causal significance of such broader problems as "political, social and psychological factors including such things as government policy, the progress of invention and the state of expectation" affecting the phenomena of economic fluctuations.[31]

[31] See his "Professor Tinbergen's Method," *Economic Journal*, September 1939.

[CHAPTER NINE]

Net Investment and Industrial Progress

Anatol Murad

CAN AN INDUSTRIALIZED ECONOMY continue indefinitely to invest in additional capital, or is there some long-run limit beyond which net investment is impossible?

This is the central question with which this essay deals. In addition, it attempts to answer two derivative questions: Must capital accumulation cease if there is no net investment? And must industrial progress languish in the absence of capital accumulation?

Traditional economics has answered the second and third questions affirmatively, but optimistically held that net investment would continue indefinitely as long as man develops new labor-saving machines and new wants.[1] The thesis developed in this paper reverses the answers. Net investment must come to an end; but cessation of net investment will be shown to be no barrier to continued capital accumulation and industrial progress.

That net investment would cease in the long run—and in a rather short long run at that—was set forth by John Maynard Keynes in the *General Theory*. In a "properly run," fully employed community, Keynes held, the marginal efficiency of capital should fall "approximately to zero within a single generation," and net investment consequently come to an end, "so that we should attain the conditions of a quasi-stationary community. . . ."[2]

But why should this happen? Keynes argued that the marginal efficiency of capital would drop to zero, and net investment consequently cease, because equipment would be accumulated until there is too much of it.[3] This explanation, however, only transfers

[1] See, for instance, Alfred Marshall, *Principles of Economics*, 8th Edition (London, Macmillan, 1930), pp. 222-23.

[2] John Maynard Keynes, *The General Theory of Employment, Interest and Money* (New York, Harcourt, Brace and Company, 1936), pp. 220-21.

[3] *Ibid.*, p. 217: ". . . capital has to be kept scarce enough in the long-period to have a marginal efficiency. . . ." Again, on p. 221: ". . . to make capital-goods so abundant that the marginal efficiency of capital is zero. . . ."

the question to the next level of analysis. In what sense, in relation to what, is there "too much" equipment? Although Keynes gave no specific answer,[4] the general tenor of his analysis suggests that he viewed deficiency of aggregate demand as the ultimate limiting factor.[5] But this argument is not admissible if a full-employment equilibrium is assumed to be the starting point, since in that case aggregate demand cannot be deficient. This is not to say that Keynes was wrong in expecting investment to cease in the long run, but only that he was too preoccupied with the short run to give a clear and satisfactory explanation for this secular atrophy of investment. Such an explanation is attempted in the following section.

A simple example may help to show why net investment must eventually cease. One hundred workers equipped only with simple tools, but with knowledge of modern industrial processes, are marooned on an island endowed with all the materials required by an industrial economy such as the workers would be capable of operating. For convenience, it is further assumed that population and technical knowledge remain unchanged.

Immediately upon arrival on the island the workers organize their productive efforts for the first year by forming two groups: an *operating force* to provide the community with consumers' goods and an *expansion force* to build capital equipment and thus expand production facilities. The relative sizes of the two forces depends on the community's willingness to "tighten the belt" in the present in order to assure itself of a larger income in the future, *i.e.*, on their propensity to consume. Assuming the average propensity to consume to be constantly 0.5,[6] 50 workers are allocated to the expansion force, the other 50 to the operating force.

During the first year the expansion force constructs a quantity of capital equipment equal to one "plant." This plant, available for use by the operating force at the beginning of the second year, is assumed to require 25 workers to operate, maintain and currently replace it.[7]

---

4 See Evsey D. Domar, "Expansion and Employment," *Amer. Econ. Rev.*, Vol. XXXVII, No. 1 (March 1947), p. 53.

5 Keynes, *op cit.*, p. 105, *et passim.*

6 This figure is assumed only to facilitate the argument.

7 Maintenance and replacement of capital is part of the process of current consumers' goods production. The cost of maintaining and replacing capital (depreciation) is, therefore, a part of the cost of consumers' goods output. Capital, once

In the second year the expansion force, still composed of 50 workers, continues to produce capital. Of the 50 workers in the operating force, 25 must be allocated to the plant completed at the end of the first year, while the remaining 25 workers continue to produce consumers' goods without benefit of capital.[8] At the beginning of the third year two plants are available for use by the operating force, each claiming 25 workers for operation (including maintenance and replacement). The entire operating force is thus required to run the two plants during the third year. The expansion force, unchanged at 50 workers, meanwhile adds a third plant to the community's productive equipment.

In the fourth year the allocation of workers must be changed. The three plants now available call for an operating force of 75 workers, leaving only 25 workers for the expansion force. In the fifth year the operating force must again be increased to utilize the additional half plant produced in the fourth year, and the expansion force correspondingly reduced. Ultimately all 100 workers must be included in the operating force and the expansion force must vanish. At that stage, under the conditions assumed, no further additions to capital could possibly increase the community's present or future capacity to produce. Capital accumulation would have reached the saturation point. New capital could be created only at the cost of abandoning existing capital of equal efficiency. Any diversion of labor from the operating force to the expansion force would therefore constitute a permanent loss to the community.[9]

What are the implications of all this as to saving and investment, if the workers receive money incomes? Net investment and saving are inextricably linked to the expansion force. Net investment, defined as *costs incurred for the purpose of making net*

---

created, is "immortal." It is not merely "used up" in the production of consumers' goods, but is "used up and recreated" in that process. Hence the replacement of worn-out equipment is a function of the operating force, not of the expansion force.

[8] Since the completed capital has increased the productivity of those using it, output of consumers' goods in the second year will be higher than in the first. This increase in productivity would make it possible to enlarge the size of the expansion force at the expense of the operating force. Historically this is what typically happens in the beginning of the industrialization process. The proportion of output devoted to net .capital formation tends at first to increase with the productivity of labor. But to avoid complications it is assumed here that the size of the expansion force remains unchanged in the second year.

[9] Cf. Alan Sweezy, "Declining Investment Opportunity," *The New Economics*, ed. Seymour Harris (New York, Alfred A. Knopf, 1947), pp. 433-34.

additions to capital, implies that labor must be assigned to the task of producing additional capital. In other words, net investment implies the need for and the existence of an expansion force.

Cessation of net investment, and hence of net saving, must mean the disappearance of the expansion force. Conversely, the disappearance of the expansion force must imply the cessation of net investment and saving.

The existence and size of an expansion force can be inferred only from the volume of net investment. No specific productive activity or group of workers can be identified as belonging to either force. Building a plant may be the work of the expansion force or of the operating force, depending on whether the cost of building the plant is incurred for the purpose of adding to the community's total production capacity or for replacement purposes. Even an unquestioned expansion in one industry may not require the activities of an expansion force; it may be accomplished at the expense of contraction in another industry. Investment in the former is then counterbalanced by disinvestment in the latter. It is not a question of which workers belong to the one force or to the other, but of the proportions of labor which are engaged, respectively, in activities which are counted as costs of current output, and in activities which are counted as costs of making net additions to capital.

In the first three years, when workers are equally divided into operating force and expansion force, one half of all costs (assuming that all workers receive equal wages) represent *net investment, i.e.,* outlays not expected to be recovered by the sale of consumers' goods. Correspondingly, one half of total money income must be saved. In the fourth year only one fourth of outlays are net investments and only one fourth of money income must be saved. In subsequent years net investment and saving must "constitute a diminishing series ending up eventually in a 100 per cent consumption-replacement economy." [10]

The tentative conclusion to be drawn from the example is that beyond a certain point—a point which may be called the point of *diminishing net investment*—the ratio of net investment to total output (I/Y) must decline and eventually fall to zero, at which point *full industrialization, i.e.,* completion of the transition from noncapital-using to capital-using production, will have

[10] Alan R. Sweezy, "Net Investment, Consumption and Full Employment. Reply." *Amer. Econ. Rev.,* Vol. XXXIV, No. 4 (Dec. 1944), p. 877.

been reached. This fundamental proposition may be called the *principle of diminishing net investment*.

Several writers have advanced this or similar theses, with various reservations and qualifications. Professor Alan R. Sweezy [11] and Mr. Nicholas Kaldor [12] should perhaps be mentioned as the foremost supporters of the view that investment opportunities are limited by the availability of labor. Professor Wright expressed the same idea, calling attention to the "fundamental proposition . . . that . . . as the stock of capital goods rises, the rate of addition to the capital stock must decline." [13] Also Keynes observes that "with a given labour force there is a definite limit to the quantity of labour embodied in roundabout processes which can be used to advantage. Apart from other considerations, there must be a due proportion between the amount of labour employed in making machines and the amount which will be employed in using them." [14] Mrs. Robinson makes a similar statement [15] without pursuing its implications. Last, but not least, Marx deserves mention as an early exponent of the view that capital accumulation must ultimately be limited by a shortage of labor. "Growth of capital," Marx wrote, "involves growth of its variable constituent or of the part invested in labour power. . . . sooner or later a point must be reached, at which the requirements of accumulation begin to surpass the . . . supply of labour. . . ." [16]

A new note was recently introduced into secular investment theory, notably by Mr. R. F. Harrod [17] and Professor Evsey D. Domar [18] who have centered attention on "the fact that invest-

[11] Alan R. Sweezy, "Declining Investment Opportunity," *ante cit.*

[12] Nicholas Kaldor, "Stability and Full Employment," *Economic Journal*, Vol. 48 (Dec. 1938), pp. 642-57.

[13] David McCord Wright, "Professor Knight on Limits to the Use of Capital," *Quarterly Journal of Economics*, Vol. LVIII, No. 3 (May 1944), pp. 337, 339.

[14] John Maynard Keynes, *op. cit.*, p. 214.

[15] Joan Robinson, *The Rate of Interest and Other Essays* (London, Macmillan & Company, Ltd., 1952), pp. 105-106.

[16] Karl Marx, *Capital* (Chicago, Charles H. Kerr & Company, 1906), Vol. I, p. 672. As Paul M. Sweezy points out, however, Marx regarded a labor shortage also as a stimulus to capital accumulation, because it would raise wages and encourage development of laborsaving machinery. (*The Theory of Capitalist Development*, New York, Oxford University Press, 1942, p. 223.)

[17] R. F. Harrod, *Toward A Dynamic Economics* (London, Macmillan and Company, Ltd., 1948); and "Notes on Trade Cycle Theory," *The Economic Journal*, Vol. LXI, No. 242 (June 1951), pp. 261-75.

[18] Evsey D. Domar, *op. cit.*; also "The Problem of Capital Accumulation," *Amer. Econ. Rev.*, Vol. XXXVIII, No. 5 (Dec. 1948), pp. 777-94.

ment not only generates income but also increases productive capacity." [19] From this they conclude that income must continuously increase in order to absorb the additional productive capacity created by new investment, even as new investment must continuously increase to assure a sufficient growth of income.

An increase in productive capacity may mean two things: an increase in productivity (output per man-hour of labor) or in the quantity of capital. The Harrod-Domar argument pertains to the latter. The s effect of investment is achieved by way of adding to the quantity of capital. But additional capital cannot yield additional output without the employment of additional labor. Investment, then, has not a twofold, but a threefold effect: (1) it generates income, (2) increases productive capacity, the use of which (3) *requires additional labor*. The twin requirements of continuously increasing net investments and continuously increasing income therefore could not be met without a continuously expanding labor supply to produce and operate continuously increasing quantities of capital.

The thesis propounded with the aid of the hypothetical example in the preceding section invites the objection, raised against all such artificial "models," that it is unrealistic. Granted that argument and conclusions are consistent on their assumptions, the assumptions may seem to vitiate them. Specifically, it may be objected that the "principle of diminishing net investment" would not hold because

(*1*) population is not stable, but growing;

(*2*) there is no fixed relation between capital and the amount of labor required for its operations, maintenance and replacement;

(*3*) capital goods are not all alike and interchangeable, but diverse and specified;

(*4*) capital accumulation may take the form of inventory accumulation and foreign investment as well as of accumulation of equipment;

(*5*) technological progress opens up unlimited investment opportunities.

[19] Evsey D. Domar, "Expansion and Employment," *ante cit.*, p. 35. See also Michael Kalecki, *Essays in the Theory of Economic Fluctuations* (New York, Farrar & Rinehart, 1939), pp. 148-49.

There are undoubtedly many other possible objections,[20] but the ones listed appear to be the most important. Let us examine each in turn.

Population and Investment

The point of diminishing investment, as well as full industrialization, may be indefinitely postponed by population increase, or more correctly by an increase in the supply of labor. This increase would have to be at a rate equal to or greater than the required rate of increase in the operating force. Under the conditions assumed for the hypothetical community, the labor force would have to increase at the rate of 50 per cent per year, indefinitely, beginning with the fourth year if the ratio of investment to total output were to continue indefinitely at 50 per cent.[21]

The rapid expansion of population in industrial nations, and especially in the United States, during the last 150 years has undoubtedly extended the opportunities for investment. Actual and prospective declines in the rate of population growth indicate that no similar stimulus to investment can be expected from this source in the future.[22]

Much attention has been given by Professor Alvin H. Hansen and others to the relation of population growth to investment.[23] Declining population growth, according to Hansen, is one of the causes of secular stagnation because it reduces *effective demand* for consumers' goods and consequently also for production instruments. To this one might object that "it is not the number of

[20] Professor Frank H. Knight and the neoclassical school which he represents would presumably reject as fallacious any attempt to analyze investment opportunities in real terms. (See, for instance, his article "Interest," in the Encyclopaedia of the Social Sciences, Vol. VIII, 1932, pp. 134, 137.)

[21] Actual I/Y in the United States from 1880-1930 averaged approximately 14 per cent. This caused "Real Estate Improvements and Equipment" to increase from roughly $30 billion to $228 billion, or more than sevenfold. (Simon Kuznets, *National Product Since 1869*, New York, National Bureau of Economic Research, 1946, p. 228.) During the same period population rose from 50 to 123 million, or two and one half times. This may indicate the disparity between the actual growth of population and the growth required to maintain indefinitely the same rate of increase in capital.

[22] See, however, Moses Abramovitz, "Economics of Growth," in *A Survey of Contemporary Economics*, Vol. II, ed. Bernard F. Haley (Homewood, Illinois, Richard D. Irwin, 1952), pp. 171-72.

[23] See for instance, Alvin H. Hansen, "Progress and Declining Population Growth," *Amer. Econ. Rev.*, Vol. XXIX, No. 1, Part 1 (March 1939), pp. 1-15.

consumers, but the number of dollars they have to spend that counts." [24] Also, the thesis that investment declines because of insufficiency of demand arising from declining population growth is open to Professor Fellner's objection that "it will not do to explain the insufficiency of investment by the insufficiency of effective demand because effective demand would be sufficient if aggregate investment were." [25] It is submitted that the true significance of declining population growth to net investment is to be found, not on the demand side, but on the supply side; not in the fact that people are consumers, but in the fact that they are producers.

Capital-Labor Ratio

A basic assumption of the example given earlier is that the quantity of capital in existence at any given time must be combined with a definite quantity of labor if it is to be fully utilized. Although this assumption must be modified, the entire argument ultimately stands or falls on its validity. If labor and capital could be combined in *any* proportions, the possibility of an insufficiency of labor, or of "excess capacity," would be ruled out. [26]

Actually it is not possible to combine a given amount of labor with unlimited amounts of capital. [27] There is of course no absolutely fixed proportion in which capital and labor must be combined; and the degree of possible variation differs from one type of capital equipment to the next. There must be one engineer and one fireman—not one half or two engineers and firemen—

[24] Emile Benoit Smullyan, "Net Investment, Consumption and Full Employment," *Amer. Econ. Rev.*, Vol. XXXIV, No. 4 (Dec. 1944), p. 874. See also Alan Sweezy, "Declining Investment Opportunity," *ante cit.*, p. 432. Joan Robinson, *op. cit.*, pp. 107-108.

[25] William Fellner, "The Capital-Output Ratio in Dynamic Economics," in *Money, Trade, and Economic Growth* in honor of John Henry Williams (New York, The Macmillan Company, 1951), p. 121.

[26] Evsey D. Domar, "Expansion and Employment," *ante cit.*, p. 44. See also Harold G. Moulton, *Controlling Factors in Economic Development* (Washington, D. C., The Brookings Institution, 1949), pp. 98-99.

[27] "One can 'add saws to a carpenter,'" as Professor Wright observes (*op. cit.*, p. 340), "but to surround him with an infinite number of the same saws and expect it to keep increasing his product seems . . . ridiculous." Professor Wright implies that it would not be ridiculous to "add saws to a carpenter" if the saws were of different types. But surely the point must soon be reached at which the carpenter would need a helper to carry the saws and find and hand him the particular saw required at the moment. Even to add different saws to a carpenter must at some point become ridiculous.

to each locomotive in operation. There may be one conductor to each passenger car or to every two or even three passenger cars— but not to 20 or 100 cars. A manufacturing plant may require 1000 workers for capacity production. Perhaps 1100 could be used if pressure of demand for its product were great; perhaps 900 would still constitute reasonably full capacity operation. But the limits would be fairly narrow.[28] Experience forces us to reject the assumption that capital can be combined with labor in any desired proportion and to affirm, on the contrary, that a fairly definite quantity of labor is required at any moment if existing capital is to be fully utilized.

Variety and Specificity of Capital Goods

The model given above assumed that there is only one type of capital good or, what comes to the same thing, that all capital goods are interchangeable. Actually, there are many different types of capital goods and, so far from being interchangeable, most can be used only for specific tasks. Does this affect or nullify the principle of diminishing net investment?

Whether capital equipment is uniform or diversified, it is still true that its use must be limited by the labor available to work it. It would not make sense for a community to build an automobile plant which, when completed, could be manned only'with workers drawn from, let us say, steel plants, thus leaving the latter idle. Of course the community could have built a smaller steel plant in order to permit some of its capital equipment to take the form of automobile-making machinery. It would then have spread its investments among different industries, but would still be limited in the aggregate amount it can invest.

Recognition of variety and specificity of capital goods affects the foregoing conclusions in one respect only; in the real world some cushion of excess capacity in each industry is justified to allow a rise in the demand for the products of a particular industry to be met by an immediate expansion of output by that industry without waiting for expansion of plant capacity. It may be "normal" for the steel industry, for instance, to operate at only 80 or 90 per cent of its capacity, the remaining 10 or 20 per cent of excess capacity being used only in times of peak activity. Most industries have some margin of excess capacity which is

[28] Nicholas Kaldor, *op. cit.*, p. 643.

regarded as normal.[29] But taking the economy as a whole, the over-all requirements for excess capacity are minor and at any rate have a limit. It is conceivable to keep "mothball war plants" in readiness [30] even as we keep a "mothball fleet," but there is bound to be some maintenance work and replacement of obsolete machines, which would limit the possibilities of investing even for such purposes. Somewhere a point of diminishing net investment must be reached.

Inventories and Foreign Investment

The principle of diminishing net investment was formulated with respect to accumulations of productive equipment—plants, machines. But capital can be accumulated also in the form of inventories and claims against foreigners. In neither of these cases does accumulated capital constitute a claim on labor. Does this invalidate the principle of diminishing net investment?

To take foreign investment first: a country could continue indefinitely to invest abroad if it found other countries willing indefinitely to buy more goods than they sell and if the people in the investing country indefinitely continued to regard their claims on foreign countries as valid even though they were never paid. Practically this is not possible. Foreign claims are liquidated by net imports or by default. Furthermore, even if one country should be able to accumulate capital in the form of claims against foreign countries for a long time, as England was in the hundred years before 1914, it is impossible for all countries to do so. The net foreign investment of one must be the disinvestment of others. In the United States, net foreign investment has accounted for only a small fraction of total capital accumulation.[31]

As to inventory accumulation, this may be significant in the short run but not in the long run. Stocks may be accumulated in

[29] Some industries must leave a large proportion of their equipment idle much of the time. Most summer resorts operate during only four months or less each year; in cold climates building equipment is idle throughout the winter, et cetera.

[30] Mr. C. E. Wilson, president of General Motors, in an address to the American Ordnance Association on October 4, 1951, suggested that in addition to its normal civilian capacity, each industry maintain special war production capacity which would remain unused in peacetime but which, in an emergency, would allow immediate transfer of labor from peace activities to war production. Construction of war production capacity, presumably at the expense of the government, could open up considerable investment opportunities. But even here the size of the available labor force would impose a limit.

[31] Simon Kuznets, op. cit., p. 228.

anticipation of higher prices or of shortages or because they could not be sold. But such accumulations will be liquidated at some later time. Long-run accumulation of inventories is chiefly related to the growing wealth and productive capacity of the community. For practical purposes, inventories may be regarded as having a fixed relation to productive equipment in the long run.[32] In the United States inventories equaled about 20 per cent of productive equipment in the period 1909-1939.[33]

Stockpiling for war purposes may open up vast investment opportunities, but here again, as in the case of expansion of war production facilities, there is bound to be a limit somewhere. The government cannot keep on making net additions to its stockpiles of metals, rubber, etc., indefinitely. It would seem, therefore, that neither foreign investment nor inventory accumulation can impair the basic long-run validity of the principle of diminishing net investment.

Technological Progress and Investment

The strongest objection to the proposition that in the long run investment opportunities are limited by the size of the labor force is that it assumes the absence of technological progress. On this assumption the proposition may be true. But do not new inventions and technological improvements in fact continually offer new opportunities for net investment? The answer generally given is that they do.[34] When, as a result of technological improvements, a given output can be produced with less labor, so the reasoning runs, the labor saved can be shifted to the construction of still more capital equipment.

This argument seems to assume that improvements lead to a saving of labor only in consumers' goods production; i.e., in the operating force. Improved shoemaking machines, for example, may double the output of shoes per man hour of labor. Without reducing the output of shoes, therefore, half the number of shoemakers could be set to work in the expansion force to produce

---

[32] See Michael Kalecki, op. cit., pp. 117-18.

[33] Simon Kuznets, op. cit., p. 228.

[34] See for example: Final Report of the Executive Secretary of the TNEC, 77th Congress, 1st Session (Washington, D. C., Government Printing Office, 1941), p. 137. Alvin H. Hansen, Business Cycles and National Income (New York, W. W. Norton and Company, 1951), p. 131. Joan Robinson, op. cit., p. 57. Alan Sweezy, "Declining Investment Opportunity," ante cit., pp. 434-35. David McC. Wright, op. cit., p. 341.

additional capital. But if productivity has doubled in shoemaking, it is likely to have doubled also in machine making. Even as improved design or new invention resulted in a machine capable of turning out twice as many *shoes* with a given amount of labor, so it is likely to result in a machine capable of turning out twice as many *shoe machines*. No workers would be released by the doubled productivity of shoe machinery, for the reason that the plant which they must operate is now twice as large.

If technological advances occurred at the same rate throughout the economy in the producers' goods industries as well as in the consumers' goods industries, no new opportunities for additional net investment would result from such advances. The notion that inventions and technological improvements open up unlimited investment opportunities implies that an undiminished (or even growing) expansion force could keep on producing additional capital equipment for an operating force which does not grow (or which may even become smaller) but which is always capable of using all the equipment because laborsaving improvements in the consumers' goods industries are always sufficient to enable the workers to take care of the additional new equipment as well as of the old.[35]

It may be contended that inventions open up new possibilities for investment because new, more efficient machines can be built to replace old, less efficient ones. This is possible, but only under the most unlikely circumstances. We must bear in mind in the

---

[35] Mr. Kaldor observes that "in order to prevent the emergence of excess capacity in equipment, the new 'machines' must be *so much* more labour-saving that the aggregate amount of labour required to work the newly installed equipment per unit of time should be no greater than the amount of labour simultaneously 'released' through the disappearance of that part of the old equipment which is worn out and has to be scrapped.

"Thus, unless Providence decrees that there should be an adequate rate of technical progress—the output capacity of the investment-goods industries determining what is adequate—there is no mechanism to ensure that the aggregate quantity of equipment which can be combined with a unit of labour should increase continuously in the same ratio—or, rather, that the number of men required per machine should decrease in the same ratio in which the number of machines increases. As investment activity continues at a high level, excess capacity of equipment is bound to make its appearance." (*Op. cit.,* pp. 652-53. His italics.)

Providence need not be invoked to maintain a long-run balance between the capital-labor ratio in machine producing on the one side and in machine operating on the other; it need be invoked only to keep the capital-labor ratio in the consumers' goods industries growing at a rate exactly sufficient to enable the operating force to absorb all the capital currently added by *net investment*. Perhaps this is what Mr. Kaldor means.

first place that replacement of equipment is part of the function of the operating force, not of the expansion force. It represents gross investment but not net investment. Secondly, it must be remembered that new inventions and technological improvements are being introduced not only through net investment but also through replacement; by the operating force as well as by the expansion force. In the early stages of industrialization, when there is as yet little capital equipment, new inventions are introduced almost exclusively by the expansion force. As capital accumulates, the replacement activities of the operating force increase and soon exceed those of the expanding force.[36] Ultimately, the expansion force vanishes and the operating force produces all equipment by way of replacement.

Inventions and technological improvements may encourage an increase in the ratio of net investment to output (I/Y) in the period preceding the point of diminishing net investment. This is the period (the first two years in our example given above) in which it is possible for I/Y to increase; and a new invention may provide the incentive which actually calls forth the additional net investment. To the extent that capital accumulation is hastened, however, the arrival of the point of diminishing net investment must be hastened too.[37] After this point has been reached, net investment must decline, inventions or no inventions.

In short, replacement of old machines by new and better ones does not give rise to net investment. In so far as the introduction of new machines does give rise to net investment, this is not by way of replacing old equipment, but of *adding* to it.

There is only one condition under which inventions and technological improvements may cause net investments to be increased (the expansion force to be enlarged) after the point of diminishing net investment has been reached, or to be resumed (the expansion force to be reconstituted) in a fully industrialized economy with an unchanging labor force: the productivity of new equipment must be so great as to justify the abandonment of part of the existing capital equipment in order to release part of the operating force for service in the expansion force to con-

[36] In the period 1919-1938, *net additions* to "Improvements and Equipment" amounted to $42 billion, *replacements* to $177 billion! (Simon Kuznets, *op. cit.*, p. 224.)
[37] Cf. Evsey D. Domar, "The Problem of Capital Accumulation," *ante cit.*, p. 779.

I

struct the new equipment. Abandonment of existing equipment would be justified if the discounted value of deferred consumers' goods output derived from immediately shifting labor to new capital construction (at the cost of suspending current production of consumers' goods) exceeded the discounted value of the gradually increasing output obtained by replacing old with new and improved equipment through the normal processes of replacement. The abandoned equipment would, of course, be worth only its scrap value. Its original construction would turn out to have been a wasted effort.

Continuation of net investment for the purpose of exploiting new inventions and technological improvements would necessitate the continual undoing of things done. It would be like building a house and immediately demolishing it to build another house of better design, only to discard it for a still better one—while the prospective occupant is camping in a tent, waiting for his house to be finished.

To justify continual scrapping of capital equipment to build better equipment would require a rate of technological progress beyond the capacity of the most inventive people. Actually technological improvements are now rarely so great as to warrant the shifting of labor from the operating force to the expansion force; and if they are, they are not likely to be recognized as such.[38] New products and new productive processes are generally introduced with sufficient gradualness [39] to allow the transition to be accomplished through normal replacement (by the operating force) and without any net investment.[40]

[38] Cf. R. G. Hawtrey, *Capital and Employment* (New York, Longmans, Green and Company, 1937), p. 46.

[39] See Rupert Maclaurin, "The Process of Technological Innovation," *Amer. Econ. Rev.*, Vol. XL, No. 1 (March 1950), p. 96, *et passim*.

[40] The automobile industry may serve as an illustration. The invention of the automobile did not cause production of horse-drawn vehicles to cease suddenly. Automobile production grew rapidly, but not so rapidly as to preclude its growth being offset by a gradual decline of the industries eventually destroyed by the automobile. As the transition from horse-drawn to motor transportation gathered momentum, some firms in the old industries disappeared, while new ones were formed in the new industry; several old firms shifted their production from old to new products (bodies, parts, etc.). To a considerable extent, therefore, the automobile industry was built up by the normal replacement of depreciated equipment in these older industries and firms with automobile production equipment.

Joseph A. Schumpeter (*Capitalism, Socialism and Democracy,* New York, Harper & Brothers, 1942, p. 114) asserted that "obviously the automobile plants were not financed from the depreciation accounts of railroads." Far from being obvious, the assertion may be wrong. It is quite likely that some of the activities of productive

Need for large-scale resumption of net investment (reconstitution of an expansion force) is more likely to arise from a sudden shift in demand than from technological improvements. If demand shifted suddenly, the additional new production instruments needed to supply the goods in greater demand could not be procured by gradual replacement of depreciated equipment in the industries affected by declining demand. Equipment in these latter industries would have to be abandoned and labor shifted from its operation to the production of new equipment. Large-scale sudden shifts in demand are often associated with war. When war breaks out, capacity to produce weapons may need to be expanded immediately and this may necessitate drawing workers away from the operation of industries turning out civilian goods. In peace time such large-scale sudden shifts are not likely to happen. Inventions and technological improvements would rarely be so revolutionary as to call for a new expansion force at the cost of a decline in current consumers' goods output and of abandonment of existing equipment.

Examination of objections to the thesis that net investment must decline after the point of diminishing net investment has been reached, has shown them to be unsubstantial. The rigid assumptions of the example given above can be relaxed without impairing the essential validity of the conclusions. Epecially it has been found that technological advance has little if any bearing on the principle of diminishing net investment. So far from assuring continued investment opportunities, technological advance speeds up the process of industrialization and thus tends to hasten the decline of investment opportunities. As to population growth, its rate could not possibly continue high enough to assure indefinite postponement of the point of diminishing net investment. We are left with the basic conclusion that the process of industrialization comprises three stages:

(*1*) the stage in which the proportion of output devoted to net investment may increase;

(*2*) the stage in which the proportion of output devoted to net investment must decrease;

---

establishments previously devoted to railroad making—machine shops for instance—were later transferred to automobile making when the rate of growth and the actual size of the railroad industry declined. This would in effect amount to the automobile industry being built up instead of the railroads being replaced, even if it were not apparent on the financial level.

(3) the stage of full industrialization in which no net investment whatever can take place.

The first stage is that in which all "underdeveloped" countries find themselves. The United States was such a country in the last century, as we shall see below. Most industrial nations, such as the United States in the first half of the present century, are in the second stage and are approaching, if they have not already reached, the third or "mature economy" stage.

The principle of diminishing net investment receives statistical confirmation from Professor Kuznets' studies of national income. His figures show that the ratio of net investment to national income in the United States rose steadily until about the turn of the century and from then on declined steadily until it was reduced to nearly nothing in the decade 1929-1938.

Net Capital Formation [41] *in Percentages of National Income*
(1929 prices)

Decade	Net Capital Formation	Decade	Net Capital Formation	Decade	Net Capital Formation
1869-78	13.7	1889-98	16.2	1914-23	11.4
1874-83	14.4	1894-03	14.8	1919-28	10.2
1879-88	14.6	1899-08	13.6	1924-33	6.0
1884-93	16.1	1904-13	13.1	1929-38	1.4
		1909-18	13.0		

Professor Kuznets minimizes the importance of the decline in the proportion of national income devoted to net investment. First, he writes that "one expects to find . . . a downtrend in the share of net capital formation." [42] The reason why one should expect a downtrend, says Professor Kuznets, is that there was "greater pressure to build up the capital structure of the country" in earlier times. If so, why was not the share of net investment highest in the earliest decades, when this pressure must have been greatest? But why should one not expect the share of net investment to *rise* as capital is accumulated, output increased, and pressure to consume lessened? According to Professor Moses Abramovitz, for instance, "the a priori expectation [is] that the

[41] Simon Kuznets, *National Income—A Summary of Findings* (New York, National Bureau of Economic Research), 1946, p. 53.
[42] *Ibid.,* p. 52.

proportion of aggregate income saved [and hence also invested] would tend to increase as per capita incomes rose." [43]

Next, Professor Kuznets brushes aside the low ratio of net investment to national income in the last two decades "which were affected by the 1929-32 depression and its aftermath." [44] But is it admissible to treat the depression as an extraneous event unconnected with the decline in net investment? Was not the Great Depression largely brought about by declining net investment? Furthermore, why did depressions not affect the share of net investment in earlier decades? The decade 1889-98 included the depression of 1893-97 and yet showed the highest proportion of net investment.

Having disposed of the embarrassing last two decades shown on his table, Professor Kuznets groups decades into three overlapping sets, *i.e.*, 1869-98, 1884-1913, 1899-1928, and finds that the average share of net investment dropped from 15 per cent in the first period to 12.2 per cent in the last period. This drop, he says, "is rather minor, and the underlying estimates are not sufficiently precise to warrant confidence in such small changes." [45] Of course one could eliminate all traces of the initial rise and subsequent decline in the share of net investment by taking an average for the entire period. As for the unreliability of estimates, it is no doubt true that estimates must be used with caution, but it is unlikely that they would be so consistently wrong from 1894 on as to show a sustained, unbroken downward trend, if there were actually no such trend. One may also ask what purpose is served by compiling such statistics, if they are as unreliable as Professor Kuznets says they are.

For whatever they are worth, the statistics support the theoretical conclusion that the proportion of output devoted to net investment must decline in a community approaching full industrialization.

What are the implications of the principle of diminishing net investment for continued industrial progress? More specifically, does the cessation of investment imply the end of capital accumulation and does the end of capital accumulation, in turn, signify the end of industrial progress?

[43] Moses Abramovitz, *op. cit.*, p. 145.
[44] Simon Kuznets, *National Income—A Summary of Findings, ante cit.*, p. 52.
[45] *Ibid.*, p. 53.

As was pointed out at the beginning of this paper, traditional economics has answered yes. A society in which there is "no more room for profitably *investing* present effort in providing for the future," wrote Marshall,[46] would be in a "stationary state" in which "the same amount of things per head of the population [is] produced in the same ways . . . for many generations together." [47] This reasoning rests on the assumptions that

(1) capital accumulation requires net investment, and that,
(2) physical productivity can be increased only through capital accumulation.[48]

To take the second of these assumptions first, most economists recognize that even in a community in which capital accumulation has ceased, progress would nevertheless result from changes in technique of production, inventions and innovations.[49] Attention has been given increasingly to the fact that inventions and innovations are likely to become less "capital-using" in an advanced industrial society.[50] This fact was long overlooked. We were accustomed to think of improvements and inventions as "capital-using," *i.e.*, requiring an increase in the ratio of capital to output (or an increase in the ratio of labor employed in intermediate production to labor employed in final consumers' goods production) [51] because in the early phases of the industrialization process, when capital theory was first formulated, this had to be and actually was so; it is also largely true for underdeveloped economies today. During the transition from *man*ufacturing to *machino*facturing, improved processes necessarily imply machine-using, *i.e.*, capital-using, processes. But once capital is in existence, improvements not requiring additional capital become possible. The reason for this is that whereas the transition to machinofacture must be made by the initial construction of ma-

[46] Alfred Marshall, *op. cit.*, p. 223. (Italics added.)
[47] *Ibid.*, p. 367. Cf. Friedrich A. von Hayek, *Pure Theory of Capital* (Chicago, University of Chicago Press, 1950), p. 14 f. C. Reinhold Noyes, "The Prospect for Economic Growth: Rejoinder," *Amer. Econ. Rev.*, Vol. XXXVIII, No. 3 (June 1948), pp. 394-96.
[48] "Any nation which fails to . . . increase its capital supply will . . . cease to raise the plane of living of the people." ". . . the formation of capital . . . involves . . . [setting] aside money income for investment." Harold G. Moulton, *The Formation of Capital* (Washington, D. C., The Brookings Institution, 1935), pp. 8, 15.
[49] *E.g.*, John Maynard Keynes, *op. cit.*, pp. 220-21.
[50] Alvin H. Hansen, *Full Recovery or Stagnation* (New York, W. W. Norton, 1938), p. 315; Joan Robinson, *op. cit.*, pp. 42 ff.
[51] Cf. Joan Robinson, *op. cit.*, p. 50.

chines, which requires net investment, improvements in machinery can be introduced via replacement, which does not require net investment. The greater the amount of accumulated capital, the larger must be the proportion of labor devoted to maintenance and replacement and the greater therefore is the opportunity for introducing improvements through this channel.

There is no reason to believe that we shall ever cease to be inventive,[52] and as long as we continue to be so we can improve our production techniques and raise our standard of living indefinitely—and without any capital accumulation.

What is more, the first assumption, too, is mistaken. Capital accumulation may continue even after net investment has ceased. This statement may seem paradoxical since net investment is often thought of as being a necessary concomitant of capital accumulation. Yet, there must be a difference between these two concepts, since otherwise it would make no sense to say that the former is necessary in order to achieve the latter. *Net investment* has already been defined as *costs* incurred for the purpose of adding to capital. *Capital accumulation,* on the other hand, is the *increase in the quantity of capital.*[53] The question, then, is: can the quantity of capital be increased without incurring costs for that purpose?

In a community which has reached the stage of full industrialization every industry, no matter whether it produces raw ma-

---

[52] In modern industry invention—the improvement of production techniques and the development of new products—has become part of the routine of current production. See Sidney D. Merlin, *The Theory of Fluctuations in Contemporary Economic Thought* (New York, Columbia University Press, 1949), p. 137.

[53] A difficulty arises in measuring the physical quantity of capital. This difficulty would not exist if there were only one kind of capital good, say a particular type of shoemaking machine. An increase in the quantity of capital could then be easily measured by counting the machines. But one cannot add shoe machines to steel plants. It would not do to reduce all capital goods to dollars and to conclude that an increase in their dollar value would measure an increase in their quantity. The dollar value of capital may change independently of changes in its quantity.

To conclude that increments in the quantity of capital are fully reflected in figures for net investment would rule out the possibility of capital accumulation without net investment. Measuring the quantity of capital by the output of goods attributable to it also is unsatisfactory because an increase in output may be due to improvements in the quality of capital without change in its quantity. The one criterion by which to measure increases in the quantity of capital would seem to be the amount of labor required to operate capital. If the operation of capital requires more labor today than yesterday, it would seem justifiable to conclude that additional capital has come into existence since yesterday. Since there is no rigid capital-labor ratio, this measure, too, is vague but nevertheless more meaningful than the others.

terials, machines, or final consumers' goods, must be regarded as engaged in producing consumers' goods. The costs incurred by each industry are part of the total cost of producing consumers' goods. The workers of all industries belong to the *operating force*.

A large part of the operating force, however, is not producing actual consumers' goods, but replacing used-up equipment (and other capital or intermediate goods). The operating force may therefore be thought of as being divided into two groups: a *production force* which is engaged in the production of final consumers' goods, and a *replacement force* which makes machines and other intermediate goods.

Now it is easily seen that consumers' goods output can be expanded as a result of new, improved machinery installed in the normal process of replacement and therefore not requiring any net investment. A new and improved shoemaking machine, for instance, may cost exactly as much in labor and materials as the old model which it replaces, but may enable the operator of the machine to double his output of shoes. If the production force can thus increase its output without net investment, it must be possible for the replacement force to do the same. Even as the output of shoes, so the output of shoemachines and of machines to make shoemachines, can be expanded indefinitely without net investment.[54] The quantity of machines may grow indefinitely without any cost being incurred for that purpose.

Although industrial effort in a fully industrialized society must be devoted entirely to production for current consumption, and consequently no part of it can be regarded as constituting "investing *present* effort in providing for the *future*," industry is still capable of further growth. Only in the beginning of the capital accumulation process is sacrificing *present* consumption

----

[54] It should be emphasized that this conclusion does not rest on the assumption that net investment is hidden in excessive depreciation and obsolescence allowances masquerading as costs of production. Depreciation allowances are assumed to amortize the cost of capital assets over the period of their usefulness. The depreciation reserve accumulated by the time a machine must be discarded supposedly equals the cost of the discarded machine.

Professor Domar assumes that depreciation refers to the "cost of replacement of the depreciated asset by another one of *equal* productive capacity." ("Expansion and Employment," *ante cit.*, p. 35. His italics.) Everyone is free to define his terms as he chooses, but Professor Domar's definition is certainly not in accordance with accounting practice. Of course this definition would equate all additions to capital with net investment even in a fully industrialized community, but net investments would be unintentional and could be inferred only from increased productive capacity.

necessary in order to enlarge *future* consumption; and the sacrifice of *present* for *future* consumption is associated with saving and net investment. But saving labor is not the same as saving income.[55] In a fully industrialized community introduction of laborsaving devices and consequent expansion of output—whether of consumers' goods or of capital goods—does not necessitate the sacrifice of present income and consequently requires no saving and investment.

The analysis presented earlier applies to any economy regardless of whether it operates under a capitalist, socialist, or any other system. The present section is devoted to some observations on the effects of declining net investment on the functioning of a capitalist economy, first in the long run and second in the short run.

Investment is an essential requirement for full employment and the key to prosperity in a capitalist economy. This is so widely and generally recognized by all economic schools and sects that it may be regarded as an axiom of modern economics. Some economists hold that not only net investment, but an increasing rate of net investment is necessary to assure continued full employment.[56]

The physical, technical limits to continued net investment, or, more specifically, the insufficiency of labor to operate ever-increasing quantities of equipment, make fulfilment of these conditions impossible. So far from increasing, net investment must diminish and ultimately cease altogether when full industrialization has been achieved. But without net investment, demand is not sufficient to keep existing capital in operation. A "mature" economy would therefore seem condemned to suffer depression and unemployment. This would be true even if saving should be reduced to zero,[57] because in the absence of net investment, profits would not be large enough to induce firms to produce at the full-employment level.[58] Besides, such a solution of the problem would not be satisfactory to investors[59] and would in fact

[55] Cf. Keynes, *op. cit.*, pp. 215-16.
[56] William T. Foster and Waddill Catchings (*Profits*, Boston, Houghton Mifflin Co., 1925), J. R. Hicks, R. F. Harrod, Evsey Domar, Eric Lundberg, and others have expressed this view. It is also implicit in Keynes' psychological law of consumption.
[57] Joan Robinson, *op. cit.*, pp. 70-71.
[58] See A. Murad, "The Sources of Profit and the Economic Revolution of Our Time," *The Southwestern Social Science Quarterly*, Vol. XXXII, No. 3 (Dec. 1951).
[59] Cf. Alan Sweezy, "Declining Investment Opportunity," *ante cit.*, p. 434.

I*

constitute abandonment of the capitalist system. To maintain full employment, mature capitalist economies will have to rely increasingly upon government consumption expenditures. Such expenditures, as Professor Galbraith, among others, has pointed out,[60] need not necessarily be for warfare but could also be directed toward increasing the welfare of the community.

We must next inquire into how these long-run effects of diminishing net investment manifest themselves in the short run. Could a shortage of labor bring about depression and unemployment? The possibility of this is doubted by most economists.[61] Preponderant opinion is that, to borrow Mrs. Robinson's phrase, "full employment is not so much a bottleneck as a powder barrel"[62] setting off inflation.

Still, it is possible for a boom to be ended by an insufficiency of labor to man additional machines. To be sure, a boom may be brought to an end by several other factors before the labor shortage gets into action. Insufficiency of demand, high wages, or bottlenecks such as limited capacity of the capital goods industries[63] have been cited as causes that kill booms before full employment is reached. These explanations are not incompatible with the labor shortage argument. A boom, as Mr. Kaldor observes, is like "a peculiar steeplechase where the horse is bound to fall at one of [several] obstacles. If it survives the first, it might be checked on the second, the third or the fourth. It is probably a rare horse which survives until the last hurdle."[64] This last hurdle is the labor shortage.

A boom is fed and kept going by investment. Initially the investments may be "autonomous," but before long the bulk of investment must be of the "induced" variety, depending on the need for additional capital in the consumers' goods industries. Such induced investment can come about only if consumers' goods industries are working at or near capacity and hence need

[60] J. K. Galbraith, "We Can Prosper Without War Orders," *New York Times*, VI, 7:1 (June 22, 1952).

[61] ". . . we might argue that . . . increasing scarcity of the labor factor might be . . . a limiting factor. However, we do not hear much of this argument and for very good reasons." J. A. Schumpeter, *op. cit.*, p. 114. ". . . it is by no means obvious through what mechanism full employment can bring a boom to an end. . . ." J. Robinson, *op. cit.*, p. 129, also pp. 80, 106.

[62] J. Robinson, *op. cit.*, p. 130.

[63] *Ibid.*, pp. 134-35, also pp. 80 ff. J. R. Hicks, *A Contribution to the Theory of the Trade Cycle* (Oxford, At the Clarendon Press, 1950), p. 129.

[64] Nicholas Kaldor, "Stability and Full Employment," *ante cit.*, p. 657.

more or are expected to need still more capital. Now, if there is already so much equipment available to the consumers' goods industries that there is not enough labor to operate it and still leave enough labor to produce additional equipment, there must be an excess of equipment somewhere—either in the producers' goods industries or in the consumers' goods industries, or in both.[65] Excess capacity must express itself in an apparent insufficiency of demand, prices being too low relative to wages, and profits consequently insufficient to justify further expansion or even maintenance of existing levels of production. Regardless of where excess capacity first appears, the result will be a falling off in net investment and a consequent reduction in income and consumption. The boom is ended, depression and unemployment appear—all because there is not enough labor to keep on expanding, even though this may not appear on the surface.[66] In this manner a labor shortage may actually cause unemployment.

Conclusions

(*1*) The relation of net investment to capital accumulation is historically and theoretically separable into three distinct stages.

The first stage extends over the period of transition from non-capital-using to capital-using methods of production. This transition can be accomplished only by shifting labor from the production of consumers' goods to the production of producers' goods. *Present* goods are sacrificed for the sake of more *future* goods through *saving* and net *investment*. The ratio of net in-

---

[65] Mr. Merlin writes that "the rate of new investment—and the boom itself—may be checked in the advanced stages of a boom as the ratio of new equipment to older equipment approaches a limiting value, *i.e.*, when new investment means that a relatively high proportion of existing equipment is rendered obsolete." (*Op. cit.*, p. 133.) This is the same as to say that equipment is excessive relative to available labor. The old equipment would not be rendered "obsolete" if there were enough labor available to operate the old as well as the new equipment. If the "obsolete" equipment continued to be used, its "obsoleteness" would encourage—not check—the rate of new investment.

[66] "The individual entrepreneur only sees that wages are high, or that product prices are low, his profits are low and his recent investment projects have turned out badly. Since it is his equipment which is redundant, he is just as likely to attribute the cause to lack of demand as to anything else. . . . It is this fact [*i.e.*, the labor shortage] that is ultimately responsible for that 'temporary exhaustion of investment opportunities' with which several economists explain the breakdown of the boom. . . ." (Nicholas Kaldor, *op. cit.*, p. 653.)

vestment to total output (I/Y) may (and generally did) increase during this first stage.

The second stage begins when the quantity of accumulated capital is so large that an increasing proportion of the total labor force must be devoted to its operation, maintenance and periodic replacement. A correspondingly smaller proportion of the labor force remains available for continued production of additional capital. The "point of diminishing net investment" has been reached. More effort is devoted to production of *present* goods, less to *future* goods. Correspondingly the ratio of saving and investment to total output (S/Y and I/Y) must decline.

The third stage is reached when production of *present* goods claims all available labor, leaving none to be set aside for the creation of additional capital to expand the flow of *future* goods. "Full industrialization" has been achieved, *i.e.*, the transition from noncapital-using to capital-using methods of production has been completed, or $I/Y = S/Y = O$.

(2) Laissez-faire capitalism, which functions only under the stimulus of investment, flourishes in the first stage, may stumble along with increasing difficulty in the second stage, but must stagnate in the third stage unless government expenditures for welfare or warfare compensate for the insufficiency of net investment.

(3) According to the "orthodox" theory of capital accumulation, economic progress—rising productivity and higher living standards—can be achieved only through capital accumulation; capital can be accumulated only through saving and net investment; and the rate of accumulation depends on the community's thriftiness. This holds true for the first stage, from which the theory sprang, but not for the second and third stages. Although in these later stages capital may be accumulated at a faster pace even than in the first stage, the net investment-output ratio (I/Y) must decline in the second stage until it reaches zero in the third stage. This apparent paradox is explained by the growing importance of capital replacement as an avenue for capital accumulation as long as technology advances. Technological improvements also may lead to expansion of output without adding to the quantity of capital. Cessation of capital accumulation, therefore, does not lead to a "stationary state," even as cessation of investment does not put an end to capital accumulation.

[CHAPTER TEN]

Distribution, Employment and Secular Growth

Kenneth K. Kurihara

IN HIS *General Theory* Keynes takes the social structure as given, with the result that the level of employment is determined independently of changes in the distribution of income. That such is a good first approximation is generally admitted on the ground that over the short run, especially without great institutional change, the distribution of income is found to remain rather stable. Over the long run, however, the whole complex of society is liable to undergo significant change. It is necessary, then, to introduce the "distribution effect" as an explicit variable in the relevant macro-economic functions affecting employment and secular growth. Only thus can we hope to mitigate those "outstanding faults of the economic society in which we live . . . its failure to provide for full employment and its arbitrary and inequitable distribution of wealth and incomes" which Keynes stresses in his concluding long-run digression.[1] But he made no analysis to justify his "operationalism" along those lines. It is the aim of this essay to analyze the relationship between income distribution and secular employment in the interest of "progressive equilibrium." [2]

To maintain the steady growth of full-employment income without inflation or deflation, some would operate on the invest-

[1] *The General Theory of Employment, Interest and Money* (Harcourt Brace, New York, 1936), p. 372.
[2] Some writers apparently do not consider such analysis fruitful. Professor D. M. Wright, for example, holds that the distribution of income and wealth is a matter for normative judgment to be considered on ethical and political grounds. See his "Income Redistribution Reconsidered," in *Income, Employment and Public Policy* (Essays In Honor of Alvin H. Hansen) (Norton, New York, 1948).

For various approaches to "progressive equilibrium" see R. F. Harrod, *Towards a Dynamic Economics* (Macmillan, London, 1948); J. R. Hicks, *A Contribution to the Theory of the Trade Cycle* (Oxford, 1950); E. D. Domar, "Expansion and Employment," *Amer. Econ. Rev.*, March, 1946; J. Robinson, *The Rate of Interest and Other Essays* (Macmillan, London, 1952); R. Eisner, "Underemployment Equilibrium Rates of Growth," *Amer. Econ. Rev.*, March 1952; K. K. Kurihara, "Secular Macroeconomic Theorems," *Rev. Econ. & Stat.*, August, 1952.

ment side of the growth equation, on the supposition that tampering with the distribution of income to lower the average propensity to save involves too many noneconomic complications as well as the possible impairment of investment incentives. This seems to be the position taken by Mr. Harrod and Professor Domar. On the other hand, Mrs. Joan Robinson suggests the possibility, and perhaps desirability, of operating on the savings side of the growth equation, for she says: "It can be plausibly argued that the phenomenon of excessive thriftiness is a product of excessive inequality, and that measures to correct inequality, which may be advocated on their own political and humanitarian merits, would, as a by-product, permanently reverse the position, and make deficient thriftiness the normal rule. There seems very little point in discussing artificial measures for absorbing excessive saving until this great question has been argued out." [3] It will be shown, however, that the above schism between the two sides of dynamic economics is more apparent than real. This we shall endeavor to do by analyzing the "distribution effect" not only on thriftiness but also on the inducement to invest—in the broad light of institutional reality and historical development.

Factors Affecting Income Distribution

It seems helpful to indicate the major determinants of income distribution before proceeding to the main business at hand. Income distribution is generally understood to mean the relative shares of the value of the total product among the factors of production.[4] This is the sense in which the "distribution effect" will be discussed throughout this paper, unless otherwise indicated. Broadly speaking, the distribution of income, as such, is under present arrangements determined by (1) the pricing of factors according to the interplay of supply and demand, and (2) the ownership of income-producing property. The following specific factors may be mentioned as affecting income distribution.

[3] See her "Mr. Harrod's Dynamics," *Econ. Journ.*, March, 1949.
[4] For broad sociological and economic determinants see M. A. Copeland, "Determinants of Distribution of Income," *Amer. Econ. Rev.*, March, 1947; also A. G. B. Fisher, "Alternative Techniques for Promoting Equality in a Capitalist Society," *ibid.*, May, 1950. For conceptual and statistical discussions see E. Lundberg, et al., *Income and Wealth: Series I* (Bowes & Bowes, Cambridge, 1951), and also National Bureau of Economic Research, *Studies in Income and Wealth*, XI, 1949.

(1) MONOPOLY. The presence of oligopsonists and monopsonists in factor markets gives rise to payment of factor prices below what is warranted by marginal productivity. For the supply of a factor curve appears to an oligopsonist or monopsonist to be so inelastic that he can always pay a lower factor price by restricting input. Likewise oligopolists and monopolists in commodity markets can charge "what the traffic will bear" by restricting output, since the demand for commodities appears to them to be also inelastic with respect to price. A given total income is likely to be more equally distributed in the absence of "the monopoly's power of making a profit merely through restricting output and employment so as to charge a scarcity price to consumers and to drive a hard bargain with labour," as Professor J. E. Meade puts it.[5] More specifically, Professor K. Galbraith has observed: "To monopoly and monopoloid forms . . . one can trace disparity in income and both a lower and a less stable consumption function than would be expected under pure competition."[6] Mrs. Joan Robinson, on the other side of the Atlantic, has expressed the similar view that "an increase in the degree of monopoly will increase thriftiness and so reduce employment, for it will alter the distribution of income unfavourably to labour."[7]

(2) THE ELASTICITY OF SUBSTITUTION BETWEEN FACTORS. The distribution of income among factors is believed to depend partly on the ease with which one factor can be substituted for another when their relative prices change as a result of a variation in the quantity of one factor relatively to that of another. If the amount of labor becomes abundant relatively to capital and therefore less expensive, labor tends to be substituted for more expensive capital in the productive process. If labor can be easily substituted for capital, the employment of labor relative to capital will increase per unit of output and the relative share of labor will increase accordingly. The unit elasticity of substitution between labor and capital[8] is sometimes said to account, in

---

[5] Cf. *Planning and the Price Mechanism* (Allen & Unwin, London, 1948), p. 64.
[6] Cf. "Monopoly and the Concentration of Economic Power," in *A Survey of Contemporary Economics,* H. S. Ellis, ed. (Blakiston, Phil., 1948), p. 111.
[7] See her *Essays in the Theory of Employment* (Blackwell, Oxford, 1947), p. 94n.
[8] For exact measurement see R. G. D. Allen, *Mathematical Analysis for Economists* (Macmillan, London, 1942), pp. 340-43; also J. R. Hicks, "Distribution and Economic Progress: A Revised Version," *Rev. Econ. Stud.,* 1936-37 (Vol. 4).

part, for the constancy of income distribution in a given situation.

(3) TECHNOLOGICAL CHANGE. Inventions and innovations affect the distribution of income, depending on whether they are "capital-saving" or "laborsaving" (capital-using) in effect. Historically, technical progress has tended to reduce the number of man-hours of work required to produce a given output, as the very term "roundabout production" suggests. If technological unemployment due to laborsaving devices has not actually resulted in an absolute reduction of labor income, it may be due to a secular rise in aggregate demand or to a simultaneous tendency to reduce man-hours of work per worker (*e.g.,* the short working-week movement).[9]

(4) THE RELATIVE AMOUNTS OF FACTORS. A factor of production which is relatively scarce generally commands a high price for its services. If, for example, the amount of labor is restricted by stationary population, strict immigration laws, the legal limitation of child and woman labor, and other long-run influences, while the amount of capital is not, both the marginal productivity of labor and the relative share of labor in a given total income tend to increase. If capital is the scarce factor, as in less developed economies, the relative share of capital tends to increase perhaps until those economies catch up with developed economies. Thus the relative opulence and poverty of productive factors in the general pattern of income distribution partly reflect the relative scarcity and abundance of those factors in a given economy.

(5) CONDITIONS OF EMPLOYMENT. Whether an economy is in conditions of persistent mass unemployment or of continuous full employment may make a significant difference to income distribution. In this regard Mrs. Joan Robinson observes that "it [mass unemployment] weakens the bargaining position of labour and makes it impossible for Trade Unions to keep monopoly profits in check." [10] This suggests that in a full-employment economy it would be easier for labor to improve its relative income position. Such an improvement may or may not actually happen, depending on the adjustment between wages and prices, public policy, and other factors. In this latter respect Dr. S. S. Alexander has made the observation that the "industrial reserve army"

---

[9] Cf. J. Robinson, *Essays in the Theory of Employment,* and also *The Rate of Interest and Other Essays,* pp. 40-51.
[10] See *The Rate of Interest and Other Essays,* p. 108.

type of opposition to full-employment measures is based on the belief that, "under conditions of full employment, management has a difficult time keeping labor under its control and labor will be in a better position to get a larger share of the total product." [11]

(6) THE TAX STRUCTURE. Another factor of mounting importance is the structure of income taxation (including individual and corporate income taxes and estate and inheritance taxes). If the tax structure is sufficiently progressive, the Lorenz curve will probably shift toward the 45° line of perfect equality by a substantial amount. That this has not happened may be attributable to the offsetting weight of regressive taxes and an increasing monopolistic concentration of income. [12] Thus Dr. A. G. B. Fisher, in his paper entitled "Alternative Techniques for Promoting Equality in a Capitalist Society," made this observation: "In many modern economies the extent to which income is being constantly redistributed by taxation is already much wider than anyone a generation ago would have thought conceivable. The really astonishing thing about the efforts so far made in this direction is, however, the slightness of their permanent effects upon the general shape of the income pyramid." [13]

(7) THE INSTITUTION OF INHERITANCE. The ownership of income-yielding assets depends largely on the institution of inheritance. The stability of income distribution over time is often explained in terms of slow changes in the ownership of inherited wealth. When and where the death duties are levied at low rates and accompanied by similar levies on gifts from the living to their heirs, the accident of birth is a governing factor in the distribution of income. This may be one element of arbitrariness unrelated to the functional distribution of income "to which Keynes alludes.

[11] See his "Opposition to Deficit Spending for the Prevention of Unemployment," in *Income, Employment and Public Policy*, p. 189. It might be added parenthetically that those who believe in the supposed economic necessity of the "reserve army" of unemployed unwittingly justify Marx's dictum that mass unemployment is "the indispensable means by which capitalists maintain their control over the labor market," to quote Dr. P. Sweezy. (See his "Keynes, the Economist," in *The New Economics*, Knopf, New York, 1948, p. 107.)

[12] Cf. R. A. Musgrave and L. Frane, "Rejoinder to Dr. Tucker," *Nat. Tax Journ.*, March, 1952; also G. H. Moore, "Secular Changes in the Distribution of Income," *Amer. Econ. Rev.*, May, 1952.

[13] A. G. B. Fisher, *op. cit.*

(8) OTHER FACTORS. A permanent change in the distribution of income is, moreover, dependent upon many noneconomic influences, especially political and humanitarian considerations. Given the common desire to minimize the dangers of too high a concentration of political power, a community may well endeavor to reduce too high a concentration of income and wealth. Given the egalitarian sentiment for ·greater equality, efforts are likely to be made to widen educational opportunity, to extend social services, to establish minimum wage legislation—all of which serve to modify the broad supply and demand forces determining the distribution of income.

With the above outline in mind, let us proceed to a consideration of the relevance of distribution to long-run equilibrium.

Distribution and Long-Run Equilibrium

Keynes poses the fundamental long-run problem of an advanced economy thus: what would happen to a long-run full-employment equilibrium, once established, if (1) that enonomy already possesses such a large accumulated stock of capital that its marginal efficiency would become negative with additional investment, (2) its monetary system cannot reduce the rate of interest below zero, and (3) the community is disposed to save a large fraction of full-employment income? [14] Having posed this problem, he expressed the fear that under the above circumstances a state of low-level employment would be the inevitable lot of economic man—a state which Professor Pigou has christened "Keynes' Day of Judgment." [15] Here at least three bases of reference are discernible. To decipher the implications of distribution for the solution of the above problem, it is useful to analyze briefly these bases of reference.

First, the "real" base of reference is the historical fact that a highly developed economy tends to accumulate more and more "roundabout" productive facilities well in excess of replacements, thus resulting in a secular decline in the rate of profit. The progressive role of "roundabout" or capitalistic production was clearly perceived by Max Weber (*The Protestant Ethic and the Spirit of Capitalism*, 1927) and J. A. Schumpeter (*The Theory of Economic Development*, 1912), though they failed to see its

[14] *General Theory*, p. 373.
[15] Cf. "Economic Progress in a Stable Environment," *Economica* 14 (1947).

grave consequences to the *endogeneous* stability of capitalism. In playing this dynamic role, however, a highly developed economy unwittingly diminishes the opportunities for further investment, since, in the words of Keynes, "the output from equipment produced today will have to compete, in the course of its life, with the output from equipment produced subsequently." [16] Short of a drastic permanent downward change in the denominator of the marginal efficiency of capital, y/p (where y is the future income of capital and p the supply price or replacement cost of capital), the numerator will become smaller to depress the ratio as net investment results in an increasing accumulation of durable equipment. That investment is, in the long run, a decreasing function of fixed capital has been recognized variously by Ricardo, Marx, and Keynes, and more recently by Dr. M. Kalecki and Mrs. Joan Robinson.[17] The only logical escape from all this is to suppose that the marginal efficiency of capital rises progressively on the a priori ground that the diminishing tendency of that capital efficiency is sufficiently counterbalanced by autonomous growth factors.[18]

The "monetary" base of reference may be seen as arising from what Keynes calls the *rentier* aspect of capitalism. Up to a certain point "finance" (like Schumpeter's famous "credit" which, together with "the entrepreneur" and "innovation," presumably explains capitalistic development) helps "industry," but beyond that point the former may seriously hinder the latter, according to Ricardo, Wicksell, and Keynes. For, to put it in Keynesian terminology, the *rentier* prevents the institutional rate of interest on money and debts from falling below a certain practical minimum, even though the marginal efficiency of capital may already be so low as to require a much lower rate for further investment. If so, the historic conflict between the rate of profit and the rate of interest, to which the above economists alluded, may well result in the triumph of the *rentier* over the entrepreneur, much to the detriment of the future of capitalism. Then Keynes' profit-maximizing equation $e(I) = r$ (where e is the marginal efficiency of capital, I the volume of investment, and r the rate of inter-

---

[16] *General Theory*, p. 141.
[17] Cf. Kalecki, *Essays in the Theory of Economic Fluctuation* (Farrar, New York, 1939); and Robinson, *The Rate of Interest and Other Essays*.
[18] On this point see K. K. Kurihara, "Secular Macroeconomic Theorems," *op. cit.*

est)[19] will be satisfied with much less real capital than is required for continuous full employment or secular growth.[20]

Lastly, there is the "socio-legal" base of reference, which is attributable to that complex of society which governs the distribution of income and which therefore predetermines the average propensity to save out of full-employment income. Keynes' policy suggestions make it unmistakably clear and operationally meaningful that the institution of inheritance and disparities of disposable incomes in a potentially wealthy economy entail the incompatibility of "the saving propensities of its wealthy members" with "the employment of its poorer members." [21] There is little doubt about a persistent tendency to excessive thriftiness in a society where people have been brought up on the classical teaching that "the abstinence of the rich" is the mainspring of progress. The theoretical possibility of the average propensity to save exceeding the average propensity to invest will remain potent as long as excessive thriftiness feeds on great inequality. It also presents a serious long-run problem in the conditions where, in the words of Keynes, "the propensity to consume and the rate of investment are not deliberately controlled in the social interest but are mainly left to the influences of *laissez-faire*." [22]

Thus capital accumulation, the *rentier* aspect, and the distribution of income are fundamental explanatory variables in Keynes' model of secular instability. These are the reasons why a full-employment equilibrium, once reached, constantly threatens to break down, and also why an advanced economy tends toward an indefinite underemployment equilibrium. This kind of endogenous explanation of secular instability is, it should be noticed, fundamentally different from the "stagnation thesis" which invokes such exogenous forces as population and technology, in two important respects. First, the former throws a searchlight

---

[19] Professor J. Tinbergen considers this equation a realistic representation of entrepreneurial decisions and motivation, as far as a private-enterprise economy is concerned. (See his "The Significance of Keynes' Theories from the Econometric Point of View," *The New Economics*, p. 225.)

[20] The argument is sometimes advanced that the "stagnation doctrine" should emphasize a "chronically low and inelastic" marginal efficiency of capital instead of too high a rate of interest. (See, *e.g.*, W. Fellner, "The Robertsonian Evolution," *Amer. Econ. Rev.*, June, 1952.) This argument, however, abstracts from the distributive aspect of the interest problem and takes the *"rentier* aspect" as given —probably in deference to the sensibilities of the *rentier*.

[21] *General Theory*, p. 31.

[22] *Op. cit.*, p. 219.

directly upon "the working of the economic engine," as Schumpeter observed in his evaluation of Keynes' "breakdown theory," [23] while the latter tends to divert attention from the endogenous defects of the economic machine to accidental non-economic forces over which the economist has little or no control. Second, the former logically leads to economic reforms in the determination of the rate of capital growth, in the monetary system, and in the distribution of income, while the latter tends to overstate the case for temporary props of a political nature. Thus it is no wonder that Keynes should suggest secular economic "operationalism" along the lines of (1) "the socially controlled rate of investment," (2) "a falling rate of interest," and (3) "the higher taxation of large incomes and inheritances." [24] Any other suggestions must assume that the invisible hand is still a reliable equilibrator, that fortuitous autonomous forces (*e.g.*, armament) making for "secular exhilaration" are here to stay, or that we can risk "throwing out the baby with the bath."

To see more clearly the relationship between distribution and employment, it is necessary to analyze the "distribution effect" on the consumption, savings and investment functions. Let us begin with the consumption function and its inverse function.

Distribution and the Consumption Function

Abstracting from its effect on consumer habits, as in most short-run discussions, one can agree that a more equal distribution of income will have no effect on total consumption or savings if the marginal propensity to consume is constant at both high and low income levels. Thus Mr. H. Lubell, in his attempt to prove the irrelevance of redistribution for the consumption function, explicitly admits that "no allowance is made for the fact that, with redistribution of income, saving habits might be materially altered." [25] Similarly, Dr. T. C. Schelling, by taking the difference in the marginal propensity to consume between wage-earn-

---

23 See his "John Maynard Keynes, 1883-1946," *Amer. Econ. Rev.*, Sept., 1946.
24 *General Theory*, p. 325, 377.
25 See his "Effects of Income Redistribution on Consumer Expenditures," *Amer. Econ. Rev.*, March, 1947. This statistical approach to "redistribution" in the sense of personal-income shifts, while it is useful in measuring the exact degree of inequality in the Lorenz-curve sense, obscures the more fundamental factoral distribution of the total product and its long-run implications for the consumption-goods vis-a-vis capital-goods structure of the economy.

ers and profit-takers as given, represents a redistribution of income from, say, profits to wages, as an addition to the wage parameter and an equal reduction in the profit parameter.[26] But it is precisely the possible effects on saving habits of changes in income distribution that is relevant to the long-run analysis. To see such effects, let us first look at income determination from the standpoint of distribution as well as of production.

Let the output of capital goods be x and their unit price p_x, the output of consumer goods y and their unit price p_y, and national income Y. Let, further, s be the constant proportion of income saved and therefore $(1-s)$ the constant proportion of income spent on consumption. Then we can write

$$Y = xp_x + yp_y = sY + (1-s)Y \qquad (1)$$

If the money wage-rate is w, the volume of employment N, and gross profits (including other property incomes) P, we can also write

$$Y = P + wN \qquad (2)$$

Dividing total employment into employment in the capital-goods industries and employment in the consumer-goods industries, we get

$$N = N_x + N_y \qquad (3)$$

From (1) and the following steps we get the rate of change of income

$$\begin{aligned}
\frac{dY}{Y} &= \frac{d(sY)}{Y} + \frac{d(1-s)Y}{Y} \\
&= s\left(\frac{d(sY)}{sY}\right) + (1-s)\left(\frac{d(1-s)Y}{(1-s)Y}\right) \\
&= s\left(\frac{d(xp_x)}{xp_x}\right) + (1-s)\left(\frac{d(yp_y)}{yp_y}\right) \qquad (1a)
\end{aligned}$$

From (2) we also get the rate of change of income

$$\frac{dY}{Y} = (1-l)\frac{dP}{P} + l\left(\frac{dw}{w} + \frac{dN}{N}\right) \qquad (2a)$$

where $l =$ the proportion of national income going to wages.

[26] Cf. *National Income Behavior* (McGraw-Hill, New York, 1951), Chap. 9.

Let the price of a unit of capital goods equal its marginal prime cost on the assumption that labor is the only prime factor of production. Then we have for capital goods

$$p_x = w \frac{dN_x}{dx}$$

and similarly for consumer goods

$$p_y = w \frac{dN_y}{dy}$$

From these conditions and equation (3) we get the rate of change of employment

$$\frac{dN}{N} = \frac{dN_x}{N} + \frac{dN_y}{N}$$

$$= \frac{xw \dfrac{dN_x}{dx}}{xN} \cdot \frac{dx}{x} + \frac{yw \dfrac{dN_y}{dy}}{xN} \cdot \frac{dy}{y}$$

$$= \frac{xp_x}{xN} \cdot \frac{dx}{x} + \frac{yp_y}{wN} \cdot \frac{dy}{y}$$

$$= \frac{s}{l} \cdot \frac{dx}{x} + \frac{1-s}{l} \cdot \frac{dy}{y} \tag{3a}$$

In the above system (2a) reflects the relative shares of wages and profits in the national income. If the proportion of national income going to wages (l) is a constant fraction, the absolute share of wage earners (wN) will depend on changes in either the money wage-rate (w) or the volume of employment (N) or both. If the proportion of total income going to wages changes according to (3a), the greater this proportion the smaller will be the volume of employment, other things being equal. However, the rate of employment will rise in the *long run* if a rise in l has the effect of increasing the average propensity to consume $(1-s)$ and therefore the rate of consumer-goods output dy/y, since $yp_y = (1-s)Y$.

Thus it is possible to represent income redistribution as a permanent change in consumer habits or, more rigorously, as a change not only in the wage parameter l but also in the consumption parameter $(1-s)$. If, for example, l changes permanently from .6 to .8 for a combination of reasons indicated earlier, $(1 - s)$ may change similarly from .75 to .9. This might be interpreted to mean that the average propensity to consume out of full-employment income is, after the redistribution, constantly 90 per cent due to the fact that the proportion of national income going to wages is constantly 80 per cent. Such an interpretation is reinforced by the observable facts that the average propensity to consume out of wage income is generally higher than that out of profit income and that well-to-do families save a larger absolute and proportionate amount of their incomes than do poor families.[27]

If significant changes in the proportion of total income going to wages do affect consumer habits, as in the above argument, it would be important to contemplate income redistribution with reference to the consumption function. In addition, there is a more compelling reason why income redistribution should be given serious attention in a long-run analysis. And that reason is what might be termed the "capital effect"[28] (in contradistinction to the "income effect") of moderate thriftiness incident to the correction of great inequality upon the marginal efficiency of capital and therefore upon the secular investment function, as will be amplified in the next section. Without an explicit treatment of that "capital effect," the usual Keynesian argument about redistributing incomes to raise the consumption function is subject to the criticism that there may be an offsetting decrease in investment as a consequence of income redistribution in favor of wages against profits. This is where a long-run analysis must be made of the relationship between distribution and investment.

---

[27] Cf. Brookings Institution, *America's Capacity to Consume* (Washington, 1934); National Resources Committee, *Consumer Expenditures in the United States: Estimates for 1935-36* (Washington, 1939); *Federal Reserve Bulletin*, August and November, 1950.

[28] Any income redistribution that significantly alters the average propensity to consume or to save will affect the secular investment function both via the "income effect" and via the "capital effect." The "income effect" refers to investment considered as an increasing function of consumption and income, $\partial I/\partial Y > 0$, while the "capital effect" deals with investment considered as a decreasing function of capital accumulation, $\partial I/\partial K < 0$. "Capital accumulation" here is limited to the growth of *fixed* capital (durable plant and equipment which is what determines the degree of "roundaboutness" and hence the historical trend of the marginal efficiency of capital in general). Capital accumulation, as such, is in turn historically predetermined by $S = I$, *ex post*. Finally the magnitude of S depends on size of income *and* the distribution of income. This subject will be treated in more detail later.

Distribution and the Investment Function

Suppose what Professor Hansen calls "a high-wage, low-profit economy" is the order of the day. Suppose, further, that the average propensity to consume is very high at all high levels of income in this high-wage, low-profit economy. What is likely to be the private inducement to investment in such an economy? Several plausible answers may be briefly appraised.

Professor Hansen himself seems satisfied to argue that the private inducement to invest is likely to be promoted in such an economy not only because consumer demand is kept up but because "there would still remain, by reason of continuous capacity output, adequate profits to sustain and motivate private enterprise." [29] Thus he equates a high-wage, low-profit economy with a regime of reasonably profitable private investment as well as with a "high-consumption, low-saving" economy, thereby arriving at the conclusion that "a high-wage, low-profit economy . . . is the goal that modern industrial communities need to reach in order to ensure adequate demand." [30] It is to be feared, however, that Professor Hansen has done less than full justice to his penetrating vision by abstracting from the "capital effect." For without an explicit statement of this effect the apparent contradiction between low profits and the unimpaired inducement to invest will remain a real contradiction. This point is made clearer in the following review of Keynes' digressive comments on the consumption-investment relation.

Keynes justifies the underconsumptionists' complaints by asserting that "capital is not a self-subsistent entity existing apart from consumption" [31] and that "since the expectation of consumption is the only *raison d'être* of employment . . . a diminished propensity to consume has *cet. par.* a depressing effect on employment." [32] These statements at best come to the familiar acceleration form $I_t = \beta(C_{t-1} - C_{t-2})$. The usual criticism that the demand for capital depends on the demand for *other* capital goods as well misses the mark. A more substantive criticism is that Keynes, while he properly criticizes underconsumptionists

[29] Cf. *Economic Policy and Full Employment* (Whittlesey, New York, 1947), pp. 48-49.
[30] *Ibid.*
[31] *General Theory,* p. 106.
[32] *Ibid.,* p. 211.

(*e.g.*, J. A. Hobson) for confusing $S = I$ with $S(Y) = \bar{I}$, nevertheless failed to see the secular significance of $S = I$ in the light of his own long-run "breakdown" theory which stresses, among others, the depressing impact of capital accumulation.[33] For if we start with the historically valid supposition that savings are actually invested, we would be in a position to argue either that the existing stock of capital is too large for further profitable investment or that the permanent reduction of excessive thriftiness and the correspondingly moderate stock of capital are conducive to a fairly high marginal efficiency of capital. This is to give prominence to the "capital effect" mentioned before. Here lies the clue to the seemingly paradoxical relationship between low profits and high investment. The apparent paradox disappears as soon as it is realized that if a regime of moderate profits is also a regime of moderate thriftiness and therefore, *ex post*, of moderate capital accumulation, the marginal efficiency of capital will not decline but, on the contrary, is more likely to increase via the usual "income effect" of high consumer demand.

Another answer is given by Professor Fellner, who points out that since "consumption is generally considered to be a more stable constituent of aggregate demand than investment," investment may be favorably affected by a small degree of uncertainty resulting from a high propensity to consume.[34] He elsewhere remarks that this psychological dependence of the inducement to invest on the steady demand for consumption is "the element of truth behind the paradox that an equitable distribution of income may be conducive to entrepreneurial interests." [35] That this is considered a paradox is once again a reflection on classical preoccupation with the principle of "derived demand" at the expense of sufficient realization that investment is a decreasing function of capital accumulation. Moreover, it is doubtful that too much significance can be attached to the stochastic connection between investment and a small degree of general

[33] Professor Domar seems to be the first to point out the secular significance of the Hobsonian supposition that savings are actually invested. (See his "Expansion and Employment," *op. cit.*, p. 52.) But he fails to note that Keynes' oversight was partly due to Hobson's erroneous attempt to apply what may be valid for long-run analysis to a short-run explanation of "Depression in Trade."

[34] Cf. "The Capital-Output Ratio in Dynamic Economics," *Money, Trade, and Economic Growth* (Macmillan, New York, 1951), p. 123.

[35] Cf. *Monetary Policies and Full Employment* (Univ. of Calif. Press, 1946), p. 44.

uncertainty inasmuch as the implied connection between uncertainty and expectations is a vague one.

It is noteworthy that Brookings Institution publications [36] are highly suggestive of the underconsumption notion that a more equitable distribution of income will increase the community's "capacity to consume" and so open up vast investment opportunities. On this line of reasoning serious arguments are sometimes advanced in support of conceivable "secular exhilaration." By contrast, the United Nations' experts would rather minimize the destabilizating effect of investment than increase investment —through measures to promote consumption. For in evaluating full-employment measures from a global point of view, the experts state: ". . . a sustained policy of raising consumers' demand would lead to a gradual adaptation of the industrial structure to a higher level of consumption and thus reduce the scope for instability emanating from the side of investment." [37] The experts seem fully alive to the declining marginal efficiency of capital that is historically observable in all the highly "industrialized countries" at whom they are directing the above policy. It is but a step from here to Professor Hansen's "high-wage, low-profit" goal.

These, then, are plausible answers to the question as to whether a "high-wage, low-profit" scheme of things is or is not conducive to secular investment. The cogency of these answers has been shown as depending, in the final analysis, upon the varying degrees of realization concerning investment as a decreasing function of capital accumulation in the historical context of a highly developed economy. It is *necessary* of course to emphasize the "income effect" of redistribution inasmuch as the growth of consumption and of income will doubtless induce investment via the acceleration principle. But unless this "income effect" is fortified against the persistent tendency of the marginal efficiency of capital to decline, secular investment will not be compatible with progressive equilibrium. This is precisely where the "capital effect" comes in. A *sufficient* explanation therefore would be that since a regime of moderate profits is likely to discourage excessive

[36] Cf., *e.g.*, H. G. Moulton, *Income and Economic Progress*, 1935, and *Capital Expansion, Employment and Stability*, 1940; M. Leven, et al., *America's Capacity to Consume*, 1934.

[37] See *National and International Measures for Full Employment* (New York, 1949), p. 37. Also see K. K. Kurihara, "The United Nations and Full Employment," *Journ. Pol. Econ.*, August, 1950.

thriftiness and, via *ex post* $S = I$, overexpansion of durable plant and equipment, the marginal efficiency of capital will be prevented from collapsing with further investment and so will give effect to the acceleration principle with further consumption and income. This is to stress the "capital effect" which Ricardo, Marx, Hobson, and Keynes had the insight to regard as a crucial explanatory variable in their long-run theories.

Thus viewed, a "high-wage, low-profit" economy would find its secular economic justification not only in sustained high consumption but also in the permanent mitigation of the depressing impact of capital accumulation—that same impact which Marx dismally viewed as the "ultimate barrier" to economic growth but which Keynes optimistically considered remediable through such a "scheme for the higher taxation of large incomes and inheritances" as would secure "a rate of accumulation not much greater than at present." [38]

Closely allied to the above discussion but more directly concerned with secular growth is the classical versus the Keynesian controversy on the question of the relationship between income distribution and capital accumulation. This question will be found to pivot around Keynes' notion of an "interest-free" society which is, in this writer's view, more fundamental than Professor Hansen's "high-wage, low-profit" economy. It will be shown that these are not alternatives but complements, but let us begin with a recapitulation of the controversy mentioned above.

The familiar classical sequence of events leading up to progress is: inequality—"the abstinence of the rich"—positive saving—net investment—progress. The validity of this logical sequence and therefore the implied justification of inequality rest on the tacit assumption of full employment or, to be more exact, an automatic, stable full-employment equilibrium with unlimited price flexibility. Here Keynes made a startling break with the classical scheme of thought by demonstrating that "up to the point where full employment prevails, the growth of capital depends not at all on a low propensity to consume but is, on the contrary, held back by it." [39]

Assume, with classical economists, that there is full employment. Now in order to produce more capital goods, less consumer

[38] *General Theory*, p. 377.
[39] *Op. cit.*, pp. 372-73.

goods will have to be produced. This done, some employed resources would be released for use in the capital-goods industries. But then such a transfer of employed resources presupposes a decrease in consumer demand. This is where inequality is considered necessary to induce "abstinence," barring a regulated pricing mechanism (involving priority allocations, etc.). Thus on the assumption of full employment due presumably to pure competition and stable equilibrium, inequality making for a high propensity to save could be logically, though perhaps not practically, defended on the ground of the supposed economic necessity of capital formation.

Now assume, with Keynes, that there is less than full employment. In this event what is needed is a high propensity to consume to stimulate the demand for capital and so to render profitable the actual utilization of available idle resources by the capital-goods industries as well as by the consumer-goods industries. A low propensity to consume, which excessive inequality nurtures, would have the contrary effect of discouraging the capital-goods industries from actually utilizing the unemployed resources available. Thus Keynes concludes that, "in contemporary conditions the growth of wealth, so far from being dependent on the abstinence of the rich, as is commonly supposed, is more likely to be impeded by it" and that "one of the chief social justifications of great inequality of wealth is, therefore, removed." [40] This disturbing conclusion has led many to question Keynes' proposition that thriftiness is inimical to capital formation. Perhaps the most serious criticism is that which comes from Professor Pigou, in his otherwise generous appraisal of Keynes' *General Theory*.[41] Let us consider his reasons in order to sharpen the issue.

First, Professor Pigou interprets Keynes as concerned with the position of "short-period equilibrium" and then argues that, "as between situations in short-period equilibrium, the quantity of investment demanded is not in any degree an increasing function of current consumption." For in equilibrium, short-period or long-period, consumption has a zero rate of change so that it cannot logically induce any investment. Mr. Harrod alludes to this as an example of failure to appreciate the implicit dynamic

---

[40] *Op. cit.*, p. 373.
[41] Cf. Pigou, *Keynes' General Theory: A Retrospect* (Macmillan, London, 1950), see esp., pp. 42–44.

theorizing so characteristic of Keynes' *General Theory*.[42] He then suggests that one should so dynamize Keynes' analysis explicitly as to mean that "a continuingly more thrifty economy would have less investment." Thus interpreted, the acceleration principle comes to the rescue. But since Keynes rules out income distribution in his short-run theory, his reference to "great inequality of wealth," etc., cannot properly be construed as having anything to do with short-period employment. In fact, the statement is made in his concluding chapter on "Social Philosophy" and in a long-run context.

Second, Professor Pigou denies, via his criticism of Keynes' "one-sided" theory of interest, the validity of the latter's proposition that thriftiness may, except in conditions of full employment, reduce investment. In the classical tradition he makes the rate of interest the main *modus operandi* of economic fluctuation. For, contrary to Keynes' liquidity-preference theory, Professor Pigou considers the rate of interest mainly as the price which equilibrates the demand for resources to invest and the readiness to abstain from present consumption. Accordingly he argues that an increase in thriftiness and therefore in savings entails a lower rate of interest (given the demand for savings) which tends to stimulate investment. Thus making the propensity to save an increasing function of the rate of interest, Professor Pigou makes a passing attempt to rehabilitate the classical theory of savings and investment, or rather of interest, and inferentially to salvage what is left of the notion that inequality is essential to capital formation and progress. Keynes himself seems to justify the classical (and Professor Pigou's) postulate that savings depend partly on the rate of interest, for in his long-run digression he says that "it may turn out that the propensity to consume will be so easily strengthened by the effects of a falling rate of interest, that full employment can be reached with a rate of accumulation little greater than at present."[43] But Professor Pigou is on weak ground when he attempts to apply to Keynes' short-run analysis what may be valid in the long run and then to declare the latter's long-run conclusion regarding the unnecessary connection between inequality and capital formation to "break down."[44]

[42] See R. F. Harrod's review of Pigou's *General Theory*, etc., in *Amer. Econ. Rev.*, Sept., 1951, pp. 665-71.   [43] *General Theory*, p. 377.

[44] Cf. Pigou, *op. cit.*, p. 44. For an extended short-run criticism of Pigou's theory see D. Patinkin, "Price Flexibility and Full Employment," *Amer. Econ. Rev.*, Sept., 1948.

There is yet another fundamental way in which distribution reacts on secular investment, namely, the underlying conflict between the rate of interest and the marginal efficiency of capital mentioned earlier. Without going into the familiar detail, it is useful to review the relationship between the rate of interest and the marginal efficiency of capital or, what is the same, between "the demand price" and "the supply price" of capital assets in general. Compare the following two identity equations:

$$Supply\ price = \frac{y_1}{1 + e} + \frac{y_2}{(1 + e)^2} + \cdots + \frac{y_n}{(1 + e)^n}$$

where y_1, y_2 and y_n refer to the prospective yields of real capital in the first year, the second year and the nth year, and e the marginal efficiency of capital as the discount factor.

$$Demand\ price = \frac{y_1}{1 + r} + \frac{y_2}{(1 + r)^2} + \cdots + \frac{y_n}{(1 + r)^n}$$

where r is the rate of interest as the discount factor, everything else being the same as in the first equation.

The first of these identity equations is relevant to *real* investment decisions, while the second is more interesting to *financial* investors. For the guiding consideration to real investors is the marginal efficiency of capital and that to their financial counterpart is the rate of interest. It is clear that the lower the interest rate, the higher will be the "demand price" or the present market value of real capital relatively to its "supply price" or replacement cost, a series of expected annual incomes being equal. It follows that the entrepreneur will increase his investment in new capital assets if it costs him less to produce them than to acquire similar existing assets yielding the same annual income, that is, if the "supply price" of capital is less than its "demand price." This is merely another way of saying that investment in new capital goods is stimulated by the marginal efficiency of capital which exceeds the rate of interest.

The above suggests both that the *rate* of interest should be made to fall faster than the marginal efficiency of capital and that interest as *unearned income* should be made to disappear, if capital growth is to be compatible with continuous full employment and if distribution is to be truly functional. In proposing the gradual "euthanasia" of the *rentier* who receives pure interest unrelated to the function of risk-taking, however, Keynes laid great stress on "the great social advantages of increasing the stock of capital." It seems worth-while to enumerate these advantages, as follows:

First, income distribution would be more genuinely related to functional "labour, including, of course, the personal services of the entrepreneur and his assistants." [45] For the owner of capital (*rentier*) would be unable, in an "interest-free" society, to exact from the user of capital (entrepreneur) an unearned surplus by compelling the latter to keep capital goods scarce enough to possess a "scarcity-value" that is in excess of the cost of production. This principle is not at all vitiated by the fact that the owner of capital may coincide with the user of capital in practice. Second, the general opprobrium occasioned by unearned income would partly disappear. For if the rate of interest is zero, the volume of investment will be pushed to the point where the marginal efficiency of capital becomes zero, with the result that the owner of capital can no longer earn pure interest any more than a competitive firm can earn "pure profit" in the long run. Thus pure interest in excess of the return in respect of risk and enterprise would cease to exist and would no longer provoke bitter resentment against the "functionless investor." Lastly, the amenities of life, of which abundant capital is technically capable, would actually become available at "a price proportional to the labour, etc., embodied in them on just the same principles as govern the prices of consumption-goods into which capital-charges enter in an insignificant degree." [46] This might mean that many "gadgets" now inaccessible to the average man would fall within the reach of his modest pocketbook.

These advantages powerfully reinforce the more obvious advantage of continuous full employment which may accompany the growth of capital unhindered by "the competition of the rate of interest on money" yet moderated by the "high-wage, low-profit" state of affairs. It may be that these effects on secular employment and functional distribution will result from a persistent "cheap money" policy that is pursued in connection with

[45] *General Theory*, pp. 313-14.
[46] *Op. cit.*, p. 221. Apropos, Mr. W. Averell Harriman reportedly alludes to the crying need of capital-poor countries for such amenities, as he says: "Bathtub isolationism is the notion that we can just go on increasing our supply of bathtubs, television sets and other conveniences and forget the rest of the world." (*New York Times*, June 25, 1952.)

a large and growing public debt. It may turn out, also, that a regime of low interest will be as instrumental in reducing thriftiness as a regime of high wages in promoting a higher level of consumption.

Postscript

Increasing the stock of capital and promoting consumption are alternatives, as Keynes thought, *only if* they are presented by abstracting from income distribution. But our analysis shows that they are really complements inasmuch as the maintenance of progressive equilibrium requires the balancing of excessive thriftiness that great inequality fosters and the deficient inducement to invest that the declining marginal efficiency of capital entails. What is more, this balancing is facilitated by a combination of a "high-wage, low-profit" economy and an "interest-free" society. It may be suggested, however, that, while theoretically complementary, increasing consumption rather than investment is likely to be considered a practical imperative if (*1*) an economy already possesses such a large accumulated stock of fixed capital as would critically depress the marginal efficiency of capital with further investment, (*2*) it is institutionally difficult to control the rate of investment directly, and (*3*) the popular will embodied in a representative government is disposed more favorably toward achieving greater equality of opportunity through a "high-wage, low-profit" scheme of things than through an "interest-free" setup.

No explicit consideration has been accorded to the possible consequences of a zero rate of interest upon the supply of capital. What of the argument that an "interest-free" society would become stagnant for lack of positive saving? Would not the long-run aim of making capital relatively abundant be defeated by a zero rate of interest? The general answer is that an "interest-free" society cannot be simply and mechanically equated with a "capital-poor" society. It is not safe to assume that income is unaltered when considering savings as an increasing function of the rate of interest. For income must decrease to diminish savings as a high rate of interest presumably encourages the readiness to save but at the same time discourages the inducement to invest in real capital. In other words, the increasing effect of a high level of income on saving may more than compensate for the decreasing

K

effect of a low rate of interest on saving, with the probable result that aggregate savings remain positive. Moreover, conditions of full employment, which the stimulating effect of a zero rate of interest on real investment would help to maintain, requires the traditional virtue of saving not only for capital growth but for averting secular inflation. There are too many motives for saving besides "a reward in the shape of interest" to warrant the apprehension that positive saving in conditions of full employment should drop to zero before capital has increased enough to be deprived of its "scarcity-value."

What now of the possibility that excessive thrift may still prevail "in a capitalist society with a perfectly equal income distribution"? This is the prognosis given by Dr. L. R. Klein.[47] He bases his estimate on the existence of "risks of the future" and "opportunities for capital accumulation" in a capitalistic economy, as well as on the hypothesis that "saving has been more closely linked to our institutions, particularly our insurance companies" than to "the existing distribution of income." It would, however, be surprising if excessive thriftiness for the sake of a "reward for waiting" could survive in the conditions envisaged by Keynes, where "a man would still be free to accumulate his earned income with a view to spending it at a later date" but where "his accumulation would not grow," [48] that is in a future capitalistic economy from which the "functionless investor" (rentier) would have disappeared. It is plausible to argue, with Dr. Klein, that saving has been due more to savings institutions than to great disparities of income, but it is equally plausible to contend, with Professor Galbraith, that "a lower and a less stable consumption" is traceable to that disparity of income which is associated with "monopoly and monopoloid forms." If so, income redistribution via a vigorous antimonopoly policy or a steeply graduated tax program cannot be ruled out as a method of encouraging consumption any more than an extensive social security program can be discarded as a means for discouraging excessive institutional saving.

Lastly, in applying such measures as antimonopoly campaigns, welfare expenditure, a persistent "cheap money" policy, progressive tax rates, and liberal dividend payments for influencing saving habits and hence secular employment and growth, it is the

[47] Cf. *The Keynesian Revolution* (Macmillan, New York, 1947), p. 138.
[48] *General Theory*, p. 221.

part of practical wisdom to proceed with due care for "the variety of life" and "valuable human activities which require the motive of money-making and the environment of private wealth-ownership for their full fruition," [49] as Keynes so aptly cautions us. With these necessary qualifications and reservations at the back of our heads, we may hope to develop a more adequate theory of employment and distribution for analyzing and remedying "the outstanding faults of the economic society in which we live," namely, to repeat, "its failure to provide for full employment and its arbitrary and inequitable distribution of wealth and incomes." Only then will distribution help rather than hinder the economic equilibrium of a dynamic, progressive society without upsetting its social equilibrium.

[49] *Op. cit.*, p. 374.

PART THREE

AGGREGATIVE ECONOMICS AND TESTING

CHAPTER ELEVEN

The Empirical Foundations of Keynesian Economics

Lawrence R. Klein

KEYNES' SYSTEM of economics is built on the foundations of several specific hypotheses concerning human behavior. The principal conclusions stand or fall on the validity of some of these hypotheses; other hypotheses contained in the system may be less strategic. Confusion apparently exists concerning such questions as:

What exactly are the Keynesian hypotheses?
Which among them are vital to the main conclusions?
To what extent are these hypotheses valid in the real world?

Through an attempted fresh restatement of some prior arguments, I shall, in this contribution, try to define sharply the Keynesian hypotheses and analyze the functioning of the model system to elucidate the more strategic hypotheses. Then I shall survey various results in the field of empirical economics, especially econometrics, and confront the hypothetical system with our present knowledge of the facts.

Three accepted pillars of the Keynesian system are (*1*) the propensity to consume, (*2*) the marginal efficiency of capital, and (*3*) liquidity-preference. From the statements in Keynes' *General Theory,* we learn that the propensity to consume is a relationship associating the community's consumption with the community's income. The relationship is assumed to be positive (higher income levels associated with higher consumption levels) with a slope everywhere less than unity. Keynes explicitly recognized that alterations in the distribution of income among the individuals of the community would affect the propensity to consume relationship but he did not develop this point in the elaboration of the workings of his model.

The concept of marginal efficiency of capital establishes a relation between outlays on new capital, expected returns from the use of new capital, and a discount or interest rate. The higher are expected returns, interest rate constant, the larger will be investment outlay. The higher is the interest rate, expected returns constant, the smaller will be investment outlay. This theory can be developed, essentially, from the theory of the profit maximizing firm.

The liquidity-preference doctrine of the *General Theory* envisages a negative relationship between the community's holdings of idle balances and the rate of interest. Moreover, this relationship is assumed to be nonlinear, falling and stretching out asymptotically just above the institutional minimum interest rate (idle cash on the horizontal axis and interest rate on the vertical axis). Keynes does not dispute the classical hypothesis that *active* balances are held in constant proportion to the level of community income, but he does make it clear that total balances, active plus idle, are not simply related to income. They are jointly related to income and the interest rate—positively related to income and negatively related to the interest rate.

In order to confront hypothetical models with the results of behavior in the real world, we must sharply formulate the models in mathematical form so that econometric methods of testing may be appropriately used. The customary mathematical exposition of the Keynesian system takes the form

(1) $\qquad C = C(i, Y); \ C_i \gtreqless 0, 0 < C_Y < 1;$

(2) $\qquad I = I(i, Y); \ I_i < 0, 0 < I_Y < 1;$

(3) $\qquad M = M(i, Y); \ M_i < 0, M_Y > 0;$

(4) $\qquad Y = C + I.$

$$
\begin{aligned}
C &= \text{consumption} \\
Y &= \text{income} \\
I &= \text{investment} \\
M &= \text{cash balances} \\
i &= \text{interest rate.}
\end{aligned}
$$

Subscripts attached to C, I and M denote partial derivatives (slopes) of the three functions.

This is an extremely useful *pedagogic* model for teaching students the main facts about the functioning of the economic mechanism, but it is surely not adequate to explain observed behavior. That is to say, if we collected statistics on the five variables from market observations, we would probably not be able to estimate four empirical relations with the properties assumed in (1)-(4) and use them for workable predictions of economic behavior. A workable model must be *dynamic* and *institutional;* it must reflect processes through time, and it must take into account the main institutional factors affecting the working of any particular system. Different features must be built into adequate models of such diverse economies as the United States, Canada, the United Kingdom, Japan, the Netherlands, etc. Models of non-capitalist societies will differ even more radically from the models of capitalist societies, with investment definitely not an endogenous magnitude.

Added variables and more explicit detail on the composition of the aggregates in (1)-(4) will also be necessary in order to develop a model with good predictive ability. Some changes of this type will affect the model in an essential way by altering principal conclusions to be derived from it. We must consider changes of this character at some length.

Empirical research is not exact. In fact, if it is to be scientifically constructed and interpreted, it must be put on a probabilistic (stochastic) base. For problems of economic analysis the Keynesian system is treated as an exact model of behavior. The empirical relations prepared to test the system are stochastic; hence we must judge acceptability or refutation of an hypothesis in a probability sense. Observed economic behavior practically never agrees exactly with a priori theory.

The model in (1)-(4) is ambiguous on the definition of units of measurement. The variables are not defined specifically as current price or "real" magnitudes. Keynes definitely measured his system in real units, wage units, but for some purposes it may not be important to distinguish between some system of "real" and current price magnitudes. Recent discussions on the role of *homogeneity* assumptions in the Keynesian system require, eventually, a positive decision on the units of measurement.

An obvious defect in the realism of the equation system (1)-(4) is the absence of any international economic relationships. The Keynesian theory was originally developed for a closed economy, but if it is to be applicable to capitalist countries other than the United States, it must contain relationships dealing with imports, exports, and other international variables. Developments in Keynesian economics after the *General Theory* have integrated the system with the workings of an open economy.

K*

The Keynesian model, then, stands as a purely pedagogic device to demonstrate the workings of an exact, static, institutionless,[1] closed, economic system whose variables consist solely of the five listed above. Our problem is to view this model as an abstraction to be tested against the realities of actual behavior. The gap between abstraction and reality must always be kept in the forefront of our minds as we carry out the confrontation of theory with empirical observation so that we can make scientific and not superficial statements about the validity or invalidity of the hypothetical system.

Keynes developed a system of static equilibrium to serve as an analytical tool in business cycle studies, although he did not devote much space in the *General Theory* to the formalities of business cycle theory. There need be no conflict between static and dynamic theories of the same system. Static theories can be dynamized in a variety of ways, and there are many plausible dynamizations of the static Keynesian system. If we start at the empirical level and estimate a dynamic statistical equation system of actual behavior, we must be able to show whether or not this system is actually a dynamization of a static Keynesian system. To put the matter in another way, the static system derived from our empirical dynamic system must not contradict the hypothesis of a static Keynesian system if the latter is to be judged acceptable. This is the type of correspondence required between abstract static models and realistic dynamic models.

Let us consider a particular example involving static and dynamic propensities to consume, or consumption functions. In addition to the effect of the income level on consumption, many students have suggested an independent effect of income change. We may write a linear consumption function involving both current and lagged income as

(5) $C_t = \alpha_0 + \alpha_1 Y_t + \alpha_2 Y_{t-1}.$

Another way of writing this same equation is

(5a) $C_t = \alpha_0 + (\alpha_1 + \alpha_2) Y_t - \alpha_2 (Y_t - Y_{t-1})$

in which consumption depends on income, Y_t, and its rate of change, $Y_t - Y_{t-1}$. The usual assumption for the dynamic model

---

[1] One institution actually accounted for in this system is the central bank. This organization is assumed to control the nominal amount of cash, thus necessitating only four relations connecting five variables.

is that a lag exists in adjusting consumption to changes in income; therefore income increases will, in the first instance, tend to be saved. Savings are positively related to income change, while consumption is negatively related, as in the preceding equation if α_2 is positive.

Equation (5) or (5a) is a dynamic relation showing the effect of lagged income or the rate of change of income. The corresponding timeless, static equation is that derived from (5) or (5a) when the rate of change of income is set equal to zero,

$$Y = Y_t = Y_{t-1}.$$

In this case the corresponding static equation is

$$C = \alpha_0 + (\alpha_1 + \alpha_2)Y.$$

As long as we have

$$0 < \alpha_1 + \alpha_2 < 1$$

there is no contradiction between real world behavior expressed in equation (5) and the standard consumption function of static Keynesian theory. Since the Keynesian theory is presented in quite general terms, with the basic mathematical functions having only a few specified properties, there is no reason to restrict the discussion to linear relations as in the above example. It is true, however, that the bulk, though not all, of statistical testing is carried out for linear functions. The particular dynamization of the consumption function used here is merely illustrative of the basic concept of correspondence between dynamic and static systems. In attempting to build a more useful dynamic model of actual behavior, we shall consider, at a later stage, alternative dynamizations which are generally consistent with the static Keynesian consumption function.

When we come to the problem of building institutional phenomena and new variables into acceptable empirical models, we shall not necessarily find that the static versions of dynamic systems agree in every detail with the abstract Keynesian system (1)-(4). Our criterion of soundness of the Keynesian model must be whether the main conclusions of the hypothetical Keynesian system remain valid. The central point of all Keynesian economics is the following:

> *The system of classical competitive equilibrium does not automatically lead to a stable solution of full employment.*

Minor changes in the system which do not alter this fundamental proposition will not be regarded as refutations of the theory. They will be regarded as refinements. It is to be observed that the central proposition of Keynesian economics does not depend on the existence of market imperfections or money illusions ruled out by the system of classical competitive equilibrium.

The meaning of full employment must be carefully explained; otherwise we shall not be able to distinguish between refinements and essential departures from the Keynesian theory in our process of empirical testing. In some analyses, full employment is identified with a given level of production. If national income is used as a measure of national production (and this may be done except for institutional complications in the matter of indirect taxes and subsidies) we may think of some level of the variable Y, say Y_0, as being a measure of full-employment output. This is a useful concept only if Y is measured in "real" units, not current price units.[2] If the system (1)-(4) is to be a "real" system, however, we lack determinacy, since either the wage rate or the price level must be treated as an explicit variable.

Equations (1), (2) and (4) could automatically be given a "real" interpretation, but if we are to write (3) as a "real" equation we must have

(3a) $$\frac{M}{p} = M(i, Y),$$

in which p is the price level and Y is a measure of real income. The institutional function of the central bank in this model is to determine M and not $\frac{M}{p}$; therefore the system is not complete if written in "real" form. Other equations must be added. The added equations will give us a framework in which to develop a more satisfactory concept of full employment. Another aspect of using a "real" system is that it possesses the homogeneity properties ascribed to economic behavior by classical economists. The absence of full-employment equilibrium in a "real" Keynesian system is then not open to the criticism that it relies for its existence on departures from classical homogeneity assump-

---

[2] A mental *tour de force* is sometimes used by defining full employment as that level of national income measured in current prices such that all further increases represent price increases alone. In a dynamic economy it is not necessarily true that fluctuations in national income below some unique level must always consist in part or whole of physical volume fluctuations.

tions. In empirical studies we must not blindly rule out the possibility that actual behavior is best expressed in terms of relations among current price variables. As a matter of fact, available statistical data do not, in general, lead us definitely to prefer one system of measurement over the other. Except where we refer later to specific empirical studies that may have used current price variables, we shall deal with systems that contain "real" relationships in equilibrium.

The pragmatic definition of full employment as meaning a particular level of real national income has at least two major defects. It assumes an unique relation between labor input and production. Other factors of production are of importance, especially capital, and there may be possibilities of technological substitution. Keynesian economics deals with a curious abstraction called the "short run" in which capital is not variable, but this abstraction cannot salvage the crude definition of full employment, since any existing item of capital can be used more or less intensively within a large degree of variation during a short period of time. The second reason for discarding the crude definition of full employment is that the labor force need not be a simple fixed number or even one depending on sociological (noneconomic) factors alone. For example, the male population between the ages of 14 and 65, corrected upwards or downwards by simple rule of thumb, is not more than a working concept for some rough policy decisions. Under pressures of movements in wages, prices, hours of work, in addition to numerous social *mores*, the labor force is capable of great variation through the employment of more or fewer women, "unemployables," overaged persons, and underaged persons.

A classical definition of full employment is that situation in which all who are willing to work at going real wage rates can find employment. This is equivalent to meaning that the observed level of employment is a point lying on the supply curve of labor. In a dynamic world, we interpret this definition as an abstraction referring only to a static system which is viewed as the equilibrium position of an associated dynamic system. The basic Keynesian hypothesis refers not to the amount of employment at each instant of time, but to the equilibrium level. It deals with underemployment equilibria.

The Keynesian system is sometimes interpreted as dependent on the assumption that labor supply is a function of the money wage rate rather than the real wage rate. If this were the case in actual fact, there would be no empirical refutation of the basic point. The classical model would simply be inapplicable to the explanation of observed behavior because by its homogeneity assumptions labor supply is a function of the real wage rate. Keynesian underemployment equilibrium may thus exist but not necessarily contradict the classical model. However, arguments will be presented below to the effect that empirical dynamic models do have basic Keynesian properties and lack basic classical properties in equilibrium. In the absence of direct data on labor supply, we are not able to state definitely that empirical results establish a labor supply relation in terms of money wage rates or real wage rates. Even without settling this point, however, we can shed light on the existence of underemployment equilibria with or without homogeneity in the labor supply equation.

In a "real" Keynesian model we have the following equations:

$$(5) \qquad C = C(i, Y)$$
$$(6) \qquad I = I(i, Y)$$
$$(7) \qquad \frac{M}{p} = M(i, Y)$$
$$(8) \qquad Y = Y(N, D)$$
$$(9) \qquad D = D(Y, K)$$
$$(10) \qquad N = N^D(w/p, D)$$
$$(11) \qquad N = N^S(w/p)$$
$$(12) \qquad Y = C + I$$
$$(13) \qquad \Delta K = I$$

In addition to variables previously defined (in real units) we now have

$$N = \text{employment}$$
$$D = \text{capital consumption}$$
$$K = \text{stock of capital}$$
$$w = \text{wage rate.}$$

The model is not precisely static, but it can be termed a trend model in which the single growing force is expressed through movements in the stock of capital. Equilibrium positions in this model should best be viewed as trend equilibria ironing out fluctuations about a growth trend instead of about a constant magnitude.

The new equations used in the expanded model are a production function (8), showing how labor input (N) and capital input (D) are transformed into output (Y); a capital consumption function (9), showing how the amount of capital used up (D) depends on the stock of capital (K) and the level of output (Y);[3] a labor demand function (10), showing how the demand for employment depends on the real wage rate and capital consumption; a labor supply function (11), showing how the supply of labor depends on the real wage rate. The last equation is a definition stating that net investment is measured as the rate of change of capital stock.

If equations (5)-(13) have a simultaneous solution with labor demand the same as labor supply, in other words, identical symbols on the left-hand sides of (10) and (11), the equilibrium is one of full employment in the strictest classical sense. All who want to work at the going real wage can find employment if the solution to the equation system provides a point on the supply curve defined by (11).

The essential point of Keynesian theory can be construed to mean that a solution does not exist, but this does not mean that we are in conflict with facts of the real world in which things do get determined. Professor Haavelmo, in discussions of the theory of employment, has put the matter neatly. He argues that certain dynamic systems, representing the real world, always have solutions provided they are in motion, but that the corresponding static systems, representing abstractions, do not possess solutions. The system fluctuates, but not about an equilibrium position. Haavelmo has made another observation that nonhomogeneous dynamic systems (containing money illusions) may correspond to static systems that have homogeneous functions in the classical sense.[4]

3 The level of output is used as a variable in (9) to indicate intensity of capital utilization. If we neglect this aspect, we can use a more familiar type of production function, $Y = Y(N, K)$.

4 T. Haavelmo, "A Note on the Theory of Investment," *Review of Economic Studies*, Vol. XVI (2), 1949-50, pp. 78-81. It should be added that classical models are not strictly homogeneous as a complete system of equations because the nominal amount of cash is determined by central bank action. The classical view is that each functional relationship describing economic behavior of people other than the banking system shall have no money illusion. Even the demand for cash has this property.

The relationship between static and dynamic systems of the same phenomena is of vital importance in singling out the essential property of the Keynesian system and in seeing how it is related to classical economics. Keynes did not explicitly develop the dynamics of his model; thus our task is to prepare realistic dynamizations and test them empirically. A dynamic model which brings out the two properties expressed by Haavelmo is one in which (10) and (11) are replaced by

$$(10a) \qquad N^D = N^D\left(\frac{w}{p}, D\right)$$

$$(11a) \qquad N^S = N^S\left(\frac{w}{p}\right)$$

$$(14) \qquad \frac{dw}{dt} = f(N^S - N^D);\ 0 \neq f(0).$$

The added equation dynamizes the system by referring to the classical type of dynamization, the law of supply and demand. It states that surpluses or deficits are cleared by movements in market prices. While both entrepreneurs and workers are assumed to behave without money illusion according to classical tenets, by virtue of the fact that real wages are chosen as the appropriate variable in (10a) and (11a), bargaining as described in (14) is in terms of money wages. This, I contend, is realistic behavior. It may be argued that wage bargaining is affected by price movements, but institutionally we observe a lag between price movements and wage adjustment; thus one could consider lagged price changes as another variable in (14). This will, in fact, be done in certain empirical models. Nevertheless, with or without a lagged price change, the dynamic system is not homogeneous. Dynamic wage bargaining introduces money illusion, but of a type that vanishes in the stationary form of the model because if

$$\frac{dw}{dt} = 0,$$

we find that all functions possess the classical homogeneity properties. The fundamental characteristic of the system is that it contains nonhomogeneous behavior functions when in motion but homogeneous functions in the static form.[5] In passing, it may be

[5] The action of the central bank is not classified as a behavior function in this statement.

pointed out that this characteristic is not necessarily in conflict with classical theory, since the homogeneity properties of that theory are not really developed beyond the static case.

The property attributed to the adjustment function f in (14)

$$0 \neq f(0)$$

shows that underemployment equilibrium is possible. If it were true that

$$0 = f(0);$$

i.e., that zero unemployment and zero wage change were compatible, we would be able to replace N^s and N^p in the static system by their common value N and admit the *possibility* of a solution to the equilibrium system (5)-(13). If a solution were to exist it would be one of full employment, since all who want to work at the going real wage could find employment.

On the other hand, if

$$0 \neq f(0);$$

an equilibrium solution of (5)-(13) does not exist. A solution may exist to the system (5)-(9), (10a), (11a), (12) and

$$0 = f(N^S - N^D).$$

The solution would not be one of full employment if

$$N^S \neq N^D.$$

In particular, underemployment equilibrium would have

$$N^S - N^D > 0.$$

By adding to the equilibrium system the equation of full employment

$$N^S = N^D,$$

we find evidence of Haavelmo's other point that the dynamic system has a solution but that the corresponding equilibrium system may not. The latter is, in this situation, overdetermined.

This version of Keynesian economics has already been presented in other publications [6] and is subsequent to previous argu-

[6] L. R. Klein, "Theories of Effective Demand and Employment," *Journal of Political Economy*, Vol. LV, 1947, pp. 108-131.

ments concerning the possibility of finding equilibrium systems not admitting a solution even when dynamic adjustment processes in the labor market are not used. It will be remarked that we stated that the equilibrium system admits the *possibility* of a solution if

$$0 = f(0).$$

The possibility is not realized unless the other equations of the system are well behaved. Previous discussion was concerned with the existence or nonexistence of an equilibrium solution as a result of the extreme interest inelasticity of savings and investment functions. If interest rates would have to fall below institutional minima in order to equate the savings and investment functions at levels of income associated with full employment in the labor market, a solution to the equilibrium equation system would not exist.[7] The institutional minimum level of interest rates is also associated with the shape of the liquidity-preference function. That function is assumed to be interest-elastic in Keynesian analysis.

Stimulated by the results obtained in the Keynesian version of the theory of employment, Pigou and others have suggested that the consumption function should contain another important variable, namely total real wealth. Pigou first used real monetary wealth, but later refinements have clarified his point to mean total real wealth. Many alterations of the consumption function to allow for income change, population growth, or income distribution do not affect the central thesis of Keynesian economics as we presented it above. However, the alteration to introduce real wealth in the consumption function does represent an essential change. Pigou argued that if unemployment were to develop, workers would offer services at reduced wage rates. The real value of wealth, measured in wage units, would rise and ultimately consumption would be stimulated enough to maintain full employment. Instead of viewing classical interest rate adjustments as the method of maintaining balance between savings and investment at full employment, the emphasis was shifted to wage rate and real wealth fluctuations to maintain the proper balance. While the effect of interest rates may be dubious, the effect of real wealth has been assumed by many students to be adequate.

[7] L. R. Klein, *The Keynesian Revolution,* Macmillan, New York, 1947.

In considering empirical studies of economic behavior to see what light they shed on the validity of the Keynesian system, we shall not be primarily interested in refinements. We shall not dwell on the fact that real world consumer behavior is affected by income change and income distribution or that investment behavior depends on profits rather than income. The truth of these facts does not contradict the principal Keynesian results. We have stated above that dynamic aspects, institutional aspects, distributional aspects and new detailed variables must all be built into the pedagogic Keynesian system to enable it to conform to real world behavior, yet these extensions do not affect the core of the theory.

More crucial properties to be empirically tested are the association of zero unemployment with zero wage change in the bargaining equation of the labor market, the interest elasticity of investment, the effect of real wealth on consumption, and the interest elasticity of the liquidity-preference function. In addition, some of the more standard and less controversial properties of the system will have to be confronted with facts if the system is to be used at all as it is presently applied. These properties consist of the existence of a relation, perhaps partial, between consumption and income with a marginal propensity to consume less than unity and a relation between holdings of idle balances and the interest rate. Some pedagogic usefulness remains if investment is regarded as a purely exogenous variable; hence it is not absolutely necessary to establish the existence of a relation between investment and profits or national income, but the models of purely exogenous investment are so far removed from reality that it is hardly worth-while to consider them in this discussion.

Before considering complex equation systems involving many relations among many variables, we shall acquire a better appreciation of the empirical foundations by considering, one at a time, each of the major relationships and its strategic assumptions.

The Consumption Function

First, as to consumption for the prewar period in the United States and in other countries, one finds a high correlation between consumer expenditures and national income, whether measured in current or constant prices. One can be misled into believing that the simplest version of the Keynesian propensity to consume, a linear relation between aggregate consumption and aggregate income with a marginal propensity to consume less than unity, provides an adequate description of behavior. This view is apparently strengthened by the cross-section relationships estimated from consumer survey data of 1935-36 in the United States. Postwar spending in this country, however, produced observations that lay far from the prewar line of relationship between consumption and income, showing the need for a more complicated relationship. Variables or phenomena that may have been omitted are income distribution, lags, wealth, population, consumer expectations and interest rate. Moreover, the relationship may not be linear.

Income distribution and nonlinearity are closely related, since a principal effect of distribution on consumption works through the differences in marginal propensity to consume at various income levels, which differences characterize nonlinearity of the spending-income relation. Aggregative time series statistics are not as revealing on these points as are micro-economic data collected in consumer surveys. Survey data show two different types of distributional effects. They show curvature in the relation between mean savings and mean income by income classes, with the marginal propensity to save rising as income rises. In addition, we find that three basic occupational groups, farmers, businessmen, and nonfarmers nonbusinessmen, show three different propensities to save (total and marginal) varying in the above order from highest to lowest. The functional distribution of income among wages, business income, and farm income is thus relevant in explaining aggregate savings behavior. Since wage income is, on the average, low relative to business income, the type of nonlinearity reflected in survey data is related to the difference in propensities to save between wage earners and businessmen. This result is also borne out in estimates from aggregative statistics for both the United States and Canada, which show a higher marginal propensity to consume out of wage than out of nonwage income.[8]

Various types of lag relationships have been considered in empirical consumption functions, all of them essential in the dynamization of static systems. Sample survey data show some

[8] See L. R. Klein, *Economic Fluctuations in the United States, 1921-1941* (Wiley, New York, 1950), pp. 68-75. T. M. Brown, "Habit Persistence and Lags in Consumer Behavior," *Econometrica*, Vol. 20, 1952, pp. 355-71.

relationship between savings or spending and income change, but the results are not unambiguous and the effects do not show up clearly except for substantial changes.[9] If the aggregative statistics are given careful statistical treatment, an income change effect on consumption is evident.[10] An entirely different type of lag has been suggested by Modigliani and Duesenberry.[11] They try to distinguish between secular and cyclical influences on the propensity to consume by using current income and the highest previous income of the community as separate variables in the consumption function. The best possible lag relation found in aggregative data, however, is that in which past consumption levels rather than past income levels influence present consumption.[12] Relations involving lagged consumption and other variables, seem to give the best bridge of the gap between prewar and postwar data. In a relation of the form

$$C_t = \alpha_0 + \alpha_1 Y_t + \alpha_2 C_{t-1}$$

in which the lag effect is expressed through past consumption, the short-run marginal propensity to consume is α_1, but the long-run or static marginal propensity is $\alpha_1/1 - \alpha_2$.

Future income expressed in the form of consumer expectations may be as relevant as past income in determining present behavior. Aggregative time series statistics are not very suitable for measuring subjective expectations of individuals. We turn to micro-economic survey data in which we find evidence of the influence of consumer expectations on savings.[13] It is an unsolved problem to develop a complete system in which expectations are endogenous. On the other hand, if we treat them as external forces influencing the propensity to consume, we are forced to modify standard Keynesian assumptions about the stability of

[9] Ruth P. Mack, "The Direction of Change in Income and the Consumption Function," *The Review of Economic Statistics*, Vol. XXX, 1948, pp. 239-58. George Katona, "Effect of Income Changes on the Rate of Saving," *The Review of Economics and Statistics*, Vol. XXXI, 1949, pp. 95-103.

[10] L. R. Klein, *op. cit.*, pp. 81-83.

[11] J. Duesenberry, *Income, Savings, and the Theory of Consumer Behavior* (Harvard Press, Cambridge, 1949). F. Modigliani, "Fluctuations in the Saving-Income Ratio: A Problem in Economic Forecasting," *Studies in Income and Wealth*, Vol. 1 (National Bureau of Economic Research, New York, 1949), pp. 371-441.

[12] See T. M. Brown, *op. cit.*, for a detailed analysis of this problem with Canadian data. See also C. Christ, "A Test of an Econometric Model for the United States, 1921-1947," *Conference on Business Cycles* (National Bureau of Economic Research, New York, 1951), pp. 35-107, eq.(6.5).

[13] L. R. Klein, "Estimating Patterns of Savings Behavior from Sample Survey Data," *Econometrica*, Vol. 19, 1951, pp. 438-54.

the consumption function. Under the impact of widespread changes in consumer expectations, which can occur within short time periods, we should find shifts in the propensity to consume. Fortunately we can still use the Keynesian framework for business cycle analysis in situations like this provided we can measure these expectations in advance. Recent developments in the field of consumer surveys through personal interviews show great promise in enabling us to handle these difficulties.

We are led to consider a trend equilibrium instead of a static equilibrium for reasons in addition to those of growth in the stock of capital. Growth in human capital, population size, is another reason, acting on the propensity to consume, for dealing with a trend equilibrium. The introduction of a smooth population trend in the consumption function is in no way incompatible with the Keynesian system of analysis. In empirical time series studies, the use of per capita variables, the size of population, or smooth time trends have been used to measure the effect of population growth on consumption.[14]

The direct influence of interest rates on saving or consumption has never been found to be of empirical significance. Moreover, there is no theoretical reason for having preconceptions that the effect of interest rates is in one direction or another. Since there are reasons why higher interest rates should stimulate saving and why they should retard saving, opposing forces tend to mask any resultant effect of significance. Debate has not centered around the influence of interest rates on saving. Instead, the influence of money market variables has been expressed through the use of cash balances as a variable in the savings function. In some cases the stock of wealth has been suggested as a more desirable variable than the stock of cash, but the analysis is much the same in either case and the aim of the proponents has been to show that market forces can bring about full employment equilibrium even if savings are interest inelastic. Empirical studies have been made using liquid rather than total wealth, but those based on consumer survey samples suggest that the results obtained would not be affected by switching from liquid to total wealth.[15]

[14] A. Smithies, "Forecasting Postwar Demand I," *Econometrica*, Vol. 13, 1945, pp. 1-14. T. Haavelmo, "Methods of Measuring the Marginal Propensity to Consume," *Journal of the American Statistical Association*, Vol. 42, 1947, pp. 105-122.
[15] L. R. Klein, "Assets Debts and Economic Behavior," *Studies in Income and Wealth*, Vol. 14, National Bureau of Economic Research, New York, 1951.

As in the case of interest rates, economic theory shows that wealth should be considered as a variable in the savings function, but it offers no convincing reason why its effect should be in one direction or another. The crucial arguments against the Keynesian hypothesis of the possibility of underemployment equilibrium have been based on the assumption that savings and wealth are negatively correlated, other things being equal. Should we expect behavior to follow the simple principle "the more one has the less one wants" or should we allow for the possibility that people raise their levels of aspiration with achievement? From another point of view we might argue that people who have accumulated wealth have done so by saving. They are in the habit of saving and will continue to do so at a high rate.[16]

The empirical evidence confirms the existence of this conflict of behavioral forces. In low income groups the effect of liquid assets on savings is significantly negative. As one moves up the income scale, the effect is attenuated and even reverses direction at high income levels.[17] This finding is of the greatest importance, because it means that the arguments against the central point of Keynesian theory based on the wealth-savings relationship are of doubtful importance. Some people react to market forces in a way to refute the Keynesian theory, while others react in a way to support it. On balance there is probably more strength to the negative than to the positive effect of wealth on savings, but the net result is that market forces are so weakened that they are not reliable instruments of adjustment. That the overall effect of liquid assets on savings is negative can be seen from the fact that equations permitting only a single direction of effect fitted to a sample covering all types of individuals show significant negative association between liquid wealth and savings.[18]

Tinbergen, in his pioneering econometric study of the United States economy, estimated a consumption function with variables, other than wealth, similar to those discussed above.[19] In

[16] For a discussion of psychological aspects of the saving-wealth relation see G. Katona, *Psychological Analyses of Economic Behavior* (McGraw-Hill, New York, 1951), pp. 167-70.

[17] L. R. Klein, *ibid.*

[18] In addition to the estimates from survey data, we find a statistically significant negative relation from time series aggregates, provided both prewar and postwar years are combined in the sample. See C. Christ, *op. cit.*

[19] J. Tinbergen, *Statistical Testing of Business-Cycle Theory*, Part II, "Business Cycles in the United States of America 1919-1932," League of Nations, Geneva, 1939.

addition he used a variable to represent capital gains. With a redefinition of personal disposable income, the Keynesian model could be revised to permit the influence of capital gains on consumption. Tinbergen's sample is heavily influenced by the 1920's in which the stock market boom in the United States possibly gives undue emphasis to the influence of capital gains. In studies of data containing more years outside this decade, capital gains do not show a similarly strong effect.

To summarize, in an aggregative econometric model, an adequate description of consumer spending behavior would require the use of variables to represent income level, income distribution, lags in behavior, population growth, and wealth.[20] These variables should produce a nonlinear consumption function—one in which the marginal propensity to consume is not constant—but this effect may be achieved by using different linear pieces, *i.e.*, by having wage, farm, and profit income as separate linear variables. Simultaneously this technique permits an effect of income distribution. Alternative representations of lags may be considered but the most useful seems to be expressible in terms of previous values of consumption. Consumer expectations are of importance but have not been introduced yet into empirical work at the aggregative level. Fortunately in practical applications of Keynesian analysis it is possible to supplement aggregative relationships containing the variables mentioned above with findings on expectations from micro-economic consumer surveys. The only empirical findings to date that are in any way contrary to the essence of Keynesian economics is the evidence on the influence of liquid wealth on saving. The empirical relationship, being mixed in direction of effect, is not clear-cut evidence against Keynesian theory. The magnitude of the marginal asset effect on savings is probably not large enough to render market forces adequate operators of adjustment towards full-employment equilibrium.

Two recent surveys of estimated consumption functions give misleading impressions that the existence of an empirical base to this Keynesian pillar is more dubious than the above discussion suggests. Mrs. Ruth Mack has surveyed contributions in the field of consumption economics and takes a pessimistic view

---

[20] It is common practice in empirical studies of consumer behavior to take account of an institutional variable like taxes by using income after taxes, disposable income, as the variable in the consumption function.

of the possibility of establishing a stable propensity to consume.[21] R. Ferber has collected a number of consumption functions fitted to prewar time series aggregates and extrapolated them mechanically into the postwar period, concluding that the extrapolations vary widely and are inaccurate.[22] Neither of these two studies is sufficiently discriminating in their choice of empirical studies for review; thus they draw upon results that are open to serious criticism from an econometric point of view. They do not examine the power of the function with lagged consumption, nor the simultaneous inclusion of the other variables cited above for inclusion in an adequate consumption function.

The Investment Function

If one views the marginal efficiency of capital simply as a scheme of making investment decisions so as to maximize profits, the variables to be used in an equation of investment behavior are well defined. With some variations in the model of maximizing behavior, different forms of the resulting investment function can be derived, but they are generally consistent with the spirit of Keynesian economics. A case can be made for assuming that aggregate investment depends on aggregate income and the interest rate. This is the form often used in the mathematical models of the Keynesian system, although an equally good argument can be made for an equation which uses profits (or nonwage income) instead of total income. In either case, the stock of capital should also be used as a variable in the equation if we are not dealing with the mythological short run. Another possibility is liquid wealth. The appropriate liquid wealth variable for the consumption function is the liquid wealth held by households for personal use. In the case of the investment function, the appropriate variable is liquid wealth held by business firms.

A strategic property of the Keynesian system is the low interest elasticity of investment, although Keynes himself did not consider this point. Empirical studies of time series data show little or no significant relation between interest and aggregate investment. In studies of particular industries in the United States,

[21] Ruth P. Mack, "Economics of Consumption," A Survey of Contemporary Economics, Vol. II (Irwin, Homewood, Ill., 1952).

[22] R. Ferber, A Study of Aggregate Consumption Functions, Technical Paper (National Bureau of Economic Research, New York, 1953).

significant interest effects have been found where capital outlay is for highly durable products lasting 20 years and longer. Both railroads and electric utilities exhibit significant interest elasticity of investment.[23] These industries are so dominated by others in investment expenditures that significant interest effects do not reveal themselves in the case of aggregate investment. It is wrong to write off interest elasticity as nil; it has definite importance in some sectors, yet interest rate adjustments in times of economic crisis are not sufficiently powerful to be used as alternatives to more direct investment policies. The marginal propensity to invest is generally estimated at some positive figure less than unity, while the stock of capital is negatively related to investment. In most studies, significant effects of cash balances have not been evident.[24]

Tinbergen, in his studies of investment behavior in particular sectors, found special variables to be at work in each case, however, his findings are not such as to contradict Keynesian theory.[25] He studied investment in the United Kingdom, France, Germany, Sweden, and the United States for periods as far distant as the latter part of the nineteenth century. His principal empirical finding is that profit (or nonlabor income) is the main determinant of investment activity. His findings on the influence of pig iron prices (proxy for capital-good prices) and interest rates are uneven. They do not show a consistent and significant pattern of effect. Tinbergen, in his particular investigations of housing and railroad investment, found results similar to those mentioned above in that interest rates prove to be more significant in those areas in which capital goods have great durability.

J. S. Pesmazoglu [26] has followed up Tinbergen's study of British investment behavior in the period 1870-1913. He, too, finds little contribution of interest rates and prices of capital goods in explaining investment fluctuations, but does find significant effects of lagged profits, lagged investment, and share prices.

[23] L. R. Klein, "Studies in Investment Behavior," *Conference on Business Cycles* (National Bureau of Economic Research, New York, 1951).
[24] L. R. Klein, *ibid.*; and *Economic Fluctuations in the United States, 1921-1941* (Wiley, New York, 1950), pp. 115-17.
[25] J. Tinbergen, *Statistical Testing of Business-Cycle Theories*, Vol. I, "A Method and Its Application to Investment Activity," League of Nations, Geneva, 1939.
[26] J. S. Pesmazoglu, "A Note on the Cyclical Fluctuations in British Home Investment, 1870-1913," *Oxford Economic Papers*, (N.S.) Vol. 3, 1951, pp. 39-61.

Profits, as distinct from Tinbergen's nonlabor income, show less importance in Pesmazoglu's equation. This is perhaps a minor point in view of the fact that share prices are quite significant in the equation. This remark is relevant in spite of the fact that he extracted the influence of profits from share prices before he put the latter variable in the investment equation.

In order to get a clear picture of investment behavior in the real world, a minimum of three types must be distinguished— inventories, plant and equipment, residential construction. The empirical results discussed above, other than Tinbergen's, are most applicable to investment in plant and equipment. Inventories are related to sales, price movements, and short-term interest rates. Behavioral lags due to stickiness or inertia in adjusting stocks are also relevant. The Keynesian theory does not give explicit treatment to types of investment, although it could without departing from its main course. Empirical inventory equations reduce to inventory-sales ratios or similarly simple equations in equilibrium form and are consequently compatible with the general type of investment equation assumed in the Keynesian model. Residential construction, in addition to being related to income and interest rates like plant and equipment investment, also depends upon specific variables in the housing market such as rents and construction costs, the stock of housing and family formation. Any special market involves special explanatory variables, but in the case of residential construction, the special forms of the equation are capable of being used as elements of a more detailed system of Keynesian economics.

Empirical studies of investment behavior from data gathered in surveys of businessmen have attempted to measure the effect of expectations on capital formation. The results obtained thus far have not been as illuminating as those showing the effect of consumer expectations on household spending or saving. Expectations of investment outlays have proved to be useful indicators of actual investment largely because of the contractual nature of investment planning. Expectations have not been studied together with other variables simultaneously in direct relation to subsequent investment outlays. Instead, deviations of actual outlays from previously stated intentions have been examined in relation to deviations of sales from prior expectations. Little correlation between the two deviates has been found, although other variables, such as size of firm or size of investment program have been shown to be significantly related to deviations from investment expectations.[27]

Results, to date, by no means negate the plausibility of the relation between profit expectations and investment outlay suggested by the principle of marginal efficiency of capital. In its purest form, in terms of subjective anticipations, this Keynesian pillar does not have much direct empirical support. However, the forms of the investment function assumed in mathematical models of Keynesian economics have substantial empirical bases. It may be mentioned that share prices or yields do, in many cases, show significant relations to investment in time series studies. Tinbergen, Pesmazoglu, and the present author have found such results in British and American data. To some extent share prices and yields reflect expected future earnings and thus lend support to the hypothesis of the theory of the marginal efficiency of capital.

The strategic role assigned to investment in causing the entire economic system to fluctuate is an important aspect of the *General Theory*. In the chapter on "Notes on the Trade Cycle," Keynes argues that shifts in the schedule of marginal efficiency of capital cause movements in output and employment. Insofar as investment behavior is shifting it is difficult to predict or mold into simple patterns. In a sense, empirical studies confirm the existence of this property of the Keynesian system. Investment equations show relatively high variability and complexity, especially when types of investment such as inventories, housing, other construction, and equipment purchases are treated separately. Although Keynes did not stress the interest inelasticity of investment, this is a crucial property that later students have built into his system and have found to be empirically sound.

The Liquidity-Preference Function

Two important aspects of liquidity-preference are the lack of constancy of the classical velocity of circulation and the high interest elasticity of the demand for cash at low interest rates.

[27] I. Friend and Jean Bronfenbrenner, "Business Investment Programs and Their Realization," *Survey of Current Business,* Vol. 30, December, 1950, pp. 11-22. An expanded paper by these authors and O. J. Firestone, "Investment Forecasting in Canada," was presented at the Midwest Meeting of the Conference on Research in Income and Wealth, September, 1951, Ann Arbor, Michigan.

Turnover rates of bank deposits have shown strong cyclical correlations. Data for the interwar period are presented in the accompanying table.

Deposit Turnover in Commercial Banks, U. S. A.
[*1919-1941*]

	Demand and Time Deposits	Demand Deposits
1919	24.5	35.0
20	23.8	35.4
21	20.8	32.6
22	21.6	34.2
23	20.8	34.1
24	20.7	34.4
25	21.7	36.3
26	22.2	37.7
27	23.4	41.0
28	26.2	46.8
29	29.9	53.6
30	22.4	40.4
31	18.1	33.2
32	14.8	27.3
33	15.3	26.8
34	16.0	26.3
35	15.8	24.9
36	16.2	24.7
37	16.1	24.7
38	14.0	21.6
39	13.6	20.2
40	12.9	18.5
41	14.0	19.4

Source: Banking and Monetary Statistics, Board of Governors of, the Federal Reserve System, Washington, D. C., 1943, p. 254.

These figures show a strong lack of constancy, even over short periods of time, provided significant fluctuations occur in national production and income. Velocity or turnover can be defined in a variety of ways, yet it does not seem that simple redefinitions will preserve constancy. For example, estimates have been prepared of currency and demand deposits in the hands of households (nonbusiness organizations). The ratio of these cash balances to disposable income show, in the following table, a similar lack of constancy.

Ratio of Household Currency and Demand Deposits
to Disposable Income, U. S. A.

1929	13.53	1939	18.00
1930	13.93	1940	18.03
1931	16.36	1941	19.41
1932	19.11		
1933	18.64		
1934	18.00	1946	33.01
1935	18.62	1947	31.40
1936	18.31	1948	26.45
1937	19.12	1949	25.70
1938	20.63	1950	24.82

In the classical model, household cash held for transaction purposes should be a constant proportion of income. Total cash holdings of households are weakly related to income, while currency
and demand deposits show a strong income orientation; yet they
do not bear a constant ratio to income.

It is undoubtedly the case, as noted above, that redefinition of
numerators and denominators of velocity ratios will not lead one
to the classical model of cash holding. A more basic revision is
needed, namely, the type that Keynes proposed in the theory of
liquidity-preference to make cash holding a function of both income and interest rates. As we shall see from a consideration of
various empirical studies, perhaps even other variables should be
included. Idle balances, as opposed to transaction balances, are
the type that Keynes theorized should be related to interest rates.
Pigou has even accepted the Keynesian proposition that velocity
is a function of interest rates. This concession is of interest since
it makes clear the proposition that important classical doctrines
are not of necessity based on the fact that cash is held in strict
proportion to income instead of as a general function of income
and interest rates (liquidity-preference theory). Certain classical
theories of price determination do depend on the constancy of
circulation velocity, but the theory of a self-adjusting economy
with full-employment equilibrium could be maintained even if
the liquidity-preference theory were correct.

It is of interest to see whether active balances depend on income and idle balances on interest rates and other variables. Alternatively, we could investigate the empirical relation between
total balances, income, interest rates, and other variables. A

second, more specific matter, is the size of the interest elasticity of liquidity-preference. Keynesian analysis of the lack of self-adjustment in the economic system has often rested partially on the assumption that liquidity-preferences are elastic at low interest rates approaching the institutional minimum.

Few empirical studies of liquidity-preference functions set out to establish a single direct relation between total cash holdings and explanatory variables. Usually an attempt is made to separate active and idle balances in the first stage of analysis. One method used for this separation is to calculate transaction velocity in a period in which it is presumed that idle balances did not exist. This would be a period of maximum velocity. Idle balances in other periods are computed as the difference between total balances and the ratio of transactions to the maximal velocity. Another possible approach is to regard currency and demand deposits as active balances. Idle balances are assumed to consist of time deposits and possibly other near money instruments, such as government bonds in the case of the United States.

In the first of studies of liquidity-preferences by a series of authors, A. J. Brown estimated the relation between British idle balances on the one hand and interest rate and price change on the other.[28] He estimated idle balances by the above-mentioned technique using maximal velocity. Brown also related total cash holdings to interest rate, price change, financial transactions, and nonfinancial transactions, but he found the total relationship less satisfactory than that using estimated idle balances alone. His study is interesting because it shows more than one alternative to cash holding—securities or goods. The strict Keynesian theory is based on the alternative between cash and securities, with interest return as the strategic variable for decision-making. Businessmen, if not households, can speculate by holding goods when prices are rising; thus price change should be a relevant variable in the liquidity-preference function. Interestingly, we find that the equilibrium form of the equation in an economic setting with no price movements reduces to the Keynesian relation between idle balances and the interest rate. There is no conflict between Brown's equation and the Keynesian theory.

A. Kisselgoff's study of business liquidity-preference in the

[28] A. J. Brown, "Interest, Prices, and the Demand Schedule for Idle Money," *Oxford Economic Papers*, No. 2, 1939, pp. 46-69.

United States is noteworthy in that it considers idle balances to depend on the profit rate (ratio of profits to net worth) as well as interest rate.[29] He calculated idle balances for his sample of manufacturing firms by the method using transaction velocity in a period when idle balances were considered to be nonexistent. Entrepreneurs can put money into their firms instead of holding idle balances. If the only way of investing in business were to purchase securities, the rates of return on securities, both equity and debt paper, would be relevant variables in the liquidity-preference function. Direct investment without the purchase of securities does, however, occur without conscious *imputation* of interest costs or equity yields, and this makes it important for Kisselgoff to consider profit in addition to interest rate in his equation. If the rate of profit on existing capital is viewed as a statistical indicator of marginal efficiency of capital and if marginal efficiency of capital equals the interest rate *in equilibrium*, Kisselgoff's function is not formally different from the Keynesian liquidity-preference function. Rather than stretch the point of complete equivalence, however, Kisselgoff's findings are important in showing the need for decomposing the theory of liquidity-preference into more specific relations for businesses, households, and financial institutions. The Keynesian aggregative theory considers only one market rate on securities, *the* interest rate, while, in reality, there are yields on equities, short-term loans, long-term loans, and other categories of financial paper. An adequate description of reality must disaggregate in the financial sector of the economy beyond the pedagogical model of Keynes.

Studies have been made of the liquidity-preference of financial institutions, and one of these is particularly relevant since it takes up the more delicate question of the shape of the liquidity-preference function. K. Philip, in a study of the liquidity-preferences of Danish banks during an unusual period of monetary expansion, finds high interest elasticity of liquidity-preference at low interest rates and large volumes of speculative cash balances.[30] He uses

[29] A. Kisselgoff, "Liquidity Preference of Large Manufacturing Corporations (1921-1939)," *Econometrica*, Vol. 13, 1945, pp. 334-44.

[30] K. Philip, "A Statistical Measurement of the Liquidity Preference of Private Banks," *The Review of Economic Studies*, Vol. XVI (2), 1949-50, pp. 71-77. For another study of banks' liquidity-preferences see A. J. Brown, "The Liquidity-Preference Schedules of the London Clearing Banks," *Oxford Economic Papers*, No. 1, 1938, pp. 49-82.

a variation on the usual method for separating balances into transactions and speculative components, but the general approach is the same as in other studies mentioned here. Although the liquidity-preference theory is not necessary for the most essential properties of Keynesian economics, high elasticity of the demand for idle balances reinforces the argument that the classical model is not self-adjusting towards full-employment equilibria.

J. Tobin has also investigated the problem of elasticity of liquidity-preference from U. S. data on the average commercial paper rate and "idle" deposits in commercial banks.[31] Idle deposits are estimated by the usual method of determining maximal velocity (in a period of no idle balances) and subtracting estimated active balances, using this velocity estimate, from total balances in each period. Tobin's scatter diagrams show high elasticity of liquidity-preference at low interest rates and large balances. M. Kalecki's theories of the connection between short and long term interest rates involve similar considerations. He starts his analysis with a J-shaped curve between transactions velocity and the short term interest rate. British data are used in his empirical study. Kalecki's J-shaped curve leads to similar results on the high elasticity of the demand for cash balances.[32]

The present author has also estimated liquidity-preference equations as components of more general econometric models of the United States.[33] A different separation between active and idle balances was used. Cash and demand deposits were regarded as active balances, related primarily to income, while time deposits were regarded as idle balances related primarily to the interest rate. The a priori separation of active and idle balances by this classification may seem open to question, although not necessarily more so than the other method adopted by the several other writers, yet statistical tests do not show any satisfactory relation of interest variables to active cash so defined or any satisfactory relation of income to idle cash so defined. These em-

[31] J. Tobin, "Liquidity Preference and Monetary Policy," *Review of Economics and Statistics*, Vol. 29, 1947, pp. 124-131.

[32] M. Kalecki, *Studies in Economic Dynamics*, Farrar & Rinehart, N. Y., 1944. See also J. N. Behrman, "The Short Term Interest Rate and the Velocity of Circulation," *Econometrica*, Vol. 16, 1948, pp. 185-190 and *Ibid. addendum*, p. 370.

[33] L. R. Klein, *Economic Fluctuations in the United States, 1921-1941*, Wiley, N. Y., 1950, pp. 109-110.

L

pirical equations are made into linear approximations; therefore, we do not find, in them, implications of infinite interest elasticity at extremely low rates of interest.

An added factor is used in the liquidity-preference equation, however. Current idle balances are related to lagged idle balances as well as interest rates. This inertia factor is introduced because people are slow to change their stocks of cash. They tend to hold the same amount as before but are willing to shift under the impact of sufficiently large movements in interest rates. Keeping in mind the fundamental relation between static and dynamic systems, we find, however, that the equations with lagged balances become like the Keynesian equilibrium equation of liquidity-preference. In the empirical linear equation

$$M_2 = 15.37 - 1.62i + 1.90(i - i_{-1}) + 0.74(M_2)_{-1} - 0.18(t - 1931),$$

the equilibrium level of the marginal interest effect is

$$-\frac{1.62}{0.26} = -6.23.$$

For the average values of i and M_2 in the sample period, the interest elasticity is -1.29.

In the United States during the last war, tremendous cash balances were accumulated, while interest rates declined only slightly or held steady. At the same time, people did not elect to shift from cash to equities or private bonds. They did accumulate large amounts of government bonds. This phenomenon can be explained either by extremely high interest elasticity of liquidity-preference or by some inertia effect in cash holding. Either linear equations with lagged balances or nonlinear relations between idle balances and the interest rate alone fit the observed data well.

Micro-economic data in sample surveys exist for studying liquidity-preference hypotheses, but no systematic investigation with this particular objective has been reported. It is generally recognized that price, wage, interest or other market elasticities cannot be estimated from isolated surveys of individuals because market variables are effectively held constant during the brief period of time when the survey is being conducted. The effects of income, asset, demographic, and anticipatory variables can, however, be studied in a single cross-section sample. Fortunately, survey data do exist which throw light on some aspects of liquidity-preference. In the repetitive sequence of annual Surveys of Consumer Finances in the United States, information on asset preferences is collected under changing economic conditions, especially price changes. Moreover, respondents in these surveys are asked direct questions on asset preferences.

Replies to questions on asset preferences show a considerable switch from assets of fixed money value to assets of fluctuating money value during an inflationary period. Results are tabulated for consumer units earning incomes of $3,000 or more per year, the portion of the population most active in savings decisions.

Investment Preferences
(percentage distribution of consumer units)

PREFERRED INVESTMENT	1949	1951	1952
Assets of fixed money value	79	69	65
Savings accounts	18	13	16
Savings bonds	54	49	43
Accounts or bonds	7	7	6
Assets of fluctuating money value	11	23	26
Common stock	2	6	8
Real Estate	9	16	17
Common stock or real estate	—	1	1
Other preferences	8	5	6
Preference not ascertained	2	3	3
	100	100	100

Source: "1952 Survey of Consumer Finances," Part I, *Federal Reserve Bulletin,* Vol. 38, July, 1952, Table 7, p. 743.

Between 1949 and 1951 there was a considerable inflationary movement as a result of the Korean War in 1950, and people reacted by shifting their preferences towards assets of fluctuating money value—nonliquid assets. This finding suggests that a dynamic liquidity-preference equation should contain the rate of change of prices as a separate variable as was done in the time-series studies of Brown and Kisselgoff.

Respondents in the Surveys of Consumer Finances were also asked to give reasons for their investment preferences. The relative frequencies of replies for those with incomes over $3,000 per year are given in the following table.

Reasons for Investment Preference
(*percentage distribution of consumer units*)

PREFERRED INVESTMENT AND REASON FOR CHOICE

Savings bonds	
Safety	28
High Yield	14
Liquidity	2
Lack of liquidity	2
Patriotism	9
Participation in payroll deduction scheme	1
Other	4
Savings account	
Safety	7
High Yield	3
Liquidity	8
Other	4
Common Stock	
High Yield	6
Inflation Hedge	3
Other	4
Real Estate	
Safety	2
High Yield	5
Inflation Hedge	3
Tangible Investment	5
Other	6
Preferences or reasons not ascertained	10

Source: Ibid., Table 10, p. 746.

These data reveal motives for holding cash or alternative assets. The purely Keynesian motives of liquidity-preference theory are clearly present. In addition one must reckon with patriotism, institutional schemes of bond sales, tangibility of assets, and safety. There is no particular problem in building these motives into the Keynesian theory, especially through the parameters of the liquidity-preference equations. Other than rate of change of prices (real estate and common stock as inflation hedges) purely economic variables are not put forward by consumers as relevant to the formation of their liquidity-preference.

There is an abundance of empirical material on liquidity-preference and in trying to give a comprehensive review of past studies, we have devoted a relatively large amount of space to this subject. We might summarize these results as follows: a variety of independent samples of data in different countries and different sectors of the economy support the main contentions of the theory of liquidity-preferences, the lack of constancy of velocity in the classical monetary equation, and the existence of a negative relation between idle balances and interest rates. Evidence exists for believing that liquidity-preferences have high interest elasticity at low interest rates, although this evidence is not conclusive since linear equations with lagged balances also fit existing data well. Separate studies have been made of liquidity-preferences of banks, business firms, and individuals. In view of the different types of economic activities pursued by these three groups, it seems to be rewarding to attempt to devise separate liquidity-preference relations to be used in each sector. Different variables will motivate banks, firms, and households in making their asset preferences.

It should be mentioned that most of the empirical work cited above, though not all, has used undeflated current value data for cash balances, income, and other variables of the analysis. Deflated data, consistent with Keynes' valuations in wage units, fit the observed data equally well.

The Labor Market Equations

If the system is to be rounded out, as was discussed at some length above, equations of production, labor demand, labor supply, and wage bargaining must also be introduced in the model. A big literature exists on the fitting of aggregative production functions, and neither the evidence on this equation nor the fine points of its formal structure need be introduced here. The properties of the labor market equations alone are more essential to the present discussion.

Results are more satisfactory in the study of labor demand than labor supply. It is difficult to assess individuals' economic motives beyond demographic forces and other factors in deciding whether or not to offer their services on the labor market. In many econometric model investigations, the labor force is taken as a datum.

If the aggregative production functions of the exponential type used so widely by P. H. Douglas and others gives a tolerably good approximation to input-output relations in the economy, it follows that profit-maximizing demand for labor will be evidenced by a fixed ratio between the wage bill and the value of output. Empirical estimates of labor demand equations derived from this line of reasoning are given in other publications of the present author.[34] Similar equations have been estimated for Canada.[35] The constancy of labor's share of national income has long been a feature of interest to economists. This type of demand function for labor depends upon the wage-price ratio and hence satisfies the classical homogeneity conditions.

G. Tintner, in a study of British statistics on wages, prices, employment, and unemployment, has considered the matter of homogeneity of labor demand and supply directly.[36] He makes labor supply and demand direct functions of wages and prices without deriving the functions from any particular model of production and profit maximization. He concludes that labor demand appears to be homogeneous in wages and prices. His supply function has dubious validity, showing a negative coefficient of real wages but he does present some small pieces of evidence that it is homogeneous.

Regardless whether supply and demand equations in the labor market are homogeneous in wages and prices, interest attaches to the bargaining equation of wage adjustment. In the author's previous studies, a relation was estimated between the annual change in wage rates on the one hand and unemployment and the lagged wage level on the other.[37] This estimated equation has the property that if the change in wage rates is set equal to zero, unemployment is greater than 3 million for average values of the lagged wage level. Christ, in his later study, estimated a similar wage adjustment equation for the labor market but added the rate of change in prices as an explanatory variable.[38] There is much merit in the latter step, although a lag should be introduced because it is characteristically true in this country that wage movements follow price movements after a delay of some months. For equilibrium, we set the rate of change in prices equal to zero. We then find a zero rate of change of wages in his equation associated with substantial unemployment (6-7 million persons) for the average level of the lagged wage rate. Similar results have

[34] L. R. Klein, *Economic Fluctuations in the United States.*
[35] T. M. Brown, *op. cit.*
[36] G. Tintner, *Econometrics*, Wiley, N. Y., 1952, pp. 143-153.
[37] L. R. Klein, *op. cit.*, p. 121.
[38] C. Christ, *op. cit.*

been found in estimated wage adjustment equations for the Canadian economy.[39]

The use of empirical equations of wage movements as a function of unemployment is not entirely satisfactory for a study of the delicate question whether zero wage change is associated with zero unemployment. The empirical equations are merely linear approximations, with greatest validity in the neighborhood of observed sample values of wage change and unemployment. If the point of zero unemployment or zero wage change is not in the cluster of sample points, it is hazardous to extrapolate the linear function to points beyond the sample range. Fortunately, however, the samples used in actual empirical determination of this equation have usually included points of zero wage change and points of low unemployment.

The Propensities to Import and Export

Keynes' analytical scheme, as developed in the *General Theory*, covered only the case of a closed economy, but was soon extended to open systems of importing and exporting economies.[40] As was customary in purely domestic Keynesian models, income was used as the principal variable in import and export demand functions. The marginal propensities to import and export were then fitted into appropriate places in various multiplier formulas.

Because of aggregation over commodity types in simple Keynesian domestic models, relative price variables have been omitted and income variables are the principal demand factors.[41] It is not strictly correct, however, in models of a closed economy, to omit relative prices of producer and consumer goods if the investment and consumption functions are treated separately. Only if these two prices are proportional to each other are we justified in neglecting their ratio as a variable in theoretical models. There is even less justification for neglecting to account for relative prices of domestic and foreign goods in import or export functions. Since the forces determining these two price

[39] The Canadian estimates have not been published but were discussed by T. M. Brown, "Canadian Experience in Forecasting from Econometric Models," at the meetings of the Econometric Society, December 1951, Boston.

[40] See L. A. Metzler, "Underemployment Equilibrium in International Trade," *Econometrica*, Vol. 10, 1942, pp. 97-112.

[41] For a discussion of aggregation and the role of relative price variables see L. R. Klein, "A Post Mortem on Transition Predictions of National Product," *Journal of Political Economy*, Vol. LIV, 1946, pp. 289-308.

levels have a measure of independence, we cannot assume that they are proportional. The failure to include relative prices as well as income effects in the foreign trade equations of Keynesian models has been misleading. For some countries like the United States, the Keynesian type of multiplier analysis is all right. It leads to the conclusion that exports are employment-creating while imports are unemployment-creating. If relative prices are used in the propensities to import or export and these functions combined with technological production functions, we find that employment may be stimulated by imports of raw materials and machinery. For many countries it is essential to disaggregate models enough to allow for types of imports and their role in the functioning of the economy.

Empirically we should find that a country's demand for imports depends upon income and relative prices of home and imported goods. Other relevant variables would be additional price ratios, foreign exchange reserves, and exports. Many countries can pay for imports only if they export or draw on previously accumulated foreign balances. These variables have been especially important in the period of dollar shortage after the war.[42] A country's exports would similarly depend on relative prices, incomes, reserves, and exports of customer countries.

In the case of the United States, estimates have been made from prewar data of the marginal propensity to import. Because of intercorrelation between price and income variables and also because of the structure of the U. S. economy, estimates of relative price elasticity have not been entirely satisfactory. The simplest Keynesian theory containing an import function with an income variable alone is perhaps realistic for this country.[43]

Tinbergen, in his elaborate econometric study of the United States, did not give explicit treatment to import and export equations, but in his subsequent study of Britain for the period 1870-1914, he found great need for import and export equations.[44] In

[42] A model systematically incorporating exchange reserves into a foreign trading system has been presented in a paper by J. J. Polak, "The Postwar International Cycle," at the meetings of the International Economic Association, Oxford, 1952.
[43] Two representative studies of the propensity to import in the United States are J. H. Adler, "United States Import Demand During the Interwar Period," *American Economic Review*, Vol. 35, 1945, pp. 418-430. R. Hinshaw, "American Prosperity and the British Balance of Payments Problem," *Review of Economic Statistics*, Vol. XXVII, 1945, pp. 1-9.
[44] J. Tinbergen, *Business Cycles in the United Kingdom, 1870-1914*, North-Holland Publishing Company, Amsterdam, 1951.

the latter study he disaggregated into separate import and export equations for consumer goods, investment goods, and raw materials. For the British economy in this classical period he found definite evidence of relative price effects on imports and exports. Exports were also tied to the volume of world trade, and capital exports. Other variables in the import equations were the level of total consumption and investment. World trade, consumption, and investment may, in a sense, be regarded as substitutes for income variables of the type now used in foreign trade equations.

T. C. Chang in a number of studies has estimated import equations for several countries.[45] His variables change from one study to the next but a representative equation uses income, relative prices, and quantity of exports. Similarly Chang and J. J. Polak have together estimated equations of imports and exports for a number of countries in a multicountry international system.[46]

T. M. Brown, in his report on econometric forecasting in Canada[47] has given various estimates of possible import demand equations. In the latest and most satisfactory version, import demand is a function of lagged nonwage disposable income, exports, and a special variable to show the effect of governmental quotas and controls. Relative prices are also used as a variable in this equation, although the coefficient is not reliably estimated. The dominant variable is lagged nonwage income, and this is, of course, reasonable in the light of the types of goods imported by Canada. This equation is probably more reliably estimated than others dealing with Canadian imports, since it is based on recently available statistics of improved quality, and since it covers both prewar and postwar observations simultaneously. Since income, though of a functional type, is the major variable, this equation can easily be worked into the usual type of aggregative Keynesian model. The other two important variables may well be regarded as exogenous to Canada; hence they present no difficulties.

These several studies have used different data, different equa-

[45] T. C. Chang, *Cyclical Movements in the Balance of Payments*, Cambridge, 1951. This is essentially an investigation of open economies in the light of the Keynesian theory of employment.

[46] T. C. Chang and J. J. Polak, "An International Economics System," paper presented at the meetings of the Econometric Society, December, 1949, New York. An abstract is published in *Econometrica*, Vol. 18, 1950, pp. 70-72.

[47] T. M. Brown, "Canadian Experience in Forecasting from Econometric Models." Paper presented at the American winter meeting of the Econometric Society, held in Boston, December 26-29, 1951.

L*

tion forms, different explanatory variables, and different degrees of disaggregation. For these reasons the results often seem divergent, yet they have a common theme that income and relative prices are dominant variables in each country's import demand equation. Depending on the special circumstances at hand, other variables such as exports, exchange reserves, foreign loans, etc., must be taken into consideration to give a full explanation of import movements. Nonetheless, builders of Keynesian theory obtain clear directions from these empirical studies on the way in which they should construct their models. The simple income-determined propensities are not adequate.

An Empirical Model of the Economy as a Whole

One by one we have surveyed statistical evidence bearing on the validity of the main pillars of Keynesian economics. The conclusion submitted here is that the theoretical system stands up well in face of the facts. From the findings that have already been discussed it is clear that the usual Keynesian models are merely pedagogical frameworks and that any careful empirical investigation must take into account all the complexities of dynamics, special institutional arrangements, and disaggregation.

The reader may well ask, however, how does it all fit together? Perhaps a brief presentation of a newly estimated model, taking account of various advances in ideas of the past five years, will answer this question and at the same time give a quick view of the complexity of a realistic model intended to be used for predictive purposes. The model to be presented below is preliminary in the sense that it contains some aggregations of detail that are intended to be eliminated as time permits. It is a model that has recently been prepared in the Research Seminar in Quantitative Economics, University of Michigan, in order to have an up-to-date model covering several postwar years, and based on the newest data in the social accounts of the United States. Until a more detailed model can be prepared, this model will be estimated from the latest available data and will be continuously checked and screened for its predictive powers. Inherent in the structure of this model are some of the features that must be built into a newly developed system of Keynesian economics, whence comes its main inspiration.

The variables are:

$C =$ consumer expenditures in billions of 1939 dollars.

$W_1 + W_2 =$ wage income in billions of dollars deflated by p.

$P =$ nonfarm, nonwage income (after depreciation and before corporate profit taxes) in billions of dollars deflated by p.

$A =$ farm income in billions of dollars deflated by p.

$D =$ capital consumption allowance.

$S_P =$ corporate savings in billions of dollars deflated by p.

$L_1 =$ year-end personal liquid assets (including government bonds) in billions of dollars deflated by p.

$N_P =$ population in millions of persons.

$I =$ gross investment in billions of 1939 dollars.

$K =$ year-end stock of capital in billions of 1939 dollars (measured from an arbitrary origin).

$i_L =$ yield on corporate bonds (long-term) in per cent.

$L_2 =$ year-end business liquid assets (including government bonds) in billions of dollars deflated by p.

$P_C =$ corporate profits (before taxes) in billions of dollars deflated by p.

$B =$ year-end accumulated corporate savings in billions of dollars deflated by p (measured from an arbitrary origin).

$W_1 =$ private wage income in billions of dollars deflated by p.

$Y + T =$ net national product in billions of 1939 dollars.

$N =$ labor force in millions of persons.

$N_W =$ number of wage earners in millions of persons.

$N_G =$ number of government employees in millions of persons.

$N_F =$ number of farmers in millions of persons.

$N_B =$ number of nonfarm entrepreneurs in millions of persons.

$h =$ index of hours worked per year (1939 base: 1.00).

$t =$ time in number of years.

$w =$ index of hourly wage rates (1939 base: 122.1).

$p =$ price index of output (1939 base: 100).

$F_I =$ imports in billions of 1939 dollars.

$p_I =$ index of import prices (1939 base: 100).

$R =$ excess reserves of banks as a percentage of total reserves.

$G =$ government purchases of goods and services in billions of 1939 dollars.

$F_E =$ exports in billions of 1939 dollars.

T = indirect taxes less subsidies in billions of dollars deflated by p.

T_C = corporate income taxes in billions of dollars deflated by p.

$W_1 + W_2 - T_W$ = disposable wage income in billions of dollars deflated by p.

$P - S_P - T_P$ = disposable nonwage nonfarm income in billions of dollars deflated by p.

$A - T_A$ = disposable farm income in billions of dollars deflated by p.

F_A = index of quantity of agricultural exports (1939 base: 100).

i_s = yield on short-term commercial paper in per cent.

The equations connecting all these variables into a system have been estimated by econometric methods which take into account the aspect of the simultaneity of the economic process. Only the estimates of the coefficients in these equations are presented here for expository purposes. A full-dress econometric discussion and all relevant error variances would be out of place in the present context. This system is, moreover, presented as a positive result. The great variety of discarded hypotheses tested and dropped will not be specifically mentioned.

The estimated equations are calculated from a sample covering the years 1929-41; 1946-50.[48]

Consumption function:

$$C = -34.5 + 0.62(W_1 + W_2 - T_W) + 0.46(P - S_P - T_P)$$
$$+ 0.39(A - T_A) + 0.23C_{-1} + 0.024(L_1)_{-1} + 0.36N_P$$

Investment function:

$$I = -16.8 + 0.76(P + A + D - T_P - T_A)_{-1} - 0.14K_{-1}$$
$$+ 0.14(L_2)_{-1}$$

Corporate savings function:

$$S_P = -2.43 + 0.86(P_C - T_C) - 0.014B_{-1}$$
$$- 0.30(P_C - T_C - S_P)_{-1}$$

Relation between corporate profits and nonwage nonfarm income:

$$P_C = -8.34 + 0.71P$$

[48] Mr. Arthur Goldberger of the staff of the Research Seminar in Quantitative Economics, University of Michigan, has prepared the basic data and carried out the computations.

Depreciation function:

$$D = 11.46 + 0.14 \, \frac{K + K_{-1}}{2}$$

Demand for labor:

$$W_1 = -2.70 + 0.36(Y + T + D - W_2) \\ + 0.14(Y + T + D - W_2)_{-1} + 0.16(t - 1929)$$

Production function:

$$Y + T + D - W_2 = -31.98 + 2.31[h(N_W - N_G) + N_E + N_F] \\ + 0.076 \, \frac{K + K_{-1}}{2} + 1.90(t - 1929)$$

Wage market adjustment:

$$w - w_{-1} = 4.11 - 0.75(N - N_W - N_E - N_F) + 0.56(p_{-1} - p_{-2}) \\ + 0.56(t - 1929)$$

Import demand function:

$$F_I = 2.09 + 0.0087(W_1 + W_2 + P + A - T_W - T_P - T_A) \, \frac{p}{p_I} \\ + 0.24(F_I)_{-1}$$

Agricultural income determination:

$$A = -4.53 + 0.25(W_1 + W_2 + P - S_P - T_W - T_P) \\ - 0.13(W_1 + W_2 + P - S_P - T_W - T_P)_{-1} + 0.009F_A$$

Household liquidity-preference function:

$$L_1 = 0.14(W_1 + W_2 + P - S_P + A - T_W - T_P - T_A) \\ + 75.0(i_L - 2.0)^{-0.84}$$

Business liquidity-preference function:

$$L_2 = -0.77 + 0.24W_1 - 0.69i_S - 0.27(p - p_{-1}) + 0.64(L_2)_{-1}$$

Relation between short- and long-term interest rates:

$$i_L = 2.66 + 0.46(i_S)_{-3} + 0.23(i_S)_{-5}$$

Money market adjustment:

$$\frac{i_S - (i_S)_{-1}}{(i_S)_{-1}} \, 100 = 6.42 - 0.55R$$

Definition of gross national product:

$$C + I + G + F_E - F_I = Y + T + D$$

Definition of national income:

$$W_1 + W_2 + P + A = Y$$

Definition of wage rate:

$$h \frac{w}{p} N_W = W_1 + W_2$$

Definition of stock of capital:

$$K - K_{-1} = I - D$$

Definition of accumulated corporate savings:

$$B - B_{-1} = S_P.$$

To convey to the reader the truly pedagogical nature of the customary versions of the Keynesian system, we should stress that this is a highly aggregative picture of the U. S. economy used only as an initial stepping stone in building a more adequate working model that will be useful in the sense of permitting us to make accurate predictions of fluctuations in the economy. Yet complex as the present model is, it stems directly from the Keynesian inspiration. It is an outgrowth of the theoretical macrodynamic models of the Keynesian system [49] and the empirical testing since 1936. It attempts to distill a workable model out of the vast amount of research stimulated by the *General Theory*.

A few comments are in order to show how the empirical work done in preparing this model aids in building a positive theory of Keynesian economics.

The consumption function takes account of functional income distribution and differences in behavior among farmers, businessmen, and all others. The influence of the past is expressed through lagged consumption. Liquid assets show a somewhat smaller marginal effect on consumption than that estimated in recent consumer surveys. To some extent this results from an intercorrelation between liquid assets and the population variable. Another contributing factor to the smaller estimate here is the absence of currency estimates in liquid asset data collected in surveys. Because of the limited magnitude of the liquid asset variable we do not regard the neoclassical modification of the Keynesian system as a matter of prime importance.

[49] Great indebtedness is also due the models of Frisch and Kalecki.

The investment function contains no interest variable. At the level of aggregation in this model, no reasonable estimates of interest coefficients have been found in a large number of trial calculations. This is the extreme version of interest inelastic investment behavior. Two wealth variables play a role, but with opposite directions of effect. The coefficient of capital stock is much more reliably estimated than that of liquid assets. The renaissance of classical arguments through the use of real wealth variables in the investment function is a matter of dubious merit. The unreliability of the liquid asset coefficient cautions us against accepting the classical argument as something that will hold with a high degree of probability. Moreover, the estimated value of the coefficient is so limited in size that the time required for the working of market adjustment processes may be too long for effectiveness.

The equation of corporate saving also has a wealth variable with a small coefficient. The effect of the past, in this equation, is expressed through the use of lagged dividends as an explanatory variable. This variable is introduced because of the tendency of corporations to try to follow a stable dividend policy.

The equations on depreciation and the relationship between corporate profits and nonwage income are of no special importance to the present discussion. They serve mainly to close the system. The production function and labor demand equation are acceptable to many theories, Keynesian or classical, and call for no comment.[50]

A labor supply equation is not explicitly introduced. At this stage, the model assumes the labor force to be an exogenous variable, but obviously this approximation eventually will have to be dropped. Regardless of our ultimate treatment of labor supply, the market adjustment equation relating wage changes to unemployment and the lagged change in prices is of the utmost importance in giving an empirical foundation to Keynesian economics. In equilibrium, this system does not associate zero unemployment with zero wage change.

The propensity to import depends both on real income and relative prices. Lagged imports show the influence of the past

[50] The particular equation of labor demand is derived from the theory of profit maximization with a logarithmic and not linear production function. In our empirical model, we regard the linear production function only as an approximation. We could have used a logarithmic function but it would have complicated other aspects of the system viewed as a unit.

on present behavior. The income effects dealt with in elaborations of Keynesian models to open economies are probably dominant in the case of United States demand and reasonably well estimated in simple equations. In other countries, the effects of terms of trade and the physical productivity of imports would have to be more carefully studied. Exports are not, in the above model, treated as an endogenous variable.

Agriculture has been singled out for explicit treatment in the estimation of consumer demand behavior. The supply and production side of agriculture is not worked out in detail in this model. One equation is simply introduced to connect agriculture with the rest of the economy and thereby retain the rudimentary properties of a closed system.

The liquidity-preference equations distinguish between household and business holdings of cash. The financial sector is not given detailed separate treatment. The speculative activities of households are assumed to involve consideration of long-term interest rates, while those of businesses are assumed to involve short-term interest rates. Businessmen speculate as well between inventories and cash, hence the use of price change as another variable in the equation for businessmen. The equation of household demand for cash shows definite nonlinearity which we have tried to approximate in our equation. The business equation uses lagged balances as an alternative mathematical construct. The empirical estimate of the household liquidity-preference equation is not very satisfactory with lagged balances in place of nonlinearity. It becomes purely an equation of serial correlation. The use of profit rates in the demand for business balances and price change in the demand for personal balances have not been experimented with in deriving the above empirical equations.

Having distinguished between long- and short-term interest rates, we need another empirical equation relating them in order to keep the system closed. The final equation, aside from definitions, has to do with the functioning of interest rates as a market mechanism to clear away surpluses or deficits of cash. The essence of the liquidity-preference theory is that the interest rate is determined, other things equal, by the forces of supply and demand on the money market. Our equation attempts to give a direct empirical expression of this method of interest rate determination.

We have taken the reader over a large area of empirical work. No matter how convinced he feels by this presentation that the Keynesian system is firmly rooted in fact, he must assuredly agree that the empirical evidence is not superficial or casual. It has been carefully studied by a variety of competent scholars, and Keynes' original intuition has yet to be shown incorrect. In a more positive sense, it stands up well before the facts of life.

CHAPTER TWELVE

Keynes versus Marx: The Methodology of Aggregates

Shigeto Tsuru

IN THE FOREWORD to her *An Essay on Marxian Economics*, Mrs. Joan Robinson writes: "Until recently, Marx used to be treated in academic circles with contemptuous silence broken only by an occasional mocking footnote." [1] Although this may well have been true in the English-speaking world, such a dictum would not apply to many other countries. Nevertheless, it is true that even in those countries where both Marxism and modern economics are equally pursued as academic disciplines, the two schools usually have not been on speaking terms with each other. One school does not understand the language of the other, and the latter would not care to understand the former. It is therefore a great tribute to Keynes that, although he himself treated Marx "with contemptuous silence, broken only by an occasional footnote," he opened a new vista in modern economics which almost naturally led to a fruitful comparison between his doctrines and those of Karl Marx. As Schumpeter wrote in his obituary essay on Keynes:

> Though Keynes's "breakdown theory" is quite different from Marx's, it has an important feature in common with the latter: in both theories, the breakdown is motivated by causes inherent to the working of the economic engine, not by the action of factors external to it. [2]

The full implication of this common feature is yet to be explored. But in a slightly narrower vein, the *rapprochement* between the two schools has been progressing mainly in the hands of Mrs. Joan Robinson, an undisputed Keynesian, whose interest appears to lie in making Marx a precursor, though imperfect, of "the

[1] Joan Robinson, *An Essay on Marxian Economics*, 1949, v. The Foreword was written in September 1941.
[2] J. A. Schumpeter, *Ten Great Economists*, 1951, p. 284.

modern theory of effective demand." [3] The similar position was also expressed by Alan Sweezy in the following words:

> Some of Marx's most important insights, ideas he was struggling to express with the inadequate analytical apparatus then available, became thoroughly clear for the first time in terms of the modern analysis [the Keynesian theory of money, income, and employment]. . . . It shows exactly how an inadequacy of investment outlets produces depression and unemployment. Marx sensed the connection but was unable with the tools at his command to work it out in detailed, systematic fashion. [4]

Lately, Mrs. Robinson has expanded her foci of comparison and given us many hints which go beyond the problem of effective demand as such. [5] We also have an article by Lawrence R. Klein, [6] which, directing our attention to Marx's theory of the falling rate of profit, [7] attempts to rewrite the Marxian scheme into an econometric model with specific "behavior equations."

Once we set our mind to reading Marx with sympathetic eyes, it is easy enough to find many points of similarities between him and Keynes. For example: the proposition to the effect that investment generates purchases without sales and so promotes boom conditions can be found in both; both repudiated the Say's law, though for slightly different reasons; Keynes' dictum that "it is preferable to regard labour . . . as the sole factor of production, operating in a given environment of technique, natural resources, capital equipment, and effective demand," [8] along with his practice of expressing economic quantities in terms of wage units, is suggestively close to Marx's theory of value; in a sense Marx foreshadows the departure which Keynes made from the orthodox theory of the rate of interest; and above all, both re-

[3] See Joan Robinson, "Marx on Unemployment," *Economic Journal*, June-September, 1941, p. 248.

[4] *American Economic Review*, March 1942, pp. 138-39 (a book review).

[5] See *An Essay on Marxian Economics*, first published in 1942, reissued in 1947 with slight alterations; *Collected Economic Papers*, 1951, especially Part III; her Introduction to Rosa Luxemburg, *The Accumulation of Capital*, 1951; and *The Rate of Interest and Other Essays*, 1952, especially pp. 90 ff.

[6] "Theories of Effective Demand and Employment," *Journal of Political Economy*, April 1947.

[7] He actually says: "The Marxian theory of the falling rate of profit is one of the first, and probably one of the best, tools for analyzing the stagnation theory." (*Ibid.*, p. 118)

[8] J. M. Keynes, *The General Theory of Employment, Interest and Money*, 1936, p. 213.

garded, though with fairly material difference in emphasis, that causes inherent to the working of the system would bring about a change from capitalism into something else.

Before we become overenthusiastic about the possibilities of establishing points of similarities between Marx and Keynes, however, we must fully acquaint ourselves with certain fundamental differences between the two, the differences which, far from political or ideological, pertain to the methodological aspect of the economic analysis and lurk often behind the formal equivalence of piecemeal propositions. My purpose in this essay is to examine such differences particularly in connection with the use of aggregates in economic analysis.

Modern society, in its economic aspect, presents itself as an interrelation of a tremendously large number of economic units. One kind or another of theoretical consolidation of these units has been practiced since the birth of economics as a scientific discipline. Doctrinal survey would reveal how, since Quesnay's time, such consolidation of economic units has undergone a historical evolution.

Products of consolidation usually pertain to society as a whole and are called, in recent economic literature, simply "aggregates." The set of aggregates most widely used in modern economic discussion is, of course, the one associated with the economics of John Maynard Keynes. Let us refer to them as "Keynesian aggregates."

It is often said that the problem of aggregates is purely definitional and that one set of aggregates, if defined in terms of objective facts, can always be translated into another set. Though this latter proposition is frequently valid,[9] it is hardly true that the problem of aggregates is purely definitional. Consolidation is a way of organizing manifold data; it is the anatomy of the economic organism. It is natural that a specific consolidation, by resulting in a correspondingly specific fixation of our subject matter, may direct attention at certain problems and away from others, and that it may even exercise an influence on the solution arrived at. To give an example, it is sufficient here to recall the terminological climate of Böhm-Bawerkian capital theory, owing to which it was long denied that the elasticity of demand for labor

[9] See Shigeto Tsuru, "On Reproduction Schemes," Appendix to P. M. Sweezy, *The Theory of Capitalist Development*, 1942.

could have a value smaller than one. To ascertain precisely at which point an error creeps in is not, alas for our science, a logical problem *simpliciter*. More than two alternative representations of a certain subject matter can not only be compatible but are often complementary, as are projections of a multidimensional object from different angles. Conflict, however, becomes especially patent when we enter the realm of practice, for there it is necessary to test empirically the relative effectiveness of alternative approaches. What may appear theoretically to be only two sides of a shield finds its counterpart in practice as two opposing policies. A recent, though a relatively minor, example of this kind is the controversy between the cost-adjustment and the effective demand schools of business cycle control. Often, of course, the conflict in practice goes deeper than here, for the fundamental reorganization of society may become involved.

Let us then begin with the Marxian aggregates and state the essentials of this system in such a way that both the contrast and the comparability with the Keynesian aggregates could be brought out in bold relief.

The principle of consolidation which Marx adopted is twofold. On the one hand, he divides all the products into producers' goods and consumers' goods. This is a division from the standpoint of *material use* of the product and actually transcends specific mode of production. That is to say, such a division exists under socialism as well as under capitalism. On the other hand, Marx divides all the products into three components of value, namely, constant capital (C), variable capital (V), and surplus value (S). This is a division which is characteristic of capitalism. Constant capital subsumes the cost of raw materials, fuel and depreciation, and is so called because these items are considered to go into the value of the product without changing their value-magnitude. Variable capital refers to capital reserved for payment of wages, and is so called because it is the category which is considered to be the source of all the new value created and thus finds its *raison d'être* only if it is variable. Surplus value is the part which, according to Marx, is a residue out of the new value created over and above the necessary payment for wages. When we apply these two principles of division to the total products of society, we obtain the following six aggregates, in which the subscript 1 refers to the producers' goods sector and the subscript 2 to the consumers' goods sector.

$$C_1 + V_1 + S_1$$
$$C_2 + V_2 + S_2$$

Here in its simplest form is a *tableau* of commodity circulation. It is a *tableau* because these six categories are mutually interrelated. The vertical division into C, V and S, which may be said to represent the "cost" structure of each sector, is actually coterminous with the horizontal division into producers' goods and consumers' goods. If we take the simplest case of circular flow and assume that both workers and capitalists consume all of their incomes, both V's and S's, while governed by the specific conditions of value relation, constitute at the same time the demand for consumers' goods. In other words, each of the six categories above constitutes at once (1) an aliquot part of the particular kind of product, *i.e.*, either producers' goods or consumers' goods, (2) a specific item in the cost structure, *i.e.*, either constant capital, variable capital, or surplus value, and finally (3) a demand for either producers' goods or consumers' goods. In this way, the tableau becomes a self-contained one in which each item of cost is in itself a demand for the product specific in the tableau. The significance of this circularity becomes obvious if we visualize a situation in the noncapitalist world. Under socialism, for example, it is conceivable that the cost of labor becomes insulated from the demand for consumers' goods by workers. The amount of purchasing power given to specific workers may be governed by principles which are not directly inherent in the cost structure. It is, in fact, one of the most important characteristics of capitalism that what is a cost item constitutes directly a demand for something. Thus the reduction of wage rates, while it may improve the cost-price maladjustment, results *ipso facto* in the shrinkage of effective demand. Marx's tableau, though quite simple, brings out this mechanism very explicitly.

Even if we advance a step toward realism and introduce the fact of saving or accumulation, the fundamental character of the tableau undergoes no change. Suppose that capitalists save a part of their surplus value and invest it in buying additional producers' goods and labor power. Then surplus value (S) divides itself into the part reserved for capitalists' consumption (S_k), the part destined to demand producers' goods (S_c), and the part destined to demand the additional labor power (S_v). And now the tableau may be rewritten as follows:

$$C_1 + V_1 + S_{k_1} + S_{c_1} + S_{v_1}$$

$$C_2 + V_2 + S_{k_2} + S_{c_2} + S_{v_2}$$

The manner in which these categories are related to each other can best be brought out by stating the condition of smooth exchange which would enable the system to go on without either overproduction or underconsumption. On the supply side we have:

Producers' goods $C_1 + V_1 + S_{k_1} + S_{c_1} + S_{v_1}$

Consumers' goods $C_2 + V_2 + S_{k_2} + S_{c_2} + S_{v_2}$

And on the demand side we have:

For producers' goods $C_1 + S_{c_1}$ from the first sector

$C_2 + S_{c_2}$ from the second sector

For consumers' goods $V_1 + S_{k_1} + S_{v_1}$ from the first sector

$V_2 + S_{k_2} + S_{v_2}$ from the second sector

In order that the supply and demand for each kind of product be equal, it will be sufficient if the equation

$$V_1 + S_{k_1} + S_{v_1} = C_2 + S_{c_2}$$

is satisfied.[10] What use we can make of this equation we shall touch upon later.

Superficially, the system of Marxian aggregates we have described above could easily be translated into Keynesian terms. Although in many ways the Keynesian aggregates are much more complex than the Marxian, in one respect they are simpler. That is, in the Keynesian system the degree of consolidation is still more thorough than in the case of Marx. Thus, to establish a bridge between the two systems, first of all we add the categories of the two sectors of Marx and obtain: ($C_1 + C_2 = C$ and so on)

$$C + V + S + S_k + S_c + S_v$$

[10] Readers can easily satisfy themselves that this is the case by equating the supply side with the demand side for each sector and cancelling the identical terms from both sides.

which is the total output, A, of Keynes.[11] His A_1, or entrepreneurial transactions, can be written as the sum of C and S_c. On the other hand, his G', or the net value conservable from what was on hand at the beginning of the period, if we may ignore his B' [12] as insignificant, is equal to the sum of C and V, while the means of production on hand at the end of the period, his G, consists of C, S_c, V and S_v. Labor power bought is included among the means of production, inasmuch as it is an asset in the sense of renderable service and may be regarded as the limiting case of "goods in process."

Equivalent expressions for such terms as user cost, U, investment, I, income, Y, saving, S, and consumption, K, can easily be derived from the above. In the definitions of Keynes:

$$U = A_1 + G' - G \quad \text{(ignoring } B')$$
$$I = G - G'$$
$$Y = A - U$$
$$S = A_1 - U$$
$$K = A - A_1$$

Translated into Marxian categories:

$$U = C - S_v$$
$$I = S_c + S_v$$
$$Y = V + S + S_v$$
$$S = S_c + S_v$$
$$K = V + S_k + S_v$$

Take for example the equality: $Y = V + S + S_v$ (in which $S = S_k + S_c + S_v$). It appears that the Keynesian Y, or national income, subsumes not only the wages-bill (V) and surplus value (S), which two exhaust the "value added" in the period, but also *additional* expenditure on labor power (S_v) paid out of the surplus value, and that "consumption" and "saving-investment" overlap to the extent of such expenditure. In other words, S_v is

---

[11] Cf. J. M. Keynes, *op. cit.*, chapter 6.
[12] B' is the sum which the entrepreneur would have spent on the maintenance and improvement of his capital equipment if he had decided not to use it to produce output.

registered twice as income and appears to be only once exchanged against goods. There is no mystery, however, once we make explicit the position of the commodity labor power in the network of circulation. In the strict logic of capitalism, additional labor power is just as much a part of the net national product as would be, for example, a new robot-machine. Two metamorphoses of S_v, therefore, have two distinct counterparts in the form of commodity, once in labor power and secondly in consumers' goods.

The Keynesian consolidation is explicit as regards the so-called "service industries" of which labor power is a constituent, but does not admit labor power, which is a "producers' good," into the category of investment goods. The difficulty is overcome, however, by imparting labor power with a character of "goods in process." The minute a new labor power is purchased, it presumably commences to take part in the process of production; and to the income, disbursed against the labor power, corresponds the limiting case of "goods in process" as a part of investment.[13]

The comparability of this kind, even if perfect, is of course not very significant. In the sections to follow I shall try to indicate some of the more important differences in methodology which should not be lost sight of in using the aggregates of either school. But here we may stretch our comparison a step further and try to see additional possibilities by way of finding formal similarities between the Marxian system and that of modern economics.

For this purpose, let us reproduce the equation

$$V_1 + S_{k_1} + S_{v_1} = C_2 + S_{c_2}$$

which, as the reader will remember, was the condition for the smooth reproduction of an economy which accumulates. Now if we define: [14]

$s =$ the rate of surplus value, or the ratio of S_1/V_1 which is assumed to be equal to S_2/V_2

[13] The point, which I developed earlier in "On Reproduction Schemes," Appendix to P. M. Sweezy, *The Theory of Capitalist Development*, 1942, received a number of criticisms, of which C. Bettelheim's "Revenu national, épargne et investissements chez Marx et chez Keynes," *Revue D'Economie Politique*, 1948, pp. 198-211, was the most prominent. To him, I answered in my "Accumulation and Consumption in the Reproduction Schema" (in Japanese), *The Economic Review*, July 1950; and to Mr. Osamu Shimomura, who also made a similar point, I answered in "Discrepancy between Income and Product" (in Japanese), *The Economic Studies Quarterly*, October, 1951.

[14] See my article "Marx's *Tableau Economique* and 'Underconsumption' Theory," *Indian Economic Review*, February, 1953.

$r_2 =$ tl e organic composition of capital, or the ratio of C_2/V_2

$h =$ the proportion between the value of variable capital in the second sector and that in the first, or the ratio of V_2 *over* V_1. (If the wage rate is the same in both sectors, it indicates the proportion in which the total labor force is divided into the two sectors.)

x_1 (or x_2) $=$ the ratio of S_{c1} (S_{c2}) over S_1 (S_2)

we may rewrite this equation as:

$$sx_1 + shx_2 - (1 + s - hr_2) = 0$$

Solving this equation for h, we obtain:

$$h = \frac{1 + s - sx_1}{sx_2 + r_2}$$

This is an equation which tells us that when there is a balanced growth in the economy the proportion in which the total labor force is divided into two sectors, producers' goods and consumers' goods, namely h, is governed in a specific manner by three factors: (*1*) the rate of surplus value, s, (*2*) the "propensity to save" or "the propensity to invest" [15] in the two sectors, x_1 and x_2, and (*3*) the organic composition of capital in the consumers' goods sector, r_2. From this equation we can say definitely that when the rate of surplus value rises, the proportion of labor force going into the consumers' goods sector has to become smaller than before, that when the "propensity to invest" rises, assuming that $x_1 = x_2$, the said proportion also has to decline, and that when the organic composition of capital in the second sector rises, the result is the same.

Now it will not be too far-fetched to compare these three factors with the famed three dynamic determinants of Harrod.[16] Our first factor here, the rate of surplus value, or s, is roughly a ratio of profit income to wage income; hence its rise corresponds exactly to what Harrod calls "the shift to profit," his second dynamic determinant. Our second factor, the "propensity to invest," or x's, is quite similar, with only inconsequential differences, to his first dynamic determinant, "the propensity to save," although the latter is formulated explicitly as a relation between two con-

[15] In the Marxian scheme the ratio of investment to the total of capitalists' income is actually larger than this, for the wages-fund for the additional labor force to be employed is also included in the category of "investment."

[16] Cf. R. F. Harrod, *The Trade Cycle*, 1936, pp. 88-101.

tiguous periods. Our third factor, the organic composition of capital in the second sector, or r_2, focuses our attention upon the relation which Harrod chooses to call "the amount of capital used in production," his third dynamic determinant. In terms of these concepts, the reader may remember, Harrod stated that:

(i) Suppose that representative income-receivers save the same proportion of their increment of income as they previously saved of the income of the day before. (ii) Suppose that there is no shift to profit. (iii) Suppose that the productive methods for which the new capital goods were designed are the same as those previously employed. On these conditions consumption on the present day will rise in the same proportion as capital goods are increased and by the same amount as that which the new capital goods were designed to provide, and this experience seems to justify the present rate of advance.[17]

Harrod is not speaking in terms of the proportion in which the total labor force is divided into the two sectors. But in both cases, that of Marx and of Harrod, the question implicitly asked is the same; namely, what are the factors which determine the proportion in which the national product is divided between consumers' goods and producers' goods as the economy advances steadily. Since the two men dealt with basically the same problem, it is not at all accidental that the correspondence between them appears to be almost perfect. What Harrod is saying in the above quotation is, in fact, what Marx would say, in our terminology, that h does not change if s, x's and r_2 remain constant. Harrod, of course, goes further and speculates for those cases where s, x's and r_2 change. For example, "if people saved a larger proportion of their increment of income or there were a shift to profit on the same day, . . . so far as these two determinants were concerned, consumption would advance less than the capital goods increased on the given day." [18] In our terminology, this means that when s and x's rise h has to decline. Harrod's reasoning concerning the case of a rise in "the amount of capital used in production" is slightly more complicated, but the conclusion comes to the same thing as the one obtained above in connection with the Marxian schema.

Thus the correspondence between the two systems is quite uncanny. But we cannot stop here. We must not fail to note the point of basic contrast between the two as regards the methodo-

[17] *Ibid.*, p. 90.   [18] *Ibid.*, p. 91.

logical position which the three determinants (s, x's and r_2) occupy. In Marx's model, they are variables or parameters implicit in the structure of his aggregates, and hence are formulated with explicit reference to the specificity of capitalism. Harrod, on the other hand, by setting these factors apart as forces independent of the system upon which they impinge, is obliged to fall back upon *a-social* generalizations for the explanation of the characteristic behavior of the determinants. Thus, the propensity to save is a "fundamental psychological law." The shift to profit and its positive sign are regarded as due to the joint operation of the laws of diminishing returns and of the diminishing elasticity of demand. And finally, the amount of capital used in production, barring short-run fluctuations, is made dependent upon inventions.

Through the apparent similarities on a certain restricted plane between Marx and Harrod, we immediately see a number of differences which are fairly basic. One of them is the difference in efficacy attributed to what may be called "parametric adjustments" in the system.

A typical capitalistic process can be visualized as that of a cluster of "parametric adjustments." Each economic unit, be it a household or a firm, is independent of each other and, being such an infinitesimal part of the whole, is typically confronted with prices, wages, the rate of interest, etc., over which each economic unit singly has no control. In other words, these quantities (prices, wages, etc.) present themselves to economic units as parameters. For its part, the economic unit has no way of perceiving directly the state of economic conditions relevant to its action *except through* its contact with those parameters. Thus it watches changes in them and adjusts itself to them presumably according to one kind or another of maximization principle. When, *e.g.*, there is an epidemic of cow disease, consumers do not and need not know about it. The number of cattle slaughtered inevitably will decline and the price of beef will rise. Consumers, finding the price of beef relatively dearer, will do this "parametric adjustment" and shift their demand to chicken or pork. So long as competition is perfect, "parameters" will reflect changes in data fully and instantaneously and call forth necessary adjustments on the part of economic units. It is in this manner that economic units, each independently enjoying the prerogative of freedom and in spite of the fact that they are separated from relevant economic data by a cloud of "parameters," are considered to comprise a society in which maximum economic welfare can be maintained even while the objective conditions keep on changing. Therefore, modern economic theory made much of the mechanism of "parametric adjustments" and has built extremely intricate doctrines around the concepts of elasticities (indicating the manner of response of economic units to parametric changes) and flexibilities (indicating the manner of response of parameters to changes in data).

In the 30's, however, the long-standing confidence in the positive function of "parameters" gradually waned. For one thing, such phenomena as rigidities of wages, inflexibility of monopoly prices and artificial control of exchange rates, coming to our attention all at once, have shaken our confidence in the presumed harmony in the system.[19] At the same time, certain statistical studies drew the attention of economists anew to the regularities of income effect which seemed to stand out much more clearly than the patterns of "parametric adjustments." In the words of Paul Samuelson:

> Among the most striking uniformities yet uncovered in economic data are the relationships between various categories of expenditure and family income. . . . In fact, so strong are these income effects that it is very difficult to find empirically the influence of price, the variable customarily related to demand by the economic theorist.[20]

In other words, the time was ripe for the emergence and rapid acceptance of the type of aggregative analysis propounded by Keynes in his *General Theory*. And for a while, there arose a sharp division among the ranks of economists between those who would emphasize the income effect and slight the problem of cost-price adjustment *and* those who would give far greater weight to the efficacy of cost-price relationships. Even then, however, the most ardent of Keynesians would not ignore entirely the rele-

[19] There is also a more general point which was expressed by N. Kaldor as follows: "It is now fairly generally recognized . . . that the price mechanism, even under the most favorable conditions, can register only some of the gains and losses which result from any particular piece of economic activity; there is a cluster of effects (what the economists call the external economies and diseconomies) which escape the net of price-cost measurement." Appendix to W. H. Beveridge, *Full Employment in a Free Society*, 1945, p. 401.
[20] Paul A. Samuelson, "A Statistical Analysis of the Consumption Function," Appendix to Chapter XI of A. H. Hansen, *Fiscal Policy and Business Cycles*, 1941, p. 250.

vance of "parametric adjustments" to many of the analytical problems. As time went on, the sharp contrast initially drawn gave way gradually to an attempt at synthesis and then to a tendency to place the crude aggregative analysis in its proper place.

The Marxian approach, on the other hand, is radically different in this regard. Marx himself was keenly aware of the important place which such categories as prices, the rate of interest, etc., occupied in the workings of a capitalist system. Thus he repeatedly brings out the point that commodities, for example, appear to be an independent entity which naturally seems to possess the attribute of price to which men passively react. He does not deny the effectiveness of price categories, nor the process of "parametric adjustments" which could be analyzed in an objective manner. But he is more concerned with the social relations among men which are hidden behind what appear to be natural attributes of things. Marx, of course, regarded the capitalist system as only one stage in the development of human societies, and he was especially eager to pin down the historically specific characteristics of capitalism as distinguished from other modes of production. Thus for him it was much less important to analyze the forces which determined the magnitude of value than to seek the reason why the product of human labor took the specific form of commodities under a capitalistic system. And his answer to this question was: "Only such products can become commodities with regard to each other as result from different kind of labor, each kind being carried on independently and for the account of private individuals." [21] In this type of society, the specific manner in which men are socially related to each other cannot be directly grasped but, instead, expresses itself through various quantitative relations among commodities, money, etc., and imparts upon the latter the appearance of being an independent social agent. Marx

[21] *Capital,* Vol. I (Kerr edition), 1918, p. 49. In similar vein he also wrote: "As a general rule, articles of utility become commodities only because they are products of private individuals or groups of individuals who carry on their work independently of each other." (*Ibid.,* pp. 83-84) Paul Sweezy elaborated on this as follows: "The exchange relation as such, apart from any consideration of the quantities involved, is an expression of the fact that individual producers, each working in isolation, are in fact working for each other. . . . What finds expression in the form of exchange value is therefore the fact that the commodities involved are the products of human labor in a society based on division of labor in which producers work privately and independently." (*The Theory of Capitalist Development,* 1942, p. 27)

characterized this deceptive aspect of the commodity society as the "fetish character of commodities." In his own words: "The character of having value, when once impressed upon products, obtains fixity only by reason of their acting and re-acting upon each other as quantities of value. These quantities vary continually, independently of the will, foresight and action of the producers. To them, their own social action takes the form of the action of objects, which rule the producers instead of being ruled by them." [22]

Marx felt it quite natural that what he called "bourgeois economists," being unable to pierce through this fetishism, were mainly concerned with the quantitative analysis of "the action of objects" which appeared to rule the producers, for they took it more or less for granted that capitalism was an immutable social relation and did not find it necessary to question the specific characteristic of the system as such. Since this was his major concern, Marx deliberately slighted the quantitative analysis of value and of its fluctuations, but developed his theory largely on the assumption of what Marshall would call "long-run normal price." Thus his discussion of *tableau économique,* which appears towards the end of the second volume of *Capital,* is conducted throughout on the assumption that commodities are exchanged strictly at their value or at "long-run normal price." In other words, "parametric adjustments" have no place in the stage of abstraction where Marx took up his aggregative analysis.

It is quite important to emphasize this point because there have been so many attempts to make mechanistic use of the Marx's tableau to prove a set of premeditated conclusions. The most visionary of these attempts is that of Henryk Grossmann, who tried to prove, on the basis of Marx's scheme of extended reproduction, the inevitability of breakdown of the capitalistic system.[23] What he did was to produce a general equation, on a

[22] *Ibid.,* p. 86.
[23] See Henryk Grossmann, *Das Akkumulations- und Zusammenbruchsgesetz des kapitalistischen Systems,* 1920. Actually, of course, his theorizing was a specific product of the contemporary controversy and perhaps should not be criticized out of that context. He was originally trying to challenge Otto Bauer by carrying out to the logical conclusion the set of assumptions which Bauer employed in criticizing Rosa Luxemburg. As such, Grossmann's critique of Bauer contained an element of truth. In fact, however, Grossmann raised to the point of absurdity the common mechanistic error of a whole train of economists starting with Tugan-Baranowsky who made Marx's tableau serve a purpose for which it was never intended.

set of rigid assumptions as to the rate of increase in wages-bill and constant capital (approximately, user cost), giving us a number of years which would elapse before capitalists' income would be no longer sufficient to cover the required amount of net investment. Using the same notation we have given earlier and designating by n the number of years before the "breakdown" comes, we may rewrite Grossmann's equation as follows: [24]

$$n = \frac{\log\left(\dfrac{s - \dfrac{Sv}{V}}{r_0 \cdot \dfrac{Sc}{C}}\right)}{\log\left(\dfrac{100 + \dfrac{Sc}{C}}{100 + \dfrac{Sv}{V}}\right)}$$

Thus if we assume, with Otto Bauer, that the rate of surplus value is unity throughout, that the organic composition of capital in the initial period is two, that constant capital increases at the annual rate of 10 per cent (i.e., $S_c/C = \dfrac{10}{100}$), and that wages-bill increases at the rate of 5 per cent (i.e., $S_v/V = \dfrac{5}{100}$), then $n = 33.5$; that is to say, after approximately 34 years capitalists' income would become insufficient to meet the required rate of accumulation.

This reasoning illustrates most strikingly the case of complete abstraction of "parametric adjustments." It is in the essence of price mechanism to register various tensions and disequilibria within the system, thus calling forth appropriate "parametric adjustments" on the part of economic units (firms and households). Convulsive movement of the economy, which we call business cycles, is nothing but an expression of such an adjustment process; and Marx would have considered absurd the extension of his logic of abstract *tableau économique* to a theory of breakdown without first going through many steps of concretization which certainly would have included the matter of "para-

[24] r_0 stands for the organic composition of capital for the economy as a whole in the initial period.

metric adjustments." In other words, it must be strictly borne in mind that Marx's scheme of reproduction, or the framework within which his aggregative analysis is conducted, is highly abstract and does not permit indiscriminate attempts at manipulation.

The caricature which Grossmann made out of the Marx's reproduction scheme is the culmination of a series of controversies conducted in terms of an all too mechanistic use of the categories in Marx's tableau. If one ignores the parametric adjustment of any sort and assumes, as Rosa Luxemburg does, that the propensity to save is always 50 per cent in both the producers' goods and the consumers' goods sectors, it will be easy enough to show, by giving appropriate arithmetic examples, that effective demand will become insufficient to absorb all the final goods produced. Rosa Luxemburg's insight in seeing this problem of effective demand is certainly not itself sterile, as Mrs. Robinson has pointed out.[25] But the use which Luxemburg made of the Marxian tableau in "proving" the point is quite arbitrary and actually oversteps the limits which Marx himself carefully imposed upon the tableau. Thus it was not difficult for Otto Bauer to "prove" the possibility of smooth reproduction on the very assumptions which Luxemburg employed, namely (1) that the propensity to invest is the same in both sectors, and (2) that the organic composition of capital rises as time goes on (or the capital-output ratio rises as time goes on).[26] So long as we confine ourselves within the logic of Marx's tableau, the smooth reproduction is possible, as we have seen earlier, if the equation

$$sx_1 + shx_2 - (1 + s - hr_2) = 0$$

is satisfied. Luxemburg's problem boils down to the question of whether this equation can be satisfied when $x_1 = x_2$ and s and r_2 rise with time. It will be easy enough to show that there is nothing in the logic of Marx's tableau to indicate that the steady growth will be upset by these assumptions.

In other words, it will not be correct to make too much use of the tableau in the form Marx left us. If we wish to address ourselves to a kind of problem with which modern economics

[25] See Joan Robinson, "Introduction to Rosa Luxemburg," *The Accumulation of Capital*, 1951.
[26] Otto Bauer, "Die Akkumulation des Kapitals," *Die Neue Zeit*, Vol. 31, No. 1, 1913.

concerns itself, Marx's reproduction scheme in itself does not give us an answer. Marxian system must be further extended by an incorporation of a theory of "parametric adjustments" in a manner consistent with the basic framework of the Marxian theory.[27]

One of the significant differences in the methodological character of aggregates between Marx and Keynes lies in the direction in which *abstraction* is carried out. Marx's intention was to represent, as simply as possible, the specific interrelation of aggregates which is characteristic of capitalism, whereas Keynesian aggregates do not necessarily concern themselves with the specificity of capitalism. They are designed primarily to assist in accounting for the level of total employment under the simple assumption that it is proportional to the net national product. A similar purpose, with differing assumptions, once gave rise to such concepts as "wage-fund" and "subsistence-fund" (Böhm-Bawerk). These concepts made us focus upon that aggregative quantity which controlled the demand for labor in capitalist society. Keynes has reoriented our attention to the other side of the shield, so to speak, namely, to the simplest functional relation between the demand for various types of goods and the level of total economic activity . . . a relation which appears to transcend the specificity of capitalism. Thus his first task was to carry through certain abstractional operations which would cut through complex appearances and to distil such aggregative quantities as might be independent of the capitalistic accounting method. The result is the Keynesian concept of national income which has only one dimension, that of being *consumable sooner or later*. The part which is consumed during a given period is called "consumption," and the remainder, in whatever physical form it may be, is called "investment." Conceptually, this set of aggregates is perfectly unambiguous. To any type of society, be it primitive-tribal or socialistic, we may apply them and refer to the ratios between them by means of such terms as "the propensity to consume," "the propensity to invest," etc. The Keynesian aggregates gain this simple unambiguity by sacrificing certain distinctions which

[27] An interesting attempt was once made by Professor Kei Shibata in this direction. See a series of articles (in English) he published in *Kyoto University Economic Review* in the first half of 1930's, or, in a more complete form, in his two-volume work: *Theoretical Economics* (in Japanese), 1935, 1936. See also my criticism on a part of his theory in "Marx's Theory of the Falling Tendency of the Rate of Profit" (in English), *The Economic Review*, July, 1951.

other systems of aggregates may be capable of making. In particular, they are indifferent to what Marx would call "the metamorphosis in the realm of commodity circulation." For example, x amount of consumers' goods can either be assumed to have been sold or unsold and national income is in no way affected. For $Y = A - U$. And y amount of producers' goods can be assumed to have been either sold or unsold and investment is in no way affected. For $I = G - G'$. Again, z amount of export could just as well have been left unsold and remained in the warehouse of disappointed sellers, and national income would have remained the same.

In fact, the contrast between Marx and Keynes can be brought out most sharply in connection with the definition of investment. The definition of investment from the Keynesian standpoint is given by Samuelson as follows: "The importance of investment consists in the fact that it involves disbursal of income to the factors of production while not at the same time bringing to the market goods which must be currently sold." [28] Thus, from this point of view, the accumulation of inventories has the same function as the construction of new plant and equipment because such accumulation no less than the latter "involves disbursal of income to the factors of production while not at the same time bringing to the market goods which must be currently sold." Export surplus has also the similar function. So does the government deficit. In other words, the Keynesian investment is defined mainly from the standpoint of its multiplier aspect and subsumes all kinds of economic acts which may be quite dissimilar to each other with respect to their productivity aspect. As such, it is no doubt a very convenient concept for the short-run analysis, especially since it is a highly operational concept and lends itself to relatively easy statistical measurement. But once we try to apply it to a slightly longer-run analysis of dynamic character, its shortcomings become immediately apparent. The failure to take note of this limitation has led Mr. Hicks, for example, to construct a highly unrealistic theory of trade cycle with the concept of "autonomous investment" which, like pyramid-building, absorbs savings without adding to productive capacity. Nowadays, of course, such unrealism is no longer tolerated by many; and we have a number of doctrines of economic dynamics, even in the

[28] P. A. Samuelson, "The Theory of Pump-priming Re-examined," *American Economic Review,* September, 1940.

camp of what may be regarded as the Keynesian school, which
give a prominent place to the productivity aspect of investment
activities. Domar's σ effect is one such example.[29] But when we
try to incorporate the productivity effect of investment into our
theory, we immediately realize that we must re-examine the concept of investment itself and make it theoretically a much more
abstract concept than when we use it in the multiplier analysis.
Pyramid building, for example, has to be deducted from it. When
we do this, we come closer to the concept of accumulation in the
Marxian tableau which is throughout expressed in terms of value
and is placed in the schema in such a way as to produce the *dual*
effect of both creating effective demand and adding to the productive capacity. The original concept of investment in the
Keynesian aggregates is indifferent to the differing effects on productivity or to occurrences of short-run character other than
those affecting the effective demand.

Apparent indifference to distinctions of this kind does not
mean, however, that the Keynesian system is altogether blind
to them. Here lurks an important difference between Keynes'
method of abstraction and that of Marx; and it is worth our brief
examination. As Marx proceeds with his model, the indifference
to certain distinctions on a given level of abstraction means the
absence of these distinctions in the model itself at that level. For
Keynes, *the very strength of his abstraction lies in the fact that
the reality in its entire complexity is contained in it though only
in one-dimensional projection.* Concretization of the system for
Marx is typically the process of successive approximation. For
Keynes, it is to change the angle of projection. Thus whatever
distinctions to which the Keynesian aggregates *appear* to be indifferent are in fact contained in them implicitly and make themselves explicit on another plane of projection. For example, instead of distinguishing in *aggregates* between investment financed
out of dishoarding and investment financed out of current saving,
Keynesians would call both of them simply investment when
projected on the plane of aggregates but would take care of the
distinction on another plane as between diminutions in liquidity-
preference and increases in the marginal efficiency schedule of
investment.

In short, in point of contrast, aggregates themselves are neutral

[29] E. D. Domar, "Expansion and Employment," *American Economic Review*,
March 1947, p. 46.

in the Keynesian system to the specificity of capitalism, viz., reduced to the simplest common denominator, as it were, for all types of society. The special relationships among aggregates which are characteristic of capitalism are squeezed implicitly into the form of functions; the consumption function, the liquidity-function, the marginal efficiency schedule of investment, etc. And by the use of such terms as "propensity" and "preference" the impression is created, if only unwittingly, that these relations among aggregates are analogous to personal reactions on the conscious level and therefore are direct, and as if they too were independent of the particular system of economy which they are used to analyze.

However, to say, for example, that the consumption function is a relation between aggregates analogous to personal reactions on the conscious level is not exactly correct. It is realized that, *theoretically speaking,* aggregate relations in modern economics are essentially *derived* relations, that is to say, deduced from household or firm relations.[30] But this fact creates a fresh theoretical problem. In the case of economic problems related to microeconomic units, the principle of maximization (whether of utility or of profit) helps us to derive a meaningful theorem, thus enabling us "to determine the nature of the changes in our unknown variables resulting from a designated change in one or more parameters."[31] A large part of the body of economic doctrines today is dependent on the use of some kind of extremum position in arriving at a *theoretical* conclusion. The aggregate relation such as a consumption function, on the other hand, has first been established as an empirical relation based upon statistical observations and has no claim for theoretical stability except as it is continually supported by facts. The failure of economic model-building in 1945 illustrates this methodological character of aggregate relations. Thus although Keynesians make much use of macro-economics, they have to fall back upon micro-economics for giving *ultimate theoretical* foundation to macro-economic theorems. It is for this reason that Duesenberry states that "aggregate relations which can be deduced from household or firm relations I shall call *fundamental* aggregate relations."[32] Thus

---

[30] See James S. Duesenberry, *Income, Saving, and the Theory of Consumer Behavior,* 1949, p. 72.
[31] P. A. Samuelson, *Foundations of Economic Analysis,* 1947, p. 7.
[32] Duesenberry, *op. cit.,* p. 72. Italics added.

the theoretical basis of Keynesian aggregates reduces itself finally
to those relations between scarce means and alternative uses
which form the foundation of modern theoretical economics and
which actually transcend any specific characteristic of capitalist
mode of production.

The Marxian aggregates, on the other hand, are not operational
as the Keynesian one. The former appear midway in Marx's
theoretical journey from the most abstract discussion of value to
the more concrete elucidation of crises and other typically capitalistic phenomena. Thus such concepts as the rate of surplus value
and the organic composition of capital which can be expressed
directly, as relations between aggregates, are not necessarily sus-
ceptible of statistical treatment. In the form presented in Marx's
tableau, aggregate relations cannot be subjected to empirical testing. They are theoretically pure concepts. For example, the reproduction scheme as discussed in the second volume of *Capital* is
constructed on the basis of the following assumptions: that all
the products are exchanged at value (*i.e.*, long run normal price);
that there are only two classes of people, capitalists and workers;
that workers consume all of their income; that there are sufficiently large numbers of capitalists in one field to permit perfect
competition to take place; that it is a closed economy; that there
are only two kinds of commodities, the producers' good and the
consumers' good and the period of turnover of capital is the
same in both sectors; that there is no change in technical coefficients; that capital does not move between the two sectors,
that is to say, the saving of the capitalists in the first sector is
invested only in the first sector, and similarly for the second;
that there is no durable capital equipment whose useful life extends beyond one period; that there are no inventories; that
money functions only as a means of circulation; and that wages
are paid in advance of the sale of the products to whose production the workers contribute. In other words, the Marxian aggregates depict the bone structure, as it were, of the capitalistic
circular flow as seen through X-ray, whereas the Keynesian
aggregates show us the delineation of our subject matter as projected on one dimensional plane.

The fact, however, that the Marxian aggregates are theoretical
does not imply that it is possible to manipulate the elements of
the tableau to prove any particular theorem which is not already

implicit in the structure of the tableau itself. In this sense, the Marxian aggregates by themselves do not claim to possess much deductive value. They are rather to serve for illustrative purposes, pointing up to us the nature of interdependence among various categories in the social circulation of a capitalist economy. And it is quite significant that in serving this purpose, the tableau is divided into two sectors of the producers' goods and the consumers' goods. This is not the same thing as the distinction between investment and consumption. This latter distinction is a division of *net* national product, whereas the former is a division of *gross* product of the society. In fact, the difference between Marx and Keynes in this respect is much more significant than is commonly supposed.

The Keynesians have made the concept of national income (or net national product) the pivot of their aggregative analysis and worked out a set of nice theoretical relations such as the multiplier, acceleration, etc., with the aid of this concept. And the rationale of using the net concept in economic analysis seems to be further reinforced by the fact that it corresponds also to the index of welfare magnitude. National income has long been a measure of economic welfare, and as such, even Marxians would not object very much. But the question is whether it is equally efficacious as *a tool in the economic analysis* of a capitalist society. To formulate our problem in terms of net concepts is as if to study the functioning of a certain organic body in terms of flows of energy which go in and come out of that body. Since this approach does not probe into the workings of internal structure of the body, it will not be possible to "tag" a particular output as coming out of a particular input. What we do is to watch at the point of spigot, so to speak, what flows in and out of the body, and relate these flows to each other. Thus any relation between aggregates, such as consumption to income, has to be regarded only in terms of "a flow during a period coincident with the flow of income during the same period." [33] The method has undoubted merits. It enables us to formulate macro-economic relations in the simplest possible manner and at the same time gives us a strategic category in the form of money flow. But at the same time it makes us close our eyes to the functioning of the internal structure itself, which, far from being solely technical, possesses

[33] A. P. Lerner, "Saving Equals Investment," *Quarterly Journal of Economics,* February 1938.

specifically economic characteristics under capitalism. It has the capacity, *e.g.*, of "making mills to make more mills" for a time. It can distend itself or shrink without necessarily registering corresponding changes in net flows. The Marxian tableau, on the other hand, focuses our attention, again in the simplest possible manner, to the logic of this internal structure under capitalism by incorporating the value relation of C plus V plus S into the tableau. This method corresponds to the basic understanding of Marx that under capitalism production is not for the purpose of ultimate consumption but for the continuous maximization of profit. The contrast in this respect is more material than it appears on the surface. Although Keynesians do say that "expenditure creates income and thus employment," they will not say that "expenditure" provides the *motivating force* of production and further production. Marx would say, however, that the competition of capital striving towards the maximization of profit provides in itself a motive force for accumulation and technical progress; and such an orientation, which dispenses with either the acceleration principle or a special theory of investment function, is directly reflected in the construction of the Marxian tableau.

It was already pointed out earlier that the tableau form of aggregates enables us to follow through the so-called dual aspect of investment, *i.e.*, the aspect of creating effective demand and that of increasing the productive capacity. It is possible for Keynesians to say that "if investment today, however large, is equal to that of yesterday, national income of today will be just equal and not any larger than that of yesterday." [34] But it will be impossible for Marxians to visualize a case of "extended reproduction" in equilibrium, *i.e.*, the case of an economy which accumulates at all, without a corresponding increase in net national product. Investment in the Marxian tableau is traced in its dual aspect to its proper destination in a manner consistent with certain significant constraints which are specified within the tableau. Furthermore, since the tableau makes explicit the relation between C and S_c (or roughly, between "user cost" and the net addition to capital), our attention can easily be directed to the position which replacement (or depreciation) occupies in the mechanism of social circulation. It is only in the recent period

[34] E. D. Domar, "Expansion and Employment," *American Economic Review,* March 1947, p. 40.

that this problem has come to be discussed as an integral part of the mechanism of a growing economy.

In parts I may have drawn too sharp a distinction between the treatment of aggregates by Marx and that by Keynes. Most of these points of difference were in fact sharp at the time when Keynes first brought out his theory of effective demand. Since that time many refinements and improvements have been added to the original scheme of simple Keynesian aggregates. Some of them have been actually in the direction of narrowing the difference between Marx and Keynes on this matter. Dissatisfaction with the analysis conducted solely in *net* concepts is a most notable example. I suspect that in future the reproduction scheme of Marx will draw the attention of a larger number of academic economists than in the 30's. But there is one last fundamental difference in methodology which still divides the modern school of economics and the Marxian. The point may be illustrated from Mr. Harrod's methodological dicta in his *Trade Cycle*. So far as we can gather from his scattered remarks in that book, his methodology may be paraphrased as follows: we go as far as we can by means of a priori method, the principal tool of which is introspection; and if a priori yields no more, we revert to observed facts and see what actually does happen. When, however, he reverts to observation, it is in order to look for an answer to a specific question which introspection alone is incapable of solving. It is characteristic of him to say, for example:

> The shift to profit has been shown . . . to depend on two factors. . . . It would be rash to say much a priori about the operation of either of these laws [the law of diminishing returns and the law of diminishing elasticity of demand] . . . But experience is that there usually is a shift to profit in a pronounced upward movement.[35]

And this is enough for him in order to assert that there is a shift to profit. But, as Schumpeter would say, "this is a problem to be solved, not a datum to be accepted." [36] The problem of social science only begins, to say the least, at the point where introspection leaves off.

What is conspicuous in Harrod is his extreme reluctance to recognize the existence of objective laws of *social* relations. It is more than a playful dictum, we may venture to guess, when he

35 Harrod, *op. cit.*, p. 92.
36 J. A. Schumpeter, *Business Cycles*, 1939, p. 188.

M*

says: "We are reluctant to suppose that man's course of endeavour can be governed by something so superficial and artificial as his own banking system." [37] If, however, society, as a subject matter of scientific endeavor, is a complex of relations qualitatively distinctive on its own level and not simply an amalgam of individuals who compose it or of atomic matter to which all existence may be reduced, it will be wisdom in methodology to presume that social relations are governed by objective laws which are not reducible to psychological and physical laws and which are beyond the reach of introspection, however discerning it may be. A theoretical edifice in social science built upon such a presumption is evidently under a handicap in developing its "analytical apparatus" if by the latter is meant an apparatus to account for the phenomena of a particular society in terms of anything but the specific laws pertaining to that society. Marx's major concern was precisely the elucidation of the specific laws pertaining to a capitalist society, and his aggregates are tools of analysis for that purpose designed primarily to lay bare the social circulation of capital.

[37] Harrod, *op. cit.,* p. 4.

CHAPTER THIRTEEN

Keynes and the Classical Tradition

Paul P. Streeten

THE PURPOSE of this essay is to bring out some of the value premises implicit in Keynes's analysis and recommendations, and to relate these premises to the great classical tradition of British economic thought.

The Harmony of Interests

The doctrine that there is a harmony of interests in society was one of the main inspirations for the formulation of economic laws. Like a leitmotif it runs through the whole of economic theory. It is so deep-rooted that some of the fiercest critics of the harmony theory were themselves its victims. The terminology changed and numerous qualifications and modifications were introduced in the course of time. Nevertheless, the common origin is clearly recognizable.

The economists inherited the doctrine from the philosophers of natural law. For Adam Smith economic laws were the decrees of a benevolent and beneficient natural order which turns man's stupid and selfish interests into the common good. Bentham no longer had Adam Smith's faith in the natural order. For him the ends which the economic system pursues are the ends of men, not of Nature. The market is a mechanism (not an organism) designed by men to serve their will.[1]

At first sight it would seem that utilitarianism made the har-

[1] It would be easy to quote numerous passages from Adam Smith's *Wealth of Nations* which could show that this contrast between his own belief in a *natural* harmony with Bentham's view of a *contrived* harmony is false. Adam Smith clearly recognized the necessity of a good deal of legislation and was certainly not naïvely optimistic about the power of uncontrolled self-interest. But, taking Smith's writings as a whole, and in particular his more general reflections, the difference in emphasis is clearly noticeable. The toughness of this belief is illustrated by the following quotation from Marshall: "This doctrine (Adam Smith's) of natural organization contains more truth of the highest importance to humanity than almost any other which is equally likely to evade the comprehension of those who discuss grave social problems without adequate study: and it has a singular fascination for earnest and thoughtful minds." (*Principles*, p. 246.)

mony doctrine redundant. The felicific calculus should have made it possible to compare pleasures and pains and to compute them in social sum. Recommendations could thus be formulated in spite of interest clashes. This appearance seems to be confirmed by the fact that Bentham attacked violently the doctrine of natural law.

Recently, Professor Viner has stressed again that Bentham was not a crude harmony theorist. Although his utilitarianism was, in spite of his protestations, inspired by, and a development of, natural law philosophy, it was a modified version. Many passages show that Bentham did not believe in the actual existence of a harmony of interests. His doctrine of legislation is an attempt to harmonize divergent interests by· setting sanctions. Professor Viner has emphasized that Bentham was aware of the gulf between private and public interest, and that he believed that it could be bridged only through education, legislation, and religion. Bentham "did prescribe limits for the field of governmental intervention in economic matters, but these limits were not . . . very narrow ones, and in any case were not so narrow as to give scope to the doctrine of the natural harmony of interests, in the sense of a harmony preordained or inherent in the nature of man living in a society unregulated by government." [2]

Yet, it would be false to conclude that Bentham recognized fully the implications of interest conflicts. He believed in harmony, though in a different sense from that used by Professor Viner.

It is useful to distinguish between a *crude* and the various versions of a *modified* harmony doctrine. According to the crude harmony doctrine the free play of self-interests automatically promotes the interest of society. There is no need for government regulation. Each, by promoting his own interest, simultaneously promotes the interest of "all" (in some significant sense).

According to the modified harmony doctrine the "interest of society," or the "interest of *all*," does not automatically coincide with the interests of each of its members, although it is in the interest of all, and in some sense also in the interest of *each*, to promote the social interest. The theory assumes different degrees

---

[2] J. Viner, "Bentham and J. S. Mill," *American Economic Review*, March 1949, p. 369. Professor L. Robbins too has again stressed that the classical economists did not believe in harmony in the sense in which the Physiocrats did. *The Theory of Economic Policy in English Classical Political Economy*, 1952.

or layers of self-interest, only one of which leads to harmony. The most commonly discussed obstacle to the realization of this kind of self-interest is ignorance, but there are others. Conflicts can arise if we think we want to follow certain courses which would not really be to our advantage.

The characteristic feature of this doctrine is that society is held to be some kind of unified body with a purpose and an interest, which are identical with private purposes and interests after the latter have been corrected and disturbing influences eliminated. The modified version of the harmony doctrine is compatible with strong authoritarian interventions and even with despotism. Individuals may be too stupid or too lazy or too misguided, too much bound by habit or enticed by temptation, to pursue their true interests (and hence the common interest) and therefore must be forced to do so.

Thus the crude version of the harmony doctrine tends to lead to a liberal laissez-faire view of policy,[3] whereas the modified version *may* provide reasons for government regulations. Harmony may have to be engineered. But according to both versions there is, actually or potentially, behind the manifold activities of individuals and groups, a coordination of activities towards a purpose. Both imply that there is a subject, a will, a plan and a rational adaptation of means towards an end in society. Society is looked upon as a super-individual [4] or a large family [5] with a

---

[3] But the liberal, laissez-faire view can also be justified on grounds of *absence* of harmony. Distrust of politics and politicians, resulting from a conviction of the selfishness and corruptibility of human beings, is perhaps a sounder basis for liberalism than purely economic arguments. The laissez-faire world, to paraphrase F. H. Bradley, is the best of all possible worlds, and everything in it is a necessary evil.

[4] The social-harmony doctrine has its equivalent in the personal sphere. The liberal view of the single human being is often blind to the tensions and conflicts which give rise to morality and overemphasizes order and consistency. This lack of imagination characteristic of the more rationalistic forms of liberalism has been analyzed by Lionel Trilling, *The Liberal Imagination*. What Noel Annan says of the moralist is also true of the economist: ". . . a humanist is always being surprised by human beings in the right way—they are always more curious and diverse than he has yet foreseen and his surprise keeps his imagination supple. The moralist who is not a humanist is always being surprised in the wrong way; he finds his moral categories too narrow to contain the variety of experience, he is shocked by what he finds. . . ." (*Leslie Stephen*, pp. 239 ff.)

[5] It is obvious that conflicts exist also within the family, and even inside an individual. Some of the criticisms therefore also apply to any view that looks upon the latter as unified systems. But there is the difference that individual actions and those of a family *are* often directed towards a purpose, whereas "the market"

unified goal which is simultaneously the (properly defined) goal of each of its members. Hence the teleological implications of such terms as "the economy," "social welfare," "economic organization," "economic function," "equilibrium," "maximum social welfare," "economic laws," etc.

Many versions of utilitarianism, in their transition from the proposition that each seeks his own happiness, to the postulate that he ought to seek the happiness of all, introduce a modified harmony doctrine. It is clear that an authoritarian, antiliberal version of utilitarianism is possible, as Bentham's views testify. But it still contains the basic assumption of interest harmony.

The rule that social happiness should be maximized requires: (1) comparisons between the happiness of different people, and (2) the imperative that whatever increases happiness on balance, subtracting losses from gains, ought to be done. The imperative (2) implies that there is always a *rational* way (which, in some interpretations means a way based on cool, enlightened self-interest) of resolving conflicts. Harmony is not automatic, but it can be contrived by careful calculation and manipulation. The "interest of society" is maximum social happiness.

More conscientious writers who felt scruples about the manner in which the promotion of the greatest social happiness could be justified to those who would suffer from it, frequently reinforced their case by an argument of which the following passage is typical:

> Moreover, each party may reflect that, in the long run of various cases, the maximum sum-total utility corresponds to the maximum individual utility. He cannot expect in the long run to obtain the larger share of the total welfare. But of all principles of distribution which would afford him now a greater, now a smaller proportion of the sum-total utility obtainable on each occasion, the principle that the collective utility should be on each occasion a maximum is most likely to afford the greatest utility in the long run to him individually.[6]

---

is not. The analogy holds only for absolute monarchies where the will of the ruler is identified with the will of the state.

On the other hand it is equally obvious that there may be interest harmony in some respects over wider areas, *e.g.*, the neighborhood, the class, the nation, perhaps even the world. The objection to the harmony doctrine is not that harmony cannot exist, but that a social analysis of interest groupings and interest conflicts is excluded by a question-begging assumption.

[6] F. Y. Edgeworth, *Papers Relating to Political Economy*, vol. ii, pp. 102-103.

Two difficulties inherent in the utilitarian philosophy have strengthened the need to have recourse to a cruder version of the harmony doctrine with its liberal policy implications, particularly in economics. The first is the impossibility to calculate and compare *in practice* the effects on happiness of a particular measure. It seems both simpler and safer to rely on the spontaneous harmony of egoisms than to perform an impossible calculation. This argument for noninterference from the complete ignorance of the effects of interference can still be found in the most up-to-date controversies.

The second aid to the cruder harmony version is the already mentioned difficulty of deriving both actual (hedonistically determined) and moral behavior from the all-powerful motives of pleasure and pain. The dangerous logical jump from "we must do what we think will please us" to "we ought to do what pleases others" is greatly eased if identity of interests can be postulated. In discussions of economic matters the otherwise helpful concept of "sympathy" is usually dropped.

What then, in the light of the above distinction, was Bentham's attitude to interest harmony? In spite of rejecting the crude version, and in spite of admitting the necessity for government intervention to enforce the greatest happiness, Bentham remained faithful to the tradition of the harmony doctrine. In his view private and sectional interests are not ultimate forces, but are the result of imperfect insight and foresight. "Vice may be defined as a miscalculation of chances," he said. Even the natural law philosophers had envisaged interest clashes which may arise from error and ignorance. Unless Bentham makes the assumption of harmony, the "public interest" which the legislator is to promote could not be objectively determined nor advanced by threats and cajoleries which reinforce self-interest. It would be impossible to say that it is desirable for each to aim at "the greatest happiness" unless harmony is assumed to start with.[7]

The quest for recommendations which can be based on a harmony of interests is as old as economic thought, and as keenly

---

[7] This, at least, would have to be the interpretation if Bentham's views are to be consistent. One could also argue that they were inconsistent. He argued both (1) that the maximization of individual happiness by each involves conflict, and (2) that it is desirable for each, and particularly the task of the legislators, to maximize the social sum of happiness. Marx made Benthamism consistent by rejecting its harmony doctrine: legislators, like businessmen, run their affairs (the state, the firms) in their own interests.

pursued today as 150 years ago. It found its crudest expression in the Physiocrats and has, in the course of time, been modified and qualified. Yet, economists have endeavored to avoid controversial judgments and to give "scientific," "objective," "unequivocal" advice, just as the natural law philosophers recommended policies because they arose "from the nature of things." When people were less sceptical about the objectivity of values, value and fact were simply equated without further discussion. Later, some justification was thought to be necessary and the distance from factual premise to value conclusion was lengthened. But it amounted merely to a widening of the diameter of a vicious circle. The utilitarian reasoning from the desired to the desirable is an example of this process. Eventually, with growing scepticism about the capacity of facts to yield imperatives, the factual side only was stressed, the value aspect was suppressed, and one hears of "scientific" advice about how to increase welfare.

Yet, at least since Jevons,[8] renunciation of the possibility to resolve conflicts by "objective" tests accompanied scientific "recommendations." Jevons, Bohm-Bawerk, Walras, Pareto, Fisher,[9] among many others, and, more recently Professor Lionel Robbins [10] rejected at some place in their writings the possibility of objective interpersonal comparisons of utility or satisfactors.

Such denials, however, did not prevent these writers from continuing to make recommendations "on economic grounds," even though it is clear that the measures recommended would involve losses for some people. Attempts were made to remove this contradiction. They usually took the form of a distinction between production (including exchange) and distribution, and thus between "efficiency" and "social justice." Pronouncements on "effi-

---

[8] "The reader will find, again, that there is never, in any single instance, an attempt made to compare the amount of feeling in one mind with that in another. I see no means by which such comparison can be accomplished. . . . Every mind is thus inscrutable to every other mind, and no common denominator of feeling seems to be possible. . . . Motives in the mind of A may give rise to phenomena which may be represented by motives in the mind of B; but between A and B there is a gulf. Hence the weighing of motives must always be confined to the bosom of the individual." Jevons, *Theory of Political Economy*, 1871, 4th edition, 1924, p. 14.

[9] Fisher regarded comparisons between the pleasures of different individuals as "mysterious" matters which "do not belong here." (*Mathematical Investigations in the Theory of Value and Prices*, 1892, pp. 99, 87). "Philosophic doubt is right and proper but the problems of life cannot and do not wait." (*Economic Essay in Honour of John Bates Clark*, p. 180).

[10] L. Robbins, *Essay on the Nature and Significance of Economic Science*.

ciency" (*i.e.*, the sphere of production) were held to be noncontroversial (*i.e.*, subject to interest harmony) while the concern for "justice" was left to the politicians, moralists, governments, etc.

The critics, on the other hand, ever since Godwin, Thompson and Hodgskin pointed out, though they were not consistent in this, that such a separation involves a circular argument, and that production cannot be conceptually separated from distribution.

Income Distribution

Keynesian theory strengthened the utilitarian tradition because it resolved one of the great moral dilemmas of the neoutilitarians. Since Bentham it was held that a more egalitarian income distribution would raise general welfare. But inequality, it was thought, is required in order to safeguard sufficient savings. Saving is the source of investment and investment is an essential condition of economic progress and of a rising standard of living of all, including the poor. Equality would defeat its own purpose by reducing the wealth not only of the rich but also of the poor.

Keynes showed that a more equal distribution raises welfare not only on the Benthamite argument that a pound transferred from a rich to a poor man reduces the utility of the former by less than it increases the utility of the latter. It would also in certain conditions speed up investment and economic progress (at any rate in the short run). He thus removed, in his own words, "one of the chief social justifications of great inequality of wealth" and thus, in the words of Schumpeter, he "smashed . . . the last pillar of the bourgeois argument . . . into dust." [11]

This argument has its forerunners among the early critics of liberal-utilitarian economics. William Thompson, whose pleas are typical of those of other socialist critics before Marx, wrote that "production would be increased, and capital accumulated with a rapidity, and to an extent, hitherto unknown" [12] if workers received the whole product of their labor and if free exchange were allowed to take place. A system in which workers receive less is restrictive, generates unemployment and waste, as well as all

[11] J. M. Keynes, *General Theory*, p. 373; Joseph A. Schumpeter in *The New Economics*, ed. by Seymour S. Harris, p. 99.
[12] William Thompson, *An Inquiry into the Principles of the Distribution of Wealth Most Conducive to Human Happiness*, 1822, ed. by William Pare, 1850, p. 175.

kinds of other vices. Greater equality, on the other hand, would set free vast productive powers, as well as all kinds of other virtues.

These early critics, like Keynes and some modern "Liberal-Socialists" (*e.g.*, Lerner, Meade) had no sympathy for detailed planning. They believed as strongly as the liberals whom they attacked in the virtues of the free market and the pricing system. What distinguished the critics from the orthodox liberals is their conviction that if only some particular institutional arrangement which causes an "artificial disturbance" could be corrected, free exchange could be relied upon to produce a social optimum.[13] The difference between the classical liberals and their critics lay in their conception of the "natural state" in which all works out for the best. The socialists, from Godwin, Thompson and Hodgskin on, attempted to show that the liberal argument, by which actual distribution was justified by competition, is circular; that legal institutions like property, contract enforcement, inheritance, and the distribution resulting from these institutions were historical, arbitrary and unjust. They argued that the "natural laws of distribution" ought to be allowed to reign. Their policies aimed at restraining restraints and thus safeguarding "real" freedom.

To the demand to reform property and inheritance laws, other critics added monopoly and the concentration of economic power. Veblen thought that if only financiers could be got out of the way the engineers could be relied upon to produce a social optimum. List, in a somewhat different tradition, believed that once manufacturing industry had been developed behind a protective tariff free trade would maximize income. Wicksell and Keynes stressed the possibility that the natural rate may diverge from the market rate of interest and that this may cause trouble. Others have emphasized wage rigidities. The common feature of all these criticisms is that the classical scheme comes into its own as soon as certain institutional "disturbances," which the classics were supposed to have ignored, were removed. The purpose of economic policy is conceived to be the removal of brakes on the free-wheeling economic process, not the provision of active power.

Like ignorance in Bentham's scheme, these obstacles were thought to prevent the achievement of an underlying harmony

---

[13] The more cautious writers usually set out a series of conditions which would have to be met before one could say that competition maximizes output.

of interests. But once they are removed, the elegant and anonymous operation of free competition could be relied upon to maximize the common welfare. Thus some of the fiercest critics of liberal doctrine tacitly accepted its fundamental tenet.

Social security measures as they are practiced today, or detailed quantitative economic planning would have been rejected by the early English socialists. On similar grounds, Keynes and some Keynesians took no great interest in the former and rejected the latter.

It may seem that Keynesian measures of regulating investment as a means of achieving and maintaining full employment represent a break with the liberal-utilitarian tradition for two reasons: first, they appear to violate the *liberal* tradition because they are interferences not only with the *distribution* but also with the *production* sphere.[14] Second, they seem to make the canons of *utilitarianism* redundant, because they appear to promote the interests of all at the expense of none.

Interference With the Sphere of Production

The unqualified laissez-faire dogma was first modified for the sphere of distribution, particularly clearly by J. S. Mill. Adam Smith and Ricardo already had drawn a sharp distinction between production (always to be understood as including exchange) and distribution. Their proof of the liberal doctrine was much more successful in relation to production than to distribution. Adam Smith's well-known theory of the division of labor was a convincing demonstration that specialization and free exchange reduce costs and increase benefits. But this proof was frequently considered to apply also without further discussion to the sphere of income and property distribution.

J. S. Mill, who was influenced by the socialist critics, challenged the principle of *laissez faire* for the sphere of distribution. But production, he still believed, should, on the whole, be left to look after itself.[15] With this qualification the doctrine entered into British welfare economics and is still widely accepted today.

[14] See above p. 351.
[15] "The laws and conditions of the Production of wealth partake of the character of physical truths. There is nothing optional or arbitrary in them. Whatever mankind produces, must be produced in the modes, and under the conditions, imposed by the constitution of external things, and by the inherent properties of their own bodily and mental structure. . . . It is not so with the Distribution of

Seen against this background, Keynes appears as a proponent of a different tradition. In some respects his views resemble those of Continental and American critics of liberalism who tried to show that production will not "look after itself." According to Keynes, government action is necessary, not only and not mainly in order to correct undesirable distributional results, but also and largely in order to maintain total effective demand and thus full employment and production.

In this respect Keynes has more in common with conservative advocates of production policies like Friedrich List than with the British classics or socialists. Both List and Keynes held that productive powers would lie stagnant unless released by certain types of state action. Both saw in the state not an agency whose activity is confined to (usually undesirable forms of) consumption and redistribution, but a powerful stimulant to production. But both also believed that, once the productive forces were released, the liberal system would work well.

Yet, from a different point of view, Keynes appears much more closely aligned with the liberals than with the antiliberals. Although List and other advocates of production policy on the one hand, and Keynes on the other, share the belief that the state has to take certain actions in order to create the right environment for private self-interest to work beneficially, there is an important difference. The Protectionists advocate interference with particular branches of production and regulation of the composition of output, whereas Keynes believed that if "we suppose the volume of output to be given, *i.e.*, to be determined by forces outside the classical scheme of thought, then there is no objection to be raised against the classical analysis of the manner in which private self-interest will determine what in particular is produced, in what proportions the factors of production will be combined to produce it, and how the value of the final product

---

wealth. That is a matter of human institution solely. The things once there, mankind, individually or collectively, can do with them as they like. . . . The distribution of wealth, therefore, depends on the laws and customs of society. The rules by which it is determined are what the opinions and feelings of the ruling portion of the community make them, and are very different in different ages and countries; and might be still more different, if mankind so chose." *Principles of Political Economy*, 1848, ed. by Ashly, 1920, II, I, 1. Adherence to the labor theory of value facilitated, of course, faith in this distinction. Computation in labor units makes it possible to give meaning to "physical output" and avoids the crucial index number problem.

will be distributed between them. . . . It is in determining the
volume, not the direction, of actual employment that the existing
system has broken down." [16]

There were, of course, many Keyneses. The Keynes of the
General Theory has, in spite of his production policies, greater
faith in *laissez faire* than the Keynes of *The End of Laissez-Faire*.
We have already noticed that their preoccupation with "artificial
disturbances" was the hallmark of those critics who remained
steeped in liberal thought in spite of their criticism of the classical
arguments. They pilloried such evils as the maldistribution of
income (the liberal socialists), monopoly, and financial ill-man-
agement (radical liberals, Veblen), etc. Keynes's analysis, faithful to this tradition, brings to light another type of obstacle to
what is believed would otherwise be the successful operation of
the market. The rigidity of the rate of interest (together, possibly,
with the rigidity of wage rates) due to speculation is another
distorting element. State interference is necessary in order to
establish, according to the *Treatise,* coincidence of the market
rate with the natural rate [17] and, according to the *General Theory*, the full-employment rate. At the same time, a series of other
"complications" are ignored.[18]

In spite of his unorthodox views on production policy, Keynes,
particularly later in life, stood faithfully in the liberal-utilitarian
tradition.[19] He was not, of course, a laissez-faire utilitarian. But
then neither was Bentham, Mill, Sidgwick or Pigou. One can

16 *General Theory,* pp. 178-79.

17 "Natural" echoes the vocabulary of eighteenth-century natural law philosophers. Analogously, the early socialists believed that the correction of the maldistribution of wealth would re-establish the "natural" state.

18 He never discusses "the complications which arise—*(1)* when the efficient units
of production are large relatively to the units of consumption, *(2)* when overhead
costs or joint costs are present, *(3)* when internal economies tend to the aggregation of production, *(4)* when time required for adjustments is long, *(5)* when
ignorance prevails over knowledge, and *(6)* when monopolies and combinations
interfere with equality in bargaining." *The End of Laissez-Faire* (1926) p. 33.
". . . I see no reason to suppose that the existing system seriously misemploys the
factors of production which are in use." *General Theory,* p. 379.

19 "Thus I agree with Gesell that the result of filling in the gaps in the classical
theory is not to dispose of the 'Manchester System,' but to indicate the nature
of the environment which the free play of the economic forces requires if it is
to realize the full potentialities of production." *General Theory,* p. 379. Of Bretton
Woods and the Anglo-American Loan Agreement he said: "Here is an attempt
to use what we have learnt from modern experience and modern analysis, not to
defeat, but to implement the wisdom of Adam Smith." *Economic Journal,* 1946,
p. 186.

believe in the greatest happiness principle without believing
that the greatest happiness is the automatic result of free market
forces. Positive government action is necessary in order to safeguard the great happiness or general welfare. The characteristic
utilitarian feature and the relic of the harmony doctrine is the
belief, which Keynes shared with Bentham and Mill, that the
economic welfare of a nation is something that the government
can and should discover and promote.[20] The *liberal* feature is
the conviction that the promotion of economic welfare requires
only a little tampering here and there, and that, for the rest, the
automatic play of self-interest is a better driving force than any
practical alternative.

Neither the utilitarian nor the liberal component of this conviction is shared, *e.g.*, by some members of the historical school,
by the Marxists, or by the Schumpeterians, who reject the notion
of a "common well-being" and who look upon government policies as the outcome of the struggle between different interests.
The conviction that national well-being is something analogous
to individual or family well-being is so deeply embedded in the
Anglo-Saxon utilitarian tradition that one tends to overlook its
metaphysical character. Antihedonist thinkers have criticized it
on logical, psychological and sociological grounds,[21] but its hold
remains strong.

[20] Keynes was not, of course, a utilitarian in the strict philosophical sense but
only in a much looser sense. He was certainly not guilty of attempting to derive
ethical propositions from descriptive propositions. Keynes's philosophical views
were greatly influenced by the teaching of G. E. Moore about the naturalistic
fallacy. Cf. "My Early Beliefs," in *Two Memoirs*. "I do not regard [the Benthamite tradition] as the worm which has been gnawing at the insides of modern
civilisation and is responsible for its present moral decay." And ". . . we are
amongst the first of our generation, perhaps alone amongst our generation, to
escape from the Benthamite tradition." *op. cit.*, p. 96.

Professor Smithies considers Keynes as a "lineal descendant of the English
Utilitarians" because "he regarded worth-while theory as a basis for programmes
of action." Arthur Smithies, "Schumpeter and Keynes," *Review of Economics and
Statistics*, May 1951, p. 164. In this sense very many are, of course, utilitarians.
Professor Smithies quotes Schumpeter's views that Mill "might have been sad-
dened by evidence of disbelief in the fundamentals of Utilitarianism, but he
would surely have been reconciled by still stronger evidence of firm adherence
to its spirit and to some of its most important practical consequences. Philosophical radicalism is obviously not dead as yet—spreading among us as it does its
generous hopes for humanity and its stout refusal to see in life but a little inter-
mezzo of irritating nonsense between eternities of death." Joseph A. Schumpeter,
Economic Journal, 1933, p. 657.

[21] Cf. Gunnar Myrdal, *The Political Element in the Development of Economic
Thought*.

Interest Harmony and Antidepression Policies

If the first objection to looking upon Keynes as a liberal and a utilitarian was that his recommendations *violate liberal* canons, the second is that they do *not require* utilitarian canons. It may appear at first sight that the whole dispute about distribution and its relation to economic welfare, which is at the heart of recent controversies in welfare economics, is irrelevant for the policies with which Keynesian economics is concerned.

In some spheres, interests seem to coincide and there, at any rate, quasi objective recommendations [22] would appear to be possible. Monetary policy is occasionally quoted as an example. Thus it might seem quite safe to say that prosperity and stability are better than depression and fluctuations, and that measures which increase and prolong general prosperity are in the general interest. Professor Frank H. Knight wrote recently: "The business cycle . . . is not a problem of conflict of interests, since practically no one profits from depressions." [23] Many of the quibbles of welfare economics about how to achieve the best allocation of given and already fully, though not optimally, employed resources may appear trivial in comparison with the problem of how to increase the employment of resources, to reduce unemployment of men and promote prosperity.

It may seem that Keynesian measures are designed to promote the "interests of all" in a sense which makes it unnecessary to compare and weight interests, since nobody is harmed. Thus even those who believe that every man's enjoyment is unique and incommensurable with any other man's could still subscribe to Keynesian measures. Surely everyone prefers prosperity to depression and stability to fluctuations, except possibly for a few speculators. If this were true, the utilitarian assumption of the comparability of individual utilities could be dropped. Measures to achieve full employment would not present any of the awkward problems of comparing and weighting which a policy of "tightening up," *i.e.*, of rendering more efficient an already fully employed economy, would have to face. It would seem that we

---

[22] They would require the value judgment that what is in the interest of each and hurts no one ought to be done.
[23] Frank H. Knight, "Economic and Social Policy in Democratic Society," *Journal of Political Economy*, December 1950, p. 520.

could increase the national cake without reducing anybody's slice.

Yet, this appearance is deceptive for at least three reasons. (1) Some people are bound to lose in any case. (2) Harmony would not prevail even if nobody were to lose pecuniarily. (3) Even if problems of redistribution could be side-stepped in the short run, they might become urgent in any long-run policy to maintain full employment. Moreover, the acceptance of Keynesian policies would, once again, bring allocative and thus distributional problems into the foreground.

In the first place, some people are bound to lose even through antidepression policies. Fixed income receivers will be worse off. It is, of course, true that they could be compensated or, if not, that their losses are negligible in comparison with the gains (which is a value judgment and involves interpersonal comparisons). There is therefore a greater degree of harmony here than in policies designed to restore, say, free trade or competition. Yet, there is hardly ever complete harmony.[24]

Second, and perhaps more important, post-Keynesian experience and controversy suggest that there is neither general agreement on Keynes's analysis nor a general harmony of those interests which are affected by Keynesian measures, quite apart from the disharmony which arises from the reduced incomes of fixed income receivers.

Opposition may arise from misunderstanding. This is possible even in the Benthamite scheme. It could, in principle, be cleared up and harmony be established. But opposition may arise in spite of, or rather because of, a full understanding of the implications of Keynesian measures. Some people oppose them because they do not want full employment, either because they believe it undermines the discipline of workers, or because they fear that, if trade unions are strengthened through full employment, the share of profits will fall; or even if it is not expected to fall, entrepreneurs may fear that their power and status in society would be reduced.[25]

Keynes himself believed more strongly in a harmony of interests in this respect than the later experience of full-employment

[24] T. Scitovsky, "The State of Welfare Economics," *American Economic Review,* June 1951.
[25] Cf. Sidney Alexander, "Opposition to Deficit Spending," in *Essays in Honour of Alvin Hansen.*

conditions would warrant. He ascribed the opposition to anti-depression policies to the stupidity of bankers and believed that the removal of risks and the increase in profits would commend these policies to entrepreneurs. In fact, their opposition is perfectly rational, both on economic and political grounds. These policies undermine their bargaining power. Decisions which in slump conditions would have been in their power become in conditions of full employment matters of government policy, such as redistribution, the rate of investment and progress.[26]

The problem has been put succinctly in a recent series of articles in *The Economist*.[27] It is argued there that the objectives of (*a*) full employment, (*b*) a stable price level, and (*c*) free collective bargaining, are incompatible. Full employment and stable prices can only be had with a loss of freedom. Stable prices and free bargaining involve unemployment, and free bargaining together with full employment spell inflation. Moreover, even if any one of these three objectives is sacrificed to the two others, in the end none may be attained.

The argument may be extended from free bargaining to freedom from state controls generally. Many consider full employment an objective which involves a sacrifice, a "price," foregone opportunities.[28] Some of these costs cannot be expressed in money terms (*e.g.*, the anticipated loss of liberty) and are, perhaps, not strictly economic. But the crucial point is that there is no harmony of interests. The situation is complicated by the necessity to compare not only the tastes of different individuals as expressed in their market choices but also their value systems. Even in the short run, a dilemma between unemployment and controls may arise, if inflation is ruled out.

A measure of agreement might perhaps be reached by drawing a distinction between antidepression policies and full-employment policies. Many who would reject the latter might accept the former, though it would be difficult to reach agreement on where the line between the two should be drawn. But there is more wide-spread agreement on the desirability of avoiding very high, long-term unemployment than on the desirability of maintaining full employment.

[26] T. Balogh, *Dollar Crisis*, pp. 79-80, 105-6.
[27] "The Uneasy Triangle," *The Economist*, August 9th, 16th, 23rd, 1952.
[28] Cf., *e.g.*, J. Viner, "Full Employment at Whatever Cost," *Quarterly Journal of Economics*, August 1950.

Even if there were complete national harmony on antidepression policies, conflict will still arise with the interests of other nations and hence with the value systems of those who have international welfare at heart. Changes in the balance of payments and changes in the terms of trade resulting from antidepression policies will have repercussions abroad. Some of these changes may be welcomed by foreigners, but others will require adjustments which they may not be willing to make. The harmony doctrine is even less plausible if we attempt to apply it to the world economy. A nation has a government which, in some conditions, might act as if the fiction of a unified body of interests were true. There is no similar international institution. In the absence of international compensation for losses the conflict of interests is sharpened and the chance to reach agreement reduced.

The third reason why Keynesian policies do not avoid interest conflicts is this: Keynes's own analysis applies to the short run. It is easier to stimulate investment sufficiently to *attain* full employment, than it is to sustain this level of investment, and thus full employment, over a prolonged period of time. In the short run investment generates income but not consumption output. In the long run, however, investment also yields increased consumption output. If the investment required to generate full-employment *income* is the same as the investment required to yield the *output* which is demanded under continued full employment, full employment will be maintained. But this would be an odd coincidence. It is quite possible that the investment required to generate full-employment income is larger than (*a*) the investment required to meet effective demand or (*b*) the investment which can be worked profitably with a given population (or a given rate of population increase). In other words, full-employment investment may fall off, either (*a*) because there is insufficient consumption demand for the goods which it helps to produce indirectly, or (*b*) because the labor force required to work in conjunction with the fixed capital equipment is too small. In either case excess capacity will emerge and investment will be reduced. It will be impossible to maintain full employment. In order to avoid case (*a*) consumption would have to be raised, and in order to avoid both (*a*) and (*b*) policies designed to transfer labor from the investment goods industries to the consumption goods trades would have to be carried out. In such a situation a redistribution of income from the wealthier to the poorer might have to play an essential part. Such a redistribution would reduce the investment required to generate income and would help to prevent the generation of excess capacity in relation to either demand or the available labor force.[29] It appears therefore that the distribution of income may play an important part in maintaining full employment over a period of time.

This type of prognosis must, however, remain highly speculative and unreliable. Policies of redistribution inevitably change not merely relative incomes but also consumption and saving habits. It is impossible to foresee the psychological and sociological factors which would influence the amount and the direction of expenditure in a society whose social structure is different from that of the existing one.

Finally, even if full agreement could be reached on antidepression policies, the wide-spread *knowledge* of Keynesian *analysis*, and the *adoption* of Keynesian *remedies* would bring the problem of interest conflicts into the forefront again, even if one could assume that it lies dormant in a world of undiagnosed and uncured unemployment.

In conditions of large-scale unemployment one group's gain need not spell another's loss. But with the adoption of antidepression policies, and a fortiori with full-employment policies, conflicts become once again acute. Measures which were before socially costless, or had a negative social cost, now involve genuine sacrifices. The question how to weigh gains against losses arises as a result of the adoption of policies which might meet with unanimous approval.

But this is not the only ground for sharpened conflicts to which a society more fully aware of its workings and more strongly determined to decide its economic fate may give rise. The conditions which most nearly approach the successful working of a harmony of egoisms were those of early and mid-Victorian society. Quasi-harmony existed then, because in their economic

---

[29] Against this, one could argue that the required transfer of resources from investment into consumption could be brought about without such drastic measures of redistribution. Alternatively, one might argue that a good deal of new investment is not geared to consumption demand and this type of investment could always be expanded. Sufficiently laborsaving investment would remove the danger of excess capacity from either cause. Investment in housing could always be increased and would reduce the danger of demand deficiency. The rate of growth of output could also be reduced by the enjoyment of more leisure.

activities as in other departments of life the Victorians accepted without much questioning certain taboos and ancient rules. The conventionalism and traditionalism characteristic of the heyday of Victorian society contributed to the formation of a tacit consensus of opinion which made for the successful working of the economic system. The mythology which fostered the idea that this was "rational" and "economic" behavior par excellence only shows how deep-seated and unconscious the acceptance of the taboos was. The gold standard, a free money market, balanced budgets, the pursuit of free competition, the acceptance of unemployment, the belief in hard work and saving, all testify to this submission to external unquestioned rules and conventions.

The quasi-harmony broke down, not because people lost their heads and indulged in a wave of irrationalism, but because they became more rational, more conscious of the working of the economic system. Less prepared to accept ancient beliefs, they stripped the structure of economic relations of the superstitions which had cemented them. With knowledge came the desire for conscious manipulation. By breaking down the tacit consensus based on convention and superstition, the conflict of interests stood more clearly revealed.

The absorption of Keynes's view is part of this process of awakening. It helped to destroy the barriers which prevented the full pursuit of a selfish manipulation of society, thus brought clashes into the open, and made government action inevitable.

Summary

We have singled out three components of the classical tradition, namely, liberalism, utilitarianism, and the harmony doctrine.

(1) Liberals are those who advocate a minimum of government interference, particularly (a) with production, both (i) in the aggregate and (ii) in particular branches; but also, to a smaller or greater extent, (b) with distribution. Critics have maintained that the distinction between production and distribution is logically invalid. In the course of time liberals have admitted increasing interference with distribution, particularly since J. S. Mill, although they insisted that "production" ought not to be thereby impaired. In a sense, even the earliest liberals advocated some government action in the field of production

(things that would otherwise not get done, *e.g.*, education, light-houses).

(*2*) Utilitarians believe that social happiness (or, more generally, welfare) should be maximized. They may be (a) liberals, *i.e.*, hold that maximization can be brought about with a minimum of government interference; or they may be (b) authoritarians, *i.e.*, believe that regulations of various kinds are necessary.

(*3*) Adherents of the harmony doctrine hold that social or public interest can be objectively determined by a careful examination of private interests. They may believe either (a) that harmony is established automatically, or (b) that it has to be engineered.

One might say that all the preceding discussion amounts to is this: If we were to draw up an *Agenda* and a *Non-Agenda* for government action, different people would, for various reasons, put different items on the one and on the other, and there are many intermediate stages between putting nothing and putting everything on the *Agenda*. Any given recommendation can be viewed in contrast to opinions on either side of this alignment, and would appear in a different light, according to whether we contrast it with extreme *laissez faire* or with extreme planning.

Although this is true, the philosophical assumptions which underlie such programs do not shade into each other with similar continuity and present more suitable criteria of distinction than the policy conclusions derived from them. These assumptions would have to form the basis of discussion, when disagreement arises.

What, then, is Keynes's position in the classical tradition?

(*1*) Keynes's thought is unmistakably in the classical liberal-utilitarian tradition. He can be considered as a harmony theorist in the sense that he looked upon the economic activities of a nation as if they were those of an individual or a family, *i.e.*, as if they had a common purpose which, properly understood, is also the purpose of each individual. The common good, public welfare, maximum output, etc., are for him meaningful concepts and desirable objectives.

(*2*) It may appear that Keynes's recommendations represent a break with the classical tradition for the paradoxical reasons (a) that they involve interference with *production*, not merely with distribution; and (b) that, by apparently promoting the interests of each and all they seem to make the *utilitarian* calculus superfluous. But (a) does not represent a break with the *harmony* tradition and the appearance of (b) is deceptive, for losses of some kinds are bound to occur.

(*3*) Advocates of production policies have often accepted the meaningfulness and desirability of maximizing the common welfare, in particular in the light of consideration 2 (b). Keynes, in particular, advocated the regulation of *aggregates* only. He stood in the *liberal* tradition in the sense that the interferences which he advocated aim at the removal of particular breaks on the free pursuit of the common good.

(*4*) For several reasons, Keynesian measures do not in fact meet with applause from all and each. (a) Some are bound to lose in any case. (b) Nonmaterial considerations may cause opposition even where there is no strictly economic loss. (c) Long-run maintenance of full employment may require redistribution.

(*5*) In a country, or in a world, pledged to full employment not only the classical problems of interest conflicts come into their own again, but new problems of the distribution of economic power and its conscious manipulation arise.

CHAPTER FOURTEEN

The Flow of Business Funds, Consumption and Investment

Lorie Tarshis

THE GROSS PRODUCT of the business sector in the United States normally accounts for about 90 per cent of the gross national product. This implies that most of the total spending stream is directed towards private business firms for the purchase of their output, and that most factor income originates in the business sector. Since business firms control the disposal of a relatively large part of the total flow of funds, their operations in this matter, as in others, come to possess a special importance for the economy. What they do with their funds—whether, for instance, they direct them so that they become a part of the income stream, or not—is likely thus to be a decisive factor in establishing the level of both consumer and business investment expenditures.

An examination of the data to be presented below will confirm this view. The propensity to consume, in the sense in which it is useful in National Income Theory, is influenced to an important degree by business decisions governing the flow of their funds. It follows that any analysis of the determinants of this propensity, or its marginal counterpart, must devote at least as much attention to developments in the business sector as to those in the personal sector. Keynes was certainly aware of this, and in his own treatment of the propensity to consume he considered, among other factors, the dividend policy of corporations and capital consumption allowances. But it is perhaps useful to restate this point and to indicate its quantitative significance, for even in a period of high personal saving, business financial practices continue to play an important role in establishing the relation between income and consumer expenditures.

And the influence the business firm exerts on the national income via its control over the flow of funds is not limited to the consumption function. The level of investment is also directly influenced by the character of this flow; and a change in its character can lead to a relatively large change in investment expenditures. As before, Keynes noted this; [1] although in his eagerness to distinguish saving and investment he seemed later to lose sight of the connection. If, then, it is true that the level of business saving influences the level of investment, we have two ways in which the character of the flow of funds through the business sector can influence income levels.

In what follows, we propose to consider some of the more important features of this flow. After describing typical patterns, we shall endeavor to account for them and to set out their chief determinants. Finally, we shall consider the significance of our findings, paying special attention to their bearing upon National Income Theory. Our data will be drawn from the United States for the period 1929-1952 (omitting the war years) and in this paper they will be aggregative in nature.

The flow of funds can be investigated from various standpoints, depending upon the question to be answered. If the problem has to do with, say, the firm's liquidity position, it would be appropriate to adopt a scheme in accordance with which cash transactions were examined with special care while other transactions were disregarded. If, instead, the question has to do with the rate of growth of new firms, a different scheme would be desirable. The specific question we have posed is about the ways in which firms, through their strategic position as recipients and disbursers of funds, can influence the level of consumer and investment expenditures; and presumably this question demands its own specific scheme of analysis. For while some of the firms' transactions and the related fund flows are directly related to these matters, not all of them are relevant. It would be desirable, on grounds of economy and simplicity, to concentrate attention upon operations that seem to affect consumer and investment expenditures directly, instead of treating *all* receipts and payments as though they were equally important for our problem. On this principle we shall direct attention mainly to transactions that appear to play a primary role in establishing consumption and investment levels. Outpayments like wages which can be expected to provide a basis for consumer purchases are, on this rule, to be considered; while others, such as using cash to build up a bank deposit, are to be disregarded. In general, then, atten-

[1] Cf. page 109, *The General Theory of Employment, Interest, and Money.*

tion is to be focussed upon those transactions or operations that affect personal income, and hence consumption, or that influence the willingness or ability of firms to undertake investment projects.

From this standpoint the decisive flows of funds have their source in the sale of final products by business concerns. These sales—to consumers, to government, to markets abroad, and to business firms on capital account [2]—measure the business gross product. The charges against the business gross product include all those disposals by the business sector that constitute income for their recipients; though not all charges give rise to such disposals. To illustrate: in 1950, the business gross product was about $253 billion. Firms which realized this sum from the sale of final products paid out for wages, salaries, rent, interest, and dividends [3] approximately $180 billion, or 71 per cent of their receipts from the sales in question. Of the remaining $73 billion, the government took roughly $45 billion in taxes; and business firms themselves retained the difference.[4] The employees, investors, creditors and landlords who received the $180 billion regarded their receipts as part of their personal income. Indeed, in 1950 these payments from the business sector made up 80 per cent of the total personal income of the economy. The importance of such disbursements in establishing the level of consumer expenditures thus becomes manifest.

The year 1950 was not unusual in respect either to the percentage of the business gross product that firms paid out in forms that constituted personal income, or to the proportion of the total personal income for which such disbursements accounted. Over the whole period 1929-1950, business firms paid out to individuals as wages, salaries, dividends, rents and so on, about 74 per cent of the sums they received for the sales of their final products; these payments in turn constituted 80 per cent of personal income, and hence provided the chief support for consumer buying.

[2] Including the value of changes in business inventories.
[3] Including the income of unincorporated enterprise which could be regarded as a combination of these various forms of income.
[4] A direct measurement of the amount retained comes to about $29 billion, instead of $28 billion. The discrepancy is accounted for in part by the arithmetical error in rounding off; in part, however, it represents a statistical error which in 1950 was nearly $2 billion.

N

Further analysis of these income-generating disbursements would be desirable in order, for example, to take account of the differences in spending that could be expected from payments received, on the one hand, by employees, and on the other by investors. It would be interesting, for instance, to investigate the reasons for the comparative stability over the years in the ratio of compensation of employees to the business gross product; the figure has not been lower than 46 per cent since 1929 nor higher than 50 per cent, and the range has been even smaller for the ratio of wages and salaries paid to the gross product of business corporations. It would be interesting, too, to look for an explanation of the fact that on the downswing the ratio of the *change* in wages and salaries paid by the business sector, to the *change* in total income originating in that sector is typically, although not always, lower than the corresponding ratio on the upswing. Answers to these questions and others like them would throw a revealing light on the whole subject—how the flow of funds through the business sector influences consumer expenditures. But unfortunately we can say no more here about the qualitative aspect of these flows, and our further remarks will be directed to their quantitative characteristics.

As we have noted, some of the charges against the business gross product do not enter into personal income. For one thing, the government levies taxes of various kinds—sales and excise taxes, contributions for employee's social security, and taxes upon corporate profits. These sums are not available to consumers.[5]

And, secondly, firms normally *retain* a part of their proceeds from sales; that is to say, they usually receive more in sales receipts than they pay out as wages, salaries, dividends and so on, and as taxes. In the following table, the charges against the business gross product are classified under three headings; those that contribute directly to personal income (and so consumption), those that represent tax payments, and finally those that constitute retentions, or as we may call them, gross business saving. It will be noticed that the sum of the three categories, each of which is estimated directly, frequently does not equal, as it should, the business gross product which is estimated independently; once again "statistical errors" explain the inequality.

[5] Except as subsequent actions by the government may make them available. But this is another matter.

TABLE I. Charges Against Business Gross Product that Constitute:
(*In billions of dollars*)

Year	Personal Income	Taxes	Gross Business Saving	Year	Personal Income	Taxes	Gross Business Saving
1929	74.1	8.4	11.7	1941	79.4	20.9	11.5
1930	65.8	8.0	8.9	1942			
1931	53.8	7.4	5.3	1943			
1932	39.7	7.2	2.7	1944			
1933	37.1	7.6	2.7	1945			
1934	42.6	8.6	4.9	1946	140.3	29.0	14.7
1935	48.6	9.2	6.4	1947	156.0	33.1	20.6
1936	54.5	10.3	6.6	1948	173.1	35.8	28.4
1937	61.6	11.7	7.8	1949	165.4	35.0	30.5
1938	54.6	11.4	8.0	1950	180.2	45.6	28.9
1939	58.8	12.2	8.5	1951	204.0*	54.2	33.0
1940	64.0	14.3	10.6	1952	213.2*	54.5	36.9

* Estimate based on incomplete data.

Perhaps the most striking feature demonstrated by these data is the steady decline over the years in the ratio of the charges against the business sector's gross product that become personal income to all such charges. Up to 1938 (except for 1934), this ratio had never fallen below 75 per cent; while from 1939 up to the present the figure has never been so high. Offsetting this decline in the business sector's contribution to personal income, has been the relatively large increase in the taxes it has paid to the government. Finally, gross business saving has remained surprisingly stable, considering the whole period; though it constituted a relatively low percentage of the business gross product in the Great Depression (but not in 1938 or 1949), in 1936 when a tax was levied on undistributed profit, and in 1945 and 1946.

The gross saving of the business sector is the difference between the business gross product and those charges against it which go either to the government, or to individuals who regard the corresponding payments as personal income. Classifying the individual items—for instance, "wages and salaries," as charges which the recipients treat as personal income; "employer contributions for social insurance" as taxes, and so on—we conclude that gross business saving is equal in amount to the sum of undistributed profits (of corporations), and capital consumption allowances. All the other charges seem to fall into one of the other two categories. However, there are some difficulties to be faced.

The first relates to the inventory valuation adjustment. In order to have a consistent set of accounts, it is necessary to correct the bookkeeping figure of profit (which normally includes some elements of inventory write-up, or its reverse, in times of changing price levels) and hence of undistributed profit, by the amount of the adjustment. Thus, if as in 1950 the books of the business community show undistributed profit at about $12.9 billion, but a sizeable part (actually, about $5.1 billion) of the firms' profits for that year is a result of nothing more than a writing-up of inventory values, the proper figure for undistributed profit is $12.9 billion minus $5.1 billion, or $7.8 billion. In some years, like 1946, 1938, 1936, 1932, 1930, the required corrections are indeed nearly as large as the unadjusted figure for undistributed profits.

A second difficulty relates to the measurement of the undistributed profits of the business sector. The measurement for the corporate sector presents no problem, except the one already noted. But no indication is given in the official National Income accounts of a corresponding sum for unincorporated enterprises. Indeed the whole of the income of such firms is treated as a part of the nation's personal income. Probably in a formal sense, this is the only procedure that can be followed, for there is no legal distinction between the personal income and the business income of the owners of such firms. Yet it is evident that these owners often do make such a distinction; and it is reasonable to conclude that their decisions reflect the ways in which they classify their income. Nevertheless, there is no way of estimating the undistributed profit of such unincorporated enterprises, and consequently the figure of business saving that must be used is too low by the amount of these excluded undistributed profits.

At the same time the figure for the Allowance for Capital Consumption seems to be too high. It includes not only the allowance for the depreciation of and accidental damage to the plant and equipment of business firms in the strict sense, but also for the depreciation of private housing and of the capital assets of nonprofit institutions. There would be no question about the propriety of including the depreciation allowance for rental housing, as a charge against the business gross product, but it seems in some ways inappropriate to do this in connection with the allowance for depreciation on owner-occupied housing.[6] Nevertheless, it is not possible to remove this element of the allowance for capital consumption, by using published data: hence, the measure of gross business saving will be somewhat distorted, but on this account it will include too much rather than too little.

It is clear that at any given level of business gross product and tax payments, the higher is business saving, the lower will be the payments from the business sector that constitute personal income. Gross business saving thus can be regarded as exerting a negative influence upon consumer expenditures. But of course it is not the only such influence. Personal saving—the difference between disposable personal income and consumer expenditures —and government taxes reduced by the amount of its transfer payments, also exert this effect. It will be worth-while to show the relative importance of business saving in holding consumer expenditures below the GNP.

Our starting point is the identity, implicit in the National Income accounts, that: the GNP minus consumer spending equals the sum of gross business saving, personal saving, and the difference between government tax receipts and its transfer payments.[7] The gap between the gross value of the total output of the economy, and what consumers take of that amount—a gap which is filled by "investment"—is a consequence of the saving done by persons and business firms, and the failure of government normally to pay out as much in the form of Transfer Payments [8] as it receives in taxes. The following table shows the amounts of these various forms of "saving"—personal, business, and government—from 1929 to 1952.

Once again, we must deal with a statistical discrepancy, for the measure of consumer expenditures to be derived by subtracting all saving from the GNP is not necessarily the same as the direct estimate of consumer spending.

The great importance of "government saving" is the most noticeable feature of the above table. In only two of the years

---

[6] Gerhard Colm estimates the capital consumption allowance on owner-occupied housing as $2.7 billion, in 1951, while the total allowance for capital consumption came, in the same year, to $24.6 billion.

[7] We shall term the difference between taxes and government transfer payments "government saving."

[8] Including interest on the national debt.

TABLE II. Composition of Saving: 1929-1952 (exc. 1941-1945)
(*In billions of dollars*)

Year	Personal Saving	Business Saving	Government Saving
1929	3.7	11.7	9.4
1930	2.9	8.9	8.9
1931	1.8	5.3	6.4
1932	— 1.4	2.7	6.4
1933	— 1.2	2.7	6.7
1934	— 0.2	4.9	7.4
1935	1.8	6.4	8.0
1936	3.6	6.6	8.3
1937	3.9	7.8	12.3
1938	1.0	8.0	11.3
1939	2.7	8.5	11.2
1940	3.7	10.6	13.4
x	x	x	x
1946	12.0	14.7	35.5
1947	3.9	20.6	42.4
1948	10.5	28.4	44.8
1949	6.7	30.5	40.8
1950	11.2	28.9	50.5
1951	17.0	33.0	55.3
1952	18.0	36.9	79.0

between 1929 and 1952 did saving of this type [9] not outrank personal and gross business saving. Of the total gross saving done in the whole period, government saving accounted for slightly more than half; between 1929 and 1940, it constituted about 51 per cent of the total, and between 1946 and 1952 almost 57 per cent of the total. Gross business saving was second in importance and except for the years of the war, it always stood higher than personal saving. For the whole period 1929-1952, the gross saving of business firms came to about 29 per cent of all saving; while personal saving accounted for only 19 per cent. Omitting the war years when personal saving was swollen by the unavailability of goods, and in other ways, gross business saving accounted for 33 per cent of all saving, while personal saving accounted for 12 per cent of the total. Before the war, gross business saving made up 39 per cent and personal saving about 10 per cent of all saving;

[9] Which includes taxes on persons, as well as those on business.

while between 1946 and 1952, the comparable figures were 31 per cent and 13 per cent respectively.[10]

Thus while gross business saving has been less important than government saving in accounting for the failure of consumers to buy up the whole output of the economy, it has been of considerably greater importance than personal saving. Yet if one were to judge their relative importance by comparing the attention each has received from economists, he would mistakenly conclude that personal saving played the more important role.[11]

Business firms have no direct control over the taxes they pay; the saving function of the government [12] depends upon tax rates and transfer payments as established by the government. The discretion of the business community extends only to the way in which the proceeds from the sale of the product, after taxes, are distributed; considering only broad categories, the decision has to do with the amount paid out to factors (including dividends), and the amount saved. The following table indicates how this decision has been made:

TABLE III. % Disposition of Business Gross Product (*Less Taxes*): 1929-1952 (exc. 1941-1945)

Year	Personal Income	Business Saving	Year	Personal Income	Business Saving
1929	86.4%	13.6%	1939	87.4%	12.6%
1930	88.1	11.9	1940	85.8	14.2
1931	91.0	9.0			
1932	93.6	6.4			
1933	93.2	6.8	1946	90.5	9.5
1934	89.7	10.3	1947	88.3	11.7
1935	88.4	11.6	1948	85.9	14.1
1936	89.2	10.8	1949	84.4	15.6
1937	88.8	11.2	1950	86.2	13.8
1938	87.2	12.8	1951	86.1	13.9
			1952	85.2	14.8

10 Of course, if the figure we have by analogy called "government saving" is not included, the importance of gross business and personal saving is enhanced. However, if that is done, the investment concept which would be required for national income analysis would be different from that which is commonly used.

11 This tendency has gone so far that very commonly the term "consumption function" is applied to the relation between disposable personal income and consumer expenditures. While it is silly to quarrel with the meaning given to a term, it might be pointed out, first, that in this sense it has quite a different meaning than it has as the Propensity to Consume in Keynes's *General Theory;* and second, that in relating consumer spending to disposable income, the concept does not cover enough territory and hence that it, along with the level of investment, are not sufficient to determine the national income.

12 It is the function which relates government saving to the gross national product.

While these results are not surprising in view of what Table I indicates, several points may be noted. Business saving as a percent of the business gross product less tax payments required by government seems to vary cyclically, generally being highest in prosperity and lowest in depression. There are exceptions to this rule, as in 1936 and 1938 when the tax on undistributed profit was imposed and then removed, and in 1949; but the general tendency is well established. Secondly, gross business saving has recently been slightly more important as a fraction of the sums available after meeting the tax bill than it was in 1929 or at any time before the end of World War II.

Of course, the firm is subject to various constraints and obligations in formulating its decisions as to how its proceeds are to be divided. In order to embark upon production it must pay the going rate of wages to employees whose number is approximately specified by the nature of its production. To escape bankruptcy, it must meet such long-term commitments as interest charges on outstanding bonds, and rentals. If preferred stock is outstanding, its management may have to pay dividends on pain of losing control. And even the dividends on its common stock may have to be above a certain level to satisfy the stockholders. Its freedom is limited, and it applies, except for minor items like executive bonuses, mainly to the dividend rate.[13]

It follows that the saving-function of the business sector is determined, once tax rates are set, within narrow limits. Given the level of sales and the wage rate, gross profits before depreciation allowances and taxes will be pretty well determined. With specified capital assets and tax rates, the firm's net profit will be established. At this point, management has discretion for it must decide how much should be paid in dividends, and hence the level of undistributed profits. Thus with a given gross business product, tax structure, wage rates, and capital assets, the level of business saving appears to depend upon management's discretion only to the extent that the dividend rate itself may be varied.

This statement is, however, too mechanical for it assumes certain relationships to be fixed which in fact are not. For one thing, profit at each level of the business gross product is not rigidly

---

[13] If a long-time period is considered, the freedom is greater. The management will then have some power in determining the firm's capital structure, and so the nature and amount of its obligations to creditors and others in the years ahead. But at any date, most of the decisions about the period directly ahead are dictated by circumstances which management inherits from the past.

determined; and for another, taxes on business profit do not depend only upon the level of profit and the tax structure. Variations in other factors can influence the results; the workings of a few are set out below.

Even with an established mark-up policy, business profits will depend on the fixed costs; and they in turn will reflect the choice of capital structure made in the past, and also any difference between today's price level and that ruling when long-term contracts were made.

Generally, if today's prices are higher than those ruling when contracts were signed, today's profits will be higher too for each level (in value terms) of the business gross product. The same rule holds for the capital consumption allowance; if capital assets were accumulated when prices were relatively low, the amount to be allowed for depreciation would be low too, and hence profits would be comparatively high. But while the first-mentioned influence would probably raise business saving at each level of the business gross product, the second would probably reduce it, since the amount by which the capital consumption allowance was unduly low would exceed the amount by which undistributed profits were, as a result, unduly high. It does not seem, however, that the net effect of a move to a different price level upon business saving could be predicted for it would depend, among other things, upon the importance of the fixed charges that entered personal income, compared with other fixed charges.

Less uncertain is the effect upon business saving of a currently changing price level. If prices are rising in one year, but not in another, and in both of them the business gross product is the same, we could expect the *unadjusted* profit level before tax in the year of rising prices to be higher than in the other. Despite this, before-tax profits adjusted for inventory revaluation should be the same. But taxes are levied on the unadjusted level of profit, and hence adjusted *net* profit would be lower in the year of rising prices. Moreover, management, though it would make some allowance in determining the dividend rate, for "fictitious" profit, would nonetheless probably pay higher dividends the higher was the level of unadjusted profit after tax. Thus in the year of rising prices, the tax collector and the stockholder would get more than in another year of steady prices and the same business gross product; accordingly undistributed profit and business saving would be lower.

The final point to notice is that if the stock of capital assets grows over time, the allowance for capital consumption will also grow. As a result, an increasing part of a certain business gross product will have to be set down under this heading, while the part assigned to profit will decline. Business saving will then gradually increase. Again, if the stock of capital were to remain constant, but a period of price stability followed a period of rising prices, the allowance for capital consumption would tend to rise, as equipment was replaced, and hence profits would fall; once again business saving would rise. These various considerations will suggest that the functional relation between the business gross product and business saving depends not only upon the relatively obvious factors such as the tax structure and management's dividend policies, but upon others as well. And bearing in mind these various factors, we would have to conclude that there was no reason to expect the business saving function to remain fixed over time, though there seems to be no convincing reason for expecting the shift to be in one direction rather than the other.

The nature of the function, its determinants being given, can be described with greater confidence. Business saving when the various determinants such as the tax structure, dividend policies, and the stock of capital goods, are constant, will move in the same direction as the business gross product. The ratio of the change in business saving to the change in the business gross product which brings it about—or in other words, the Marginal Propensity of Business to Save—depends primarily upon three relations: (i) the marginal effect of a change in business gross product upon profits before tax; (ii) the marginal tax rate on profits; and (iii) the marginal dividend rate from profits after tax. To illustrate: if the first expression has a value of .35, the second of .50, and the third of .30, the marginal propensity to save, if we can take the change in the capital consumption allowance to be zero, as in this context we should, would come to $12\frac{1}{4}$ ($=(.35)(1-.50)$ $(1-.3)$).

Unfortunately we cannot get an accurate impression of the actual value of this ratio by considering the statistical record, for as we have noted, there is no reason to suppose that the function itself has remained constant from one year to the next. Still, an examination of the relative changes in the two measures may give us at least a rough idea of the magnitude we seek. Moreover, if we discover occasions when the ratios of change are out of line with those found most of the time, we may conclude that the function itself has altered, and seek an explanation.[14]

The relevant data are found in the table which follows:

TABLE IV. Changes in Business Gross Product & Gross Business Saving (*In billions of dollars*)

Years	(1) Business Gross Product	(2) Gross Business Saving	Ratio of (2) to (1)	
1929-30	−12.3	−2.8	22.8%	
1930-31	−14.3	−3.6	25.2%	
1931-32	−16.7	−2.6	15.6%	1929-33: 19.7%
1932-33	− 2.5	0	—	
1933-34	+ 8.1	+2.2	27.2%	
1934-35	+ 6.8	+1.5	22.0%	
1935-36	+ 8.8	+0.2	2.3%	
1936-37	+ 7.8	+1.2	15.4%	
1937-38	− 6.2	+0.2	x	1933-40: 18.6%
1938-39	+ 6.6	+0.5	7.6%	
1939-40	9.6	+2.1	21.9%	
1947-48	+24.1	+7.8	32.4%	
1948-49	− 4.1	+2.1	x	
1949-50	+22.6	−1.6	x	1947-52: 20.7%
1950-51	+38.3	+4.1	10.7%	
1951-52	+13.8	+3.9	28.3%	

With minor exceptions the change in business saving was the same in direction as the change in the business gross product. The exceptions are easy to understand. Between 1937 and 1938 there was a fall in the business gross product and yet business saving rose very slightly; the most important factor in explaining this was, probably, the virtual abolition of the tax on undistributed profit; in addition the tax on corporate profits and dividends was based upon a figure for profits that was about 25 per cent lower than the "true" (*i.e.*, "adjusted for inventory valuation") level. Again between 1945 and 1946 the direction of the changes was different, for while the business gross product increased, busi-

---

[14] Of course, unless the function were linear, we should not expect the value of the marginal propensity to save to be always the same, even though the function itself did not shift.

ness saving fell. The explanation appears to be that book profits in 1946 were greatly in excess of the adjusted level; and taxes and dividends were based substantially upon the book figures. Hence they were out of line with the real figure, and undistributed profits (adjusted) were therefore unduly low. Though a similar situation ruled in 1947 and 1948, the ratio of changes (between 1946 and 1947 and 1947 and 1948) in business saving and business gross product was scarcely affected. The next year saw however the opposite situation; with book profits somewhat below the adjusted figure, taxes and dividends were unduly low too. As a result, even though there was a decline in the business gross product from the year before, the level of business saving rose. And finally in 1950, the situation was again reversed; with price inflation, book profits were a good deal higher than "real" profits; and so, therefore, were dividends and taxes on corporate profit. As a result, adjusted undistributed profits in 1950 were below the level for 1949 despite the increase in the business gross product.

If we omit from consideration the years in which the inventory valuation adjustment was relatively large, and those when the tax on undistributed profits was imposed or removed, we have the following results: the total change from year to year, disregarding signs, in the business gross product was $166 billion, and the change in business saving was $32.6 billion. If we can suppose that the influence of other factors upon the business saving function more or less cancelled out [15] we may conclude that the marginal propensity of business to save was about 20 per cent. Let us accept this figure as giving at least a general picture of the magnitude.

It is interesting to compare this figure with the corresponding ones for government and personal saving. Using the same procedures, we find that the marginal propensity of persons to save (against their disposable personal income) was roughly 18.0 per cent; the marginal propensity of government to save (against the gross national product) was about 22 per cent. But these figures do not describe the role played by business firms, government, and individuals, in accounting for changes in the gap between the GNP and consumer expenditures, when the GNP itself

---

[15] The increasing allowance for capital consumption was offset, in direction at least, by the increase in the tax rate on corporate profits.

changes. The point can be most clearly seen as follows: between 1929 and 1930, the Gross National Product fell by $12.9 billion, while consumer expenditures fell by $8 billion. The gap between the GNP and consumption thus fell by $4.9 billion. Such a reduction in the gap meant a decline in total saving: business, government, and personal. Actually personal saving fell by $0.8 billion, or·16.3 per cent of the total decline; government saving declined by $0.7 billion, or 14.3 per cent; and business saving fell by $2.9 billion, or 60 per cent of the total.[16] Making similar calculations for all the years 1929-1952 (omitting 1941-1946) we have the following results:

Between 1929 and 1933, changes in business saving accounted for 54 per cent of the changes in total saving; with the decline in personal saving accounting for about 30 per cent of the total and the reduction in government saving for 16 per cent. Between 1933 and 1940, the rise in business saving accounted for 40 per cent of the total; the rise in "government saving" for 35.5 per cent, while the increase in personal saving amounted to nearly 25 per cent of the total increase. It is not instructive to examine the data for the war years for light on our problem. The very great increase in taxes, and the inability of consumers to buy as much as they wanted, were so important that they obscured all else. From 1947[17] to 1952, the increase in business saving came to 24 per cent. The increase in personal saving amounted to 23 per cent; and the increase in government saving was most important, accounting for the remaining 53 per cent of the increase in total saving.[18]

In each period the change in business saving was somewhat more important than the change in personal saving. Considering all these periods, the sum of year-to-year changes in gross business saving was about 30 per cent greater than the sum of such changes in personal saving; considering the prewar period only, changes in gross business saving were about twice as important as changes in personal saving. Hence, in dealing with the multiplier effect, it is evident that the tendency for business saving to

16 There is an unassigned $0.5 billion decline in saving, indicated in the official data by an increase in the statistical discrepancy.
17 To choose for the beginning of the period this year when individuals saved very little as they tried to make good various wartime deficiencies leads to an overstatement of the "normal" rise in personal saving.
18 Had the period ended with 1950, before the great tax increase required to finance the defense program became effective, the role of each sector in accounting for the total increase in saving would have been: government, 35 per cent; business, 34 per cent; and personal, 31 per cent.

change with changes in the business gross product (and the GNP) must be carefully noted.

The importance of gross business saving in determining the level of consumer expenditures and changes in that level when there is a change in income cannot be questioned; but it may be argued that by dealing with the gross rather than the net concept, the role of business saving has been exaggerated. Certainly if we set *net* business saving against personal and government saving, our answer would be quite different from that reached above. In most years personal saving was higher than the undistributed profit of corporations; however, we must remember the fact that this way of measuring net business saving means that the saving of unincorporated business is treated as part of personal saving.[19]

This criticism certainly cannot be dismissed. For some purposes, indeed, the appropriate concepts do seem to be net business saving and net investment. But for our study which, among other things, must deal with the decision-making process for private investment, and which has for its main interest an analysis of the factors determining the level of activity, it seems clear that the more fruitful concepts are gross private investment, and hence gross business saving.

By comparing business, personal, and government saving, we have perhaps created the impression that the level of each is independent of the others. But such an impression would be incorrect. For one thing, as consideration of the income identities will show, the sum of personal, business, and government saving must be identically equal to the sum of gross private investment (including net foreign investment), and government expenditures upon goods and services. Thus given the level of investment (in the most general sense) when the levels of any two types of saving are known, the third is determined too. For another, it is clear that a change in the saving function in one sector will lead to changes in the saving functions in the others. Thus, if there should be a reduction in tax rates on corporate profits, government saving would fall while business and personal saving would rise, since higher profits after tax would lead to higher dividends and hence higher personal saving, and also to higher undis-

[19] The *changes* in net business saving were, however, greater than the *changes* in personal saving up to the war.

tributed profits.[20] Or if management should decide to pay out more in dividends from a certain level of corporate profits, there would be a reduction in business saving offset (if investment is not affected) by increases in personal and government saving.

There are still other possibilities to be explored for mutual interaction among the saving functions of the three sectors. For instance, an increase in business saving may lead to a rise in stock prices—at any rate, it should, though an increase in dividends is more likely, in fact, to produce this effect. But if stock prices rise, individuals probably would be disposed to save less from any given level of disposable income. Hence personal saving might decline not only because of the reduction in disposable income, but also because of the capital gains that would, if our supposition is correct, be enjoyed. The effect of a change in the business saving function upon personal saving, and consumer expenditures may thus be quite complex. Nevertheless there are certainly more reasons for expecting a change in the propensity of business to save to bring about a change in the opposite direction in consumption than its reverse.

Gross business saving is equal in amount to the sum of the capital consumption allowances and undistributed profit. But this does not mean that firms save their undistributed profit—an item which is after all entered on the debit side of the balance sheet. When firms save there must be an increase in their assets (and the increase in their undistributed profits, or surplus, and reserves for depreciation are the *offsetting* entries) or a decrease in their liabilities. When gross business saving is positive, business assets, measured at cost, increase, or business liabilities fall. If gross business investment is zero, then the assets that must increase when gross business saving is positive, are cash and accounts receivable, or at least this is so until a positive decision to do something with the funds is made.[21] How they use these assets—whether to finance the purchase or repair of plant and equipment, to build up bank deposits or a portfolio of securities, or to pay off debts, is a matter which we must consider.

Bearing in mind the obstacles that generally check investment

20 If we can assume that investment would be unaffected, the sum of the changes in the three types of saving would have to come to zero.
21 This is not the place to consider where these additional assets will come from, but the question obviously demands attention.

when firms must finance their expenditures by borrowing or raising money through the stock market, it seems that high gross business saving encourages investment expenditures. To a brief discussion of these obstacles we must now turn our attention.

A convenient starting-point is the simple statement that a firm will undertake an investment program provided it can borrow money at an interest rate lower than the prospective yield on the project. While various modifications are required, the fact remains that no project on which the prospective yield is less than the interest rate will be undertaken, if the firm must borrow to finance it. But in fact the conditions are far more stringent. For one thing, an allowance would be made for risk—in this context for the risk that the estimate of yield is incorrect. Bearing in mind the common business rule that the purchase of a capital asset is undertaken only when there is a reasonable assurance that its cost will be fully recovered in a period far shorter than its life, it is clear that the allowance for risk is frequently very high—perhaps a multiple of the interest rate. Then there is the further risk to be considered which management understandably deems very important, the enhanced danger of bankruptcy with every increase in the firm's debt. Considering this risk too, management may require an anticipated rate of return far above the interest rate as compensation. If the firm is already in debt, it may not be able in any case to borrow, except by issuing junior bonds, since it has perhaps agreed to protect its present creditors by refraining from adding anything which possesses claims as high as theirs against its assets. Or if the ratio of the firm's debt to its liquid (or other) assets exceeds the figure which large lenders find prudent, it may not be able to get money by floating a new bond issue on any reasonable terms. For these and other reasons, firms may require a very high prospective yield before they will consider embarking on a project that has to be financed by borrowing. It may be noted in passing that if the obstacle to financing a project in this way has been too low a ratio of liquid assets to debt, positive business saving over a period would weaken it, and thus perhaps encourage investment.

The first has, however, another external source of funds—floating new stock on the market.[22]

The criterion by which the firm would be expected to make its

[22] It is true that to many smaller firms this alternative is not a real one. We may deal with such cases by treating the net issue price as very low.

decision about projects to be financed in this way is quite different from that discussed above; indeed it is doubtful that anything useful can be said about the interest rate (or its equivalent) that is implied by the dividend rate on the stock. If management is acting in the interests of its stockholders,[23] it will undertake to float a new issue to finance a project when the ratio of the addition to profit to be expected on existing assets exceeds the ratio of the amount of new stock to be issued to the amount of stock presently outstanding.[24] If the new profit could be expected to add 40 per cent to the firm's profits, after tax, and if it could be financed by increasing the outstanding stock by only 30 per cent, it would be to the present stockholders' advantage to have this program adopted—unless there were some other program that was even more attractive. It follows then that for a given expectation of additional earnings on the project, the market is unfavorable—whether low or high—if management feels that the price per share is unduly low considering the earnings prospects on existing assets.[25] When depression gives way to prosperity, it is likely to favor this kind of program, for while the expectation of earnings on present assets is likely to rise, the ratio of the cost of the project to the additional earnings it can be expected to produce is likely to fall, and meanwhile the prices of the stock would assuredly increase. But even in prosperity, projects that promise a high yield may not be undertaken if they are to be financed by new stock issues.

This conclusion can be simply illustrated with the following data: suppose a project is under consideration which could be undertaken at the cost of $100 million. Suppose that it would promise a high yield—say 20 per cent a year, or $20 million additional profit. Next, suppose that the firm's existing assets are expected to earn $50 million in a year and that there are 1,000,000 shares out. Finally, suppose that the market price of the stock, and the net price on a new issue is $200. To finance the new project, the shares outstanding would have to be increased by

---

[23] Assuming that interest to be the maximum earnings, including undistributed profit, per share of outstanding stock.

[24] This is a necessary condition. But other ways of financing the project may be available, and if one of them is superior this particular program would not be adopted.

[25] The price must exceed the product of expected earnings per share on present assets times the ratio of the cost of the project to the additional earnings it can be expected to produce.

50 per cent, while the earnings would increase, if the project were undertaken, by only 40 per cent. This would imply a reduction in earnings per share, and so the decision would be negative. In this case, the price per share—only four times the expected earnings per share on existing assets—would be too low, and the project would not be started even if it promised a high yield.

There are other reasons,·too, why management might be unwilling to embark upon a project to be financed by a stock issue even when earnings prospects are favorable. It might fear, for example, that with more stock outstanding, it might lose control. Or it might wish to avoid disclosures of information such as would be required if a new issue were publicly offered. Or it may be interested not so much in the earnings of its present stockholders as in their capital gains. Thus, as with projects to be financed by borrowing, there are many circumstances in which, even though projects could be expected to have a high yield, they would not be undertaken if they had to be financed through stock issues.

However, when firms are saving heavily, they can finance many projects without appealing to the market. In such a period, they find themselves with liquid assets which they are free to use as they please. Presumably these can be employed to pay for investment goods which are intrinsically attractive but which would not be bought if recourse to the financial market were necessary. But the question still remains as to whether the firms would decide to use their funds in this way.

Once again we shall assume that, dividends having been determined, management seeks to maximize prospective earnings per share. If so, it should seek to use the funds that are becoming available with this goal in mind. One possibility is, of course, to pay off debt—although the terms of previous loans may penalize or limit redemption before maturity. And the gains from doing so may not in any case be much greater than the *net* interest saved.[26] Another possibility is to acquire assets such as bonds and stock. This program is open to the objection that the yield on high-grade securities is likely to be very low, while management might be subjected to criticism if more speculative purchases

---

[26] There may also be some reduction in the risk of financial disaster, but the reduction in risk where debt is reduced from, say, $50 million to $20 million would probably be much less than the increase in risk from an increase in debt from $50 million to $80 million.

proved unsuccessful. To hold cash will, of course, be free from risk, but the absence of yield should, when other opportunities are available, limit such holdings.

The alternative to all of these ways of using the accumulating funds is, of course, to employ them to finance the purchase of new plant and equipment, or the replacement of old, and the accumulation of inventories. The "costs" to the firm of such investment expenditures are the earnings that might have been obtained by using the funds in some different way, but since, as we have seen, these earnings are likely to be quite low, this constitutes a relatively minor deterrent. It follows then that many investment projects which would not have been undertaken if their financing had had to be done through the market may prove attractive if they can be carried out with funds retained from operations.

The case for supposing that business investment expenditures would be stimulated by high business saving is further strengthened when attention is directed to corporate profits tax legislation as it applies to "closely-held corporations." In these cases the Treasury may levy a penalty when it believes that earnings are being retained in order to ease the burden of the personal income tax for the owners. But in the administration of this clause, the firm generally can escape the penalty if it can show that retained earnings were used to finance capital expenditures. Investment projects for such firms probably can be done at a negative cost, and the conditions for undertaking them are then very mild.

There is, however, one caution to be noted. The saving of business firms may not be well distributed in the sense that firms which have projects to be undertaken may not be able to retain enough funds to finance them, while those which have been able to save substantial amounts may not have any worthwhile projects at hand. A high level of business saving will prove more effective in stimulating investment when the saving is done by firms which are considering expansion, and perhaps especially by firms which have no access to outside financing. However, in the normal course of events, when there is an increase in aggregate business saving, almost all firms share in the rise. Hence, we may conclude that a change in business saving will lead to a change in the same direction in investment.

The total effect upon investment and the gross national product of a given change in business saving will differ, depending upon the reason for the change. Thus, if business saving increases because management adopts a more cautious dividend policy, the influences are mixed—the effect of greater ease in financing being partly offset by the effect of a reduction in the consumption function. If, instead, business saving increases because of a cut in tax rates, there is no offset to consider; and if the increase accompanies an increase in the gross national product, then there is a two-fold stimulus to investment. Yet, even in the least favorable case, a change in business saving would be likely to lead to a change in the same direction in investment expenditures.

A brief consideration of the implications of our results for the theory of income determination is desirable. There are several points worth making.

For one thing, a realistic study of the consumption function must consider the role of business in its determination. And since the value of the marginal propensity to consume is also affected by business practices, a study of the multiplier process must, if it is to be realistic, take into account the effect on business saving of a change in the business gross product.

For another, even though we accept the view that a change in business saving will lead to a change in the same direction in investment, this does not imply a return to Say's law and its consequences. There is no reason to suppose that every *attempt* to save more succeeds, or that if it does succeed, it leads to an equal increase in investment. An equilibrium at a less-than-full-capacity income level can thus be established.

Another consequence bearing upon the stability of the system also follows: with the marginal propensity of business to save having a significant value, there is a tendency for any change in the gross national product to become cumulative. For example, with a rising level of activity, firms would find, in the increased ease of financing, a further inducement to increase their investment spending. Financial factors thus would be expected to strengthen the conventional acceleration effect. Fortunately there is some reason to suppose that the marginal propensity of business to save becomes particularly low in depression and, if this is so, the effectiveness of the accelerator diminishes once activity falls far enough.[27]

[27] The policy implications—maintaining prosperity by lowering corporate profits tax rates—are interesting.

Keynes has given us a powerful tool for analyzing national income determination. But it was not a finished piece of equipment, as he knew perfectly well. Various refinements are still needed and it seems that one such improvement will be to allow for the ways in which the business firm by virtue of its control over the flow of funds can influence the level of income.

CHAPTER FIFTEEN

Utility Analysis and the Consumption Function: An Interpretation of Cross-Section Data[1]

Franco Modigliani[2] *and Richard Brumberg*

Introduction

OF JOHN MAYNARD KEYNES' many hypotheses, the one that has been subject to the most intensive empirical study is the relation between income and consumption. By now, his generalization is familiar to all:

> The fundamental psychological law, upon which we are entitled to depend with great confidence both *a priori* from our knowledge of human nature and from the detailed facts of experience, is that men are disposed, as a rule and on the average, to increase their consumption as their income increases, but not by as much as the increase in their income.[3]

The study of the consumption function has undoubtedly yielded some of the highest correlations as well as some of the most embarrassing forecasts in the history of economics. Yet the interest in the subject continues unabated since, if it were possible to establish the existence of a stable relation between consumption, income, and other relevant variables and to estimate its parameters, such a relation would represent an invaluable tool for economic policy and forecasting.

[1] We are indebted to several colleagues, and especially to Messrs. R. Cyert, of Carnegie Institute of Technology, and C. Christ, of the Johns Hopkins University, for reading the manuscript and making valuable suggestions.

[2] My contribution to this paper is a direct outgrowth of the research carried out as director of the project on "Expectations and Business Fluctuations" financed by a grant of the Merrill Foundation for the Advancement of Financial Knowledge. I should particularly like to call attention to the relation between consumption, assets, income expectations, and the life cycle of income as developed in this paper and the relation between production, inventories, sales expectations, and the seasonal cycle of sales as developed in my joint paper with O. H. Sauerlender, "The Use of Expectations and Plans of Firms for Short Term Forecasting," *Studies in Income and Wealth*, Vol. XVII, in course of publication.

[3] John Maynard Keynes, *The General Theory of Employment, Interest, and Money*, 1936, p. 96.

The work done in this area during the last few years has taken two directions.[4] One has consisted in extensive correlations of data on aggregate consumption, or saving, with income and a large collection of additional miscellaneous variables. The second direction has been the exploitation of cross-section data. Old material has been reworked and new information collected. The most elaborate of the new studies have been those of the Survey Research Center of the University of Michigan. As in the time series analysis, more and more variables have been included, or are proposed for inclusion, in order to discover stable relations.[5]

By now the amount of empirical facts that has been collected is truly impressive; if anything, we seem to be in imminent danger of being smothered under them. What is, however, still conspicuously missing is a general analytical framework which will link together these facts, reconcile the apparent contradictions, and provide a satisfactory bridge between cross-sectional findings and the findings of aggregative time series analysis.

It is our purpose to attempt to provide such an analytical framework through the use of the well-developed tools of marginal utility analysis. We have shown elsewhere[6] that the application of this instrument proves of great help in integrating and reconciling most of the known findings of aggregative time series analysis. In this paper, we shall attempt to show how the same model of individual behavior can be applied to the analysis of cross-section data. We hope to demonstrate that this model provides a consistent, if somewhat novel, interpretation of the existing data and suggests promising directions for further empirical work.

[4] For two excellent bibliographies in this field, see: G. H. Orcutt and A. D. Roy, "A Bibliography of the Consumption Function," University of Cambridge, Department of Applied Economics, mimeographed release, 1949; and *Bibliography on Income and Wealth, 1937-1947*, edited by Daniel Creamer, International Association for Research in Income and Wealth, 1952.

[5] For example, see Lawrence R. Klein, "Savings Concepts and Their Relation to Economic Policy: The Viewpoint of a User of Savings Statistics," paper delivered at the Conference on Savings, Inflation, and Economic Progress, University of Minnesota, 1952.

[6] Franco Modigliani and Richard Brumberg, "Utility Analysis and Aggregate Consumption Functions: An Attempt at Integration," a forthcoming study.

Part I: THEORETICAL FOUNDATIONS

I.1 Utility Analysis and the Motives for Saving

Our starting point will be the accepted theory of consumer's choice. The implications of this theory have been so incompletely recognized in the empirically-oriented literature of recent years, that it will be useful to retrace briefly the received doctrine.[7]

Consider the following variables:

c_t consumption of the individual during the t-th year (or other specified interval) of his life, where t is measured from the beginning of the earning span;

y_t income (other than interest) in the t-th year (for an individual of age t, y_t and c_t denote current income and consumption, while y_τ and c_τ, for $\tau > t$, denote expected income and planned consumption in the τ-th year):

s_t saving in the t-th year;

a_t assets at beginning of age period t;

r the rate of interest;

N the earning span;

M the retirement span; and

L the life span of economic significance in this context, that is, $N + M$.

It is assumed that the individual receives utility only from present and prospective consumption and from assets to be bequeathed. If we assume further that the price level of consumables is not expected to change appreciably over the balance of the life span, so that the volume of consumption is uniquely related to its value, then for an individual of age t, the utility function can be written as

$$(1.1) \qquad U = U(c_t, c_{t+1}, \cdots c_L, a_{L+1}).$$

This function is to be maximized subject to the budget constraint, which, if the rate of interest, r, is not expected to change appreciably over the balance of the life span, can be expressed by means of the equation

[7] For an extensive application of marginal utility analysis to the theory of saving see the valuable contributions of Umberto Ricci, dating almost thirty years back: "L'offerta del Risparmio," Part I, *Giornale degli Economisti*, Feb. 1926, pp. 73-101; Part II, *ibid.*, March, 1926, pp. 117-147; and "Ancora Sull'Offerta del Risparmio," *ibid.*, Sept. 1927, pp. 481-504.

$$(1.2) \qquad a_t + \sum_{\tau=t}^{N} \frac{y_\tau}{(1+r)^{\tau+1-t}} = \frac{a_{L+1}}{(1+r)^{L+1-t}} + \sum_{\tau=t}^{L} \frac{c_\tau}{(1+r)^{\tau+1-t}} . [8]$$

For the utility function (1.1) to be maximized, the quantities c_τ and a_{L+1} must be such as to satisfy the first order conditions:

$$(1.3) \qquad \begin{cases} \dfrac{\partial U}{\partial c_\tau} = \dfrac{\lambda}{(1+r)^{\tau+1-t}} \; ; \quad \tau = t, t+1, \cdots, L \\[2ex] \dfrac{\partial U}{\partial a_{L+1}} = \dfrac{\lambda}{(1+r)^{L+1-t}} \end{cases}$$

where λ represents a Lagrange multiplier. The equation (1.3), together with (1.2), yields a system of $L - t + 3$ simultaneous equations to determine $L - t + 1$ $\bar{c}_\tau$'s, $\bar{a}_{L+1}$ and $\bar{\lambda}$, the barred symbols being used to characterize the maximizing value of the corresponding variable.

If current income, $y_t + ra_t$, is unequal to c_t, the individual will be currently saving (or dissaving); and similarly, if $y_\tau + ra_\tau$ is not equal to $\bar{c}_\tau$, the individual will be planning to save (or dissave) at age τ. The traditional model suggests that we may usefully distinguish two separate reasons for such inequalities to arise. We refer to these reasons as the "motives for saving." [9]

I The first of these motives is the desire to add to the estate for the benefit of one's heirs; it arises when $\bar{a}_{L+1}$ is greater than a_t. Under this condition $y_\tau + ra_\tau$ must exceed $\bar{c}_\tau$ for at least some $\tau \geqq t$.

II The second motive arises out of the fact that the pattern of current and prospective income receipts will generally not coincide with the preferred consumption, $\bar{c}_\tau$, for all $\tau \geqq t$. This clearly represents an independent motive in that it can account for positive (or negative) saving in any subinterval of the life span, even in the absence of the first motive.

It is precisely on this point that a really important lesson can be learned by taking a fresh look at the traditional theory of the household; according to this theory there need not be any close and simple relation between consumption in a given short period

[8] See, for instance, J. Mosak, *General Equilibrium Theory in International Trade*, Ch. VI, especially pp. 116-117.
[9] Cf. Keynes, *op. cit.*, p. 107.

and income in the same period. The rate of consumption in any given period is a facet of a plan which extends over the balance of the individual's life, while the income accruing within the same period is but one element which contributes to the shaping of such a plan. This lesson seems to have been largely lost in much of the empirically-oriented discussion of recent years, in the course of which an overwhelming stress has been placed on the role of current income, or of income during a short interval centering on the corresponding consumption interval, almost to the exclusion of any other variable.

Before proceeding further with the implications of our model, it is necessary to devote brief attention to one conceivably important element that we have neglected so far, namely, the phenomenon of uncertainty. No attempt will be made in this paper to introduce uncertainty in the analysis in a really rigorous fashion. The reason for this procedure is simple; we believe that for the purposes in which we are interested, a satisfactory theory can be developed without seriously coming to grips with this rather formidable problem. An examination of the considerations that support this conclusion, however, is best postponed until we have fully explored the implications of our model under certainty. We may simply note at this point that the presence of uncertainty might be expected to give rise to two additional motives for saving:

III   The precautionary motive, *i.e.*, the desire to accumulate assets through saving to meet possible emergencies, whose occurrence, nature, and timing cannot be perfectly foreseen. Such emergencies might take the form of a temporary fall in income below the planned level or of temporary consumption requirements over and above the anticipated level. In both cases the achievement of the optimum consumption level might depend on the availability of previously acquired assets.

IV   Finally, as a result of the presence of uncertainty, it is necessary, or at least cheaper, to have an equity in certain kinds of assets before an individual can receive services from them. These assets are consumers' durable goods. If there were no uncertainty, a person could borrow the whole sum necessary to purchase the assets (the debt cancelling the increase in real asset holdings), and pay off the loans as the assets are consumed. In the real world, however, the uncertainty as to the individual's ability to pay forces the individual to hold at least a partial equity in these assets.

While we have thus come to distinguish four separate motives for saving, we should not forget that any one asset in the individual's "portfolio" may, and usually will, satisfy more than one motive simultaneously. For example, the ownership of a house is a source of current services; it may be used to satisfy part of the consumption planned for after retirement; it may be bequeathed; and, finally, it is a source of funds in emergencies. It follows that any possession which can be turned into cash will serve at least one of the four motives and should accordingly be treated as an asset. These possessions include, in particular, equities in unconsumed durable goods.

Saving and dissaving can then usefully be defined as the positive, or negative, change in the net worth of an individual during a specified time period. Correspondingly, consumption will be defined as the expenditure on nondurable goods and services—adjusted for changes in consumers' inventories—plus current depreciations of direct-service-yielding durable goods.[10]

As we shall see, the fact that assets are capable of satisfying more than one motive simultaneously provides the foundation for our earlier statement that it should be possible to neglect the phenomenon of uncertainty without too serious consequences. But a fuller development of this point will have to wait until later.

I.2   Some Further Assumptions and Their Implications

The currently accepted theory of the household, even in the very general formulation used so far, has begun to broaden our view of saving behavior. It is, however, too general to be really useful in empirical research. If we are to derive from it some propositions specific enough to be amenable to at least indirect

[10] Quite recently, many others have advocated this definition. See, for instance, Kenneth Boulding, *A Reconstruction of Economics*, Ch. 8; Mary W. Smelker, "The Problem of Estimating Spending and Saving in Long-Range Projections," Conference on Research in Income and Wealth (preliminary), p. 35; Raymond W. Goldsmith, "Trends and Structural Changes in Saving in the 20th Century," Conference on Savings, Inflation, and Economic Progress, University of Minnesota, 1951; James N. Morgan, "The Structure of Aggregate Personal Saving," *Journal of Political Economy*, Dec. 1951; and William Hamburger, "Consumption and Wealth," unpublished Ph.D. dissertation, The University of Chicago, 1951.

empirical tests, it will be necessary to narrow it down by introducing some further assumptions about the nature of the utility function (see Assumption II below). For convenience of exposition, however, we shall also find it useful to introduce several additional assumptions whose only purpose is to simplify the problem by reducing it to its essentials. These assumptions will enable us to derive some very simple relations between saving, income, and other relevant variables, and it will appear that the implications of these relations are consistent with much of the available empirical evidence. While some of the simplifying assumptions we are about to introduce are obviously unrealistic, the reader should not be unduly disturbed by them. In the first place we have shown elsewhere[11] that most of these assumptions (except Assumption II) can be greatly relaxed or eliminated altogether, complicating the algebra but without significantly affecting the conclusions. In the second place, the question of just which aspects of reality are essential to the construction of a theory is primarily a pragmatic one. If the theory proves useful in explaining the essential features of the phenomena under consideration in spite of the simplifications assumed, then these simplifications are thereby justified.

It may be well to recall, first, that one simplifying assumption has already been made use of in developing our basic model of equation (I.1) to (I.3); this is the assumption that (on the average) the price level of consumables is not expected to change appreciably over time. The first of our remaining assumptions will consist in disregarding altogether what we have called the "estate motive." Specifically, we shall assume that the typical household, whose behavior is described by equations (I.1) to (I.3), does not inherit assets to any significant extent and in turn does not plan on leaving assets to its heirs. These conditions can be formally stated as:

ASSUMPTION I: $a_1 = 0,$ $\bar{a}_{L+1} = 0.$[12]

[11] Modigliani and Brumberg, *op. cit.*

[12] The assumption $\bar{a}_{L+1} = 0$ might be stated more elegantly in terms of the following two:

$$\text{(a) } \frac{\partial U}{\partial a_{L+1}} \equiv 0; \qquad \text{(b) } a_{L+1} \geqq 0.$$

The first of these equations specifies certain properties of the utility function U; the second states an institutional fact the individual must take into account in his planning, namely that our economic, legal, and ethical system is set up so as to make it rather difficult to get away without paying one's debts. The addition of these two equations to our previous system implies $\bar{a}_{L+1} = 0$.

Assumption I, together with equation (I.2), implies that our household, in addition to having no inherited assets at the beginning of its life, also does not receive any gift or inheritance at any other point of its life; it can only accumulate assets through its own saving.

From Assumption I and equation (I.2), it follows immediately that current and future planned consumption must be functions of current and expected (discounted) income plus initial assets, *i.e.*,

$$\bar{c}_\tau = f(v_t, t, \tau), \qquad \tau = t, t+1, \cdots, L;$$

where

$$v_t = \sum_{\tau=t}^{N} \frac{y_\tau}{(1+r)^{\tau+1-t}} + a_t,$$

and t denotes again the present age of the individual.[13]

Now what can be said about the nature of the function f? Or, to reformulate the question, suppose that, on the expectation that his total resources would amount to v_t, and with a given interest rate, our individual had decided to distribute his consumption according to the pattern represented by $\bar{c}_\tau$. Suppose further that, before carrying out his plan, he is led to expect that his resources will amount not to v_t but, say, to $v_t + \Delta v_t$. Should we then expect him to allocate the additional income to increase consumption in any specific period of his remaining life (*e.g.*, his early years, or his late years, or his middle years), relative to all other periods, or can we expect him to allocate it so as to increase all consumptions roughly in the same proportion?

We are inclined to feel that the second alternative is fairly reasonable; or, at any rate, we are unable to think of any systematic factor that would tend to favor any particular period relative to any other. And for this reason we are willing to assume that the second answer, even if it is not true for every individual, is true on the average.[14] This gives rise to our second assumption, the only one that is really fundamental for our entire construction, namely:

ASSUMPTION II: The utility function is such that the *proportion* of his total resources that an individual plans to devote to

---

[13] The fact that $a_1 = 0$ by Assumption I of course does not imply $a_t = 0$.

[14] The expression "on the average" here means that if we aggregate a large number of individuals chosen at random, their aggregate consumption will behave approximately as though each individual behaved in the postulated way.

consumption in any given year τ of his remaining life is determined only by his tastes and not by the size of his resources. Symbolically, this assumption can be represented by the following equation:

$$(I.4) \qquad \bar{c}_\tau = \gamma_\tau^t v_t, \qquad \tau = t, t + 1, \cdots, L$$

where, for given t and τ the quantity γ_τ^t depends on the specific form of the function U and on the rate of interest r, but *is independent of "total resources,"* v_t.

As a result of well-known properties of homogeneous functions, it can readily be shown that a sufficient condition for Assumption II to hold is that the utility function U be homogeneous (of any positive degree) in the variables $c_t, c_{t-1}, \cdots, c_L$.[15]

The remaining two assumptions are not essential to the argument, but are introduced for convenience of exposition.[16]

ASSUMPTION III: The interest rate is zero, *i.e.*, $r = 0$.

As a result of this assumption, the expression

$$v_t = \sum_{\tau=t}^{N} \frac{y_\tau}{(1 + r)^{\tau+1-t}} + a_t$$

can be rewritten as $y_t + (N - t)y_t^e + a_t$, where

$$y_t^e = \left(\sum_{\tau=t+1}^{N} y_t \right) \Big/ \ (N - t),$$

represents the average income expected over the balance of the earning span.

---

[15] More generally, it is sufficient that the utility index be any monotonic increasing function of a function U homogeneous in $c_t, \ldots, c_L$. This assumption can also be stated in terms of properties of the indifference map relating consumption in different periods. The postulated map has the property that tangents to successive indifference curves through the points where such curves are pierced by any one arbitrary radius vector are parallel to each other.

It may also be worth noting that a simple form of the utility index U satisfying our assumption is the following:

$$U = \log U = \alpha_0 + \sum_{\tau=t}^{L} \alpha_\tau \log c_\tau$$

since U is clearly homogeneous in $c_t, \ldots, c_L$. The above expression in turn has the same form as the well-known Weber Law of psychophysics, if we regard U as a measure of the intensity of the sensation and c as the intensity of the stimulus. One may well speculate whether we have here something of deeper significance than a mere formal analogy.

[16] For a discussion of the effects of removing them, see Modigliani and Brumberg, *op. cit.* Also, see various footnotes below.

Equation (I.4) now reduces to:

$$(1.4') \qquad \bar{c}_\tau = \gamma_\tau^t [y_t + (N - t)y_t^e + a_t]$$

which implies

$$\sum_{\tau=t}^{L} c_\tau = [y_t + (N - t)y_t^e + a_t] \sum_{\tau=t}^{L} \gamma_\tau^t.$$

Furthermore, taking into account Assumption I ($\bar{a}_{L+1} = 0$) we also have

$$(I.5) \qquad \sum_{\tau=t}^{L} c_\tau = y_t + (N - t)y_t^e + a_t.$$

From (I.4') and (I.5) it then follows that

$$(I.6) \qquad \sum_{\tau=t}^{L} \gamma_\tau^t = 1.$$

ASSUMPTION IV: All the γ_τ^t are equal; $i.e.$, our hypothetical prototype plans to consume his income at an even rate throughout the balance of his life.

Let γ_t denote the common values of the γ_τ^t for an individual of age t. From (I.6) we then have

$$(I.7) \qquad \sum_{\tau=t}^{L} \gamma_\tau^t = (L + 1 - t)\gamma_t = 1;$$

or,

$$\gamma_\tau^t = \gamma_t = \frac{1}{L + 1 - t} \equiv \frac{1}{L_t},$$

where $L_t \equiv L + 1 - t$ denotes the remaining life span at age t.

Part II: IMPLICATIONS OF THE THEORY AND THE EMPIRICAL EVIDENCE

II.1   The Individual Consumption Function and the Cross-section Consumption-Income Relation

Substituting for γ_τ^t in equations (I.4') the value given by (I.7), we establish immediately the individual consumption function, $i.e.$, the relation between $current$ consumption and the factors determining it:

$$(II.1) \qquad c = c(y, y^e, a, t) = \frac{1}{L_t} y + \frac{(N - t)}{L_t} y^e + \frac{1}{L_t} a;$$

where the undated variables are understood to relate to the current period.[17] According to equation (II.1), current consumption is a linear and homogeneous function of current income, expected average income, and initial assets, with coefficients depending on the age of the household.

The corresponding expression for saving is

$$(II.2) \qquad s = y - c = \frac{\dot{L} - t}{L_t} y - \frac{N - t}{L_t} y^e - \frac{1}{L_t} a.$$

In principle, equations (II.1) and (II.2) could be directly tested; but they cannot easily be checked against existing published data because, to our knowledge, data providing joint information on age, assets (which here means *net worth and not just liquid assets*), and average expected income, do not exist.[18] We must, therefore, see whether we can derive from our model some further implications of a type suitable for at least indirect testing in terms of the available data. Since most of these data give us information about the relation between consumption in a given short interval and income over the same interval (or some small neighborhood thereof) we must seek what implications can be deduced as to the relations between these variables.

If the marginal propensity to consume is defined literally as the increment in the current consumption of the household accompanying an increment in its current income, divided by the increment in income, keeping other things constant, then, according to equation (II.1), this quantity would be $\dfrac{\partial c}{\partial y} = \dfrac{1}{L_t}$, which is independent of income but dependent on age. The consumption function (II.1) would be represented by a straight line with the above slope and an intercept $\dfrac{(N - t)y^e + a}{L_t}$; and, since this intercept can be assumed positive,[19] the proportion of income saved should tend to rise with income.

---

[17] For an individual of age $t > N$, by assumption, $y = y^e = 0$ and only the last term on the right-hand side of (II.1) remains.

[18] The valuable work in progress at the Survey Research Center of the University of Michigan gives hope that the variety of data required for such a test may sometime become available. Clearly, the problem of measuring average expected future income may prove a serious challenge. On this point, however, see text below and the Appendix.

[19] Obviously, both y^e and a will generally be nonnegative.

In order to get some feeling as to the quantitative implications of our results, let us say that the earning span, N, is of the order of 40 years, the retirement span, M, 10 years, and therefore the total active life span, L, of the order of 50 years. These figures are not supposed to be anything more than a very rough guess and their only purpose is to give us some notion of the magnitudes involved. On the basis of these figures, the marginal propensity to consume would lie somewhere between a minimum of 1/50, or 2 per cent, and a maximum of 1/11, or 9 per cent, depending on age.

These figures seem unreasonably small. This is because the above definition of the marginal propensity to consume is clearly not a very reasonable one. A change in the current income of the household will generally tend to be accompanied by a change in its expected income, y^e, so that there is little sense in including ye among the things that are supposed to be constant as y changes. Note, however, that the same objection does not apply to a, for a denotes initial assets and, for a given household, assets at the beginning of the current period necessarily represent a constant.

Once we recognize that y^e is generally a function of y, the marginal propensity to consume at age t may be defined as

(II.3)
$$\frac{dc}{dy} = \frac{1}{L_t} + \frac{N-t}{L_t}\frac{dy^e}{dy} .$$

Since $\dfrac{dy^e}{dy}$ would generally tend to lie between 0 and 1,[20] the marginal propensity to consume would fall for different individuals between a minimum of 1/50 and a maximum of 4/5, depending both on age and on the value of $\dfrac{dy^e}{dy}$.

Unfortunately, the empirical validity of these statements cannot be tested from observations of actual individual behavior. The reason is that consumption and income can only have a *single* value for a *given individual at a given age*. To be sure, we might be able to observe the behavior of an individual whose income had changed in time; but, even if we could control the value of y^e, we could not keep constant his age nor probably his initial assets (*i.e.*, assets at the beginning of each consumption period). The only way we could possibly check these conclusions is by observing the behavior of (average) consumption of *different*

[20] See below, Section 3, especially footnote 39.

o

households at different income levels, *i.e.*, by observing the "cross-section" average and marginal rate of consumption with respect to income.[21]

Suppose we make these observations and, for the sake of simplicity, suppose further that all the households we examine have approximately the same age and in every case $y = y^e$. Should we then expect the marginal rate of consumption to be $\dfrac{N - t + 1}{L_t}$, as equation (II.3) would seem to imply? The answer is no; the individual marginal propensity to consume cannot be simply identified with the cross-section marginal rate of consumption. Turning back to equation (II.1), we can easily see that (if all individuals behave according to this equation) the cross-section marginal rate of consumption should be

$$\text{(II.4)} \qquad \frac{d'c}{d'y} = \frac{N + 1 - t}{L_t} + \frac{1}{L_t}\frac{d'a}{d'y},$$

where the differential operator d' is used to denote cross-section differentials. Although $\dfrac{da}{dy}$ must be zero for an individual, there is no reason why the cross-section rate of change, $\dfrac{d'a}{d'y}$, should also be zero. Quite the contrary. Our model leads us to expect a very definite relation between the (average) net worth of households at a given income level and the income level itself, which relation we now proceed to explore.

II.2   *The Equilibrium Income-Asset-Age Relation and the Consumption-Income Relation in a Stationary and Nonstationary Cross Section*

To see clearly the implications of our model it will be useful to examine at first the nature of the cross-section relation between consumption and income in a special case which we shall call a

---

[21] We speak here advisedly of average and marginal rate of consumption, rather than of "cross-section marginal propensity to consume," for, as will become clear, the use of the latter term is likely only to encourage a serious and already too frequent type of confusion. The word "propensity" denotes a psychological disposition and should refer to the way in which a *given* individual reacts to different stimuli, and not to the way in which *different* individuals react to different stimuli. The differential reaction of different individuals in relation to different stimuli may give us information about the individual propensity, but it is not, in itself, a propensity.

cross section of "stationary" households. A household will be said to be in stationary position if it satisfies the following two conditions: (a) at the beginning of its active life it expects a constant income throughout its earning span; and (b) at every point of its life cycle it finds that its original expectations are completely fulfilled in the sense that its past and current income are as originally expected and its expectations for the future also coincide with its original expectations.[22] From equations (I.4) and (I.7) (since by assumption $y_1^e = y_1$ and $a_1 = 0$) we see that for such a household the consumption plan at age 1, which we denote by $\bar{c}_\tau^1$, must be

$$(\text{II.5}')\qquad \bar{c}_\tau^1 = \frac{N}{L}\,y_1, \qquad\qquad \tau = 1, 2, \cdots, L;$$

and the saving plan

$$(\text{II.5}'')\qquad \bar{s}_\tau^1 = \begin{cases} \dfrac{M}{L}\,y_1, & \tau = 1, 2, \cdots, N \\[2mm] -\dfrac{N}{L}\,y_1, & \tau = N+1, N+2, \cdots, L. \end{cases}$$

Finally, the asset plan, which is the sum of planned savings, must be

$$(\text{II.5}''')\qquad \bar{a}_\tau^1 = \begin{cases} \dfrac{(\tau-1)M}{L}\,y_1, & \tau = 1, 2, \cdots, N \\[2mm] \dfrac{N(L+1-\tau)}{L}\,y_1, & \tau = N+1, N+2, \cdots, L. \end{cases}$$

We will make use of equation (II.5''') to define the notion of "stationary equilibrium" assets. We say that initial asset holdings at age t, a_t, are in equilibrium relative to any given level of income, y, if

$$(\text{II.6})\qquad a_t = a(y,t) = \begin{cases} \dfrac{(t-1)M}{L}\,y, & t = 1, 2, \cdots, N \\[2mm] \dfrac{N(L+1-t)}{L}\,y, & t = N+1, N+2, \cdots, L. \end{cases}$$

Now it can readily be shown that for households fulfilling the stationary conditions and behaving according to equation (II.1),

[22] For a generalization of the notion of stationary household, see below footnote 25.

assets, at any age, will coincide precisely with those planned at age 1.[23] But, by definition, for a household of age $t \leqq N$ in stationary position, current income, y, equals y_1; it follows that its assets at the beginning of the current period must be

$$(\text{II.8}) \qquad a = \bar{a}_t^1 = a(y_1, t) = a(y,t) = \frac{(t-1)M}{L} y, \qquad t \leqq N$$

which exhibits explicitly the relation between current initial assets, income, and age. Substituting from (II.8) into (II.1) and (II.2) and remembering that, by assumption, income expectations coincide with current income, we find for any age $t \leqq N$,

$$(\text{II.9}) \qquad c = \frac{N}{L} y, \qquad s = \frac{M}{L} y;$$

i.e., for households fulfilling the stationary conditions and within the earning span, current consumption and saving are proportional to the current income.[24]

---

[23] This proposition may be established by mathematical induction. Suppose that the proposition holds for t, i.e., that

$$(\text{II.7}) \qquad a_t = \bar{a}_t^1 = \frac{(t-1)M}{L} y_1;$$

then, since by assumption

$$y_t = y_t^e = y_1, \qquad t \leqq N - 1,$$

we have, from (II.2),

$$s_t = \frac{M}{L} y_1$$

and

$$a_{t+1} = a_t + s_t = \frac{(t-1)M}{L} y_1 + \frac{M}{L} y_1 = \frac{tM}{L} y_1 = \bar{a}_{t+1}^1.$$

Thus, if equation (II.7) holds for t it holds also for $t + 1$. But equation (11.7) holds for $t = 1$, since

$$a_1 = 0 = \frac{(L-1)M}{L} y_1 = \bar{a}_1^1.$$

Hence, equation (II.7) holds for all $t \leqq N$. By similar reasoning, it can be shown that it holds also for $N + 1 \leqq t \leqq L$.

[24] While this result implies that, at zero income, consumption itself would have to be zero, it should be remembered that, under our stationary assumptions, the current level of income coincides with the level received in the past and expected in the future. A household whose income is permanently zero could hardly survive as a separate unit. Or, to put it differently, a household, within its earning span, whose current income is zero or negative cannot possibly be in stationary equilibrium.

At first sight this conclusion may appear to have little empirical meaning, since the notion of a stationary household is a theoretical limiting concept with little operational content. But our result need not be interpreted literally. Clearly our model has the following very significant implication: if we take a cross section of households within their earning span, which are reasonably well adjusted to the current level of income (in the sense, that, for each household, current income is close to the level the household has received in the past and it expects to receive in the future), then we should find that the proportion of income saved is substantially the same at all levels of income.[25] Even this more general conclusion is not easy to test from available data. Yet we shall be able to show presently that some rather striking evidence in support of this implication of our model is provided by certain recent studies.

From the result just established it follows directly 'that, if our sample consisted primarily of households in stationary position, then the cross-section rate of change of consumption with respect to income, $\frac{d'c}{d'y}$, is entirely different from the individual marginal propensity to consume defined by equation (II.3). According to equation (II.9) the cross-section rate of change must be $\frac{N}{L}$, a result which can also be derived from equation (II.4), by observing that, for stationary households, equation (II.8) holds so that, for

[25] It can be shown that if we eliminate Assumption III, our model still implies that, for a stationary cross section, the proportion of income saved is independent of income; however, this proportion will tend to rise with age, up to retirement. The conclusion that the proportion of income saved is independent of income, given age, also continues to hold if we relax our Assumption IV and assume only that there exists a typical pattern of allocation of resources to current and future consumption which does not necessarily involve a constant planned rate of consumption over time. Finally this conclusion also remains valid if we recognize the existence of a typical life pattern of income and redefine a stationary household as one who expects its income not to be constant over time but rather to follow the normal life pattern, and whose expectations are continuously fulfilled in the sense stated in part (b) of the original definition in the text. Just what effects these two relaxations would have on the relation between the proportion of income saved and age depends, of course, on the specific shape of the pattern of allocation of resources to consumption over the life cycle and on the shape of the life pattern of income. Note, however, that since the line of relation between saving and income *for each* age group is supposed, in any event, to go through the origin, even if we fail to stratify by age, the regression of consumption on income should tend to be linear (though not homoscedastic) and a regression line fitted to the data should tend to go approximately through the origin.

given age t, $\dfrac{d'a}{d'y} = \dfrac{(t-1)M}{L_1}$. Note, in particular, that (a) the individual marginal propensity varies with age, whereas the cross-section rate of change is independent of the age composition of the sample (provided all households are within the earning span); and (b) the slope of the cross-section line could not even be expected to represent some average of the marginal propensities at various ages. Indeed, even under unity elasticity of expectations, the marginal propensity at any age (except age 1) is less than N/L.[26]

In general, however, a random sample would not consist entirely, or even primarily, of households in stationary position. Let us therefore proceed to the more general case and see what we can learn from our model about the behavior of households who are not in stationary equilibrium.

Making use of the definition of $a(y,t)$ given in (II.6), the individual saving function (II.2) can be rewritten in the following useful form:

$$(\text{II.2}') \quad s = \frac{M}{L} y^e + \frac{L-t}{L_t} (y - y^e) - \frac{1}{L_t} [a - a(y^e,t)]$$

$$= \frac{M}{L} y + \frac{N(L-t) - M}{LL_t} (y - y^e) - \frac{1}{L_t} [a - a(y^e,t)].$$

The quantity $(y - y^e)$, representing the excess of current income over the average level expected in the future, may be called the "nonpermanent component of income" [27] (which may be positive or negative). Similarly, the quantity $[a - a(y^e,t)]$, representing the difference between actual initial assets and the volume of assets which would be carried by an individual fully adjusted to the "permanent" component of income y^e, may be called the "imbalance in initial assets" or also "excess assets" relative to the permanent component of income.

[26] As we have seen, under the assumption $y^e = y$ $\left(\text{and therefore } \dfrac{dy^e}{dy} = 1\right)$ the individual marginal propensity to consume is $\dfrac{N - t + 1}{L_t}$, which reaches a maximum for $t = 1$, the maximum being $\dfrac{N}{L}$.

[27] Cf. M. Friedman and S. Kuznets, *Income from Independent Professional Practice*, pp. 325 ff.

The first form of equation (II.2′) states the proposition that saving is equal to: (1) a constant fraction of the permanent component of income (independent of both age and income) which fraction is precisely the stationary equilibrium saving ratio; plus (2) a fraction of the nonpermanent component of income [this fraction is independent of income but depends on age and is larger, in fact much larger, than the fraction under (1)]; minus (3) a fraction, depending only on age, of excess assets. A similar interpretation can be given to the second form of (II.2′).

Equation (II.2′) is useful for examining the behavior of an individual, who, after having been in stationary equilibrium up to age $t - 1$, experiences an unexpected increase in income at age t so that $y_t > y_{t-1}^e = y_{t-1}$. Here we must distinguish two possibilities. Suppose, first, the increase is viewed as being strictly temporary so that $y_t^e = y_{t-1}^e = y_{t-1}$. In this case $a_t = a(y_t^e,t)$.[28] There is no imbalance in assets and, therefore, the third term is zero. But the second term will be positive since a share of current income, amounting to $y_t - y_{t-1}$, represents a nonpermanent component. Because our individual will be saving an abnormally large share of this portion of his income, his saving ratio will rise above the normal figure $\dfrac{M}{L}$. This ratio will in fact be higher, the higher the share of current income which is nonpermanent, or, which is equivalent in this case, the higher the percentage increase in income.[29] Let us next suppose that the current increase in income causes him to raise his expectations; and consider the limiting case where $y_t^e = y_t$, i.e., the elasticity of expectations is unity.

In this case the transitory component is, of course, zero; but now the third term becomes positive, reflecting an insufficiency of assets relative to the new and higher income expectation. Accordingly, the saving ratio rises again above the normal level $\dfrac{M}{L}$ by an extent which is greater the greater the percentage increase in income. Moreover, as we might expect, the fact that expectations have followed income causes the increase in the

---

[28] Since the individual was in stationary equilibrium up to the end of period $t - 1$, we must have $a_t = a(y_{t-1}, t)$ and, by assumption, $y_{t-1} = y_t^e$.

[29] From the last equality in equation (II.2′) and with $y_t^e = y_{t-1}$, we derive immediately

$$\frac{s_t}{y_t} = \frac{M}{L} + \frac{N(L - t) - M}{LL_t}\left(\frac{y_t - y_{t-1}}{y_t}\right).$$

saving ratio to be somewhat smaller than in the previous case.[30]

Our model implies, then, that a household whose current income unexpectedly rises above the previous "accustomed" level (where the term "accustomed" refers to the average expected income to which the household was adjusted), will save a proportion of its income larger than it was saving before the change and also larger than is presently saved by the permanent inhabitants of the income bracket into which the household now enters. The statement, of course, holds in reverse for a fall in income.[31]

II.3 A Reinterpretation of the Cross-section Relation Between Consumption and Income

The propositions we have just established are not easy to test directly with existing data, since such data do not usually provide information on the "accustomed" level but, at best, only on the level of income during a previous short period. However, even this type of information should be useful, at least for an indirect test of our conclusions. For, suppose we divide all the households into three groups: (1) those whose income has increased in the current year; (2) those whose income is approximately unchanged; and (3) those whose income has fallen. Then, unless most of the income changes just happen to be such as to return the recipients to an accustomed level from which they had earlier departed,[32] group (1) should contain a greater proportion of people whose income is above the accustomed level than group (2) and, a fortiori, than group (3). Hence, according to our model, the households in group (1) whose income has risen should save, on the average, a larger proportion of income than those in group (2), which in turn should save a larger proportion than those in group (3). It is well known that this proposition is overwhelmingly

[30] From equation (II.2'), with $y_i^e = y_{t-1}$ and since $a_t = \dfrac{(t-1)M}{L} y_{t-1}$, we derive,

$$\frac{s_t}{y_t} = \frac{M}{L} + \frac{(t-1)M}{LL_t}\left(\frac{y_t - y_{t-1}}{y_t}\right).$$

It is easily verified that the right-hand side of this expression is necessarily smaller than the corresponding expression given in the preceding note.

[31] This conclusion fails to hold only if the elasticity of expectations is substantially greater than unity.

[32] More precisely, unless there is a very strong correlation between the current change in income, $y - y_{-1}$, on the one hand, and the difference between the previous "accustomed" level and the previous year income, $y_{-1}^e - y_{-1}$, on the other.

supported by empirical evidence.[33] Even where some apparent exceptions have been reported, these have occurred largely because of the inclusion in expenditure of current outlays for durable goods which we do not include in consumption as far as they result in an increase in net worth.[34]

We will readily recognize that the proposition we have just derived is far from novel; but notice that our model suggests an explanation that is quite different from the one usually advanced. According to the usual explanation, which is already to be found in the *General Theory* (p. 97), consumer expenditure habits are sticky and only adjust with a lag to the changed circumstances; in the meantime, savings, which are considered as a passive residual, absorb a large share of the changed income. In our model, on the other hand, savings tend to go up either because the new level of income is regarded as (partly or wholly) transitory or, to the extent that it is regarded as permanent, because the initial asset holdings are now out of line with the revised outlook. If the outlook has improved, assets are too low to enable the household to live for the rest of its expected life on a scale commensurate with the new level of income; if the income outlook has deteriorated, then, in order for the household to achieve the optimum consumption plan consistent with the new outlook, it is not necessary to add to assets at the same rate as before, and perhaps even an immediate drawing-down of assets to support consumption may be called for.

We feel that this alternative interpretation has merits. While not denying that the conventional explanation in terms of habit persistence may have some validity, we feel that it has been made to bear too heavy a weight. We all know that there are hundreds of things that we would be eager to buy, or do, "if only we could afford them," and nearly as many places where we could "cut corners" if it were really necessary. Therefore, as long as we are dealing with moderate variations in income (variations whose possibility we had already envisaged at least in our day-dreams),

[33] See, for instance, G. Katona and J. Fisher, "Postwar Changes in the Income of Identical Consumer Units," *Studies in Income and Wealth*, Vol. XIII, pp. 62-122; G. Katona, "Effect of Income Changes on the Rate of Saving," *The Review of Economics and Statistics*, May, 1949, pp. 95-103; W. W. Cochrane, "Family Budgets—a Moving Picture," *loc. cit.*, Aug., 1947, pp. 189-198; R. P. Mack, "The Direction of Change in Income and the Consumption Function," *loc. cit.*, Nov., 1948, pp. 239-258.

[34] Katona and Fisher, *ibid.*, especially Section D, pp. 97-101; and G. Katona, *ibid.*

there is not likely to be any significant lag in the adjustment of total expenditure. Of course, there may be significant lags (and leads) in certain types of expenditures: moving to a more exclusive neighborhood may take years to be realized, but meanwhile that dreamed-of vacation trip may come off at once.[35]

Our discussion of the effect of income changes enables us to proceed to an analysis of the cross-section relation between current consumption and current income that we should expect to find, and actually do find, in a random sample which does not consist primarily of households in stationary position.

As is well known, budget studies typically show that the proportion of income saved, far from being constant, tends to rise from a very low or even negative figure at low levels of income to a large positive figure in the highest brackets. These findings are by no means inconsistent with our earlier results concerning the saving-income relation for a stationary cross section. Quite the contrary; the observed relation is precisely what we should expect on the basis of our model when we remember that, in the type of economies to which these budget data mostly refer, individual incomes are subject to short-term fluctuations, so that current income generally will tend to differ more or less markedly from the previous accustomed level and from current income expectations. Such fluctuations may vary in intensity according to time, place, occupation, and other characteristics of the sample covered, but they will never be entirely absent and frequently will be substantial.

[35] It is, in principle, possible to design an experiment to test which of the two hypotheses represents a better explanation of the observed behavior. One possible test might be as follows. Select the set of households whose income has changed unexpectedly in the given year T, and who expect the change to be permanent. Consider next the subset whose income in the immediately following years remains at the new level and whose expectations are therefore fulfilled. If the traditional explanation is the correct one, then by the year $T + 1$ saving should revert to the average level prevailing for all households who have been for two or more years in the income brackets into which our households have moved. On the other hand, if our hypothesis is correct, the saving of our subset of households should, in the years following T, continue to remain higher, on the average, than the saving of the households who have been *permanent* inhabitants of the relevant brackets. Furthermore, under our model, the difference between the saving of the new and the original inhabitants should tend to remain greater the more advanced the age of the household in the year T. Needless to say, the data for such a test are not available at this time and the case for our explanation must rest for the moment on the evidence that supports our model as a whole. The purpose of describing a possible experiment is to emphasize the fact that the two alternative hypotheses have implications that are, in principle, observationally distinguishable. Some of these implications are, in fact, of immediate relevance for aggregative time series analysis.

The very same reasoning we have used in the discussion of the effect of income changes leads to the conclusion that, in the presence of short-term fluctuations, the highest income brackets may be expected to contain the largest proportion of households whose current income is above the accustomed level and whose saving is, therefore, abnormally large. Conversely, the lowest income brackets may be expected to contain the largest proportion of people whose current income is below the accustomed level and whose saving is, therefore, abnormally low. As a result of the presence of these groups, which are not fully adjusted to the current level of income, in the lowest brackets the proportion of income saved will be lower, and in the highest brackets it will be higher than the normal figure (M/L in our model) which we should expect to be saved by the permanent inhabitants of these respective brackets. Thus, the proportion of income saved will tend to rise with income, and the cross-section relation between consumption and income will tend to be represented by a line obtained by rotating the stationary line clockwise around a fixed point whose x and y coordinates coincide approximately with the average value of income and consumption respectively.

While the general line of argument developed above is not new,[36] it may be useful to clarify it by means of a graphical illustration developed in Figures 1 and 2. We will start out by analyzing a cross section of households all belonging to a single age group within the earning span, and will examine first the consumption-income relation; once we have established this relation, the saving-income relation can easily be derived from it.

Our consumption function (II.1) can be rewritten in a form analogous to the saving function (II.2′), namely:

$$(\text{II.1}') \quad c = \frac{N}{L} y^e + \frac{1}{L_t}(y - y^e) + \frac{1}{L_t}[a - a(y^e, t)]$$

$$= \frac{N}{L}\left\{ y^e + \frac{L}{NL_t}(y - {}^e) + \hbar\, \frac{L}{NL_t}[a - a(y^e, t)] \right\}$$

In the construction of our figures, we shall find it convenient to have a symbol to represent the expression in braces; let us denote it by $p = p(y, y^e, t, a)$. This expression may be regarded as

[36] See, for instance, the brilliant paper of William Vickrey, "Resource Distribution Patterns and the Classification of Families," *Studies in Income and Wealth*, Vol. X, pp. 260-329; Ruth P. Mack, *op. cit.*, and the contributions of Margaret G. Reid quoted in the next section.

the stationary equivalent income of the current set of values y, y^e, t and a, for the household, in the sense that, if the household were fully adjusted to a level of income $p = p(y, y^e, t, a)$, then it would behave in the same way as it currently does. Let us further denote by the symbol $\bar{x}(y)$ the average value of any variable x for all the members of a given income bracket, y. Then the proportion of income consumed by the aggregate of all households whose current income is y is, clearly, $\bar{c}(y)/y$. Our problem is, therefore, that of establishing the relation between $\bar{c}(y)$ and y. But, according to (II.1'), $\bar{c}(y)$ is proportional to $\bar{p}(y)$ whose be-

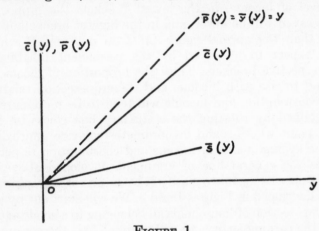

FIGURE 1

havior, in turn, as we see, depends on that of $\bar{y}^e(y)$ and $\bar{a}(y)$. We must therefore fix our attention on the behavior of these last two quantities.

In the case of a *stationary* cross section, illustrated in Figure 1, we know that for *every* household, $y^e = y$ and also $a = a(y^e, t)$. It follows that, for *every* household, $p = y$, and therefore the average value of p in any income bracket y, $\bar{p}(y)$, is also equal to y, *i.e.*, $\bar{p}(y) = y$. Thus, the cross-section relation between $\bar{p}(y)$ and y is represented by a line of slope one through the origin—the dashed line of our Figure 1. The consumption-income relation is now obtained by multiplying each ordinate of this line by the constant N/L, with the result represented by the upper solid line. Because the $\bar{p}(y)$ line goes through the origin, so does the consumption-income relation, $\bar{c}(y)$, and the elasticity of consumption with respect to income is unity. These same propositions hold equally for the saving-income relation, $\bar{s}(y)$ (lower solid line of Figure 1), obtained by subtracting $\bar{c}(y)$ from y. This merely illustrates a result established in the preceding section.

Let us consider now what we may expect to happen if income is subject to short-term fluctuations, a case illustrated in Figure 2.

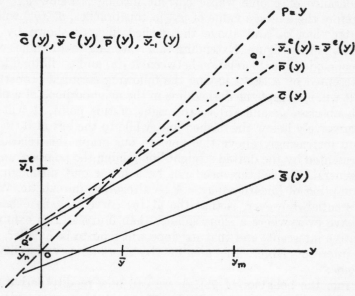

FIGURE 2

We may assume for expository convenience that on the average these fluctuations cancel out so that average current income, $\bar{y}$, is the same as the average future income expected in the year before by the sample as a whole, $\bar{y}^e_{-1}$. But, because of the presence of short-term variations, this equality will not hold for individual households; for some households current income will be higher than y^e_{-1}, while for others it will be lower. As a result of these fluctuations, as we have already argued, in the highest income brackets there will be a predominance of households whose current income is above y^e_{-1}. This, in turn, means that in these brackets the average value of $y^e_{-1}, \bar{y}^e_{-1}(y)$, will be less than y itself;[37] in terms

[37] The specific "technical" assumption underlying the entire discussion can be formulated thus:

(II.10) $$y_i = y^e_{-1i} + \epsilon_i$$

where the subscript i denotes the i-th household and the random term ϵ is assumed

of our graph, $\bar{y}^e_{-1}(y)$ will fall below the dashed line, which represents the line of slope one through the origin. For instance, corresponding to the highest income bracket shown, $y_m, \bar{y}^e_{-1}(\bar{y}_m)$ may be represented by a point such as q in our graph. Conversely, in the lowest income bracket shown, y_n, there will tend to be a preponderance of people whose current income is below y^e_{-1}, and therefore the average value of y^e_{-1} in this bracket, $\bar{y}^e_{-1}(y_n)$ will be greater than y_n and above the dashed line, as shown by the point q', in the figure. Extending this reasoning to all values of y, we conclude that the relation between $\bar{y}^e_{-1}(y)$ and y will tend to be represented by a curve having the following essential properties: (a) it will intercept the dashed line in the neighborhood of a point with abscissa $\bar{y}$; and (b) to the right of this point, it will fall progressively below the dashed line, while to the left of it, it will stand increasingly above this line. In our graph this relation is represented by the dotted straight line joining the points q' and q; in general, the relation need not be a linear one, although the assumption of linearity may not be altogether unrealistic. What is essential, however, is that the $\bar{y}^e_{-1}(y)$ curve may be expected to have everywhere a slope smaller than unity and to exhibit a positive intercept; and that its slope will tend to be smaller, and its intercept larger, the greater the short-term variability of income.

From the behavior of $\bar{y}^e_{-1}(y)$, we can now readily derive that of $\bar{y}^e(y)$, which is the quantity we are really interested in. The latter variable is related to $\bar{y}^e_{-1}(y)$ and to y itself through the elasticity of income expectations. The elasticity of expectations relevant to our analysis can be defined as the percentage change in income expectation over the two years in question, $\dfrac{y^e - y^e_{-1}}{y^e_{-1}}$,

---

to have zero mean and to be independent of y_{-1}. From (II.10), making use of a well-known proposition of correlation theory, we deduce

(II.10′) $\qquad \bar{y}^e_{-1}(y) = \alpha + \beta y; \qquad \beta = r^2_{yy_{-1}}{}^e, \quad \alpha = \bar{y}^e_{-1} - \beta \bar{y}$

Clearly, β is necessarily less than one and α is necessarily positive (since, by assumption, $\bar{y}^e_{-1} = \bar{y}$). A more general and realistic stochastic assumption than the one just formulated would be the following:

$$y_i = k y^e_{-1i}(1 + \epsilon_i{}^*),$$

ϵ' having the same properties as ϵ in (II.10). Since this assumption would complicate the analysis considerably (e.g., it would destroy the linearity of (II.10′)) without affecting the essence of our argument, it has seemed preferable to base our discussion in this paper on equation (II.10).

divided by the corresponding percentage difference between current income and the previous year's expectation, $\dfrac{y - y^e_{-1}}{y^e_{-1}}$.

If we denote this elasticity by the symbol E, we have

(II.11) $$E = \frac{y^e - y^e_{-1}}{y - y^e_{-1}},^{38}$$

which in turn implies:

(II.11′) $y^e = y^e_{-1} + E(y - y^e_{-1}) = (1 - E)y^e_{-1} + Ey;$

i.e., the current income expectation is a weighted average of the previous expectation and current income, with weights depending on the elasticity of expectation. If E is close to zero, current income will have little influence in reshaping expectations and y^e will be close to y^e_{-1}; if, at the other extreme, E is close to unity then current expectations will be determined primarily by the recent behavior of income. From (II.11′) we readily deduce the relation between $\bar{y}^e(y)$ and $\bar{y}^e_{-1}(y)$, namely:

(II.12) $$\bar{y}^e(y) = \bar{y}^e_{-1}(y) + E[y - \bar{y}^e_{-1}(y)].^{39}$$

[38] This definition is not altogether satisfactory for an individual household since y may have been expected to be different from y^e_{-1} (which is the average income expected over the entire balance of the earning span); in this case the fact that y differs from y^e_{-1} need not generate any revision of expectations, *i.e.*, y^e may be equal to y^e_{-1}. As an alternative definition that would give more adequate recognition to the causal relation between the behavior of current income and changes in expectations, we may suggest the following:

$$E = \frac{y^e - y^e_{-1}}{y^e_{-1}} \bigg/ \frac{y - y^{e(t)}_{-1}}{y^{e(t)}_{-1}},$$

where $y^{e(t)}_{-1}$ denotes the income expected in the previous year for the current year. However, when we aggregate a large number of households, it is not unreasonable to expect that, on the average $y^{e(t)}_{-1} = y^e_{-1}$, in which case our alternative definition leads back to equation (II.11) in the text.

[39] In deriving (II.12) from (II.11), we are implicitly assuming that the average value of E is approximately the same at all levels of income, an assumption that does not seem unreasonable for the specific stochastic model with which we are presently dealing. A more general formulation of (II.12), which may be especially useful in establishing a connection between cross-section and aggregative time-series analysis, might be as follows:

(II.12′) $\bar{y}^e(y) = \bar{y}^e_{-1}(y) + E_1[y - \bar{y}^e_{-1}(y)] + E_2(\bar{y} - \bar{y}^e_{-1}),$

which states that individual expectations depend not only on the behavior of individual income but also on that of average income for the entire community, $\bar{y}$. This hypothesis is supported by the consideration that changes in aggregate income may well represent a more reliable indicator for the future than just a change in individual

Equation (II.12) admits of a very simple graphical interpretation. Suppose, first, that E is zero: then $\bar{y}^e(y)$ coincides with $\bar{y}^e_{-1}(y)$, the dotted line of Figure 2. Next, suppose E is positive but less than one; then, for any value of y, $\bar{y}^e(y)$, if it were drawn, would lie between y and $\bar{y}^e_{-1}(y)$, i.e., between the dashed and the dotted line and precisely E per cent of the way from the dotted to the dashed line. Finally, if E is greater than one, or less than zero, then $\bar{y}^e(y)$ will fall outside the band marked off by our two lines. The last two cases, however, may be regarded as extremely unlikely, when one remembers that y^e and y^e_{-1} are defined as expectations about the average level of income over the entire balance of the earning span.[40] In our graph we have assumed a zero value for E so that $\bar{y}^e(y)$ coincides with $\bar{y}^e_{-1}(y)$; this assumption has been chosen not because we think it is realistic but only because it eliminates the necessity of showing a separate curve in our figure. In general, we should rather expect E to be positive but less than one, so that the $\bar{y}^e(y)$ curve would fall between the dotted and the dashed line. *The slope and intercept of this curve will thus depend on the degree of short-term variability of income* [which determines the shape of $\bar{y}^e_{-1}(y)$] *and on the elasticity of expectations.* But note that where short-run fluctuations play a

---

income. It follows from (II.12') that the elasticity of expectation for the community as a whole is

$$\frac{\bar{y}^e - \bar{y}^e_{-1}}{\bar{y} - \bar{y}^e_{-1}} = E_1 + E_2,$$

an expression that could be close to unity even if, as seems likely, E_1 is much smaller than one. On the other hand, it can be easily verified that if (II.12') holds, with $E_2 \neq 0$, the elasticity of expectation as defined by (II.11) will generally change from income bracket to income bracket unless $\bar{y} = \bar{y}^e_{-1}$, an equality which has been explicitly assumed for the purposes of our discussion in the text and which makes (II.12') identical with (II.12).

[40] Such cases are of course not impossible for an individual household; all we claim is that they are unlikely for the average of all households falling in a given income bracket. (See, however, footnote 38.)

There is, of course, no opportunity to test the above statement from available data, since no attempt has yet been made, to our knowledge, to secure information on y^e and y^e_{-1}. Data such as those collected by the Survey Research Center on income expectations for the following year, and presented, for example, in G. Katona, *Psychological Analysis of Economic Behavior*, p. 120, have only a rather remote connection with our concepts. In terms of our notation, these data refer to y_{iT}, y_{iT-1}, and $y_{iT}^{e(T+1)}$, where T denotes the calendar year of the survey. If one is willing to make the rather risky assumption that $y_{iT}^{e(T+1)} = y_{iT}^e$, and the even more risky one that $y_{iT-1} = y_{iT-1}^e$, then it can be inferred from Katona's tabulations that the proportion of households with E greater than one has been somewhat under 20 per cent, and fairly stable, in the surveys for which data are presented.

large role, as might be the case, say, for a sample of farmers, the elasticity of expectations may, itself, be expected to be small on the average, since current income will contain little new reliable information on the basis of which to reshape the previous expectation about average future income, y^e_{-1}. Hence, a large short-term variability of income will tend to depress the slope, and raise the intercept, of $\bar{y}^e(y)$ for two reasons: (1) because it pulls the $\bar{y}^e(y)$ closer to $\bar{y}^e_{-1}(y)$, and (2) because it diminishes the slope of $\bar{y}^e_{-1}(y)$.

We have thus exhibited the behavior of the first component of $\bar{p}(y)$. As we see from (II.1'), the second component is very simple to handle; it represents again a fraction, $\dfrac{L}{NL_t}$, of the difference between y and $\bar{y}^e(y)$, i.e., of the distance from the dotted to the dashed line. Furthermore, for any reasonable assumption about the values of L and N, this fraction is quite small within the earning span. Thus, the sum of the first two terms of $\bar{p}(y)$ could be represented by a new line falling somewhere between the dashed and the dotted line but very close to the latter. Since it would be so close, this new line is not shown separately in our figure and we will assume that the line $\overline{q'q}$ represents already the sum of the first two components.

We may now proceed to the last component of $\bar{p}(y)$ which measures the (average) unbalance in assets at each current income level. A repetition of the familiar reasoning suggests once more that in the highest income brackets there should tend to be an abnormally large proportion of households whose current income expectation is higher than it had been in the past and for whom, accordingly, current assets are low relative to the current expectation y^e; and that the opposite should be true in the lowest income brackets. Hence, the last term will again be negative for sufficiently large values of y and positive for 'sufficiently small values. The zero point is again likely to occur for a value of y close to $\bar{y}$, although its location may vary depending on the previous history of the economy (especially the history of the last t years).[41] In any event $\bar{p}(y)$, which is obtained by

---

[41] The average gap between initial assets, a, and the stationary equilibrium value,

$$a(y^e, t) = \frac{(t-1)M}{L} y^e,$$

at any given level of income, can be derived from the stochastic assumption intro-

adding this last term to the previous two, will tend to have a slope everywhere smaller than our dotted line and a larger intercept; its graph may therefore look something like the dashed-dotted line of Figure 2.

We are now ready to exhibit the consumption-income relation $\bar{c}(y)$, which is obtained simply by multiplying the ordinates of $\bar{p}(y)$ by the constant, N/L. The result is represented by the upper solid line. As we intended to show, it is a line much flatter than the stationary cross-section line of Figure 1 (from which it can be obtained by rotation around its point $(\bar{y}, \bar{y}^e)$) and it exhibits the large positive intercept characteristic of budget data. In other words, in the presence of short-term fluctuations in income, the proportion of income consumed will tend to fall with income and the elasticity of consumption with respect to

---

duced in footnote 36, with the addition of an analogous stochastic assumption as to the relation between a and y^e_{-1}, namely

(II.13) $$y^e_{-1i} = \lambda x_i + \omega_i,$$

where $$x_i = a_i \bigg/ \frac{(t-1)M}{L}, \qquad E(\omega_i) = 0, \quad E(\omega_i x_i) = 0.$$

x_i may be regarded as a function of the income expectations held by the household during all previous years of its active life.

From (II.13), we derive

(II.14) $$\bar{x}(y^e_{-1}) = \mu + \nu y^e_{-1}; \qquad \nu = r^2 x_{y^e_{-1}}/\lambda, \quad \mu = \bar{x} - \nu \bar{y}^e_{-1}.$$

Since in a growing economy $\lambda = \bar{y}^e_{-1}/\bar{x}_i$ may be expected to be at least as high as unity, we must have $0 \leq \nu \leq 1$, $\mu \geq 0$. From (II.14) and the definition of x_i, we obtain

$$\bar{a}(y) = \frac{(t-1)M}{L} \bar{x}(y) = \frac{(t-1)M}{L} [\mu + \nu \bar{y}^e_{-1}(y)].$$

Finally, taking into consideration the definition of $a(y^e, t)$, and using equation (II.12), we derive

$$E\{[a - a(y^e, t)] | y\} = \bar{a}(y) - \frac{(t-1)M}{L} \bar{y}^e(y)$$

$$= \frac{(t-1)M}{L} [\mu + (\nu - 1 + E)\bar{y}^e_{-1}(y) - Ey],$$

which can be expressed entirely in terms of y by making use of equation (II.10′). The above expression must fall as income rises, as stated in the text, since its derivative with respect to y is proportional to $-[E(1 - \beta) + \beta(1 - \nu)]$, which is necessarily negative (provided $E > 0$, which is assumed). In fact, we can establish that

$$E\{[a - a(y^e, t)] | y\} \gtreqless 0$$

as

$$y \lesseqgtr \bar{y} \left[1 - \frac{\lambda - 1}{\lambda[E(1 - \beta + \beta(1 - \nu))]} \right],$$

which shows explicitly the level of income at which the average gap between a and $a(y^e, t)$ is zero.

income will be less than one. Another important result we have established is that the elasticity of consumption with respect to income should depend, according to our theory, on three major factors which are capable of variation in different samples. This elasticity depends, inversely, on (a) the degree of short-term variability of income; (b) the magnitude of variations over time in the permanent component of income that give rise to unbalances in the relation between assets holdings and the permanent component itself; and (c) directly, on the elasticity of income expectations.[42] Given the magnitude of these three factors, the elasticity should depend also on the age of the households in the sample since, as we see from equation (II.1'), the coefficient of the second and third components of p vary with age. This point, however, will receive proper attention in the next section.

In our discussion so far we have been concerned with a cross section of households within the earning span. The effect of the inclusion of retired households in the sample can readily be established. According to our model, these households should have, on the average, levels of consumption not very different from the over-all average,[43] while, at the same time, earning incomes well below average (in our present simplified version, no income at all). The inclusion of these households, therefore, will have the effect of raising still further the $\bar{c}(y)$ curves for low levels of y, thereby increasing its general tilting and possibly making it convex to the income axis.[44]

[42] We have seen that a high elasticity of expectations tends to pull $\bar{y}^e(y)$ closer to the 45-degree line; at the same time, however, it will tend to flatten the $p(y)$ curve relative to the $\bar{y}^e(y)$ curve, for, if assets are approximately adjusted to y^e_{-1}, then the larger the gap between y^e and y_{-1}, the larger will tend to be the unbalance in assets. Since, however, the second effect does not quite offset the first (see the discussion of Section II.2, especially page 20), a high value of E will, on the whole, increase the slope and reduce the intercept of $p(y)$ and thus of $\bar{c}(y)$.

[43] They may, in fact, have an average consumption level below the over-all average for two reasons: (a) because it seems likely that the level of consumption planned for after retirement will, on the whole, tend to be smaller than the average level during the earning span; (b) because of the secular rise in income per capita which characterizes most of the economies for which we have budget data. See, on this point, Modigliani and Brumberg, op. cit.

[44] Our statements about retired households find strong support in the data on the size distribution of income by age, reported by Janet A. Fisher, in "Income, Spending, and Saving Patterns of Consumer Units in Different Age Groups," Studies in Income and Wealth, Vol. XV, especially Tables 1 and 2, pp. 81 and 82. Actually, these tables are likely to overestimate the income (used in our sense) of elderly people, since income, there, is defined to include such items as pensions and retirement pay (p. 81, footnote 6). These inclusions also reduce the usefulness of the information on saving

Summing up, the typical findings of budget studies as to the relation between consumption, saving, and income in a given year, or some other short interval of time, are precisely what they should be according to our model. But, as we see, the interpretation of these findings that follows from our model is radically different from the one generally accepted. According to the usual interpretation, these findings show that the proportion of income saved rises with the economic status of the household. According to our model, on the other hand, they only show that households whose income is above the level to which they are adjusted save an abnormally large proportion and those whose income is below this level save an abnormally low proportion, or even dissave.

To be sure, up to this point, we have done little more than to show that the findings of budget data are consistent with either interpretation. It may be objected that this demonstration is an insufficient ground for discarding the old and widely accepted explanation for our new and radically different one. It would seem that, to support our claims, we should be able to produce some crucial tests, the result of which will enable us to discriminate between the two competing explanations. We believe that the remarkable piece of research recently reported on by Margaret G. Reid, discussed in the next section, comes as close to providing such a test as seems feasible with the kind of data that are presently available.[45]

---

and dissaving by age groups presented in Table 11 (p. 93). Even with the upward-biased definition of income, the proportion of positive savers is smaller in the age group 65 and over than in any other group except the group 18 to 24. For this latter group, of course, the figures are seriously affected by the inclusion of durable goods purchases in consumption. Presumably, had our definitions of income and saving been adopted, the relative scarcity of savers and predominance of dissavers in the elderly group would be much more pronounced.

[45] These results were first reported in a brief communication presented at the Conference on Saving, Inflation and Economic Progress, University of Minnesota, in May, 1952. The authors have also had the opportunity to consult a preliminary draft on "The Relation of the Within-Group Permanent Component of Income to the Income Elasticity of Expenditures," and have had the benefit of extensive discussion and consultations with Miss Reid. The hypothesis tested in the above-mentioned paper had already been partly anticipated in Reid's earlier contribution, "Effect of Income Concept upon Expenditure Curves of Farm Families," *Studies in Income and Wealth*, Vol. XV, especially pp. 133-139.

II.4 Some Evidence on the Constancy of the Saving Ratio for a Stationary Cross Section

In order to understand the foundations of Reid's highly ingenious techniques and the meaning of her results, we must turn back to our Figures 1 and 2, and to the reasoning underlying their construction. Suppose that, somehow, we had been able to locate a sample of households, within their earning span, each of which fulfilled completely our stationary specifications. For *every* member of this sample, because of the complete absence of short-term income fluctuations, we would have the chain of equalities $y = y^e = y^e_{-1} = y_{-1}$ so that the correlation between current and previous income, $r_{yy_{-1}}$, would be unity. Furthermore, if our theory is correct, the elasticity of consumption with respect to current income, η_{cy}, would also be unity. Moreover, this conclusion would continue to hold if the above chain of equalities were replaced by "proportionality," *i.e.*, $y = \dfrac{y^e}{k_1} = \dfrac{y^e_{-1}}{k_2} = \dfrac{y_{-1}}{k_3}$.

In this case, all the households are out of stationary equilibrium but, so to speak, by the same proportion; this would affect the slope of the $\bar{c}(y)$ curve of Figure 1, but not its intercept, so that the consumption-income elasticity would remain unity.[46]

Now, since information on the permanent component of income and the degree of adjustment to it is not available, it is impossible to locate a sample fulfilling exactly our specifications. On the other hand, it may not be impossible to find one for which short-term

---

[46] If the equalities are replaced by proportionality, the correlation $r_{yy_{-1}}$ remains unity. Furthermore, replacing in (II.1) y^e by $k_i y$, and a by

$$\frac{(t-1)M}{L} \nu y^e_{-1} = \frac{(t-1)M\nu k_2}{L} y,$$

(since by assumption, up to the beginning of the current year the assets of every household are proportional to the stationary equilibrium value, ν being the proportionality factor and having the same meaning as in note 41), we obtain

$$c = \frac{L + L(N-t)k_1 + M(t-1)\nu k_2}{LL_t} y,$$

so that, for any given age t, the consumption-income relation is still a straight line through the origin and therefore η_{cy} is still unity. Since, however, the slope varies with age, if we fail to stratify by age, we may find that the computed value of η_{cy} is not exactly one, even for a stationary cross section. On the other hand, it can be verified, from the above expression, that the variation in slope with age is likely to be rather small so that, in fact, η_{cy} should be quite close to unity, unless k_2 and ν are substantially different from unity, an unlikely case except in deep depression or at the peak of a boom.

fluctuations are of relatively minor importance and current income is relatively close to the level to which the household is adjusted. These conditions might be satisfied, for instance, by a sample of government employees or of college professors. For such a sample we would expect to find a correlation between current and previous income, $r_{yy_{-1}}$, close to unity and, *if our model is correct*, an elasticity of consumption with respect to income, η_{cy}, close to unity. At the other extreme, for a group of households for which random short-term fluctuations play a dominant role, say, a sample of farmers over a wide geographical region, we would have a low value of $r_{yy_{-1}}$ and, as we know from the analysis of Figure 2, a low elasticity of consumption with respect to income. This implication of our model clearly forms the basis for a crucial experiment; this experiment has not been carried out as such, although we look forward to its being performed in the near future by anyone having the resources and interest. Meanwhile, Reid's method is very similar to the comparison we have just proposed. The discussion that has led us to the formulation of our crucial experiment suggests that the correlation between current and previous income can be taken as indirect, approximate measure of the degree to which the current income of each household is close to the level to which the household is adjusted (or to a constant multiple of this level—see previous paragraph). In the first place, this correlation is a very good direct measure of strictly short-term fluctuations which, as we have seen, control the relation between $\bar{y}^e(y)$ and y. Secondly, it seems reasonable to expect that the gap between $\bar{p}(y)$ and $\bar{y}^e(y)$ will, itself, tend to be smaller the smaller the short-run variability of income; for, when incomes are basically stable, there should also be less opportunity for significant discrepancies between the permanent component of income and assets to develop. Thus, when the correlation between current and previous income is high, $\bar{p}(y)$ itself should tend to be close to y. The $\bar{p}(y)$ and $\bar{c}(y)$ curves should, therefore, be similar to those of Figure 1, and the elasticity of consumption with respect to income should be close to unity. Conversely, when the correlation between current and previous income is small, evidencing the presence of pronounced short-term fluctuations, the $\bar{y}^e(y)$, $\bar{p}(y)$, and $\bar{c}(y)$ curves should be similar to those shown in Figure 2, and the elasticity of consumption with respect to income should be well below unity.

Hence, if we take several samples of households and, for each of these samples, we compute (a) the correlation between current and previous income, $r_{yy_{-1}}$ and (b) the elasticity of consumption with respect to income, we should find a clear positive rank correlation between the two above-mentioned statistics and, furthermore, η_{cy} should approach unity as $r_{yy_{-1}}$ approaches unity. In essence, this is precisely the test Reid has carried out and her results clearly confirm our inference. The fact that for none of her groups $r_{yy_{-1}}$ is, or could be expected to be, as high as unity prevents η_{cy} from ever reaching the theoretical stationary value of unity; but her data do show that, in the few cases where r comes close to one, η_{cy} is also impressively close to unity. According to Reid's results η_{cy} ranges from a value as low as .1 for r in the order of .2 to values as high as .8 for the highest values of r, which are in the order of .8.[47]

The above discussion is, of course, not intended as an exhaustive account of Reid's techniques and many valuable results; for this purpose the reader is referred to her forthcoming publications. Nevertheless, the brief sketch presented should be sufficient to indicate why her results seem to us to represent as impressive a confirmation of one important implication of our theory, at the micro-economic level, as one may hope to find at this time.

In addition to the test just described, there are several other, partly older, findings that support our model and acquire new meaning in the light of it.

According to our model the typical findings of budget studies as to the relation between consumption and income are basically due to the fact that, in the presence of short-term fluctuations, income over a short interval is a poor and *seriously biased* measure of the accustomed level. In the previous test the extent of this bias was measured by the correlation $r_{yy_{-1}}$; the higher the correlation, the smaller the bias and, therefore, the higher the elasticity of consumption with respect to income. Margaret Reid and a few others have suggested and tested alternative methods of getting a more reliable index of the accustomed level than current income and, invariably, it is found that when consumption is related to such a measure, the elasticity of consumption with

---

[47] The figures just quoted are in part approximate since Reid has not used the statistic $r_{yy_{-1}}$ but, instead, one closely related to it. Although we do not have specific information on the age composition of the samples, we understand that retired households, if any, represent a negligible proportion of the samples.

respect to it rises markedly above the consumption-current income elasticity, and comes close, frequently remarkably close, to unity.[48]

Another set of results that supports our model is that reported in the classical contribution of Dorothy S. Brady and Rose D. Friedman, "Savings and the Income Distribution." [49] As is well known, their major finding is that the saving ratio appears to bear a much more stable relation to the position of the income recipient in the income distribution than to the absolute level of income itself. In other words, the proportion of income saved in a *given decile* varies much less over time and space than the proportion of income saved at a *given level of income*. It is not difficult to see that these results are what one would expect if our model is correct. As should be clear from the reasoning we have followed in developing our Figure 2, the relative frequency of households in a given income bracket whose income is below or above their accustomed level, depends, not on the absolute level of income, but, rather, on the position of the income bracket relative to the average income. For example, in a given

[48] See, for instance, Josephine H. Staab, "Income-Expenditure Relations of Farm Families Using Three Bases of Classification," Ph.D. dissertation, The University of Chicago, 1952; Reid, *op. cit.* (several new experiments are also reported in Reid's preliminary draft quoted above); Vickrey, *op. cit.* In essence Vickrey's point is that consumption is more reliable than current income as a measure of the permanent component of income (p. 273) and he suggests, accordingly, that the individual marginal propensity to consume (with respect to the permanent component) can be estimated more reliably by relating consumption (per equivalent adult), c, to $\bar{y}(c)$ than by relating $\bar{c}(y)$ to y, as has been usually done. It can be shown that Vickrey's suggestions receive a good deal of support from our model (with the addition of the stochastic assumptions introduced in various footnotes above) in that the relation between c and $\bar{y}(c)$ should be very similar to that between c and our quantity p. In particular, c should be nearly proportional to $\bar{y}(c)$, a conclusion that Vickrey himself did not reach but which is well supported by his own tabulations. A double logarithmic plot of c against $\bar{y}(c)$, based on his data, reveals an extremely close linear relationship with a slope remarkably close to unity. (We have estimated this slope, by graphical methods, at .97.) On the other hand, using the conventional plot, $\bar{c}(y)$ against y, the slope for the same data can be estimated at somewhat below .85, and, in addition, the scatter around the line of relationship is distinctly wider than for the first mentioned plot.

In the contribution under discussion Vickrey has also been very much concerned with the influence of the size composition of the household on saving behavior. This is a point which, because of limitations of space, we have been forced to neglect in the present paper. We will merely indicate, at this point, that our central hypothesis (that the essential purpose of saving is the smoothing of the major and minor variations that occur in the income stream in the course of the life cycle) provides a framework within which the influence of family size can be readily analyzed. We hope to develop this point in later contributions.

[49] *Studies in Income and Wealth*, Vol. X, pp. 247-265.

income bracket, say $10,000, we should expect to find a large proportion of people whose accustomed level is less than $10,000 if, say, the average income is $2,000 and the level $10,000 is in the top decile; while, in this same bracket, we should expect to find a small proportion of people whose accustomed level is below $10,000 if the community average income were, say, $50,000 so that the $10,000 bracket is in the lowest income decile. More generally, it can be shown that provided, as seems likely, there is a fairly stable relation between average income in a given decile and the over-all average income, then the saving ratio, in a given decile, would depend primarily on the (relative) short-term variability of income.[50] Thus, if we compare, over time or space, groups for which the (relative) variability of income is not very different, the proportion of income saved in any given decile should be roughly the same for every group. As an example, we can compare the behavior of nonfarm families in different regions and at different points in time (see Brady and Friedman, Charts 1 through 4) and we find our inference confirmed. Furthermore, within a group, the greater the variability in income, the greater

[50] Making use of equations (II.10'), (II.12) and the expression for $\bar{a}(y)$ derived in note 41, our cross-section income-consumption relation can be reduced to the form

$$\bar{c}(y) = A + By = A^*\bar{y} + By,$$

where A^* and B depend on the coefficients E, α, β, λ, μ, ν we have introduced earlier, and on age. These coefficients, in turn, depend primarily on the variability of income as measured by $r_{yy}{}^e{}_{-1}$ and $r_{xy}{}^e{}_{-1}$, and, probably to a lesser extent, on the long-term trend of income (which affects λ, μ and ν) and on the cyclical position of the economy (which affects α and β and possibly E). Hence, if we have various samples of households for each of which the variability of income is approximately the same, the coefficients A^* and B should also be approximately the same for each sample, especially if the samples in question do not differ too markedly with respect to age, composition and the cyclical position of total income. Denoting by $\bar{c}_i$ and $\bar{y}_i$ the average value of consumption and income for all households falling in the i-th quantile of a given sample, we must have

$$\bar{c}_i = A^*\bar{y} + B\bar{y}_i.$$

If, furthermore, for each of the samples compared $\bar{y}_i/\bar{y}$ is approximately constant, so that we can write $\bar{y}_i = k_i\bar{y}$, we obtain

$$\bar{c}_i/\bar{y}_i = \overline{(c/y)}_i = \frac{A^*}{k_i} + B,$$

i.e., the proportion of income consumed in a given quantile, i, should be approximately the same for all samples compared, as stated in the text. We may add that, if we replace our simple stochastic assumption (II.10) by the more realistic one suggested at the end of note 37, the conclusion stated in the text would still stand, although the relation between $\overline{(c/y)}_i$ and i would be more complex than indicated by the right-hand side of the above equation.

should be the variation in the saving ratio as between the lower and the upper deciles. This inference, too, is supported by comparison of nonfarm and farm groups (compare Chart 2 with Chart 5).

It will be recognized that our theory offers an explanation for the Brady-Friedman findings that is fundamentally different from the social-psychological explanation that has been advanced heretofore.[51] Although our current interpretation is much simpler and integrates these findings with many others without recourse to additional postulates, we do not wish to deny that the earlier explanation may have some validity.

One more finding of some significance has to do with the relation between the elasticity of consumption with respect to income on the one hand and age on the other, to which reference has been made earlier. It can be shown that the slope of $\bar{c}(y)$ should tend to fall, and its intercept to rise, with age, unless, on the average, the elasticity of income expectations is extremely low, say, in the neighborhood of zero.[52] Since such a low average elasticity of expectations is rather unlikely to prevail, especially in a basically growing economy, we should generally expect the elasticity of consumption with respect to income to fall with age. This conclusion finds empirical support in the findings reported by Janet Fisher.[53] Our theory provides a common-sense explanation for her empirical finding. The increase in expected income, y^e, which accompanies the change in current income, produces a relatively larger increase in the anticipated total resources of a younger than of an older household, if E is above the minimal value, because of the greater number of years over which the

---

[51] For example, see James Duesenberry, *Income, Saving and the Theory of Consumer Behavior*.

[52] Making use of equations (II.10'), (II.12) and of the expression for $\bar{a}(y)$ of note 41, it can be verified that

$$\frac{\partial^2 \bar{c}(y)}{\partial y \, \partial t} < 0,$$

i.e., the slope of the cross-section consumption-income relation falls with age, provided

$$E > \frac{1}{M+1} - \frac{M\beta(1-\nu)}{(M+1)(1-\beta)}.$$

A very similar condition on E must be satisfied in order for the constant term to rise with age. Since $1/(M+1)$ should be in the order of 0.1, and β and ν are typically smaller than unity, the right-hand side of the above inequality cannot significantly exceed zero and is, in fact, likely to be negative.

[53] *Op. cit.*, p. 90 and p. 99.

higher level of income will be received. To give a specific illustration, suppose that $E = 1$, and that y, and therefore also y^e, increase by one unit. For a household of age $N - 1$, which has only one year to go before retirement, total resources, v_{N-1}, increase by only two units, and these two units have to be spread over the remaining two years of earning and M years of retirement. Therefore consumption rises by only $\dfrac{2}{M + 1}$. At the other extreme, if the household had age 1, its total anticipated resources rise by N units, to be spread over $N + M$ years. Hence, current consumption rises by $\dfrac{N}{N + M}$ units. By a similar reasoning, one can conclude that the depressing effect on current consumption of the unbalance in assets that has been created by the change in income is greater the older the household, because of the smaller number of years available to the household to redress the unbalance.

In conclusion then, there is already ample evidence, and from widely different sources, which is consistent with the most distinctive implications we have derived so far from our theory and which is not equally consistent or, at any rate, readily explainable in terms of any other single set of hypotheses that, to our knowledge, has been advanced so far.

II.5 *Individual Saving, Assets, and Age*

In recent years a good deal of attention has been devoted to the influence of assets on consumption, and attempts have been made at estimating the cross-section relation between these variables on the expectation that the parameters obtained would yield information on the time-series relation. Our theory has something to contribute as to the pitfalls of such an attempt. To begin with, it suggests that the relevant concept of assets is *net worth;* unfortunately, most of the recent empirical work has concentrated instead on liquid assets, a variable which, according to our model, bears no definite relation to consumption, except perhaps as a very imperfect proxy for net worth.

But even if information on net worth were available, knowledge of the variation in consumption as between different households having different asset holdings, would give very little (and that little would be biased) information as to how a household would react if its assets were increased unexpectedly by a given amount, say, by an anonymous gift of the usual benevolent millionaire or, to take a more fashionable example, by an unexpected fall in the price level of consumables. This failing occurs because the observed asset holdings do not just happen to be there; instead, they reflect the life plan of the individual, which in turn depends on income and income expectations.

To interpret the positive correlation between assets and consumption as implying that people consume more *because* they have more assets would be only slightly less inaccurate than the inverse inference that people have higher assets because they consume more. The point is that both consumption and assets are greatly affected by the other variables: income, income expectations,[54] and age.

It may be objected that we are destroying a straw man; anyone studying the effect of assets would have sense enough to control the effect of, say, income. This may well be true, yet we feel that the above paragraph contains a useful lesson as to the relation between assets and consumption plans that one may too easily forget. For instance, the statement which has been repeated *ad nauseam* that in the early postwar years people bought durable goods lavishly *because* they had such large holdings of liquid assets (which may even find some apparent confirmation in survey results) might well stand a good deal of re-examination along the lines indicated above.

But our model tells us that it is not enough to control income or even income expectations. As it is brought out clearly by our analysis of the stationary case, assets depend also on age (see equation II.8); and this implication of our model is one for which scattered supporting empirical information is available.[55] Further-

[54] There is ample evidence of a very pronounced correlation between assets and income, at least as far as liquid assets are concerned. See, for example, Lawrence Klein, "Assets, Debts, and Economic Behavior," *Studies in Income and Wealth*, Vol. XIV, Table 1, p. 209; and Fisher, *op. cit.*, Table 6, p. 86.

[55] Gustave Cassel, *The Theory of Social Economy*, 1932 ed., p. 244; Horst Mender-hausen and Raymond W. Goldsmith, "Measuring Estate Tax Wealth," *Studies in Income and Wealth*, Vol. XIV, Table 4, p. 140; and Fisher, *loc. cit.* The most systematic information we have found on this subject is that presented by Janet Fisher, although, unfortunately, her most interesting tabulations relate to liquid assets only. For this reason we will not attempt an extensive comparison of her findings with our theory. We may point out, however, that in terms of liquid assets, her data agree remarkably well with our theory in several respects. For example, a comparison of the mean income ratio (Table 1, p. 81) with the mean ratio of liquid asset holdings (Table 4, p. 84) by age groups, reveals that the ratio of assets per spending unit to

more, as we have seen, our hypothetical household goes on consuming a constant fraction of income (equation II.9) even though its assets continue to rise, and reach their peak just before retirement; the rise in assets relative to income does not depress saving because it is part and parcel of the life plan. In other words, higher assets do not necessarily affect saving; they do so only if, on account of unexpected variations, assets turn out to be out of line with income and age: it is only an excess (or shortage) of assets that affects the saving ratio (see equation II.2').[56]

Finally, we can see from our equation (II.1) that the cross-section marginal rate of change of consumption (or saving) with respect to asset holdings (income and income expectations constant) could not yield a reliable estimate of the marginal propensity to consume with respect to assets. The reason is simple. From (II.1), it follows that this marginal propensity is

$$(\text{II.15}) \qquad \frac{\partial c}{\partial a} = -\frac{\partial s}{\partial a} = \frac{1}{L_t}.$$

This expression is independent of assets and income but depends on age. We cannot, therefore, properly speak of *the* marginal propensity to consume with respect to assets, as this quantity will vary substantially from age group to age group, tending to increase with age.

Let us finally remember that, in order to compute the individual marginal propensity from cross-section data, it is also not sufficient to control age by introducing this variable linearly in a linear regression of consumption on income and assets,[57] for,

---

income per spending unit rises steadily with age. For the age group 45-64, which is her oldest group wherein active households presumably predominate, this ratio is nearly three times as large as for her youngest group, 18-24. For the age group 65-and-over, wherein, presumably, retired people predominate, the ratio nearly doubles again. This very high ratio is precisely what should be expected from our model where assets are drawn down slowly but income falls much faster with retirement. In terms of assets, rather than of the income/asset ratio, the peak should be reached just before retirement. Confirmation of this inference is found in the tabulations of Table 5 (p. 85).

Also suggestive of this relation is the complaint by Lawrence Klein, "Assets, Debts, and Economic Behavior," that: "There is some indication that the influence of age on savings may be obscured by a significant positive correlation between (L/Y) and a" (where Y = income, L = liquid assets, and a = age of the spending-unit head in years)."

[56] All this has, of course, some significant implications about the "Pigou effect" which are developed in Modigliani and Brumberg, *op. cit.*

[57] Cf. Klein, *ibid.*, pp. 220 ff.

according to our model, age does not enter in a linear fashion. The only way of estimating the marginal propensity at various ages and, in the process, test equation (II.15) is to carry out a full stratification by age groups (or some equivalent procedure). It is to be hoped that data for such a test may sometime be available.[58]

II.6   Uncertainty, Saving, and the Composition of Assets

The analysis of the previous sections is helpful in providing a justification for our earlier contention that the phenomenon of uncertainty can be neglected without seriously affecting the usefulness of the analysis.

As we have seen, even under the assumption of certainty there are sufficient incentives for the household to accumulate assets at a rapid rate during the early years of its life. Since the assets thus accumulated can be used to acquire durable goods and are also available as a general reserve against emergency, it would appear that the last two motives (p. 392), which are the result of uncertainty, need not affect significantly the saving behavior.[59]

To be sure, though assets can satisfy several purposes, their efficiency will not be the same in this respect. For instance, those assets which are best suited to satisfy the fourth motive are frequently not very well suited to satisfy the third. Accordingly, variations in the relative urgency of our four motives as between different individuals, and at various points of the life cycle for the same individual, will be reflected in the composition of the balance-sheet. This composition will also be affected by the current and prospective total resources, by the nature of the available alternatives, and, last but not least, by "social" pressures. Cautious individuals will hold relatively more liquid assets. Individuals with large means will tend to hold more durable goods. Examples of social pressure on the type of assets held are

[58] More generally, the essential implication of our theory that should be tested is that the (average) relation between consumption and net worth, given income and income expectations, is linear and with a slope which tends to grow with the age of the household. The specific value of the slope given by (II.15) depends on Assumptions III and IV which are convenient for exposition but are not essential to the theory.

[59] In the very early years these motives might possibly lead to a somewhat faster rate of accumulation than might occur otherwise. On the other hand, in his early years, an individual may feel less of a need for precautionary assets since, being a better risk, he will be in a better position to borrow, and may also be able to rely, for emergencies, on his relatives.

also not far to seek; witness the scramble for common stock during the 'twenties and the adoption of television after the Second World War.[60]

As to the effect of the life cycle on the composition of the "portfolio," one might expect that during the period of family formation people will put most of their savings into durables. Automobiles, refrigerators, stoves, and other appliances are felt to be essential to the establishment of an American household. After the initial purchase of durables, although depreciated goods are to be replaced and some additional goods are to be bought, savings flow into other kinds of assets. Various liquid assets may be acquired. The acquisition of a house, which requires (except for the recent G.I. housing) a prior large stock of cash, can be expected to occur throughout the life span. These generalizations are borne out by the existing data.[61]

In conclusion, uncertainty as well as many other factors must be recognized as being of great importance if one is interested in developing a satisfactory theory of the composition of the "portfolio" or, which is equivalent, of the rate of addition to the specific assets. They do not seem to be essential, however, for the development of a useful theory of the factors controlling the over-all rate of saving. Needless to say, the final justification of this statement must rest on whether or not our theory proves helpful in explaining facts which are presently known or will be revealed by further empirical work. The results so far are encouraging.

II.7   Summary

On the basis of the received theory of consumer's choice, plus one major assumption as to the properties of the utility function, we have been able to derive a simple model of individual saving behavior which is capable of accounting for the most significant

[60] Cf. Boulding, *op. cit.*, Ch. 3 and Ch. 5 for a novel approach to the choice of asset combinations. See also J. Marshack, "Money and the Theory of Assets," *Econometrica*, Oct. 1938, pp. 311-325.

Because durable goods generally seem more vulnerable to social pressure than the forms of saving that make up the ordinary (*e.g.*, Department of Commerce) definition, it is easy to see why they have been thought of as consumption. Keynes enforced the definition only by his interest in the modes of saving not necessarily matched by investment. However, the idea of ostentatious durables typifying "conspicuous consumption" preceded the *General Theory* by many years.

[61] See: Dorothy S. Brady, "An Analysis of Saving on the Basis of Consumer Expenditure Data," *Saving and Capital Market Study*, Section 3, R. W. Goldsmith, Director, preliminary; and Fisher, *op. cit.*, Tables 4, 5, and 6, pp. 85-89.

findings of many cross-section studies. Inasmuch as this model has been shown elsewhere to be equally consistent with the major findings of time-series analysis, we seem to be near the ultimate goal of a unified, and yet simple, theory of the consumption function.

The results of our labor basically confirm the propositions put forward by Keynes in *The General Theory*. At the same time, we take some satisfaction in having been able to tie this aspect of his analysis into the mainstream of economic theory by replacing his mysterious psychological law with the principle that men are disposed, as a rule and on the average, to be forward-looking animals.[62] We depart from Keynes, however, on his contention of "a greater *proportion* of income being saved as real income increases" (p. 97, italics his). We claim instead that the *proportion of income saved is essentially independent of income;* and that systematic deviations of the saving ratio from the normal level are largely accounted for by the fact that short-term fluctuations of income around the basic earning capacity of the household, as well as gradual changes in this earning capacity, may cause accumulated savings to get out of line with current income and age. The common sense of our claim rests largely on two propositions: (a) that the major purpose of saving is to provide a cushion against the major variations in income that typically occur during the life cycle of the household as well as against less systematic short-term fluctuations in income and needs; (b) that the provisions the household would wish to make, and can afford to make, for retirement as well as for emergencies, must be basically proportional, on the average, to its basic earning capacity, while the number of years over which these provisions can be made is largely independent of income levels. We have shown that our claim is strongly supported by budget data when these data are properly analyzed.

In *The General Theory*, Keynes did not put much emphasis on the proposition quoted above. But in the literature that followed, the assumption that the proportion of income saved must rise with income has frequently been regarded as one of the essential aspects of his theory and, as such, it has played an important role

---

[62] Our conclusions are also in complete agreement with B. Ohlin's brief but illuminating remarks and criticism of Keynes developed in "Some Notes on the Stockholm Theory of Savings and Investment," reprinted in *Readings in Business Cycle Theory;* see especially pp. 98-100.

in Keynesian analysis and its applications to economic policy and forecasting.

The task of developing the policy implications of our analysis falls outside the scope of this paper. We may, nonetheless, point out, as an example, that our new understanding of the determinants of saving behavior casts some doubts on the effectiveness of a policy of income redistribution for the purpose of reducing the average propensity to save.

Finally, we hope our study has proved useful in pointing out the many pitfalls inherent in inferences derived from cross-section data without the guidance of a clear theoretical framework. For instance, we must take a dim view of the attempts that have been made at deriving the time-series average and marginal propensity to save from the cross-section relation between saving and income. *The individual marginal propensity cannot, generally, be identified with the cross-section rate of change;* in fact, as we have seen, these two parameters need not bear any definite and stable relation to one another. We have further shown elsewhere[63] that the individual marginal propensity to save bears, in turn, a very complex relation to the time-series marginal propensity and hardly any relation at all to the time-series average propensity.

Needless to say, many implications of our theory remain to be tested. In fact, it is a merit of our hypothesis that it leads to many deductions that are subject to empirical tests and therefore to contradiction. We would be the first to be surprised if all the implications of the theory turned out to be supported by future tests. We are confident, however, that a sufficient number will find confirmation to show that we have succeeded in isolating a major determinant of a very complex phenomenon.

Appendix

Some Suggestions for the Adaptation of our Model to Quantitative Tests and Some Further Empirical Evidence

Of the many cross-section studies of saving behavior in recent years, the one that comes closest to testing the hypothesis represented by our equations (II.1) and (II.2) is the extensive quantitative analysis reported by Lawrence R. Klein in "Assets, Debts and Economic Behavior," *op. cit.* (see especially pp. 220-227 and

[63] Modigliani and Brumberg, *op. cit.*

P

the brief but illuminating comment of A. Hart, *ibid.*, p. 228). In this appendix we shall attempt to provide a brief systematic comparison of his quantitative findings with the quantitative implications of our theory.

We have already pointed out the many shortcomings of his analysis for the purpose of testing our theory, both in terms of definitions of variables and of the form of the equation finally tested. Because of these shortcomings, the result of our comparison can have at best only a symptomatic value. In fact, the major justification for what follows is its possible usefulness in indicating the type of adaptations that might be required for the purpose of carrying out statistical tests of our model.

Making use of the identity $N - t \equiv \dfrac{N(L - t)}{L} - \dfrac{Mt}{L}$, our equation (II.2) can be altered to the form

$$(A.1) \qquad s_i = \frac{L - t_i}{L_i} y_i - \frac{N(L - t_i)}{LL_i} y_i^e - \frac{a_i}{L_i} + \frac{M}{LL_i} t_i y_i^e,$$

where the subscript i denotes the i-th household, and L_i is an abbreviation for $L + 1 - t_i$.

Unfortunately, the variable y_i^e is usually unknown. Some information on it might be gathered by appropriate questions analogous to the question on short-term income expectations which has already been asked in the past. Klein himself, however, has not made use of this possible source of information in the study in progress. We must, therefore, find some way of relating y_i^e to the variables actually used by Klein, which are also those most commonly available.

It is clear that y^e must bear a fairly close and reasonably stable relation to current income, y. In fact, at various points in the text we have suggested that the relation between these two variables may be expressed by the equation

$$(A.2) \qquad \begin{cases} y^e = (1 - E)y^e_{-1} + Ey + A + U \\ = (1 - E)(\alpha + \beta y) + Ey + U', \end{cases}$$

where A is a constant for a given sample (though subject to variation over time); E is the elasticity of income expectations defined by equation (II.11); U and $U' = (1 - E)\epsilon' + U$ are random errors; α, β are defined by equations (II.10′); and ϵ' is the random component of that equation.

If we also have information on previous year's income, y_{-1}, we can clearly exploit this information to get a better estimate of y^e_{-1}, and (A.2) then takes the form

(A.3) $$y^e \doteq \alpha^* + \beta_1 y + \beta_2 y_{-1} + U^*.$$

The coefficients of this equation, as well as the random component U^*, depend again on the short-term variability of income as measured by the correlation $r_{yy_{-1}}$, on the variance of U and on the elasticity of expectations E. It is not worth-while, however, to derive here this relation explicitly.

Substituting for y^e from (A.3) into (A.1), and rearranging terms (and neglecting the error term which is proportional to U^*) we get:

(A.4) $$\left\{ \begin{aligned} s_i = &- \frac{(N-t_i)\alpha^*}{L_i} + \frac{(L-t_i)(L-N\beta_1)-L(N-t_i)\beta_2}{LL_i} y_i \\ &- \frac{a_i}{L_i} + \frac{(N-t_i)\beta_2}{L_i}(y_i-y_{-1i}) + \frac{M\beta_1}{LL_i} t_i y_i. \end{aligned} \right.$$

Finally, dividing through by y_i and making use of the identity $L \equiv M + N$, we obtain the result[64]

(A.5) $$\left\{ \begin{aligned} \frac{s_i}{y_i} = &\frac{(L_i-1)(L-N\beta_1)-L(L_i-M-1)\beta_2}{LL_i} \\ &- \frac{(L_i-M-1)\alpha^*}{L_i}\frac{1}{y_i} - \frac{1}{L_i}\frac{a_i}{y_i} \\ &+ \frac{(N-t_i)\beta_2}{L_i}(y_i-y_{-1i})/y_i + \frac{M\beta_1}{LL_i} t_i. \end{aligned} \right.$$

If the quantity L_i were a constant, this equation would be identical in form with the equation Klein proposed to test;[65] although, in the actual statistical test he has found it convenient to approximate the first two terms by an expression of the form $\lambda + \mu \log y_i$, and the variable $\dfrac{y_i - y_{-1i}}{y_i}$ by $\dfrac{y_i - y_{-1i}}{y_{-1i}}$.

[64] The division by y_i creates certain statistical problems in connection with the random term; this difficulty can be handled by an appropriate modification of equation (A.2) or (A.3) which need not be discussed here since it would greatly complicate the presentation without basically affecting the conclusions.

[65] p. 220.

If we now look at Klein's results, we can take courage from the fact that all his coefficients have at least the sign required by our model; namely, a positive sign for income, income change, and age (t in our notation, a in Klein's) and negative for assets $\left(\dfrac{a}{y} \text{ in our notation, } \dfrac{L}{Y} \text{ in Klein's}\right)$. This result is of some significance, especially in the case of the age variable. According to our model, the positive sign of this coefficient reflects the fact that within the earning span, for a given level of income and assets, the older the household the smaller will tend to be its resources per remaining year of life, and therefore the smaller the consumption (*i.e.*, the higher the saving).

It would be interesting to compare the size of Klein's coefficients with the values implied by our model. At this point, however, we must remember that the analogy between Klein's equation and our equation (A.5) is more formal than real; for Klein treats his coefficients as if they were constant, whereas, according to our model, they are all functions of age since they all involve the quantity L_i. Consideration of the sensitivity of the coefficients of our equation to variations in t suggests that the error involved in treating them as constants might be quite serious. We must further remember that the specific value of the coefficients in (A.5) is based on Assumptions III and IV. As we have repeatedly indicated, these Assumptions are introduced for expository convenience but are not an essential part of our model. With the elimination of Assumption III and the relaxation of IV, along the lines suggested in footnote 25, the form of our equations and the sign of the coefficients are unchanged, but the value of these coefficients is not necessarily that given in equation (A.5), nor is it possible to deduce these values entirely on a priori grounds, except within broad limits.

We might, nonetheless, attempt a comparison, for whatever it is worth, by replacing the variable t_i in the expression L_i by a constant, say, by its average value in Klein's sample. Unfortunately, this average is not published, but we should not go far wrong by putting it at between 15 and 25 and computing a range for each coefficient using these two values." We must also take a guess at the value of β_1 and β_2. These quantities, it will be noted, are not observable. On the basis of an analysis of factors controlling these coefficients we suggest, however, that a value in the order of .5 to .6 for β_1 and of .2 and .3 for β_2, is not likely to be far from the mark. Using our standard assumption as to the value of L and N, we then get the following comparison:

Coefficient of	Klein's estimates[66]	Our Model (linear approximation)
Assets	−.21; −.25	−.04 to −.03
	(.02) (.03)	
Income change	.03; .07	.1 to .2
	(.05) (.06)	
Age	.0013; .0055	.003 to .0045
	(.0022) (.0024)	

The age coefficient falls squarely within the range of Klein's results and nothing further need be said about it. The coefficient of income change estimated from the sample is lower than we should have expected, although, at least in one case, the difference from our estimate is well within the range of the standard error.[67] In the case of assets, however, the statistical coefficient is clearly far too great. A large part of this disparity is due, we suggest, to the fact that Klein's variable L represents liquid assets whereas our variable a represents net worth, which is clearly, on the average, several times as large as liquid assets. Hence, if liquid assets holdings are a reasonably good index of total net worth, Klein's coefficient would have to be a large multiple of ours.[68] While it is doubtful that this multiple could be as large as 6 or 7, there seems little doubt that this correction would cut the excess of Klein's coefficient over the theoretical value very substantially, probably to well within one half.[69]

[66] Figures in parentheses represent the standard errors. The two figures in this column represent the parameters of the equation for "Home Owners" and "Renters," respectively (*op. cit.*, p. 221). Since the completion of this Appendix, Mr. Klein has kindly informed us that the average age for the two samples combined is 46 years; this implies an average age, since entering the labor force, in the order of 20 to 25 years, which is within the assumed range.

[67] We suspect that expressing income change in terms of y_{-1} instead of y may also contribute to the discrepancy.

[68] If this explanation is correct, it would also follow that Klein's coefficient greatly overestimates the effect on consumption of an increase in assets due, say, to an unanticipated fall in the price level of consumables. In any event, as already pointed out, the relation between the cross section and the time-series marginal propensity is a complex one. In the companion paper quoted earlier, we have shown that the time-series marginal propensity to consume with respect to net worth should be in the order of 0.1.

[69] There is also reason to believe that failure to take into account properly the age variable may lead to an appreciable upward bias in the asset coefficient if the cross section includes retired people. Since we do not know whether Klein's sample does have a significant representation of retired households we cannot say whether this explanation is relevant.

Unfortunately, no definite statement can be made about the coefficient of income and the constant term on account of the logarithmic transformation introduced by Klein. However, approximate computations we have made suggest that these coefficients are in line with our theory in the case of his first equation and somewhat too large (in absolute terms) for the second.

It would thus appear that, at least in terms of orders of magnitude, Klein's findings agree with the implications of our model. We hasten to repeat that the comparison has very limited significance and its results must be taken with a good deal of salt; yet Klein's estimates, just as the many other empirical data we have been able to locate, would seem to warrant the feeling that we are on the right track.

INDEX

GEORGE ALLEN & UNWIN LTD
London: 40 Museum Street, W.C.1
Auckland: 24 Wyndham Street
Bombay: 15 Graham Road, Ballard Estate, Bombay 1
Buenos Aires: Escritorio 454-459, Florida 165
Calcutta: 17 Chittaranjan Avenue, Calcutta 13
Cape Town: 109 Long Street
Hong Kong: F1/12 Mirador Mansions, Kowloon
Ibadan: P.O. Box 62
Karachi: Karachi Chambers, McLeod Road
Madras: Mohan Mansion, 38c Mount Road, Madras 6
Mexico: Villalongin 32-10, Piso, Mexico 5, D.F.
Nairobi: P.O. Box 12446
New Delhi: 13-14 Ajmeri Gate Extension, New Delhi 1
São Paulo: Avenida 9 de Julho 1138-Ap. 51
Singapore: 36c Prinsep Street, Singapore 7
Sydney, N.S.W.: Bradbury House, 55 York Street
Toronto: 91 Wellington Street West

Monetary Theory and Public Policy

KENNETH K. KURIHARA   *5th Impression. Demy 8vo. 30s. net*

Monetary Theory and Public Policy treats systematically the important concepts of modern economic theory, particularly as these concepts apply to problems of money and banking and to related public policy, both national and international. The latest developments in monetary theory, Keynesian and non-Keynesian, are discussed.

Part One is concerned with money and general prices, with problems of inflation as well as those of depression. Inflation is discussed in terms of modern monetary theory rather than in terms of the traditional quantity theory, that is, as an integral part of the general theory of effective demand.

Part Two deals with interest, the consumption function, the savings-investment equilibrium, and related policy discussions. Here the Keynesian and non-Keynesian contributions to economic theory are examined in considerable detail to facilitate later policy consideration.

Part Three provides an application of the Keynesian "income-expenditure" approach to an "open system" economy with foreign economic relations. Various theories about the external value of money, the roles of the International Bank and the International Monetary Fund, the international aspects of depression, the problems of a chronic dollar shortage, and related problems of international currency and finance are considered against the background of the changing international setting.

"Mr. Kurihara is a highly competent economist, with an unusual capacity for relating and synthesizing theories developed by different thinkers . . . He has a gift for translating the theoretical into the institutional; he neither leaves value judgments out of the picture nor confuses them with analysis . . . The job is very neatly done."   *The Economist*

Readings in Monetary Theory

American Economic Association Series   *3rd Impression. Demy 8vo. 35s. net*

This addition to the series of republished articles sponsored by the American Economic Association contains the most important articles on monetary theory and policy published since 1900. A complete bibliography adds its value for students or for reference use.

Amongst the eminent contributors are J. R. Hicks, J. E. Meade, R. G. Hawtrey, D. H. Robertson, A. G. Pigou, and Gustav Cassel.

Ten Great Economists

J. SCHUMPETER   *2nd Impression. Demy 8vo. 25s. net*

In this collection of essays one of the greatest economists of our day has written brilliant· evaluations of the men most influential in shaping economic thought during the past century. The papers, gathered together in book form for the first time, are biographical in character but with a penetrating critical approach that makes them classics in their field.

The "ten great economists" are, in chronological order, Karl Marx, Marie Esprit Leon Walras, Carl Menger, Alfred Marshall, Vilfredo Pareto, Eugen von Böhm-Bawerk, Frank William Taussig, Irving Fisher, Wesley Clair Mitchell, and John Maynard Keynes. An appendix includes George Frederic Knapp, Friedrich von Wieser, and Ladislaus von Bortkiewicz. Each of the essays, with the exception of the one on Marx, was written for an economic journal, either to celebrate an anniversary or on the occasion of the death of an economist. The essay on Karl Marx is Part I of Schumpeter's *Capitalism, Socialism and Democracy*, and gives a comprehensive treatment of Marx as prophet, sociologist, economist, and teacher.

A particular warmth and interest is given to these biographical essays by the author's having known, with the exception of Marx, each of the subjects personally. Professor Schumpeter's awareness of the contributions of these men, not only to economics but also to the main current of thought in our century, will make this book important to economists and to everyone seeking to understand our times.

"This is an illuminating, stimulating and highly civilized book."
                                                              The Economist

Theory of Economic Growth

PROFESSOR W. ARTHUR LEWIS   *5th Impression. Demy 8vo. 30s. net*

'Let us take a plunge and say that it is as good a book as its most obvious predecessors in the genre: Smith's *Wealth of Nations*, part of Mill's *Principles* and Marshall's *Industry and the Trade*. Of these it most resembles—in its orthodoxy, completeness, eclecticism, reliability and inevitable originality—Mill's *Principles*.'
                                          Times Educational Supplement

'A working handbook for statesmen as well as a detached study.'
                                                              The Economist

Utility and all That

D. H. ROBERTSON   *3rd Impression. Demy 8vo.* 18s. *net*

The appearance of a new book by Professor Robertson is an event, the more welcome for its extreme rarity. The present collection of his writings between the years 1945 and 1950 offers an acute running commentary on the march of economic events in the post-war world. At the same time it gives the views of one of our foremost economists on some recent developments in economic theory. As always, the products of Professor Robertson's incisive mind are couched in a style of almost deceptive ease and charm.

"This book is for the most part a penetrating commentary on various aspects of recent economic controversy but the victims, eminent and less eminent, who receive Professor Robertson's well-directed shafts, will receive them with a grin. Economists and libraries will acquire this book as a matter of course and generations of students will be indebted to the author for rescuing his essays from the pages of more or less obscure learned journals."   *The Statist*

The Principles of Economic Planning

PROFESSOR W. ARTHUR LEWIS *7th Impression. Demy 8vo.* 7s. 6d. *net*

The author, in this brief exposition of the principles of economic planning for the citizen interested in our present political and economic difficulties, shows that the issue is not *whether* to plan, but *how* to plan. He suggests that our planning should be done as far as possible through the budget and that other forms of control should be relegated to a subsidiary position. He does not argue for complete State control which he feels is inimical both to true Socialism and public good, but for a system of controls which would combine and encourage the best features of *laissez faire* and State planning.

The book shows that it is possible and desirable for the State to plan by inducement rather than by direction by using its power to manipulate the market to secure its objectives.

GEORGE ALLEN AND UNWIN LTD